T0321791

Modern Technologies for Big Data Classification and Clustering

Hari Seetha
Vellore Institute of Technology–Andhra Pradesh, India

M. Narasimha Murty
Indian Institute of Science, India

B. K. Tripathy
VIT University, India

A volume in the Advances in Data
Mining and Database Management
(ADMDM) Book Series

Published in the United States of America by
    IGI Global
    Information Science Reference (an imprint of IGI Global)
    701 E. Chocolate Avenue
    Hershey PA, USA 17033
    Tel: 717-533-8845
    Fax: 717-533-8661
    E-mail: cust@igi-global.com
    Web site: http://www.igi-global.com

Library of Congress Cataloging-in-Publication Data

Names: Seetha, Hari, 1970- editor. | Murty, M. Narasimha, editor. | Tripathy,
  B. K., 1957- editor.
Title: Modern technologies for big data classification and clustering / Hari
  Seetha, M. Narasimha Murty, and B.K. Tripathy, editors.
Description: Hershey, PA : Information Science Reference, [2018]
Identifiers: LCCN 2017010783| ISBN 9781522528050 (hardcover) | ISBN
  9781522528067 (ebook)
Subjects: LCSH: Big data. | Data mining. | Cluster analysis. |
  Classification--Nonbook materials. | Document clustering.
Classification: LCC QA76.9.B45 M63 2018 | DDC 005.7--dc23 LC record available at https://lccn.
loc.gov/2017010783

This book is published in the IGI Global book series Advances in Data Mining and Database Management (ADMDM) (ISSN: 2327-1981; eISSN: 2327-199X)

British Cataloguing in Publication Data
A Cataloguing in Publication record for this book is available from the British Library.

All work contributed to this book is new, previously-unpublished material.
The views expressed in this book are those of the authors, but not necessarily of the publisher.

For electronic access to this publication, please contact: eresources@igi-global.com.

Advances in Data Mining and Database Management (ADMDM) Book Series

ISSN:2327-1981
EISSN:2327-199X

Editor-in-Chief: David Taniar, Monash University, Australia

MISSION

With the large amounts of information available to organizations in today's digital world, there is a need for continual research surrounding emerging methods and tools for collecting, analyzing, and storing data.

The **Advances in Data Mining & Database Management (ADMDM)** series aims to bring together research in information retrieval, data analysis, data warehousing, and related areas in order to become an ideal resource for those working and studying in these fields. IT professionals, software engineers, academicians and upper-level students will find titles within the ADMDM book series particularly useful for staying up-to-date on emerging research, theories, and applications in the fields of data mining and database management.

COVERAGE

- Sequence Analysis
- Educational Data Mining
- Cluster Analysis
- Heterogeneous and Distributed Databases
- Neural Networks
- Database Testing
- Factor Analysis
- Quantitative Structure–Activity Relationship
- Predictive analysis
- Web Mining

IGI Global is currently accepting manuscripts for publication within this series. To submit a proposal for a volume in this series, please contact our Acquisition Editors at Acquisitions@igi-global.com or visit: http://www.igi-global.com/publish/.

Titles in this Series

For a list of additional titles in this series, please visit:
http://www.igi-global.com/book-series/advances-data-mining-database-management/37146

Data Visualization and Statistical Literacy for Open and Big Data
Theodosia Prodromou (University of New England, Australia)
Information Science Reference • ©2017 • 365pp • H/C (ISBN: 9781522525127) • US $205.00

Web Semantics for Textual and Visual Information Retrieval
Aarti Singh (Guru Nanak Girls College, Yamuna Nagar, India) Nilanjan Dey (Techno India College of Technology, India) Amira S. Ashour (Tanta University, Egypt & Taif University, Saudi Arabia) and V. Santhi (VIT University, India)
Information Science Reference • ©2017 • 290pp • H/C (ISBN: 9781522524830) • US $185.00

Advancing Cloud Database Systems and Capacity Planning With Dynamic Applications
Narendra Kumar Kamila (C.V. Raman College of Engineering, India)
Information Science Reference • ©2017 • 430pp • H/C (ISBN: 9781522520139) • US $210.00

Web Data Mining and the Development of Knowledge-Based Decision Support Systems
G. Sreedhar (Rashtriya Sanskrit Vidyapeetha (Deemed University), India)
Information Science Reference • ©2017 • 409pp • H/C (ISBN: 9781522518778) • US $165.00

Intelligent Multidimensional Data Clustering and Analysis
Siddhartha Bhattacharyya (RCC Institute of Information Technology, India) Sourav De (Cooch Behar Government Engineering College, India) Indrajit Pan (RCC Institute of Information Technology, India) and Paramartha Dutta (Visva-Bharati University, India)
Information Science Reference • ©2017 • 450pp • H/C (ISBN: 9781522517764) • US $210.00

Emerging Trends in the Development and Application of Composite Indicators
Veljko Jeremic (University of Belgrade, Serbia) Zoran Radojicic (University of Belgrade, Serbia) and Marina Dobrota (University of Belgrade, Serbia)
Information Science Reference • ©2017 • 402pp • H/C (ISBN: 9781522507147) • US $205.00

For an enitre list of titles in this series, please visit:
http://www.igi-global.com/book-series/advances-data-mining-database-management/37146

701 East Chocolate Avenue, Hershey, PA 17033, USA
Tel: 717-533-8845 x100 • Fax: 717-533-8661
E-Mail: cust@igi-global.com • www.igi-global.com

Table of Contents

Detailed Table of Contents

Chapter 1
B. K. Tripathy, VIT University, India
Hari Seetha, Vellore Institute of Technology – Andhra Pradesh, India
M. N. Murty, IISC Bangalore, India

Data clustering plays a very important role in Data mining, machine learning and Image processing areas. As modern day databases have inherent uncertainties, many uncertainty-based data clustering algorithms have been developed in this direction. These algorithms are fuzzy c-means, rough c-means, intuitionistic fuzzy c-means and the means like rough fuzzy c-means, rough intuitionistic fuzzy c-means which base on hybrid models. Also, we find many variants of these algorithms which improve them in different directions like their Kernelised versions, possibilistic versions, and possibilistic Kernelised versions. However, all the above algorithms are not effective on big data for various reasons. So, researchers have been trying for the past few years to improve these algorithms in order they can be applied to cluster big data. The algorithms are relatively few in comparison to those for datasets of reasonable size. It is our aim in this chapter to present the uncertainty based clustering algorithms developed so far and proposes a few new algorithms which can be developed further.

Chapter 2
Ashok Kumar J, Anna University, India
Abirami S, Anna University, India
Tina Esther Trueman, Anna University, India

Sentiment analysis is one of the most important applications in the field of text mining. It computes people's opinions, comments, posts, reviews, evaluations, and emotions which are expressed on products, sales, services, individuals, organizations, etc. Nowadays, large amounts of structured and unstructured data are being produced on the web. The categorizing and grouping of these data become a real-world problem. In this chapter, the authors address the current research in this field, issues and the problem of sentiment analysis on Big Data for classification and clustering. It suggests new methods, applications, algorithm extensions of classification and clustering and software tools in the field of sentiment analysis.

Chapter 3

R. Raj Kumar, RGMCET, India
P. Viswanath, IIITS Chittoor, India
C. Shoba Bindu, JNTUA, India

A large dataset is not preferable as it increases computational burden on the methods operating over it. Given the Large dataset, it is always interesting that whether one can generate smaller dataset which is a subset or a set (cardinality should be less when compare to original dataset) of extracted patterns from that large dataset. The patterns in the subset are representatives of the patterns in the original dataset. The subset (set) of representing patterns forms the Prototype set. Forming Prototype set is broadly categorized into two types. 1) Prototype set which is a proper subset of original dataset. 2) Prototype set which contains patterns extracted by using the patterns in the original dataset. This process of reducing the training set can also be done with the features of the training set. The authors discuss the reduction of the datasets in the both directions. These methods are well known as Data Compaction Techniques.

Chapter 4

Anu Singha, South Asian University, India
Phub Namgay, Sherubtse College, Royal University of Bhutan, Bhutan

A tool which algorithmically traces the effectiveness of the text files would be helpful in determining whether the text file have all the characteristic of important concepts. Every text source is build up on key phrases, and these paramount phrases follow a certain grammatical linguistic pattern widely used. An enormous amount of information can be derived from these key concepts for the further analysis such as their dispersion, relationship among the concepts etc. The relationship among the key concepts can be used to draw a concept graphs. So, this chapter presents a detailed methodologies and technologies which evaluate the effectiveness of the extracted information from text files.

Chapter 5

Chitrakala S, Anna University, India

Analyzing Social network data using Big Data Tools and techniques promises to provide information that could be of use in recommendation systems, personalized service and many other applications. A few of the analytics that do this include sentiment analysis, trending topic analysis, topic modeling, information diffusion modeling, provenance determination and social influence study. Twitter Data Analysis involves analyzing data specifically obtained from Twitter, both tweets and the topology. There are three major classifications on the type of analysis being performed such as Content based, Network based and Hybrid analysis. Trending Topic Analysis in the context of Content based static data analysis and Influence Maximization in the context of Hybrid analysis on data streams using the power of Big Data Analytics are discussed. A novel solution to Trending Topic analysis to generate topic evolved, conflict-free sequential sub summaries and influence maximization to handle streaming data are explained with experimental results.

Chapter 6

Sushruta Mishra, KIIT University, India
Brojo Kishore Mishra, C. V. Raman College of Engineering, India
Hrudaya Kumar Tripathy, KIIT University, India
Monalisa Mishra, C. V. Raman College of Engineering, India
Bijayalaxmi Panda, BPUT Rourkela, India

Social network analysis (SNA) is the analysis of social communication through network and graph theory. In our chapter the application of SNA has been explored in telecommunication domain. Telecom data consist of Customer data and Call Detail Data (CDR). The proposed work, considers the attributes of call detail data and customer data as different relationship types to model our Multi-relational Telecommunication social network. Typical work on social network analysis includes the discovery of group of customers who shares similar properties. A new challenge is the mining of hidden communities on such heterogeneous social networks, to group the customers as churners and non-churners in Telecommunication social network. After the analysis of the available data we constructed a Weights Multi-relational Social Network, in which each relation carry a different weight, representing how close two customers are with one another. The centrality measures depict the intensity of the customer closeness, hence we can determine the customer who influence the other customer to churn.

Spatial dataset, which is becoming nontraditional due to the increase in usage of social media sensor networks, gaming and many other new emerging technologies and applications. The wide variety of sensors are used in solving real time problems like natural calamities, traffic analysis, analyzing climatic conditions and the usage of GPS, GPRS in mobile phones all together creates huge amount of spatial data which really exceeds the traditional spatial data analytics platform and become spatial big data .Spatial big data provide new demanding situations for their size, analysis, and exploration. This chapter discusses about the analysis of spatial data and how it gets descriptive manipulation, so that one can understand how multi variant variables get interact with each other along with the different visualization tools which make the understanding of spatial data easier.

Social network analysis is one of the emerging research areas in the modern world. Social networks can be adapted to all the sectors by using graph theory concepts such as transportation networks, collaboration networks, and biological networks and so on. The most important property of social networks is community, collection of nodes with dense connections inside and sparse connections at outside. Community detection is similar to clustering analysis and has many applications in the real-time world such as recommendation systems, target marketing and so on. Community detection algorithms are broadly classified into two categories. One is disjoint community detection algorithms and the other is overlapping community detection algorithms. This chapter reviews overlapping community detection algorithms with their strengths and limitations. To evaluate these algorithms, a popular synthetic network generator, i.e., LFR benchmark generator and the new extended quality measures are discussed in detail.

With reducing cost of storage devices, increasing amounts of data is being stored and processed for extracting intelligence. Classification and clustering have been two major approaches in generating data abstraction. Over the last few years, text data is dominating the types of data shared and stored. Some of the sources of such datasets are mobile data, e-commerce, and wide-range of continuously expanding social-networking services. Within each of these sources, the nature of data differs drastically from formal language text to Twitter or SMS slangs thereby leading to the need for different ways of processing the data for making meaningful summarization. Such summaries could effectively be used for business advantage. Processing of such data requires identifying appropriate set of features both for efficiency and effectiveness. In the current Chapter, we propose to discuss approaches to text feature selection and make a comparative study.

Chapter 10
Vignesh U, VIT University, India
Parvathi R, VIT University, India

The chapter deals with the big data in biology. The largest collection of biological data maintenance paves the way for big data analytics and big data mining due to its inefficiency in finding noisy and voluminous data from normal database management systems. This provides the domains such as bioinformatics, image informatics, clinical informatics, public health informatics, etc. for big data analytics to achieve better results with higher efficiency and accuracy in clustering, classification and association mining. The complexity measures of the health care data leads to EHR (Evidence-based HealthcaRe) technology for maintenance. EHR includes major challenges such as patient details in structured and unstructured format, medical image data mining, genome analysis and patient communications analysis through sensors – biomarkers, etc. The big biological data have many complications in their data management and maintenance especially after completing the latest genome sequencing technology, next generation sequencing which provides large data in zettabyte size.

Preface

The rapid growth in digitalization, the technology advancement in data collection tools led to the explosive growth of large volumes of data—both structured and unstructured—which moves fast. The traditional database systems are incapable to store, manage and process such voluminous data. The efficient and effective analysis of such data is the need of the day as all he organizations are drowning in data and require proper mechanisms that provide insights of such large data for better decision making. Classification and clustering are such methods that extract some useful information from large structured and unstructured data sets.

Today the problem is not only about handling large volumes of data but also about processing different types of data. The data generated by various flights, social media such as Facebook, Twitter, blogs, Google+, which include numeric, text data and multimedia data, time series data such as stock exchange data, electricity consumption data, genomic data, health care data, sensor data, hyper spectral image data, online transaction data (e.g., Amazon, Flipkart), online research publications and so on. With increase in the Internet of Things applications the amount of the data being generated will further increase.

There is an imminent need to process such wide variety of data. New algorithms, technologies and infrastructure are essential which have the capabilities in analysing such data in contrast to traditional methods. Novel pre-processing methods are required that reduce the time and complexity in preparing such variety of data for analysis. The important components of big data ecosystem, as per 2011 McKinsey Global Institute report, include machine learning, natural language processing, A/B testing as techniques for data analysis; technologies like business intelligence, cloud computing and visualization such as graphs, charts, etc.; classification, clustering, pattern recognition, deep learning, predictive analytics, distributed systems (Map Reduce), No SQL technologies, Apache SPARK, are other technologies that deal with big data.

The contributed volume consists of 10 chapters written by experts from industry and academia. The motivation for editing this book is to enable the readers to understand the multidisciplinary nature of the Big Data and its applications as well as the challenges in various fields.

Clustering the real-world data is essential for better visualization and interpretation of data. Most of the real-world data is uncertain and dealing with uncertainty is a challenging task. As a result, the uncertainty based models available, like the fuzzy set, rough set, intuitionistic fuzzy set, neural networks and their hybrid combinations were used by several researchers in developing data clustering algorithms. Perhaps the sequence started with the development of fuzzy c-means algorithm by Ruspini in 1967, as an extension of the hard c-means algorithm. A major breakthrough in the development of clustering algorithms came when in 1981; J. Bezdek introduced the concept of objective function for fuzzy c-means and through minimisation of this objective function subject to the regular constraints for fuzzy c-means. This technique was followed later in most of the clustering algorithms to follow thereafter. The Euclidean distance function used to measure the similarity between data points leads to the problem of linear separability. So, kernels functions have been used in its place and kernelized clustering algorithms have been proposed. Also, beside c-means several other algorithms like the k-mode, k-median and k-Medoid algorithms are also in vogue. At the arrival of large datasets, all these algorithms have been found to be inadequate to handle such datasets. So, researchers have tried to extend these algorithms to make them suitable to the situation. Many of these algorithms are incremental in nature. In some cases parallel implementations were done and in some cases the MapReduce technique developed by Google was used. In the first chapter of this volume, an exhaustive study of these algorithms is done and their strength and weaknesses have been analysed. In some sense the development of clustering algorithms for large datasets is in its preliminary stage as large datasets have several other characteristics beyond its size, which are needed to be handled in addition to the size of these datasets. Some prospective research directions citing many such problems for further study have been mentioned at the end of this chapter besides an exhaustive list of source materials being provided as references.

Sentiment analysis, also known as opinion mining is one of the most important research fields in Information Processing, Text mining, and Linguistics. Information shared in online social networks. It contains useful information about products, sales, service, individuals, organizations, Governments, policies, politics, etc. Information in sentiment analysis is expressed in the form of an objective statement or a subjective statement. The objective statement refers to some factual information and subjective statement refers to personal feelings such as love, joy, surprise, anger, sadness, and fear. These data come under big data because of their volume, variety, and velocity. From another angle, we see that it can be treated as software as a service, platform as a service and infrastructure as a service. Which are services under big and hence are responsible to create opportunities and pose challenge to extract valuable information.

Sentiment analysis is one of the most important applications in the field of text mining. It is a process of categorizing the opinion of the writer as positive, negative or neutral. Sentiment analysis in social media is very important as it helps us to improve services provided to customers, success of a product or campaign success etc. It computes people's opinions, comments, posts, reviews, evaluations, and emotions which are expressed on products, sales, services, individuals, organizations, etc. Nowadays, large amounts of structured and unstructured data are being produced on the web. The categorization and grouping of these data has become a real-world problem.

In the second chapter of this volume, the authors address the current research in this field, issues and the problem of sentiment analysis on Big Data for classification and clustering. In this chapter, new methods, applications, algorithmic extensions of classification and clustering along with the associate software tools involved under sentiment analysis are discussed. Topics like Symmetric Matrix-based predictive classifier, Comparative experiments using supervised learning, Classifier ensembles, Ranked Word Graph for Sentiment polarity Classification, Sentiment Classification via Social context regularization, Context-Based Sentiment analysis, Semi-supervised subjective feature weighting and intelligent modelling, Cross-lingual sentiment classification: Similarity discovery, Supervised study weighting scheme, SVM with the linear kernel as the classification model, unsupervised dependency parsing-based text classification method, SACI (Sentiment Analysis by Collective Inspection), and a lexicon-based unsupervised method form the contents of this chapter. Big data classification and clustering techniques for mining from big data are presented with critical analysis. It starts with three machine learning approaches of supervised, semi-supervised and unsupervised methods for big data are presented The. Topics under supervised sentiment learning methods discussed includes Naive Bayes method, maximum entropy method, support vector machine, stochastic gradient descent method, n-gram based character language model, cross-domain sentiment classification, ranked WordNet graph, structured microblog sentiment classification, a multi-label classification based approach, BBS based sentiment classification, a fuzzy conceptualization model, supervised term weighting method, feature relation network based sentiment classification, a verb-oriented approach, meta-level sentiment models for big data, emotion topic model, syntax tree pruning and tree kernel based sentiment classification, morphemes based sentiment classification, joint sentiment – topic model, a dependency tree based approach, improved word-of-mouth sentiment classification, and a deep belief network based sentiment classification. Similarly, semi-supervised sentiment learning methods analysed include Semi-supervised dimensionality reduction, topic-adaptive sentiment classification (TASC), multi-dimensional classification, active deep learning method, and fuzzy deep belief networks. The unsupervised sentiment learning methods discussed include clustering sentiment based on graph similarity, unsupervised artificial neural networks, unsupervised multi-class sentiment learning, an entropic measure based clustering, and unsupervised cross-lingual topic model.

The ensemble-based approaches, which perform multiple learning algorithms for better performance, comprising of sentiment analysis using classifier ensembles and lexicons, a multi-objective weighted voting ensemble classifier based on differential evolution algorithm; random subspace method, feature ensemble plus sample selection (SS-FE) approach, and an unbalanced sentiment classification using ensemble learning are discussed. Some proposals for future work involving the topics; hybrid approaches, extensions of clustering and classification, applications of sentiment analysis on big data, and software tools from the big data perspective, their empirical verification using different data sets, development of different software tools for performance measure are presented, which provide some directions to budding researchers in the field.

Data compaction is the reduction of the number of data elements, bandwidth, cost, and time for the generation, transmission, and storage of data without loss of information by eliminating unnecessary redundancy, removing irrelevancy, or using special coding. In Chapter 3 of this volume various data compaction techniques are presented. The topics presented include variations of the Nearest Neighbour methods along with their advantages and disadvantages, data compaction techniques which use Prototype selection like the CNN, MCNN or OCNN and the methods PCA or LDA which deal with dimensionality. When both cardinality and dimensionality of the data set are considered together, any of the methods CNN, MCNN or OCNN can be combined with the methods PCA or LDA. This is termed as data compaction using Prototype selection and Feature selection. In this chapter the effectiveness and usefulness of prototype selection and feature selection methods were elucidated. Experiments have been carried out and results are expatiated. These methods are helpful to the researchers where there is necessity of reducing the data size. Some future directions of research under data compaction techniques are also proposed here. It is suggested that the CNN or MCNN methods which require single scan of the data set can be improved. Also, it is added that the OCNN algorithm can be modified to reduce its time complexity. Some further reading directions are provided for readers who are interested to get details on the topics covered here along with their chronological developments and critical analysis.

With the rise of modern technology, paper-based text files are being replaced by electronic version and is easily available online. Though the readers embrace comfort and portability provided by electronic version of the text files, paper based text files are still popular. Unlike decades back, text files in any field of study is readily available now. With the demand for text files rising, the qualities of the text files are compromised. With the decline rate reading habits, readers hardly spent some time to evaluate the content of the file due to lack of patience. It necessitates developing techniques which analyze the effectiveness of text files in detail. The readers will be helped through this technique in finding the suitable text files according to their needs depending upon their comprehension capability.

Such a tool which algorithmically traces the effectiveness the text files would be helpful in determining whether the text file have all the characteristic of a good source. Every file is build up on key concepts, and these key concepts form the foundation of a good source. The text sources that contain concepts that share some common properties and semantically related are more lucid and intelligible than those text sources which contain many unrelated concepts. These paramount phrases follow a certain grammatical linguistic pattern widely used. An enormous amount of information can be derived from these key concepts for the further analysis such as their dispersion across the file, relationship among the concepts, etc. Such analysis will help in better assessment of the text file. The relationship among the key concepts can be used to draw a concept graphs. Since we live in an increasingly visual society, pictorial representation of the key concepts as a graph would help the readers in easily judging the text source and their content.

In Chapter 4 of this volume, methodologies depending on the key concepts for retrieval of text files are presented. The authors analyse the techniques for examining the key concepts in the text files and present some of the different tools used in natural language processing along with a detailed discussion on their uses and implementation methods. The focus is on key concepts basing upon the terminological noun phrases, which upon extraction, can be further analysed to check the credibility of the text file in conveying the required set of information to the readers. It is based on the intuition that a source which contains right set of related key concepts is more beneficial and comprehensible. The set of key concept which form the cornerstone of a text file can be further used to draw concept graphs. The noun phrases from the candidate set of extracted phrases form the nodes of the graph and the relationship that exists between the nodes can be denoted by a link between the concept pairs. The 'in' degree and 'out' degree of each vertex of the graph i.e., the noun phrases can be used to determine the most important key concepts. Such representation of the source in a visual form helps readers in easily judging and grasping the key concepts. This ultimately serves as a preface to the text files and reduces the cognitive burden of the readers.

It is argued that although the selection of key concepts from the text files is the main point in information retrieval, selecting a good text file is of utmost importance as the ability to figure out the key concepts has been a big hurdle and troubling task. Recognizing the importance of key concepts, devising such methodologies, technologies, and the linguistic patterns to extract the key concepts from a text file and evaluate the text file based on key concepts is of immense importance. This chapter highlights the importance, techniques and approaches in selecting a good text file and retrieving useful information from these files. An exhaustive bibliography of resources on these concepts is also a hall mark of this chapter.

One of the outcomes of the popularity of online social networks is the development of a new field, social network analysis (SNA). This field studies not just the structure of social network but also the behaviour of the people who belong to it. One social network that has become popular for analysis is Twitter. Tweets based on a specific topic of interest, once extracted can be analysed and the results obtained can be used in many applications. Twitter Data Analysis has gained much popularity nowadays as obtaining information from Twitter makes it possible for vendors to provide personalized solutions to their customers and unlike other social networks, most accounts of Twitter are public, making it possible to obtain the necessary data. Also, the limitation imposed upon the number of characters ensures that one can quickly cover many twits in a short period of time, process them to get useful information quickly and react to these twits. The three forms of twitter analysis are content based analysis, network based analysis and hybrid analysis. Content based analysis techniques rely solely on the tweets/text produced, network based analysis depends upon the structures of the networks used. As is well known by now, hybrid techniques are more effective than their individual components if formed suitably. So, a combination of the above two analysis techniques which is often more suitable is termed as hybrid analysis. In Chapter 5 of this volume techniques/methodologies in Twitter Data Analysis and its significance are discussed. The basic intention of this chapter is to show how analytical techniques namely Trending Topic Analysis and Influence Maximization can be utilized to study and mine significant information from a social network such as Twitter. Some illustrative applications in real life business value use cases is detailed. The authors believe that these illustrations would trigger ideas for researchers in various fields.

To be precise, a study on Trending Topic Analysis technique which is a content based static data analysis is emphasized accounting to the urging need of a complete analysed summary of the topic under interest, presented in a topic evolved manner. Another study is on the Influence maximization technique which is a hybrid data analysis is discussed. It is important as it provides a way to find a small set of users, thus reducing the cost of promoting a product or campaign while simultaneously maximizing the spread of word about them. Distinguishing and critical aspect of the proposed Influence Maximization methodology is that it follows a Big Data approach enhancing its significance many folds.

Social Network Analysis (SNA) can be described as the process of defining social communication by the help of network and graph theory. The network structure is characterized in terms of actors, people or things associated by ties or links. Social network analysis is described by different social media networks, collaboration graphs, kinship. The representation of network is done through a diagram called sociogram, where nodes are represented as points and links as lines. A social network can be established between person, groups or organizations. It indicates the ways in which they are connected through various social familiarities ranging from casual acquaintance to close familiar bonds. Different scenarios such as email traffic, disease transmission, and criminal activity can be modelled using social networks. The co-ordination and flow between people, groups, organizations, or other resources information sharing is analysed by Social network analysis. People in the network represented as nodes and groups, while the links show relationships or flows between the nodes. A mathematical or graphical analysis of human relationship can be established by Social network analysis. This method is also used as Organizational Network Analysis by Management consultants for business clients. Social structure of the organization is described by groupings. As a whole the behaviour of the network is explained by number, size, and connections between sub-groupings in a network. Some of the features of sub-group structure can define the behaviour of the network by solving following questions. Several queries like, how fast will things move across the actors in the network and is it most likely that conflicts will involve multiple groups, or two factions, what is the extent of overlapping of the sub-groups and social structures can be raised under the circumstances. The analysis is preceded by the basic approaches for collecting data, which are in the form of questionnaires, interviews, observations, and some other secondary sources.

In Chapter 6 of this edited volume the focus is on our Multi-relational Telecommunication social network, where attributes of call detail data and customer data as different relationship types are modelled. After the analysis of the available data we constructed a Weights Multi-relational Social Network, in which each relation carry a different weight, representing how close two customers are with one another. The centrality measures depicts the intensity of the customer closeness, hence it can be found that the customer who influence the other customer to churn. Our second study comprises analysis of various structural properties of the SMS graph, including the in-degree distribution, out degree distribution, connected components and cliques. From the study on connected components, it has been found that almost 70% of the components are of size two, i.e., maximum user communication takes place in isolated pairs. One of the possible uses of the degree distribution is to develop a traffic plan which benefits the users as well as the service providers. Information Dissemination is another possible application of connected and strongly connected components. In a commercial network, the service providers would like to exploit the social networking aspects, and try to achieve maximum spread of information from minimum resources using underlying social dynamics. So, this chapter will be helpful to all of them.

As a result of generation of enormous amount of data created due to the increase of various other gadgets and advancement in technologies, each and every field need a data analytics in order to do make better decisions or to make more profit or to get the best opinion out of it. One of the major sources of generation of big data is the social media, which never fails to create tons and tons of data every day, out of this the spatial data which is created at the rate of terabytes. Due to the creation of such huge data, the data mining activity is getting hyperactive by various data mining approaches and algorithms. One of the special cases in remote sensing data analysis is spatial data analysis. The data collected from the space via satellites and meteorological data detected by the sensors to determine land and sea perceptions are making handling spatial data a huge one. The investigations of such substantial data display their own difficulties, despite the fact that with exceedingly capable processors and rapid data access conceivable shortly. Geospatial Data has always been Big Data. Now Big Data Analytics for geospatial data is available to allow users to analyze massive volumes of geospatial data. Petabyte archives for remotely sensed Geo data were being planned in the 1980s, and growth has met expectations. Add to this the ever-increasing volume and reliability of real time sensor observations, the need for high performance, big data analytics for modelling and simulation of geospatially enabled content is greater than ever. Workstations capable of fast geometric processing of vector Geo data brought a revolution in GIS. Now big processing through cloud computing and analytics can make greater sense of data and deliver the promised value of imagery and all other types of geospatial information. Cloud initiatives have accelerated lightweight client access to powerful processing services hosted in remote locations. The recent ESA/ESRIN "Big Data from Space" event addressed challenges posed by policies for dissemination, data search, sharing, transfer, mining, analysis, fusion and visualization. Chapter 7 of this volume deals with big data approach of handling spatial data is discussed along with the visualization technique. The Hadoop framework which provides various ways to handle the spatial data and also the map reduce framework which is explained here paves way to the emergence of different algorithms for handling the spatial data which acts as the base. The spatial Hadoop and apache mahout environment are becoming more and more curious and lot of researches getting emerged in it. When coming to visualization, whatever is done should get a shape and a view which is only possible through the visualization tools. The tools discussed in this chapter also did not reach its heights and further researches are carried out and most user friendly visualization tools has to be created in order to view the results of big data and also one of the open challenge of Hadoop framework is security in handling the spatial data.

As social networks are getting more popular, analyzing such networks has become one of the most important issues in various areas. In the era of big data, the amount of available data is growing unprecedentedly. Thus, data analysis techniques need very scalable approaches that can cope with huge network datasets. The significance of big data has attracted the concern of governments, companies and scientific institutions. The voluminous data available in social network sites and web like Facebook, Twitter, Instagram, LinkedIn, Weibo, World Wide Web and Wikipedia can be treated as bi data. This data can be represented as a graph/ Network, where nodes denote persons or pages, while edges represent the relationship between persons or pages. This relationship represents following in Twitter, friendship in Facebook, professional connections in LinkedIn, hyperlinks in WWW. This data may constitute several communities based interactions between people or entities. The members of community have some common interests such as movies, travel, photography, music, novels etc. and hence, they tend to interact more frequently within the community than the outside. Finding Communities in social networks is similar to Graph clustering problem, hence, it can also be called as big graph clustering with respect to larger networks. In Chapter 8 of this work, the features like community detection, detection of overlapping of various communities and their evaluation are presented and analysed.

Some research directions outlined in this chapter are as follows. Most of the research in community detection is done for unweighted and undirected networks only. Hence, there is a scope for future work in this area by developing algorithms for weighted and directed, attributed, bipartite networks. Scalability of the algorithm is also another research direction in this area because the number of nodes and edges in a real world social network are increasing rapidly. Moreover, social networks are dynamic in nature that means they evolve over time. Hence, community detection in dynamic networks is a challenging task for future work.

In Chapter 9, the focus is on feature selection for large datasets. General feature selection approaches, issues that are specific to text feature selection and experimental comparison of some text feature selection approaches on a common dataset are discussed. The work forms a brief study of feature selection algorithms. Relevant celebrated works that focused on different aspects of feature selection ranging from specific methods, feature selection metrics, theoretical frameworks, empirical studies, feature selection studies in relation to text mining, text categorization, similarity preserving, etc., are provided.

Bioinformatics is an interdisciplinary area that deals with the biology, computer and statistics. It involves the major aspects of genomics and proteomics with the genome sequencing, which are very sensitive in nature as representing the individual letter for a single nucleotide in case of DNA sequencing. Since 1970, the biological databases are digitized and their sensitivity factors with efficiency are maintained in a perfect manner but due to the vast amount of increasing data the maintenance aspect and extraction of information from gene expression becomes so complex, thus the big data gives the better results for these problems in an accurate manner. So, one needs to deal with information efficiently, accurately and in a faster manner by saving enormous time with biological data sets.

In the final chapter of this volume, analysis, interpretation, and visualization of big biological data produced by high throughput technologies such as next generation sequencing, microarray etc. are covered efficiently. It provides a framework for integrating new computational tools. NGS data are aligned by proposed alignment tool pairwise-multiple alignment tool. NGS data undergo assembly process with new proposed algorithm package gene assembler. A new machine learning approaches for re-sequenced genomes are included to detect polymorphism and structural variant. The resultant analyzed data are visualized using tabular and graphical method with inclusion of new packages of big data visualization using python language. The users will able to connect to the large high amounts of data dumped in the public databases like PDB, NCBI, and from several other available online databases.

This book should be useful for computing science students, application developers, data scientists, business analysts, business professionals, data analysts, statisticians, scientists and researchers working in the fields of data mining, big data analytics, machine learning, information retrieval, knowledge based systems and visualization. Since big data analytics is growing as a multidisciplinary field various technologies that could enlighten academicians and professionals becomes essential.

The editors will feel that their efforts have been duly rewarded if it serves the needs of students, the practitioners and researchers in the field of big data.

Hari Seetha
Vellore Institute of Technology-Andhra Pradesh, India

M. N. Murty
Indian Institute of Science, India

B. K. Tripathy
VIT University, India

Chapter 1
Uncertainty–Based Clustering Algorithms for Large Data Sets

B. K. Tripathy
VIT University, India

Hari Seetha
Vellore Institute of Technology – Andhra Pradesh, India

M. N. Murty
IISC Bangalore, India

ABSTRACT

Data clustering plays a very important role in Data mining, machine learning and Image processing areas. As modern day databases have inherent uncertainties, many uncertainty-based data clustering algorithms have been developed in this direction. These algorithms are fuzzy c-means, rough c-means, intuitionistic fuzzy c-means and the means like rough fuzzy c-means, rough intuitionistic fuzzy c-means which base on hybrid models. Also, we find many variants of these algorithms which improve them in different directions like their Kernelised versions, possibilistic versions, and possibilistic Kernelised versions. However, all the above algorithms are not effective on big data for various reasons. So, researchers have been trying for the past few years to improve these algorithms in order they can be applied to cluster big data. The algorithms are relatively few in comparison to those for datasets of reasonable size. It is our aim in this chapter to present the uncertainty based clustering algorithms developed so far and proposes a few new algorithms which can be developed further.

DOI: 10.4018/978-1-5225-2805-0.ch001

An intelligent being cannot treat every object it sees as a unique entity unlike anything else in the universe. It has to put objects in categories so that it may apply its hard-won knowledge about similar objects encountered in the past, to the object at hand. – Steven Pinker, How the Mind Works, 1997

1. INTRODUCTION

We are living in a world full of data. Every day, people deal with different types of data coming from all types of measurements and observations. Data describe the characteristics of a living species, depict the properties of a natural phenomenon, summarize the results of a scientific experiment, and record the dynamics of a running machinery system. More importantly, data provide a basis for further analysis, reasoning, decisions, and ultimately, for the understanding of all kinds of objects and phenomena. One of the most important of the myriad of data analysis activities is to classify or group data into a set of categories or clusters. Data objects that are classified in the same group should display similar properties based on some criteria. Actually, as one of the most primitive activities of human beings (Anderberg, 1973; Everitt et al., 2001), classification plays an important and indispensable role in the long history of human development. In order to learn a new object or understand a new phenomenon, people always try to identify descriptive feature and further compare these features with those of known objects or phenomena, based on their similarity or dissimilarity, generalized as proximity, according to some certain standards or rules. As an example, all natural objects are basically classified into three groups: animal, plant, and mineral. According to the biological taxonomy, all animals are further classified into categories of kingdom, phylum, class, order, family, genus, and species, from general to specific. Thus, we have animals named tigers, lions, wolves, dogs, horses, sheep, cats, mice, and so on. Actually, naming and classifying are essentially synonymous, according to Everitt et al. (2001), with such classification information at hand, we can infer the properties of a specific object based on the category to which it belongs. For instance, when we see a seal lying easily on the ground, we know immediately that it is a good swimmer without really seeing it swim.

Basically, classification systems are either supervised or unsupervised, depending on whether they assign new data objects to one of a finite number of discrete supervised classes or unsupervised categories, respectively (Bishop, 1995; Cherkassky and Mulier, 1998; Duda et al., 2001).

A cluster is a collection of data elements that are similar to each other but dissimilar to elements in other clusters. A vast amount of data is generated and made available across multiple sources. It is practically impossible to manually analyze the myriad of data and select the data that is required to perform a particular task. Hence, a mechanism that can classify the data according to some criteria in which only the classes of interest are selected and rests are rejected is essential. Clustering techniques are applied in the analysis of statistical data used in fields such as machine learning, pattern recognition, image analysis, information retrieval, and bioinformatics and is a major task in exploratory data mining (Bezdek and Pal 1998, Tou and Gonzalez 1974). A wide number of clustering algorithms have been proposed to suit the requirements in each field of its application.

The first and perhaps the most common clustering algorithm is Hard C-Means (HCM). However, uncertainty has become an integral part of modern day databases. There are many uncertainty based models in literature like the fuzzy sets introduced by Zadeh (1965), the rough sets introduced by Pawlak (1982), the intuitionistic fuzzy sets introduced by Atanassov (1986) and their hybrid models like the rough fuzzy sets and fuzzy rough sets introduced by Dubois and Prade (1990) and the rough intuitionistic fuzzy sets introduced by Saleha et al. (2002) and intuitionistic fuzzy rough sets introduced by Tripathy et al (2002). Several modifications to HCM framework led to the development of various uncertainty based C-Means algorithms such as Fuzzy C-means (FCM) (Ruspini, 1970, Bezdek, 1981), Rough C-Means (RCM) (Lingras et al, 2004, Peters, 2006), Rough-Fuzzy C-Means (RFCM) (Mitra et al, 2006, Maji and Pal 2007), Intuitionistic Fuzzy C-Means (IFCM) (Chaira 2011) and Rough Intuitionistic Fuzzy C-Means (Tripathy et al. 2013). It has been established that RIFCM works better than all the other c-means algorithms for numeric data sets. The combination of fuzzy or intuitionistic fuzzy techniques with the rough set techniques take care of graded membership and graded non-membership of objects in clusters and the uncertainty through the boundary regions. It was observed later that the behaviour of RIFCM fluctuates over image datasets (Srujan et al 2017a). However, this is because of the selection of initial solutions. Now a day, genetic algorithms are used to find an optimal initial solution. It has been observed that taking the firefly algorithm to select the initial solutions shows that RIFCM is the best among all the algorithms discussed above for both numerical and image data sets (Namdev et al 2016; Srujan et al 2017a, 2017b).

The process of grouping a set of physical or abstract objects into classes of similar objects is called clustering. It is an exploratory procedure that searches for "natural" structure within a data set. This process involves sorting the data cases or objects into groups or clusters so that objects in the same cluster are more like one another than they are like objects in another cluster. The sorting occurs on the basis of similarities calculated from the data; no assumptions about the structure of the data are made. A cluster of data objects can be treated collectively as one group and so may be considered as a form of data compression (Priyadarishini et al 2011). Although classification is an effective means for distinguishing groups or classes of objects, it requires the often costly collection and labelling of a large set of training tuples or patterns, which the classifier uses to model each group (Priyadarishini et al 2011). A number of algorithms for clustering categorical data have been proposed such as K-Means, Expectation-Maximization (EM) Algorithm, Association Rule, K-Modes, K-Prototypes, CACTUS (Clustering Categorical Data Using Summaries), ROCK (Robust Clustering using Links), STIRR (Sieving Through Iterated Relational Reinforcement), LCBCDC (Link Clustering Based Categorical Data Clustering), fuzzy K-modes algorithm, fuzzy centroids algorithm etc.. These algorithms require multiple runs to establish the stability needed to obtain a satisfactory value for one parameter. While these methods make important contributions to the issue of clustering categorical data, they are not designed to handle uncertainty in the clustering process. In order to handle this situation many clustering based algorithms have been established using uncertainty based models. One such model is rough set theory. Rough sets theory is a new mathematical tool to handle uncertainty and incomplete information. Polish mathematician Pawlak Z initially proposed it (Pawlak and Skowron, 2007a). The theory consists of finite sets, equivalence relations and cardinality concepts. A principal goal of rough set theoretic analysis is to synthesize or construct approximations (upper and lower) offsets concepts from the acquired data. Rough set theory clarifies set-theoretic characteristics of the classes over combinatorial patterns of the attributes. This theory can be used to acquire some sets of attributes for classification and can also evaluate the degree of the attributes of database that are able to classify data. Basically, when using rough sets, the data itself is used to come up with the approximation in order to deal with the imprecision within. It can therefore be considered a self-sufficient discipline (Pawlak and Skowron 2007b, 2007c). Unlike fuzzy set based approaches, rough sets have no requirement on domain expertise to assign the fuzzy membership. This is an important issue in many real world applications where there is often no sharp boundary between clusters (Parmar et.al 2007). Still, it may provide satisfactory results for rough clustering. They call this algorithm as MMR (Min-Min Roughness) Clustering is useful for data reduction, image segmentation, medical analysis, weather forecasting and text mining etc. In practical application, the data sets contain numerical and categorical (nominal) data in general. Accordingly, clustering algorithm is required to able to deal with both numerical data and categorical data. The algorithm established is not suitable to handle hybrid datasets. In order to tackle such situations MMR algorithm was extended by Kumar et al (Kumar and Tripathy, 2009) when they introduced the MMeR (Min-Mean Roughness) algorithm. Besides being applicable to hybrid data sets, this algorithm refines the selection of attribute concept used in MMR. MMeR was further extended to develop the SDR (Standard deviation Roughness) in (Tripathy et al, 2011a) and SSDR (Standard deviation- Standard deviation Roughness) in (Tripathy et al, 2011b). However, it has been observed that SSDR does not have much improvement over SDR.

1.1. Applications of Clustering

Clustering has been applied in a wide variety of fields, as illustrated below with a number of typical applications (Anderberg, 1973; Everitt et al., 2001; Hartigan, 1975).

1. Engineering (computational intelligence, machine learning, pattern recognition, mechanical engineering, electrical engineering). Typical applications of clustering in engineering range from biometric recognition and speech recognition, to radar signal analysis, information compression, and noise removal.
2. Computer sciences. We have seen more and more applications of clustering in web mining, spatial database analysis, information retrieval, textual document collection, and image segmentation.
3. Life and medical sciences (genetics, biology, microbiology, palaeontology, psychiatry, clinic, phylogeny, pathology). These areas consist of the major applications of clustering in its early stage and will continue to be one of the main playing fields for clustering algorithms. Important applications include taxonomy definition, gene and protein function identification, disease diagnosis and treatment, and so on.
4. Astronomy and earth sciences (geography, geology, remote sensing). Clustering can be used to classify stars and planets, investigate land formations, partition regions and cities, and study river and mountain systems.
5. Social sciences (sociology, psychology, archaeology, anthropology, education). Interesting applications can be found in behaviour pattern analysis, relation identification among different cultures, construction of evolutionary history of languages, analysis of social networks, archaeological finding and artifact classification, and the study of criminal psychology.
6. Economics (marketing, business). Applications in customer characteristics and purchasing pattern recognition, grouping of firms, and stock trend analysis all benefit from the use of cluster analysis.

Cluster analysis is a basic human mental activity and consists of research developed across a wide variety of communities. Accordingly, cluster analysis has many alternative names differing from one discipline to another. In biology and ecology, cluster analysis is more often known as numerical taxonomy. Researchers in computational intelligence and machine learning are more likely to use the terms unsupervised learning or learning without a teacher. In social science, typological analysis is preferred, while in graph theory, partition is usually employed. This diversity reflects the important position of clustering in scientific research. On the other hand, it causes confusion because of the differing terminologies and goals. Frequently, similar theories or algorithms are redeveloped several times in different disciplines due to the lack of good communication, which causes unnecessary burdens and wastes time.

2. TYPES OF CLUSTERING ALGORITHMS FOR LARGE DATA

We divide and discuss the algorithms in large - scale data clustering in the following categories:

- Random sampling
- Data condensation
- Density-based approaches
- Grid-based approaches
- Divide and conquer
- Incremental learning
- Model Based

Many proposed algorithms combine more than one method to be scalable to large - scale data cluster analysis and thus belong to at least two categories above. For example, the algorithm DENCLUE relies on both density – based and grid-based notions of clustering. The algorithm FC processes data points in an incremental way, and it also represents cluster information with a series of grids.

2.1. Random Sampling Methods

Clustering algorithms that use a random sampling approach in large - scale data clustering are applied to a random sample of the original data set instead of the entire data set. The key point of the random sampling approach is that an appropriate - sized sample can maintain the important geometrical properties of potential clusters, while greatly reducing the requirement for both computational time and storage space. The lower bound of the minimum sample size can be estimated in terms of Chertoff bounds, given the low probability that clusters are missing in the sample set (Guha et al., 1998).

2.2. Condensation-Based Methods

Condensation-based approaches perform clustering by using the calculated summary statistics of the original data rather than the entire data set. In this way, the requirement for the storage of and the frequent operations on the large volume of data is greatly reduced and large - scale data sets can be clustered with reasonable time and space efficiency. The algorithm BIRCH (Balanced Iterative Reducing and Clustering using Hierarchies) (Zhang et al., 1996) is such an example, which has an important impact on many other condensation-based methods.

BIRCH is local (as opposed to global) in that each clustering decision is made without scanning all data points or all currently existing clusters. It uses measurements that reflect the natural closeness of points, and at the same time, can be incrementally maintained during the clustering process. 1 BIRCH exploits the observation that the data space is usually not uniformly occupied, and hence not every data point is equally important for clustering purposes. A dense region of points is treated collectively as a single cluster. Points in sparse regions are treated as outliers and removed optionally. BIRCH makes full use of available memory to derive the finest possible sub-clusters (to ensure accuracy) while minimizing I/O costs (to ensure efficiency). The clustering and reducing process is organized and characterized by the use of an in-memory, height balanced and highly-occupied tree structure. Due to these features, its running time is linearly scalable. If the final two phases are omitted, BIRCH is an incremental method that does not require the whole dataset in advance, and only scans the dataset once.

2.3. Density-Based Methods

Density-based approaches rely on the density of data points for clustering and have the advantage of generating clusters with arbitrary shapes and good scalability. The density of points within a cluster is considerably higher than the density of points outside of the cluster. Specifically, the algorithm DBSCAN (Density Based Spatial Clustering of Applications with Noise) (Ester et al., 1996) implements the concept of density—reachability and density—connectivity to define clusters.

Such points are known as core points. If two core points are within each other's neighborhood, they belong to the same cluster. It also can be seen that density -reachability is symmetric for core points. In comparison, there exist two other types of data points, border points and noise points. Border points, those on the border of a cluster, do not contain enough points in their neighborhood to be the core points, but they belong to the neighborhood of some core points. The points that are neither core points nor border points are regarded as noise.

Here, data objects are separated based on their regions of density, connectivity and boundary. They are closely related to point-nearest neighbours. A cluster, defined as a connected dense component, grows in any direction that density leads to. As a result density-based algorithms are capable of discovering clusters of arbitrary shapes. These algorithms have the inherent property that they provide protection against outliers. Thus the overall density of a point is analysed to determine the functions of datasets that influence a particular data point. DBSCAN, OPTICS, DBCLASD and DENCLUE are algorithms that use such a method to filter out outliers and discover clusters of arbitrary shape.

2.4. Grid-Based Methods

Grid-based approaches divide a data space into a set of cells or cubes by a grid. This space partitioning is then used as a basis for determining the final data partitioning. The algorithm STING (STatistical INformation Grid) (Wang et al., 1997) uses a hierarchical structure within the division of the data space. Cells are constructed at different levels in the hierarchy corresponding to different resolutions. The hierarchy starts with one cell at the root level and each cell at a higher level has l children (four by default). Information in each cell is stored in terms of a feature independent parameter, i.e., the number of points in the cell, and feature dependent parameters, i.e., mean, standard deviation, minimum, maximum, and distribution type. Parameters at higher - level cells can be obtained from parameters at lower - level cells. Cells that are relevant to certain conditions are determined based on their data summaries, and only those cells that are children of the relevant cells are further examined. After the bottom level is reached, a breadth - first search can be used to find the clusters that have densities greater than a pre-specified threshold. Thus, STING combines both data condensation and density-based clustering strategies. The clusters formed by STING can approximate the result from DBSCAN when the granularity of the bottom level approaches zero (Wang et al., 1997). STING achieves faster performance in simulation studies than other algorithms, such as BIRCH. STING is also extended as STING+ (Wang et al., 1999) to deal with dynamically evolving spatial data while maintaining the similar hierarchical structure. STING+ supports user - defined triggers, which are decomposed into sub - triggers associated with cells in the hierarchy. STING+ considers four categories of triggers based on the absolute or relative condition on certain regions or features. Wave Cluster (Sheikholeslami et al., 1998) considers clustering data in the feature space from a signal processing perspective. Cluster boundaries, which display rapid changes in the distribution of data points, correspond to the high - frequency parts of the signal, while the interiors of clusters, which have high densities, correspond to the low frequency parts of the signal with high amplitude. Signal processing techniques, such as wavelet transform, can be used to identify the different frequency sub-bands of the signal and therefore generate the clusters. Wavelet transform demonstrates many desirable properties in cluster identification, particularly with the benefits of effective filters, outlier detection, and multi - resolution analysis. For example, the hat – shaped filters make the clusters more distinguishable by emphasizing dense regions while suppressing less dense areas in the boundaries. Low - pass filters have the advantage of automatically eliminating noise and outliers. Multi – resolution representation of a signal with wavelet transform allows the identification of clusters at different scales, i.e., coarse, medium, and fine. The size of the grid will vary corresponding to different scales of transform.

The performance of a grid-based method depends on the size of the grid, which is usually much less than the size of the database. However, for highly irregular data distributions, using a single uniform grid may not be sufficient to obtain the required clustering quality or fulfil the time requirement. Wave-Cluster is another example of this category.

2.5. Divide and Conquer

When the size of a data set is too large to be stored in the main memory, it is possible to divide the data into different subsets that can fi t the main memory and to use the selected cluster algorithm separately to these subsets. Clusters are identified in the transformed feature space. The assignment of data points to the corresponding clusters is achieved via a lookup table, which associate cells in the original feature space with cells in the transformed feature space. Clustering result is obtained by merging the previously formed clusters. This approach is known as "divide and conquer" (Guha et al., 2003; Jain et al., 1999). Specifically, given a data set with N points stored in a secondary memory, the divide - and - conquer algorithm first divides the entire data set into r subsets with approximately similar sizes. Each of the subsets is then loaded into the main memory and is divided into a certain number of clusters with a clustering algorithm. Representative points of these clusters, such as the centers of the clusters, are then picked for further clustering. These representatives may be weighted based on some rule, e.g., the centers of the clusters could be weighted by the number of points belonging to them (Guha et al., 2003). The algorithm repeatedly clusters the representatives obtained from the clusters in the previous level until the highest level is reached. The data points are then put into corresponding clusters formed at the highest level based on the representatives at different levels. Stahl (1986) illustrated a two - level divide - and - conquer clustering algorithm applied to a data set with 2,000 data points. The leader algorithm (Duda et al., 2001) is first used to form a large number of clusters from the original data.

The obtained representatives of these clusters are then clustered with a hierarchical clustering algorithm.

2.6. Incremental Clustering

In contrast to batch clustering, which requires loading the entire data set into the main memory, an incremental or online clustering approach does not require the storage of all these data points, instead handling the data set one point at a time. If the current data point displays enough closeness to an existent cluster according to some predefined criteria, it is assigned to the cluster. Otherwise, a new cluster is created to represent the point. Because only the representation of each cluster must be stored in the memory, an incremental clustering strategy saves a great deal of space. A typical example that is based on incremental learning is the adaptive resonance theory (ART) family (Carpenter and Grossberg, 1987, 1990). Several other clustering algorithms, such as DBCLASD and FC, also process the input data points incrementally. As previously mentioned, one of the major problems for incremental clustering algorithms is that they are order dependent, which means that different presentation orders of the input points cause different partitions of the data set (Carpenter and Grossberg, 1987; Moore, 1989). Obviously, this is not an appealing property because of the problem caused in cluster validation. DBCLASD (Xu et al., 1998) uses two methods to decrease the reliance on data ordering. The first heuristic retains the unsuccessful candidates rather than discarding them and then tries them again to the clusters. The second heuristic allows data points to change their cluster membership.

2.7. Model-Based Algorithms

These methods optimize the fit between the given data and some mathematical model. It is based on the assumption that the data is generated by a mixture of underlying probability distributions. Also, during the process the number of clusters is supposed to be generated using standard statistics where the outliers are being considered. This guarantees the robustness of the algorithm. The two standard approaches use are; statistical and neural networks based. MCLUST, COBWEB and EM are the three best known algorithms under this category. In addition there are SOMs under the neural network approaches. Probability measures are used to determine the clusters in the statistical approach. Thus, the derived concepts are represented by probabilistic descriptions. On the other hand, a set of connected input/output pairs are used in the neural network approach. Among the several properties of neural network approach which have made this approach popular are; they have distributed processing architecture and are inherently parallel, the learning of neural networks through weight adjustments help is fitting the data better and they process numerical data and the object patterns are represented by quantitative measures only. These features are helpful as normally one comes across numerical data and other data can be transformed to numeric.

3. CHARACTERISTICS OF BIG DATA

Although big data in the early stage were described through their vast size, there are several characteristics which describe the concept more accurately. The presence of one or more of these characteristics puts a data set under big data. These are termed as the five Vs to characterise big data and are Volume, Velocity, Variety, Veracity and Value.

3.1. Volume

This refers to the largeness of the dataset in terms of size. There are several sources of data generation now a day like e-mails, Facebook, twitter messages, photos, videos, sensor data and satellite data. This increasingly makes data sets too large to store and analyse using traditional database technology. The traditional data clustering algorithms are not suitable to be applied to these datasets. In order to make an algorithm suitable for such datasets, the algorithm must have techniques to handle size of dataset, handling their high dimensionalities and handling outliers/noisy data. There will always data sets that are too large for any given computer. So, instead of increasing the storage capacity of computers, it is desirable to develop method which are extensible to very large data sets (Cutting et al, 1992; Baeza-Yates, 1999; Ribeiro- Neto, 1999).

3.2. Variety

It refers to the different types of data in the dataset. The various types may be numerical, categorical or hierarchical. In order to handle this characteristic of data sets an algorithm must consider the type of the data set and cluster shape. In the past we focused on structured data that neatly fits into tables or relational databases. Things have changed over the past few years and a large number of data sets are now unstructured, and therefore can't easily be put into tables. The data sets obtained from social media, video sequences and photos obtained from some sources like the satellite fall into this category.

3.3. Velocity

It refers to the speed at which new data is generated and the speed at which data moves around. The social media messages go viral in seconds, the credit card transactions are checked for fraudulent activities very quickly, or the milliseconds it takes trading systems to analyse social media networks to pick up signals that trigger decisions to buy or sell shares. Big data technology allows us now to analyse the data while it is being generated, without ever putting it into databases. A clustering algorithm must be of reasonably low complexity and its run time should be fast.

3.4. Veracity

It refers to the messiness or trustworthiness of the data. With many forms of big data, quality and accuracy are less controllable. We find the Twitter posts with hash tags, abbreviations, typos and colloquial speech as well as the reliability and accuracy of content, there are problems with the trust and accuracy. So, big data clustering algorithms should be capable of dealing with these types of data.

3.5. Value

It is all well and good having access to big data but unless we can turn it into value it is useless. So you can safely argue that 'value' is the most important V of Big Data. Data is only as valuable as the business outcomes it makes possible. It is important that businesses make a business case for any attempt to collect and leverage big data. It is so easy to fall into the buzz trap and embark on big data initiatives without a clear understanding of costs and benefits. It is how we make use of data that allows us to fully recognise its true value and potential to improve our decision-making capabilities and, from a business stand point, measure it against the result of positive business outcomes.

4. CHARACTERISTICS OF A GOOD LARGE DATA CLUSTERING ALGORITHM (FAHAD ET AL., 2014)

Basing upon the characteristics of big data, Fahad et al have presented the following as characteristics of a good big data algorithm:

4.1. Type of Dataset

The data clustering algorithms mostly take care of numerical or categorical data sets as their domain of application. However, the datasets cannot be of one type only. It may be a hybrid data set. Even if in some cases it is manipulated to transform one type of dataset to the other or converting the typical attributes from one category to another, these are not natural. It has been observed that algorithms which work perfectly on one type of data perform poorly on hybrid datasets. So, algorithms should be developed to handle hybrid data sets from the beginning.

4.2. Size of Dataset

It has been observed that some of the clustering algorithms which are very much effective on small datasets fare poorly or not applicable as the size of the dataset increases. The vice versa also occurs sometimes. So, the data size must be kept in mind while developing a clustering algorithm

4.3. Input Parameter

A large number of parameters may affect the functionality of a clustering algorithm. So, a minimum number of parameters are always preferable.

4.4. Handling Outliers/Noisy Data

The dataset in most of the real life situations may not be pure. The outliers in the noisy dataset create a lot of problems for a clustering algorithm. It becomes difficult to put an object into a cluster.

4.5. Time Complexity

In many cases the algorithms are to be run several times to improve the clustering quality. So, a low time complexity is desirable. High complexity may make it inefficient to apply for large datasets.

4.6. Stability

It is desirable that the output remains same for a clustering algorithm irrespective of the order in which the patterns are input. This provides stability to the clustering algorithm.

4.7. Handling High Dimensionality

Many of the real life data sets have high dimensionality or have high number of features. Dimensionality reduction is the process of removing un-important or less important features so that the analysis performed on the rest of the features is enough to shed light on the study. Also, as the number of dimensions increase the data become increasingly sparse. It leads to the unpleasant situation that the measurement of distances between pairs of points becomes meaningless. So, the big data clustering algorithms should take care of high dimensionality, may be with a possible filtering of dimensions in the beginning.

5. DIFFERENT BIG DATA CLUSTERING ALGORITHMS

In this section we present the big data clustering algorithms based on uncertainty based models developed so far. These algorithms can be categorised as incremental or specific.

5.1. Fuzzy C-Means Algorithms for Large Data

Over the years, since the development of the fuzzy C-means (Ruspini 1970, Bezdek 1981), several algorithms have been proposed with different applications in view using different uncertainty based models like intuitionistic fuzzy sets (Atanassov, 1986), rough sets (Pawlak, 1982), rough fuzzy sets (Dubois and Prade, 1990), rough Intuitionistic Fuzzy sets (Saleh et al, 2011).

Following the incremental approach, FCM has been extended so that it can be applicable to large data sets. Kothari et al (2014) have used random sampling techniques so that the extended Fuzzy C-means algorithm is applicable for large dataset. However, one of the finest approaches to extend Fuzzy C-Means algorithm for very large data is due to (Havens et al, 2012).

In this paper the authors have proposed three different approaches aimed at extending the FCM clustering to large data. These three approaches are:

- Sampling followed by non-iterative extension.
- Incremental techniques that make one sequential pass through subsets of the data.
- Kernelised versions of FCM that provide approximations based on sampling, including three proposed algorithms.

An easy approach to attend to very large datasets is to take sample the dataset and then use FCM to compute the cluster centres of the sampled data. It has been observed that if the data were sufficiently sampled, the error between the cluster centre locations produced by clustering the entire dataset and the locations produced by clustering the sampled data should be small. This approach is called the random sampled and extended approach and the corresponding algorithm is called as rseFCM. The literal FCM, called LFCM, the 'c' number of centres are selected at random. In this algorithm each object is considered equally important in the clustering solution. The weighted FCM (wFCM) model introduces weights that define the relative importance of each object in the clustering solution.

One of the most well-known methods for fuzzy clustering of very large data is the generalised extensible fast FCM (geFFCM) (Hathaway and Bezdek, 2006). This algorithm uses statistics-based progressive sampling to produce a reduced dataset that is large enough to capture the overall nature of the data. It then clusters this reduced dataset and non-iteratively extends the partition to the full dataset. However, the sampling method used in geFFCM can be inefficient and in some cases the data reduction is not sufficient for VL data.

Other leading algorithms include single-pass FCM (spFCM) (Hore et al, 2007) and online FCM (oFCM) (Hore et al, 2009), which are incremental algorithms to compute an approximate FCM solution. The spFCM algorithm computes the new cluster centres by feeding forward the cluster centres from the previous iteration into the data being clustered. Unlike spFCM, the oFCM clusters all s subsets of objects separately and then aggregates the s sets of cluster centres at the end. The bit-reduced FCM (brFCM) (Eschrich et al, 2003) algorithm uses a binning strategy for data reduction. The brFCM algorithm was designed to address the problem of clustering in large images. The brFCM begins by binning the input data X into a reduced set X', where X' is the set of bin centres. This reduced set X' is then clustered using wFCM, where the weights are the number of objects in each bin. A kernel-based strategy which is called approximate kernel FCM (akFCM) was developed in (Chitta et al, 2011, Havens et al, 2011), which relies on a numerical approximation that uses sampled rows of the kernel matrix to estimate the solution to a c-means problem. The spkFCM and okFCM algorithms were introduced in (Havens et al, 2012). A comparative analysis of the group of algorithms wFCM, LFCM, rseFCM, spFCM, oFCM, brFCM and an extended algorithm is provided in Table 1 in terms of their time and space complexity.

Table 2 presenta the time and space complexities of the group of algorithms wkFCM, kFCM, rsekFCM, akFCM, spkFCM, okFCM and an extended algorithm.

In the above tables, we have:

Table 1. Space and time complexities of vector data algorithms

Algorithms	Time Complexity	Space Complexity
wFCM, LFCM	$O(tc^2dn)$	O((d + c)n)
rseFCM	$O(tc^2dn \ / \ s)$	O((d + c)(n/s))
spFCM	$O(tc^2dn)$	O((d + c)(n/s))
oFCM	$O(tc^2dn)$	O((d + c)(n/s)+cs)
brFCM	$O(tc^2ds)$ +bin	O((d + c)s)
Extension	$O(c^2dn)$	O(cn)

Table 2. Space and time complexities of kernel algorithms

Algorithms	Time Complexity	Space Complexity
wkFCM, kFCM	$O(tcn^2)$	$O(n^2)$
rsekFCM	$O(tcn^2 \ / \ s^2)$	$O(n^2 \ / \ s^2)$
spkFCM	$O(tcn^2 \ / \ s)$	$O(n^2 \ / \ s^2)$
okFCM	$O(tcn^2 \ / \ s + tc^3s^2)$	$O(n^2 \ / \ s^2 + s^2)$
akFCM	$O(n^3 \ / \ s^2 + tcn^2 \ / \ s)$	$O(n^2 \ / \ s)$
Extension	O(cn)	O(cn)

c = The number of clusters
n = The size of the data set
s = The number of equal sized subsets of the integers {1, 2… n}
d = The number of features of the data set

In the above study, time is not the predominant problem and accuracy and feasibility are the main focus points. Basing upon the load ability of data into memory and some other factors the algorithms can be selected.

This process is summarised in the form of a figure in (Havens et al 2012, Figure 7).

5.2. Intuitionistic Fuzzy C-Means Algorithm for Large Data

It is well known that the intuitionistic fuzzy set model (Atanassov, 1986) is superior to the fuzzy set model (Zadeh, 1965). Hence the fuzzy c-means clustering algorithms have been extended to develop the corresponding intuitionistic fuzzy c-means algorithms for data clustering. In (Tripathy et al, 2016) a novel algorithm is proposed where the data chunks are initially identified by Mapper class in Hadoop framework. The clusters along with arbitrary centroids serve as input to mapper class. The centroids are updated at the end of each of the iterations of IFCM. This is done just after the reducer class merges the chunks. Applying IFCM alone on large data is less efficient and process become cumbersome. This drawback can be overcome by using Hadoop. It helps tremendously for computing better clusters effectively and reaches local optima efficiently. The performance of HIFCM is compared with those of parallel k-means (PKM) and modified parallel k-means (MPKM) algorithms introduced by Mathew and Vijayakumar (Mathew et al, 2014) and it was observed experimentally that HIFCM performs better than both these algorithms.

5.3. A MapReduce-Based Fuzzy C-Means Clustering Algorithm (Ludwig, 2015)

An efficient approach in big data clustering is to build efficient and effective parallel clustering algorithms. MapReduce methodology introduced by Google (Dean and Ghemawat, 2004) is used in most of these algorithms. First, we provide a review of the Crisp clustering algorithms, which are developed by using MapReduce framework, in order to make them applicable for large data sets.

The original DBSCAN algorithm had drawbacks like, data balancing and scalability. An efficient algorithm called Mr-dbscan, which handles these issues was introduced in (He et al, 2014).In this the sequential processing is replaced with parallelised implementation, which takes care of scalability. It has been found to be suitable to handle imbalanced data.

A parallel clustering algorithm, which locates the centroids by calculating the weighted average of each individual cluster points via the Map function and then uses the reduce function to assign new centroids to each data point based upon distance calculations is introduced in (Zhao et al, 2009). A MapReduce iterative refinement technique is applied to locate the final centroids. This approach helps in processing data of reasonably large size. Similarly, the problem of document clustering using the MapReduce-based K-means is proposed in (Zhou et al, 2011). The authors compare a non-parallelised version of K-means with a parallelised version of K-means to show the significant improvement in the speed of execution. Also, it is shown that the algorithm performs well in terms of accuracy for the text clustering task.

A method called the ensemble learning bagging method, which uses MapReduce in K-means (Li et al, 2011) handles the instability and sensitivity to outliers problem efficiently. It may be noted that bagging is one of the most popular type of ensemble techniques. A Self-Organising Map (SOM) is an unsupervised neural network that projects high-dimensional data onto a low-dimensional grid. MapReduce was used in a modified SOM to work with large datasets in (Nair et al, 2011). In (Ene et al, 2011), the authors used an ant colony approach to decompose the big data into several data partitions to be used in parallel clustering. The MapReduce framework is used here.

Since the introduction of the objective function approach by Bezdek (Bezdek, 1981), most of the fuzzy clustering algorithms are based on the optimization of the objective function

$$J = \sum_{i=1}^{n} \sum_{j=1}^{c} (\mu_{ij})^m d^2(x_i, C_j)$$

where n is the number of data items, c is the number of clusters, x_i is the ith data item, C_j is the jth cluster and μ_{ij} is the membership value of x_i in C_j and $d(x_i, C_j)$ is the distance of x_i from the centre of the cluster C_j. Also, some modifications to this objective function is considered some times.

With the advent of large data sets, these algorithms became more or less unsuitable for clustering these data sets and needed to be improved or modified. We have discussed some of these extensions above. One of the approaches to extend FCM is to use parallelisation. One such extensions was done in (Modenesi et al, 2007) where the concept of Message Passing Routines (MPI) was used. The parallelisation was achieved three master/slave processes. The first one was computing the centroids. The second one takes care of computing distances, updates the centroids and prepares the partition matrix. The last one computes the validity index. However, the MapReduce environment decomposes the large computations into several independent Map functions. This approach is fault tolerant. This is the approach used in (Ludwig, 2015). The basic functionality is that the input is taken as a set of (key, value) pairs. The algorithm to be parallelised needs to be expressed by Map and Reduce functions. The Map function takes an input pair and returns a set of intermediate (key, value) pairs. The framework then groups all intermediate values associated with the same intermediate key and passes them to the Reduce function. The reduce function uses the intermediate key and set of values for that key. These values are merged together to form a smaller set of values. The intermediate values are forwarded to the Reduce function via an iterator. There are five algorithms. Algorithm 1 is the main procedure of the algorithm (called MR-FCM). The second one describes the procedure for the Map function of the first MapReduce job. The third one describes the procedure how merging of intermediate centroid matrices is done by the Reduce function of the first MapReduce function. The fourth one describes how the Map function of the second MapReduce job and the final algorithm deals with the reduce function of the second MapReduce function. The accuracy of the MR-FCM algorithm has been found to be satisfactory through experimental analysis. However, this paper does not cover the purity and scalability of the algorithm. Also, it was not tested with big data sets having multiple GBs of data.

5.4. Extension of Probabilistic Clustering to Large Data Sets (Hathaway & Bezdek, 2006)

The extensible methods of clustering are supposed to handle large or very large data sets. Instead of dealing with these data sets, many approaches deal with their sub-samples. So, Very Large $\supset$ Large $\supset$ Sub-sample .Two algorithms for large data sets, called the generalised extended fast fuzzy c-means (geFFCM) and a probabilistic algorithm called generalised extended fast expectation maximization (geFEM) have been proposed in (Hathaway and Bezdek, 2006). Both these methods work on the principle of selecting a sample form the data set, cluster it and then extend the result to the original data set. There is a fundamental difference between the two methods. In case of a large data set the clustering obtained by application of literal FCM (LFCM), i.e. the FCM being applied to the whole sample data set and its extension to the whole data set can be compared with the result obtained when LFCM is applied to the whole data set, the quality of the extended approach can be ascertained. This is not possible for a very large data set. So, the confidence on the accuracy of geFFCM is based on its verified results for various experiments carried out on the large data sets.

It has been stated in (Ganti, 1999a) that an algorithm is said to be scalable if its runtime complexity increases linearly with the number of records of input data. It has been argued in (Hathaway and Bezdek, 2006) that scalability alone is not enough as although FCM is scalable in the above sense it is slow in processing a lot of samples. Making the clustering algorithms faster is not a solution to the problem of handling very large data as these data sets cannot be processed at a time.

Also, it has been observed by several authors that progressive sampling approach leads to more efficient algorithms than the literal approaches under many circumstances (Provost et al, 1999). Another approach is due to (Meek et al, 2002) in which samples are used for expectation-maximization clustering. However, unlike these two approaches due to (provost et al, 1999) and (Meek et al, 2002), in the geFFCM algorithm (Hathaway et al, 2006) clustering never starts until an adequate sample is selected. Once an adequate sample is selected, single run of the algorithm is carried out over the selected sample and solutions to the remaining samples are approximated relying upon extensibility.

Single pass algorithms start by selecting a random subset of the whole data set which can be stored in memory and cluster it, summarize and then one of the many possible strategies is applied. This process is continued until the data set is exhausted. The hard c-means algorithm is used to determine the partition matrices for each of the subsets and then these matrices are concatenated. However, there is no guarantee in this approach the final matrix obtained be a valid partition of the whole data set.

The extensible fast fuzzy c-means introduced in (Shankar and Pal, 1994) is an evolution of the progressive sampling method. In FFCM the LFCM is applied to a sequence of extended partitions generated from the whole data set. The terminating condition for this approach is that the successive extended partitions differ by a predefined threshold value. Another algorithm similar to eFFCM is the multistage random sampling fuzzy c-means (mrFCM) (Cheng et al, 1995). As mrFCM runs on the whole data set, eFFCM is faster than mrFCM. Another extension of FCM, the bit reduction FCM (brFCM) introduced by Eschrich et al (2003) attains excellent average speed up factors over LFCM. It is distantly related to approximate FCM (AFCM) algorithm. The algorithm extensible fast fuzzy c-means clustering(eFFCM) introduced in (Pal and Bezdek, 2002) uses the progressive sampling which terminates with a subsample of pixels that is representative of all pixels in the image. After that LFCM is applied to the set of feature vectors corresponding to the subsample. Finally, the extensibility property of FCM is used to extend the clusters to the rest of the image. It was experimentally established in (Pal and Bezdek, 2002) that extended partition of image data can be a very accurate approximation to the literal partition. The generalised eFFCM (geFFCM) differs from eFFCM in four ways.

- The subsample selection and enhancement is using sampling without replacement.
- The selection is based on various subsets of all features.
- It uses bins of unequal width derived from the initial subsample.
- It uses only the divergence test under statistical test.

The experimental analysis confirms the following characteristics of geFFCM.

- It is applicable to non-image data.
- It is well suited for continuous or discrete data having a large number of distinct feature values.

- With a suitable restriction on the bins, it can also be applied to coarse data exhibiting only a small number of distinct feature values.
- Termination of progressive sampling is controlled by the choice made by the user.

It is noted that the methods of subsampling and extension are equally effective for acceleration, approximation and extension to very large data of any extensible clustering algorithm but not just to FCM.

5.5. Hadoop-Based Uncertain Possibilistic Kernelized C-Means Algorithms for Image Segmentation and a Comparative Analysis

To measure the distance between two data points a metric called Euclidean distance is used in clustering. But a major limitation to this metric is that it can only segregate the points which are linearly separable. This problem is overcome by using kernel function which ensures that data points are separable by creation of non-linear separators (Zhang et al 2002, Zhou et al 2008). Using the kernel metric, recently, a kernel based rough intuitionistic fuzzy c-means algorithm (KRIFCM) has been proposed by (Tripathy et al, 2014a) and they confirmed its superiority over RFCM, KRFCM and RIFCM using standard clustering accuracy metrics like Davies Bouldin (DB) and Dunn (D) Indices (Davis et al 1979, Dunn 1973).

When considering FCM algorithm it is known that cumulative membership of object over the classes is 1. This condition prevents meaningless outcomes by restricting a solution in which all the memberships could be 0 hence it also enables to express memberships as probabilities. Since the stated constraint ensures that membership values are associated to one another, this makes it inappropriate for situations when the membership value symbolizes "typicality". Possibilistic approach for clustering was proposed by Krishnapuram and Keller (Krishnapuram et al 1993, 1996) using the concept of typicality. In this approach the constraint imposed on the sum of membership values is reduced signifying that each membership can lie between 0 and a constant denoted as c. The membership rating of an object to a cluster is called typicality of that object. In 1997, Pal et al. (Pal et al, 2005) introduced a fuzzy-possibilistic c-means (FPCM) technique which could produce typicality as well as membership value during clustering. In FPCM, constraint applied on typicality ensures that for a cluster the sum of typicalities over all the instances is 1, this makes FPCM less susceptible to problem of coincidental cluster in PCM and FCM's probabilistic restriction problem. Later, Anuradha et al. introduced PRCM which was based on rough sets and Tripathy at al. introduced PRFCM (Tripathy et al, 2014b) and PRIFCM (Tripathy et al, 2015). They established its superiority over PRCM, RCM and RFCM algorithms.

In Tripathy et al (2016) three hybrid clustering algorithms were introduced by combining rough, fuzzy, and intuitionistic fuzzy with possibilistic approach and kernelized distance functions. These are PKRCM, PKRFCM and PKRIFCM. The performances of these algorithms were compared with the algorithms of other families of algorithms; the typical hybrid algorithms RCM, RFCM, RIFCM; their kernelized versions KRCM, KRFCM, KRIFCM and their possibilistic versions PRCM, PRFCM, PRIFCM. Out of several kernel functions available, three algorithms were selected for this study; namely the Radial Basis, the Gaussian and the hyper tangent. So, the number of possibilities for comparison becomes multiplied. Also, an effort was made to find out the most suitable of the three kernels for the segmentation of these images.

Definition 1: Kernel Distance

Let 'a' denote a data point. Then transformation of 'a' to the feature plane which possess higher dimensionality be denoted by $\varphi(a)$. Description of inner product space is given by $K(a,b) = \langle \varphi(a), \varphi(b) \rangle$. Let $a = (a_1, a_2, \ldots a_n)$ and $b = (b_1, b_2, \ldots b_n)$ are two points in the n-dimensional space. Kernel functions used in this paper are stated as follows:

- Radial Basis Kernel

$$R(a,b) = \exp\left(-\sum_{i=1}^{n}(a_i^{\,p} - b_i^{\,p})^q / 2\sigma^2\right) \tag{2}$$

In this paper all the implementations of all the algorithms corresponding to Radial Basis Kernel have been done using p=2 and q=2 in equation (2).

- Gaussian Kernel (RBF with p=1 and q=2)

$$G(a,b) = \exp\left(-\sum_{i=1}^{n}(a_i - b_i)^2 / 2\sigma^2\right) \tag{3}$$

- Hyper-Tangent Kernel

$$H(a,b) = 1 - \tanh\left(-\sum_{i=1}^{n}(a_i - b_i)^2 / 2\sigma^2\right) \qquad (4)$$

where

$$\sigma^2 = \frac{1}{N}\sum_{i=1}^{N}|| a_i - a' ||^2$$

and

$$a' = \frac{1}{N}\sum_{i=1}^{N}a_i \qquad (5)$$

For all the kernels functions, N denotes the total number of existing data points and $|| x - y ||$ denotes the Euclidean distance between points x and y which pertain to Euclidean metric space. By [7, 30] D(a, b) denotes the complete form of kernel distance function where D(a, b) = K(a, a) + K(b, b) – 2K(a, b) and when similarity property (i.e. K(a, a) =1) is applied, we get:

$$D(a,b) = 2(1 - K(a,b)) \qquad (6)$$

Instead of merely displaying images to the user, treating a huge number of images as data is a new idea. In recent times storage and processing of an image has been considerably expensive. One of the major problems today is to process millions of images in the shortest amount of time and that too very cheaply. Industries are in the need of cheap frameworks which can ensure this cumbersome task; in this regard ApacheTM Hadoop comes to rescue. ApacheTM Hadoop in an open source framework for distributed computing of very large datasets and that too on commodity hardware. It is known for its capability to handle hardware failures efficiently. Each system in the distributed environment is known as node. Combination of all the nodes in the system is called as a cluster. The framework has been developed in Java and follows a map-reduce paradigm for processing the data. In this paradigm, the first step is fragmentation of data. This fragmentation ensures distribution of data on multiple nodes in the cluster. Each node then performs its task separately and the processed data is integrated as a whole in the reduce step. The problems like failure of nodes are automatically handled in the course of processing by the framework itself. All this makes Hadoop a tremendously ambidextrous and flexible platform.

One of the most challenging aspects of data mining is analysis of unstructured data. Currently, image data is growing at a brisk rate and we are in the need of algorithms which can find meaningful insights in the growing volume of primarily unstructured image data. A medium resolution satellite image with 2000 X 2000 pixels contains 40 lakh data points, even if 1 lakh such images have to be analysed collectively then it would account for tremendous processing power. If the analysis is primarily a clustering task then high accuracy also becomes an equally important requirement. Hence if efficient machine learning techniques can be applied in distributed framework then we will be able to sense resourceful information from huge volumes of images in considerably less time. Not all algorithms can be devised to work with the map-reduce paradigm of Hadoop. However, if one can organize an algorithm that can harmonize with this paradigm decently then it would add a high value to the processing efficiency.

Moving a step further in the process of hybridization of techniques and models that concepts kernel as similarity measure, the possibilistic approach and the uncertainty based models; fuzzy set, intuitionistic fuzzy set and rough set is possible. If this resulting hybrid combination can be incorporated to synchronize with the distributed architecture of Hadoop, an immensely efficient clustering technique can be comprehended. In order to realize this, in this paper we introduced three such algorithms called the Hadoop based possibilistic kernelized rough c-means (HPKRCM), Hadoop based possibilistic kernelized rough fuzzy c-means (HPKRFCM) and Hadoop based possibilistic kernelized rough intuitionistic fuzzy c-means (HPKRIFCM). Also, we try for three variations of each of these algorithms by taking three different types of kernels; the Radial basis, the Gaussian and the hyper tangent kernels. The basic aim is to compare the efficiency of the algorithms and find out which of the kernels is most appropriate under which real life applications. Also, the aim is to compare these algorithms with the basic hybrid algorithms as discussed earlier. In order to make our study extensive on images we have selected images from four different categories of real life set ups; namely a metal coin, a MRI image, Cancerous blood cells and a satellite image.

Four different types of input images were considered as input to all these algorithms. These are images of a metal coin, a MRI image, cancerous blood cells and a satellite image. In fact, in earlier studies also similar images were taken into consideration in papers related to the families of hybrid models stated above. Since images are being considered as inputs, more than the output images it was decided to take the help of several indices proposed to determine the efficiencies of data clustering algorithms; namely the Davis and Bouldin (DB) (1979), Dunn (D) (1973), Alpha (α), rho (ρ), alpha star (α^*) and gamma (γ) (Davis et al 1979, Dunn et al 1973, Maji et al 2007). The number of clusters selected was four and five. Also, as visual aid, they have provided the bar diagrams for all the six indexes and all the algorithms for each of the four input images. In addition to all these, pixel clustering images for brain MRI image was considered, to show the cluster formation in each of the cases taken for comparison. Our experimental analysis shows that the hyper tangent kernel is the best one when applied along with PKRIFCM algorithm. Our observation confirms with that of Chaira (Chaira 2015), who established that for IFCM the hyper tangent kernel provides the best results for MRI images. Among several observations obtained, we find that the HPKRIFCM algorithm with the hyper tangent kernel performs the best for MRI images.

6. SCOPE FOR FUTURE STUDY

As we have seen above the data clustering algorithms developed so far are not adequate and there are still a lot many algorithms developed for normal data sets to be either improved or improved by applying some techniques like the ones presented in section 5 to make them suitable for clustering large data sets. It is suggested to extend all the algorithms presented in section 5 except the one considered in section 5.5 as follows.

- The rough set based algorithms.
- The hybrid rough fuzzy algorithms.
- The hybrid rough intuitionistic fuzzy algorithms.
- The Kernelised versions of the algorithms.
- The possibilistic versions of all the algorithms.

7. CONCLUSION

In this chapter our main goal was to present the clustering processes available for large data sets, which cannot be clustered by using the available algorithms which are applicable to datasets of reasonable sizes and complexities. We introduced the different approaches available to date in modifying some of the algorithms in order to make them suitable to handle the large datasets. One of the mostly tackled algorithms is the fuzzy C-means. There is a plethora of algorithms, which are extension of FCM like FFCM,eFFCM, mrFFCM, brFFCM, geFFCM, AFCM, MR-FCM, spFCM., oFCM, wFCM, akFCM, spkFCM, okFCM and rseFCM. We touched each of these algorithms with references to original papers from where further details of these algorithms can be found out. In section 5.6, we presented several algorithms based upon hybrid models such as RFCM, RIFCM, their kernelized versions (with three kernels being taken) KRFCM, KRIFCM; their possibilistic versions PRFCM,

PRIFCM; their possibilistic kernelized versions PKRFCM, PKRIFCM and all with respect to the Hadoop platform. Also, a comparative analysis of these algorithms is presented. Finally, some research directions is also proposed. However, we cannot say that the process is over by any means. There are a lot of algorithms involving other uncertainty based models which can be extended or modified to have better algorithms in future.

REFERENCES

Aggarwal, C., Han, J., Wang, J., & Yu, P. (2003). A framework for clustering evolving data streams. *Proc. Int. Conf. Very Large Databases*, 81–92. doi:10.1016/B978-012722442-8/50016-1

Anderberg, M. R. (1973). *Cluster analysis for applications*. Academic Press.

Baeza-Yates, R., & Ribeiro-Neto, B. (1999). *Modern Information retrieval*. Reading, MA: Addison Wesley Longman.

Bezdek, J. C. (1981). Pattern recognition with Fuzzy Objective Function Algorithms. Kluwer Academic Publishers.

Bu, H., Howe, B., Balazinska, M., & Ernst, M. D. (2010). HaLoop: Efficient Iterative Data Processing on Large Clusters. Proceedings of the VLDB Endowment, 3(1), 285-296.

Can, F. (1993). Incremental clustering for dynamic information processing. *ACM Transactions on Information Systems*, *11*(2), 143–164. doi:10.1145/130226.134466

Can, F., Fox, E., Snavely, C., & France, R. (1995). Incremental clustering for very large document databases: Initial MARIAN experience. *Information Sciences*, *84*(1–2), 101–114. doi:10.1016/0020-0255(94)00111-N

Carpenter, G. A., & Grossberg, S. (1987). A massively parallel architecture for a self-organizing neural pattern recognition machine. *Computer Vision Graphics and Image Processing*, *37*(1), 54–115. doi:10.1016/S0734-189X(87)80014-2

Carpenter, G. A., & Grossberg, S. (1990). ART 3: Hierarchical search using chemical transmitters in self–organizing pattern recognition architectures. *Neural Networks*, *3*(2), 129–152. doi:10.1016/0893-6080(90)90085-Y

Chaira, T. (2015). *Medical Image Processing: Advanced Fuzzy Set Theoretic Techniques*. CRC Press.

Cheng, T. W., Goldgof, D. B., & Hall, L. O. (1995). Fast clustering with application to fuzzy rule generation. *Proceedings of the IEEE international Conference on Fuzzy Systems*, 2289-2295.

Chitta, R., Jin, R., Havens, T., & Jain, A. (2011). Approximate kernel k-means: Solutions to large scale kernel clustering. Proc. ACM SIGKDD Conf. Knowl Discovery and Data Mining, 895-903.

Cordeiro, F., Traina, C. Jr, Traina, A. J. M., Lopez, J., Kang, U., & Taloutsos, C. (2011). Clustering very large multi-dimensional datasets with MapReduce. *Proceedings of KDD'11*, 690-698.

Cutting, D. R., Karger, D. R., Pederson, J. O., & Tukey, J. W. (1992). Scatter/gather: a cluster-based approach to browsing large document collections. Proceedings of the ACM SIGIR'92, 318-329.

Davis, D. L., & Bouldin, D. W. (1979). A cluster separation measure. *IEEE Transactions on Pattern Analysis and Machine Intelligence, PAMI-1*(2), 224–227. doi:10.1109/TPAMI.1979.4766909 PMID:21868852

Dean, J., & Ghemawat, S. (2004). MapReduce: simplified data processing on large clusters. *Proceedings of the 6th conference on Symposium on Operating Systems Design and Implementation*, 6, 10.

Dubois, D., & Prade, H. (1990). Rough Fuzzy Sets and Fuzzy Rough Sets. *International Journal of General Systems, 17*(2-3), 191–209. doi:10.1080/03081079008935107

Dunn, J. C. (1973). *A fuzzy relative of the ISODATA process and its use in detecting compact well-separated clusters*. Academic Press.

Ene, A., Im, S., & Moseley, B. (2011). Fast clustering using MapReduce. *Proceedings of KDD'11*, 681-689.

Ester, M., Kriegel, H. P., Sander, J., & Xu, X. (1996). A Density-Based Algorithm for Discovering Clusters in Large Spatial Databases with Noise. *Proceedings of KDD-96*, 226–231.

Esterich, S., & Ke, J. (2003). Fast accurate fuzzy clustering through data reduction. *IEEE Transactions on Fuzzy Systems, 11*(2), 262–269. doi:10.1109/TFUZZ.2003.809902

Everitt, B. J. & Marina E. W. (2002). Psychomotor Stimulant Addiction: A Neural Systems Perspective. *The Journal of Neuroscience, 22*(9), 3312–3320.

Everitt, B. S., Landau, S., Leese, M., & Daniel, S. (2011). *Cluster Analysis* (5th ed.). John Wiley & Sons, Ltd. doi:10.1002/9780470977811

Fahad, A., Alshatri, N., Tari, Z., Alamri, A., Khalil, I., Zomaya, A. Y., & Boura, A. et al. (2014). A Survey of Clustering Algorithms for Big Data: Taxonomy and Empirical Analysis. *IEEE Transactions on Emerging Topics in Computing, 2*(3), 267–279. doi:10.1109/TETC.2014.2330519

Ganti, V., Gehrke, J., & Ramakrishnan, R. (1999a). Mining very large databases. *Computer, 32*(August), 38–45. doi:10.1109/2.781633

Ganti, V., Ramakrishnan, R., Gehrke, J., Powel, A. L., & French, J. C. (1999b) Clustering large datasets in arbitrary metric spaces. *Proceedings of the 14th international conference on Data Engineering*, 502-511. doi:10.1109/ICDE.1999.754966

Guha, S., Meyerson, A., Mishra, N., Motwani, R., & OCallaghan, L. (2003). Clustering data streams: Theory and practice. *IEEE Transactions on Knowledge and Data Engineering, 15*(3), 515–528. doi:10.1109/TKDE.2003.1198387

Guha, S., Rastogi, R., & Shim, K. (1998). CURE: An efficient clustering algorithm for large databases. *Proceedings of ACM SIGMOD*, 73–84 doi:10.1145/276304.276312

Guha, S., Rastogi, R., & Shim, K. (2000). ROCK: A Robust Clustering Algorithm for Categorical Attributes. *15th International Conference on Data Engineering*, 512-521. doi:10.1016/S0306-4379(00)00022-3

HarPeled, S., & Mazumdar, S. (2004). On core sets for K-means and k-median clustering. *Proc. ACM Symposium on Theory Compute*, 291–300.

Hartigan, J. A. (1975). Clustering Algorithms. John Wiley & Sons, Inc.

Hathaway, R., & Bezdek, Z. (2006). Extending fuzzy and probabilistic clustering to very large data sets. *Computational Statistics & Data Analysis, 51*(1), 215–234. doi:10.1016/j.csda.2006.02.008

Havens, T. C., Bezdek, J. C., Leckie, C., Hall, L. O., & Palaniswami, M. (2012). Fuzzy c-Means Algorithms for Very Large Data. *IEEE Transactions on Fuzzy Systems, 20*(6), 1130–1146. doi:10.1109/TFUZZ.2012.2201485

Havens, T. C., Chitta, R., Jain, A. K., & Rong, J. (2011). Speedup of fuzzy and possibilistic kernel C-Means for Large scale clustering. *2011 IEEE International Conference on Fuzzy Systems (FUZZ)*, 463-470. doi:10.1109/FUZZY.2011.6007618

He, Y., Tan, H., Luo, W., Feng, S., & Fan, J. (2014). Mr-dB scan: a scalable MapReduce based dB scan algorithm for heavily skewed data. *Frontiers of Computer Science, 8*(1), 83-99.

Hore, P., Hall, L., & Goldgof, D. (2007). Single pass fuzzy c-means. *Proc. IEEE Int. Conf. Fuzzy Syst.*, 1-7.

Hore, P., Hall, L., Goldgof, D., Gu, Y., & Maudsley, A. (2009). A scalable framework for segmenting magnetic resonance images, J. Signal process. *Syst.*, *54*(1-3), 183–203.

Huang, Z. (1997). Clustering Large Data Sets With Mixed Numeric And Categorical Values. *Proceedings of the first Pacific-Asia Conference on Knowledge Discovery and Data Mining.*

Jain, A. K., & Dubes, R. C. (1988). *Algorithms for clustering Data.* Upper Saddle River, NJ: Prentice-Hall, Inc.

Kothari, D., Narayanan, S. T., & Devi, K. K. (2014). Extended Fuzzy C-Means with Random Sampling Techniques for Clustering Large Data. *Int. Jour. of Innovative Research in Advanced Engineering*, *3*(1), 1–4.

Krishnapuram, R., & Keller, J. M. (1993). A Possibilistic Approach to Clustering. *IEEE Transactions on Fuzzy Systems*, *1*(2), 98–110. doi:10.1109/91.227387

Krishnapuram, R., & Keller, J. M. (1996). The possibilistic c-means algorithm: Insights and recommendations. Fuzzy Systems. *IEEE Transactions on*, *4*(3), 385–393.

Li, H. G., Wu, G. Q., Hu, X. G., Zhang, J., Li, L., & Wu, X. (2011). K-means clustering with bagging and MapReduce. *Proceedings of the 2011 44th Hawaii International conference on System Sciences*, 1-8.

Liao, L., & Lin, T. (2007). A fast constrained fuzzy kernel clustering algorithm for MRI brain image segmentation. *Proc. Int. Conf. Wavelet Analysis and Pattern Recognition*, 82–87.

Lingras, P., & West, C. (2004). Interval Set Clustering of Web Users with Rough K-Means. *Journal of Intelligent Information Systems*, *23*(1), 5–16. doi:10.1023/B:JIIS.0000029668.88665.1a

Ludwig, S. A. (2015). MapReduce-based Fuzzy C-Means Clustering Algorithm: Implementation and Scalability. *Int. Jour. of Machine Learning and Cybernetics*, *6*(6), 923–934. doi:10.1007/s13042-015-0367-0

Maji, P., & Pal, S. K. (2007). RFCM: A Hybrid Clustering Algorithm using rough and fuzzy set. *Fundamenta Informaticae*, *8*(4), 475–496.

Mathew, J., & Vijayakumar, R. (2014). Scalable parallel clustering approach for large data using parallel K-means and firefly algorithms. *Proceedings of International Conference on High Computing and Applications*, 1–8.

McQueen, J. (1967). Some Methods for Classification and Analysis of Multivariate Observations. *Proc. Fifth Berkeley Symposium on Mathematics Statistics and Probability*, 281–297.

Meek, C., Thiesson, B., & Heckerman, D. (2002). The learning curve sampling method applied to model based clustering. *Journal of Machine Learning Research*, 2, 397–418.

Mitra, S., Banka, H., & Pedrycz, W. (2006). Rough-Fuzzy Collaborative Clustering. *IEEE Transactions on Systems, Man, and Cybernetics. Part B, Cybernetics*, 36(4), 795–805. doi:10.1109/TSMCB.2005.863371 PMID:16903365

Modenesi, M. V., Costa, M. C. A., Evsukoff, A. G., & Ebecken, N. F. (2007). Parallel Fuzz C-means Cluster Analysis. In *Lecture Notes in Computer Science on High Performance Computing for Computational Science- VECPAR*. Springer.

Nair, S., & Mehta, J. (2011). Clustering with apache Hadoo. *Proceedings of the International Conference, Workshop on Emerging Trends in technology, ICWET'11*, 505-509.

Namdev, A., & Tripathy, B. K. (2016). Scalable Rough C-Means clustering using Firefly algorithm. *International Journal of Computer Science and Business Informatics*, 16(2), 1–14.

Ng, R. T., & Han, J. (1994). Efficient and Effective clustering methods for spatial data mining. *Proceedings of the 20th international conference on very large databases*, 144-155.

Orlandia, R., Lai, Y., & Lee, W. (2005). Clustering high dimensional data using an efficient and effective data space reduction. *Proc. ACM Conference on Information and Knowledge Management*, 201–208.

Pal, N. R., Pal, K., Keller, J. M., & Bezdek, J. C. (2005). A Possibilistic Fuzzy C-Means Clustering Algorithm. *IEEE Transactions on Fuzzy Systems*, 13(4), 517–530. doi:10.1109/TFUZZ.2004.840099

Papadimitriou, S., & Sun, J. (2008). Disco: distributed co-clustering with MapReduce: A case study towards petabyte-scale end-to-end mining. *Proc. of the IEEE ICDM'08*, 512–521. doi:10.1109/ICDM.2008.142

Pawlak, Z. (1991). *Rough Sets, Theoretical Aspects of Reasoning about Data*. Dordrecht, The Netherlands: Kluwer.

Ruspini, E. H. (1970). Numerical methods for fuzzy clustering. *Information Sciences*, 2(3), 319–350. doi:10.1016/S0020-0255(70)80056-1

Saleha, R., Haider, J. N., & Danish, N. (2002). Rough Intuitionistic Fuzzy Sets. *Proceedings of the 8th Int. conf. on Fuzzy Theory and Technology (FT & T)*.

Shankar, B. U., & Pal, N. (1994). FFCM: An effective approach for large data sets. *Proc. Int. Conf. Fuzzy Logic, Neural Nets, Soft Computing*, 332.

Srujan, C., Jain, A., & Tripathy, B. K. (2017). Image segmentation using Hybridized Firefly Algorithm and Intuitionistic Fuzzy C-Means. *First International Conference on Smart Systems, Innovation and Computing*. Manipal University.

Srujan, C., Jain, A., & Tripathy, B. K. (2017). Stabilizing Rough Set Based Clustering Algorithms using Firefly Algorithm over Image Datasets. *Second International Conference on Information and Communication technology for Intelligent Systems*.

Tripathy, B. K., Bhargava, R., Tripathy, A., Dhull, R., Verma, E., & Swarnalatha, P. (2013). *Rough Intuitionistic Fuzzy C-Means Algorithm and a Comparative Analysis in proceedings of ACM Compute 2013*. VIT University.

Tripathy, B. K., & Ghosh, A. (2011a). SDR: An algorithm for clustering categorical data using rough set theory. Recent Advances in Intelligent Computational Systems (RAICS), 2011 IEEE, Trivandrum, 867-872.

Tripathy, B. K., & Ghosh, A. (2011b). SSDR: An Algorithm for Clustering Categorical Data Using Rough Set Theory. *Advances in Applied Science Research, 2*(3), 314–326.

Tripathy, B. K., & Ghosh, A. (2012). Data Clustering Algorithms Using Rough Sets. Handbook of Research on Computational Intelligence for Engineering, Science, and Business, 297.

Tripathy, B. K., Ghosh, S. K., & Jena, S. P. (2002). Intuitionistic Fuzzy Rough Sets. *Notes on Intuitionistic Fuzzy Sets (Bulgaria), 8*(1), 1–18.

Tripathy, B. K., Goyal, A., Chowdhury, R., & Patra, A. S. (2017). *MMeMeR: An Algorithm for Clustering Heterogeneous Data using Rough Set Theory*. Communicated to International Journal of Intelligent Systems and Applications.

Tripathy, B. K., Goyal, A., & Patra, A. S. (2016). Clustering Categorical Data Using Intuitionistic Fuzzy K-mode. *International Journal of Pharmacy and Technology, 8*(3), 16688–16701.

Tripathy, B. K., Goyal, A., & Patra, A. S. (2016). A Comparative Analysis of Rough Intuitionistic Fuzzy K-mode for Clustering Categorical Data. *Research Journal of Pharmaceutical, Biological and Chemical Sciences, 7*(5), 2787–2802.

Tripathy, B. K., & Kumar, M. S. P. (2009). MMeR: An algorithm for clustering Heterogeneous data using rough Set Theory. *International Journal of Rapid Manufacturing*, *1*(2), 189–207. doi:10.1504/IJRAPIDM.2009.029382

Tripathy, B. K., & Mittal, D. (2016). Hadoop based Uncertain Possibilistic Kernelized C-Means Algorithms for Image Segmentation and a Comparative analysis. *Applied Soft Computing*, *46*, 886–923. doi:10.1016/j.asoc.2016.01.045

Tripathy, B. K., Mittal, D., & Hudedagaddi, D. P. (2016). Hadoop with Intuitionistic Fuzzy C-Means for Clustering in Big Data. *Proceedings of the International Congress on Information and Communication Technology*, 599-610. doi:10.1007/978-981-10-0767-5_62

Tripathy, B. K., Tripathy, A. & Govindarajulu, K. (2014b). Possibilistic rough fuzzy C-means algorithm in data clustering and image segmentation. *Proceedings of the IEEE ICCIC2014*, 981-986.

Tripathy, B. K., Tripathy, A. & Govindarajulu, K. (2015). On PRIFCM Algorithm for Data Clustering, Image Segmentation and Comparative Analysis. *Proceedings of the IEEE IACC2015*, 333 – 336.

Tripathy, B. K., Tripathy, A., Govindarajulu, K., & Bhargav, R. (2014a). On Kernel Based Rough Intuitionistic Fuzzy C-means Algorithm and a Comparative Analysis. Advanced Computing, Networking and Informatics, 1, 349-359.

Xu, X., Ester, M., Kriegel, H. P., & Sander, J. (1998). A Distribution-Based Clustering Algorithm for Mining in Large Spatial Databases. *Proceedings of 14th International Conference on Data Engineering (ICDE'98)*.

Yang, J., & Li, X. (2013). MapReduce based method for big data semantic clustering. *Proceedings of the 2013 IEEE International Conference on Systems, Man and Cybernetics, SMC'13*, 2814-2819. doi:10.1109/SMC.2013.480

Zadeh, L. A. (1965). Fuzzy Sets. *Information and Control*, *8*(11), 338–353. doi:10.1016/S0019-9958(65)90241-X

Zhang, D., & Chen, S. (2002). Fuzzy Clustering Using Kernel Method. *Proceedings of the international conference on control and automation*, 123–127.

Zhang, T., Ramakrishnan, R., & Livny, M. (1996). BIRCH: An efficient data clustering method for very large databases. *Proc. ACM SIGMOD Int. Conf. Management Data*, 103–114. doi:10.1145/233269.233324

Zhao, W., Ma, H., & He, Q. (2009). *Parallel k-means clustering based on MapReduce. In proceedings of the CloudCom'09* (pp. 674–679). Berlin, Heidelberg: Springer Verlag.

Zhou, P., Lei, J., & Ye, W. (2011). Large-scale data sets clustering based on MapReduce and Hadoop, Computational. *Information Systems*, *7*(16), 5956–5963.

Zhou, T., Zhang, Y., Lu, H., Deng, F., & Wang, F. (2008). Rough Cluster Algorithm Based on Kernel Function. In G. Wang, T. Li, J. W. Grzymala-Busse, D. Miao, A. Skowron, & Y. Yao (Eds.), *RSKT 2008, LNAI* (Vol. 5009, pp. 172–179). doi:10.1007/978-3-540-79721-0_27

KEY TERMS AND DEFINITIONS

Fuzzy Sets: It is a generalisation of the crisp sets where the membership of elements in the collection is assigned any value in [0, 1] instead of only '0' or '1' in crisp sets. The change of membership is gradual rather than being sudden.

Intuitionistic Fuzzy Sets: It is a generalisation of fuzzy sets by defining a general non-membership value to elements instead of assuming that the non-membership is one's complement of the membership value.

Large Data: Data set being high in volume beyond the capacity of certain storage space or having complex characteristics.

Uncertain: The fact of being not sure about a state or conclusion.

Chapter 2
Sentiment Mining Approaches for Big Data Classification and Clustering

Ashok Kumar J
Anna University, India

Abirami S
Anna University, India

Tina Esther Trueman
Anna University, India

ABSTRACT

Sentiment analysis is one of the most important applications in the field of text mining. It computes people's opinions, comments, posts, reviews, evaluations, and emotions which are expressed on products, sales, services, individuals, organizations, etc. Nowadays, large amounts of structured and unstructured data are being produced on the web. The categorizing and grouping of these data become a real-world problem. In this chapter, the authors address the current research in this field, issues and the problem of sentiment analysis on Big Data for classification and clustering. It suggests new methods, applications, algorithm extensions of classification and clustering and software tools in the field of sentiment analysis.

DOI: 10.4018/978-1-5225-2805-0.ch002

INTRODUCTION

Sentiment analysis (also called opinion mining) is one of the most important research fields in Information Processing, Text mining, and Linguistics. Information shared in online social networks (forums, blogs, etc.) contain useful information about products, sales, service, individuals, organizations, Governments, policies, politics, etc. This information is expressed in two ways namely, an objective statement and a subjective statement. The objective statement refers to some factual information and subjective statement refers to personal feelings such as love, joy, surprise, anger, sadness, and fear. The amount of information collected in terms of volume, variety, and velocity is called Big Data. It can be treated as software as a service, platform as a service and infrastructure as a service. Based on these services, big data creates opportunities and challenges to extract valuable information.

This chapter addresses the sentiment classification and clustering techniques, such as Machine learning based approach, lexicon-based approach, and the hybrid approach. These in turn include techniques like Symmetric Matrix-based predictive classifier, Comparative experiments using supervised learning, Classifier ensembles, Ranked Word Graph for Sentiment polarity Classification, Sentiment Classification via Social context regularization, Context-Based Sentiment analysis, Semi-supervised subjective feature weighting and intelligent modelling, Cross-lingual sentiment classification: Similarity discovery, Supervised study weighting scheme, SVM with the linear kernel as the classification model, unsupervised dependency parsing-based text classification method, SACI (Sentiment Analysis by Collective Inspection), and a lexicon-based unsupervised method.

PROBLEM OF SENTIMENT ANALYSIS ON BIG DATA

Big data creates new challenges on data processing, data storage, data representation, pattern mining, visualization, etc (Gema Bello-Orgaz et al., 2016) in the field of data mining, machine learning, natural language processing, text mining, social networks, and sentiment analysis. The rapid growth of unstructured data in social networking, blogs, reviews, posts, comments, and tweets are the most important source for sentiment analysis (Changli Zhang et al., 2008). Further, sentiment analysis problems focus on different levels namely Document level, Sentence level, and aspect level (R Feldman, 2013). The document-level sentiment analyzes a piece of information. It represents multiple opinions, but not a single opinion view. Document level sentiment analysis hides insights and useful information by reducing a whole document into a single opinion. Sentence level expresses overall opinions of each sentence. Aspect level exactly expresses what people likes or dislikes. For instance, a single review of BMW 1 Series car is analyzed as shown in Figure 1. The sentences are numbered in parenthesis.

The classification and clustering techniques are required to provide meaningful information for those polarity data. The data can be classified and clustered into positive, negative, and neutral polarities. Sentiment analysis refers to a classification problem due to the prediction of polarity words such as positive, negative and neutral. The accuracy, data size, data sparsity, and sarcasm are the main issues in sentiment mining classification and clustering. Therefore, sentiment classification aims to mine the written documents (comments, posts, reviews, tweets, etc.) about a products or services and classifying the documents into positive or negative opinions (Qiang Ye et al., 2014, Yanghui Rao et al., 2014). Sentiment clustering aims to group the written documents. The general framework for sentiment analysis on Bigdata is shown in Figure 2.

MACHINE-LEARNING-BASED APPROACH

Machine learning approach is applicable to opinion mining problem. Determining positive or negative polarity is viewed as a former binary classification problem. Machine learning methods perform better predictions than the former methods by using the labeled, semi-labeled and unlabeled data [3]. In this approach, the supervised, semi-supervised and unsupervised learning methods are explained in the context of sentiment mining approach for big data.

Figure 1. A single review sentiment detection at different levels

The car is small and very fun to drive (1). The 128i engine has plenty of power (2). Very comfortable seats (sports option) (3). The rear seats have more room that you may think and gave to the car a great practical aspect (4). Trunk space also is not too bad, but it is a fun car (5). Inside noise, with the top up or down, is very low (6). No annoying rattles. Fuel economy: just ok(7). The fuel tank is small. The Ipod option works well (8).	*Document level*	*Positive*
	Sentence level	*(1), (3), (4), (5), (7), and (8) express positive opinions, (2) and (6) express none (objective information)*
	Aspect level	*Car (1,5), space (4,5), room (4), chest(5), and box (5)express positive opinions, Sport (3), Noise (6), fuel oil (7, 8), economy (7), and tank (8) express none*

Figure 2. A general framework for sentiment analysis on Bigdata

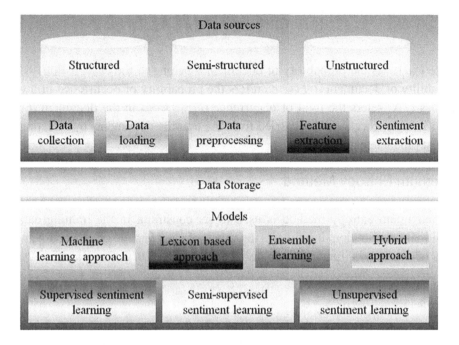

Supervised Sentiment Learning

Supervised sentiment learning is the machine learning based approach. This system learns from labeled training data. Various supervised sentiment learning methods are discussed as follows.

Naive Bayes Method

Naive Bayes is a probabilistic model based on Bayes' rule. This model is used to predict the most likely class for a new document, and it performs well for text classification as well as training purposes in many domains. The documents are generated as multinomial event model by considering word frequency information. A document is represented as a sequence of words from BOW (Bag of Words). The probability of an event is obtained in a document based on the following equation (Qiang Ye et al., 2014, Abinash Tripathy et al., 2016, Changli Zhang et al., 2008, Rui Xia et al., 2011).

$$P(d_i|c_j) = P(|d_i|)|d_i|! \prod_{t=1}^{|V|} \frac{P(w_t|c_j)^{N_{it}}}{N_{it}!}$$

where $P(d_i|c_j)$ is the probability of document d belong to the class c $P(|d_i|)$ is the probability of document d $P(w_t|c_j)$ refers the probability of occurrence of a word in class c. N_{it} refers the total of occurrence of the word in the document d_i. The classification process can be carried from the training documents by selecting the highest probable class.

Maximum Entropy Method

The maximum entropy method is used to set constraint in the training data on conditional distribution. It estimates the values of class b in the given document a in terms of exponential function (Abinash Tripathy et al., 2016, Rui Xia et al., 2011).

$$P_{ME}(b|a) = \frac{1}{Z(a)} \exp\left\{\sum_i \lambda_i f_i(a,b)\right\}$$

such that

$$f_i(a,b) = \begin{cases} 1, & a = a_i \text{ and } b = b_i, \\ 0, & other, \end{cases}$$

where $P_{ME}(a|b)$ is the probability of class b in the given document a. $Z(a)$ is the normalizing factor. $f_i(a, b)$ is the feature in class b and document a. One represents the occurrence of class b in the given document a. λ_i represents the weight coefficient. The weight is calculated based on the frequent occurrence of a feature in a class a. The highest word frequencies are considered for classification.

Support Vector Machine Method

Support Vector Machine (SVM) is effectively used for classifying the features in a hyperplane by using weights. It separates the documents into positive and negative training class with maximum margin. SVM outperforms Naive Bayes method. The maximum margin determines the distance from decision boundary to the closest data point. These data points are called as support vectors (Qiang Ye et al., 2014, Abinash Tripathy et al., 2016, Rui Xia et al., 2011, Ahmed Alsaffar et al., 2014).

Let D = {(x_i, y_i)}, $i = 1, 2, 3, \ldots$ be the training set with labeled pair. Where $x_i \in R^n$ and $y_i \in \{+1, -1\}$. The positive and negative classes are named as +1 and -1. Let g(x) = w$^T\phi$ (x) + b be the discriminant function. Where the parameter w and b represent the weight vector and bias. These parameters are learned automatically on the training set following the optimization problem by

$$\min \frac{1}{2} w^T w + C \sum_{i=1}^{n} \xi_i$$

such that

$$\begin{cases} y_i g(x_i) \geq 1 - \xi_i, \\ \xi_i \geq 0, i = 1, 2, .., n, \end{cases}$$

where ξ represents the slack variables and C represent the penalty coefficient or regularization factor. SVM becomes minimization problem. The solution is associated with the Lagrange multiplier α_i and kernel function as expressed in the following equation. In the text classification problems, the linear kernel is always used to due to the high dimensional feature space.

$$g(x) = \sum_{i=1}^{\tilde{N}} \alpha_i y_i K(\tilde{x}_i, x).$$

Stochastic Gradient Descent (SGD) Method

Stochastic gradient descent method is a gradient descent optimization method (Abinash Tripathy et al., 2016, Leon Bottou, 2012). It is used to find maximums or minimums by iteration when the training data set is large. Let (x, y) be a pair of an arbitrary input (x) and a scalar output (y), and $l(y\hat{}, y)$ be a loss function. Let $f \in F$ be a family of F functions f$_w$(x) by a weight vector w. The average over the unknown distribution dP(z) on sample $z_1, \ldots, z_n$.

$$E(f) = \int l(f(x), y) \, dP(z) E_n(f) = \frac{1}{n} \sum_{i=1}^{n} l(f(x_i), y_i)$$

where $E(f)$ is the expected risk for generalization performance. $E_n(f)$ is the empirical risk for training set performance. In statistical learning, the empirical risk is minimized instead of the expected risk by choosing the family F. The minimization of the empirical risk $E_n(f)$ using gradient descent (GD):

$$w_{t+1} = w_t - \gamma \frac{1}{n} \sum_{i=1}^{n} \nabla_w Q(z_i, w_t),$$

where γ refers the chosen learning rate and w_0 refer the initial estimate. This algorithm achieves linear convergence when γ is sufficiently small. i.e., $-\log \rho \sim t$, where ρ is the residual error. The scalar learning rate is replacing by a positive definite matrix Γ_t to obtain the better optimization algorithms. The inverse of the Hessian cost at the optimum.

$$w_{t+1} = w_t - \Gamma_t \frac{1}{n} \sum_{i=1}^{n} \nabla_w Q(z_i, w_t).$$

where w_0 is the initial estimate sufficiently close to the optimum. This second order gradient descent achieves quadratic convergence. It reaches the optimum after a single iteration. Otherwise, $-\log \rho \sim t$. Stochastic gradient descent method estimates each iteration on the basis of single randomly picked example z_t instead of computing the gradient of empirical risk $E_n(f)$.

$$w_{t+1} = w_t - \gamma_t \nabla_w Q\left(z_t, w_t\right)$$

where $\{w_t, t = 1, 2, \dots\}$ is the stochastic process depends on randomly picked example for each iteration. $Q(z_t, w_t)$ is the risk minimization. γ_t is the learning rate. If γ_t decreases slowly, w_t decreases equally slowly. If γ_t decreases too quickly, w_t reaches the optimum at the significant amount of time.

N-Gram-Based Character Language Model

The N-gram based character language model is a new model derived from the N-gram language models (Qiang Ye et al., 2014, Abinash Tripathy et al., 2016). This model takes characters as letters, space, or symbols instead of words in the algorithm. In this model, a probability distribution $p(s)$ is defined for strings $s \in \Sigma*$. Where $\Sigma*$ is a fixed alphabet character. The chain rule for a character c and string s is defined as:

$$p(sc) = p(s).p(c \mid s)$$

The N-gram Markovian assumption for n-1 characters and the maximum likelihood estimator for N-grams are:

$$p(c_n \mid s_{c1}, ...c_{n-1}) = p(c_n \mid c_1...cn - 1)$$

$$\hat{p}_{ML}(c \mid s) = \frac{C(sc)}{\sum_c C(sc)}$$

where $p\hat{}_{ML}(c \mid s)$ is the probability of maximum likelihood for a character c in the string s. $C(sc)$ is the number of observed sequence sc in the training data. $\Sigma_c C(sc)$ is the number of single-character extensions of sc.

Cross-Domain Sentiment Classification

Words can be used to express different opinions in different domains. For instance, consider two specific domains, the namely source domain D_{src} and target domain D_{tar} (Sinno Jialin Pan et al., 2010). Let $D_{src} = \{(x_i, y_i)\}$, $i = 1, 2, ..., n$ be the set of labeled sentiment data, and $D_{tar} = \{x_i\}$, $i = 1, 2, ..., n$ be the some unlabeled sentiment data. The cross-domain sentiment classification learns a classifier to predict the sentiment polarity of unseen data from D_{tar}. Assume that the sentiment classifier f is a linear function as expressed by the following equation:

$$y = f(x) = sign(xw^T)$$

where $x \in \mathbb{R}^{1 \times m}$. If $xw^T \geq 0$, then $sign(xw^T)$ is assigned as positive score $+1$. If $xw^T \leq 0$, then $sign(xw^T)$ is assigned as negative score -1. w is the weight vector learned through the training data.

Sinno Jialin Pan et al. (2010) proposed a framework to achieve the targets based on identifying domain-independent features and a spectral feature alignment algorithm. They presented three strategies to select domain-independent features. (1). Domain-independent features are selected based on their frequency in both source domain and target domain. (2). Domain-independent features are selected based on the mutual independence between features and labels on the source domain data. (3). Domain-independent features are selected based on the modified mutual information criteria between features and domains. These strategies were used to construct a bipartite graph for identifying domain-independent and domain specific features. A spectral clustering algorithm was used to align domain-specific features. The selected features are augmented for cross-domain sentiment classification. Their experiment showed that spectral domain-specific feature alignment outperformed using the labeled data and unlabeled data in the target domain.

Marc Franco-Salvador et al. (2015) proposed a knowledge-enhanced meta-classifier for single and cross-domain sentiment classification. This new method combines different types of approaches namely, bag-of-words, n-grams or lexical resource-based classifiers. They performed word sense disambiguation using the BabelNet multilingual semantic network to generate independent features. Using these independent features, a semantic network was allowed to obtain vocabulary expansion-based classifier. Their result proved that the knowledge-enhanced meta-classifier performs better than the state-of-the-art.

Ranked WordNet Graph

Ranked WordNet graph system computes the positive or negative values in sentiment classification (Arturo Montejo-Ráez et al., 2014). The polarity is measured in a real value interval [-1, +1]. The values greater than zero represents positive emotion, less than zero represents negative emotion, and zero represents neutral. Therefore, the Ranked WordNet graph system is represented as a function $p: t \rightarrow R$ such that $p(t) \in [-1, +1]$. Where $p(t)$ is the function on a text. A few elements of information is used for deciding the texts as positive or negative. This method expands the few concepts to calculate polarity of tweets, posts, etc.

Personalized Page Vectors is generated as a sequence of WordNet synsets with weights for each tweet or post, etc, in the random walk algorithm. In the graph of WordNet, nodes are represented as synsets and axes are represented as semantic relations, and terms are represented as tweets, posts, etc. Synsets are selected to the closest sense for each term iteration. Valued nodes are retrieved based on a number of iterations or a convergence of weights. Mathematically, let G be the WordNet graph and N be the vertices { $v_1, v_2,...v_N$ } representing all synsets, and M be a $N \times N$ probability matrix for all possible relations between synsets. If $M_{ij} = 0$, there is no relationship exists between the vertices v_i and v_j. If $M_{ij} = 1/d_i$, there is a relationship between the vertices v_i and v_j. d_i is the number of relations going from node i, which is also called the outdegree of v_i. The synsets score values are computed for vector P in the recursive equation:

$$P = \alpha MP + (1 - \alpha)v$$

In the above equation, αMP represents the values across the graph with propagation, $(1-\alpha)v$ represents a way to reach new nodes randomly without propagation. The vector v represents N elements with a value of 1/N. In the graph, any node is reachable according to the α factor. This factor value is set manually between 0.85 and 0.95, i.e. close to 1.0. Therefore, a tiny weight is given to any node. The solution considers a maximum number of iterations or convergence criteria in the given equation. If four valid terms are correctly identified such as nouns, adjectives or verbs, the initial weight ¼ is assigned to the term nodes uniformly. The term nodes are connected to the synsets and part of the whole graph. The WordNet 3.0 version has been used in this method.

The SentiWordNet scores and weights associated to synsets are compared to obtain the final polarity score as expressed by the following equation:

$$p = \frac{r.s}{\left| t \right|}$$

where p refers the final polarity score, r refers the weights associated to synsets by the random walk algorithm for each tweet text over WordNet, s represents the polarity score obtained from SentiWordNet, and t represents the set of concepts in the tweet. Moreover, the average of the product between the associated weights obtained by the random walk algorithm and the difference of positive and negative SentiWordNet scores is calculated by:

$$p = \frac{\sum_{\forall s \in t} rw_s . (swn_s + -swn_s -)}{\left| t \right|}$$

where s represents the synset in the tweet t, rw_s represents the weights associated with synsets after the random walk algorithm for each tweet over WordNet, $swn_s +$ represents positive synset score and $swn_s -$ represents negative synset scores retrieved from SentiWordNet.

Structured Microblog Sentiment Classification

Structured microblog sentiment classification (SMSC) explains how to incorporate social contexts such as topic context, user context, friend context into sentiment classification (Fangzhao Wu et al., 2016). (i). Topic context is used to indicate whether two microblog messages have similar opinions related to the same topic. Let $M \in \mathbb{R}^{N \times N_T}$ be the message – topic matrix. Where N and N_T represent the number of messages and topics. If $M_{ij} = 1$, then the message i is related to topic j. If $M_{ij} = 0$, then the message i is not related to the topic j. Then the connection matrix of topic context is defined as $T = M \times M \; \mathbb{R}^{N \times N}$. The diagonal elements set zeros in T, If T_{ij} is greater than zero, then the two messages i and j are related to the same topic. T_{ij} indicates the number of topics that both messages i and j share. Otherwise, T_{ij} is zero. (ii). User context is used to indicate an individual's opinion related to the same topic or target. Let $P \in \mathbb{R}^{N \times N}_{U}$ be the message-user matrix. Where N_U refers the number of users in the dataset. If $P_{ij} = 1$, then the message i is posted by the user j. If $P_{ij} = 0$, then the message i is not posted by the user j. Then the user context -connection matrix is expressed as $U = (P \times P^T) \bigcirc T \in \mathbb{R}^{N \times N}$. Where $\bigcirc$ is the Hadamard product. It is represented as entrywise product matrices and $(A \bigcirc B)_{ij} = A_{ij} \times B_{ij}$. $P \times P^T$ is represented as a matrix to indicate whether two messages are posted by the same user. U represents that two messages are posted by the same user at the same time to similar topic or target. If U_{ij} is greater than zero, then the two message i and j are posted by the same user to the same topic. Otherwise, U_{ij} is zero. (iii). Friend context is used to indicate friends' similar opinions to the same topic. Let $S \in \mathbb{R}^{N_U \times N_U}$ be the social relation matrix between users. If $S_{ij} = 1$, then there is a relation with the user i and j. If $S_{ij} = 0$, then there is no relation between the user i and j. Then the friend context-connection matrix is expressed as $F = (P \times S \times P^T) \bigcirc T \in \mathbb{R}^{N \times N}$. Where $P \times S \times P^T$ is represented as a matrix to indicate whether two messages are posted by the two users with social relations. If F_{ij} is greater than zero, then the message i and j are posted by the two users at the same time to the same topic. Otherwise, F_{ij} is zero.

Let N be the microblog messages, and $m_i \in \mathbb{R}^{D \times 1}$, $i = 1, 2, ..., N$ be the extracted feature vectors from microblogs, Where D refers the number of features in microblogs. Microblog messages need to be classified as positive or negative. If its sentiment score is great than zero, then it is classified as positive. If its sentiment score is less than zero, then it is classified as negative. Let $x_i \in \mathbb{R}$, $i = 1, 2, ..., N$ be the final sentiment score generated by SMSC framework. SMSC model is formulated to assign similar sentiment scores to microblog messages connected by social contexts and to respect the content-based sentiment predictions:

$$\arg \min_{x} L = \frac{1}{2} \sum_{i=1}^{N} (x_i - h(m_i))^2 + \alpha \sum_{i=1}^{N} \sum_{i \neq j} U_{ij} |x_i - x_j| + \beta \sum_{i=1}^{N} \sum_{i \neq j} F_{ij} |x_i - x_j|$$

where $x \in \mathbb{R}^{N \times 1}$ refers the vector representation of x_i, $i = 1, 2, ..., N$. α and β represents the nonnegative regularization coefficients. $U \in \mathbb{R}^{N \times N}$ and $F \in \mathbb{R}^{N \times N}$ represent the user context and friend context.

A Multi-Label Classification-Based Approach

Multi-label classification is used to classify an instance into a set of labels rather than one label. It has two main methods namely, problem transformation methods and algorithm adaption methods. First, the problem transformation method is used to transform the multiple-label training data into single-label data. Then the method learns a single-label classifier from the transformed data. Shuhua Monica Liu et al. (2015) proposed the multilabel classification based approach for microblogs. This approach was implemented based on three components namely, text segmentation, feature extraction, and multi-label classification. They empirically compared the performance of the proposed approach with 11 multi-label sentiment classification methods.

BBS-Based Sentiment Classification

Weitong Huang et al. (2008) studied BBS (an electronic information center) based user behavior and opinions by using ARC-BC text classification algorithm. Theis algorithm was implemented based on associated rules. It divides the user opinions into three categories namely, support, opposes and neutral. The authors showed very practical significance results for making the decision to government, the network purification, and prosperity, and building a harmonious society.

Other Supervised Sentiment Learning

Zhi-Hong Deng et al. (2014) proposed a supervised term weighting scheme to improve the performance of sentiment analysis. This method was implemented based on two factors namely, the importance of a term in a document and importance of a term for expressing sentiment. The authors employed functions based on term frequency to compute importance of a term in a document, and seven statistical functions to compute importance of a term for expressing sentiment from training document with labeled categories. They proved that the proposed method achieves the best accuracy on two datasets out of three datasets. In (Sheng-Tun Li & Fu-Ching Tsai, 2013), a novel classification framework was proposed using fuzzy formal concept analysis. The proposed framework conceptualizes documents into concepts. The authors evaluated the performance of the framework on two opinion polarity datasets. The results revealed that the proposed framework decreases the sensitivity to noise. In (Ting-Chun Peng & Chia-Chun Shih, 2010), an unsupervised snippet-based sentiment classification method was proposed to unknown sentiment phrases. This method uses the Reference Word Pairs (RWPs) instead of semantic orientation methods to predict sentiment phrases. The authors extracted sentiment phrases in each review by means of Parts-of-Speech (POS) rules. The authors utilized top-N relevant snippets returned by the search engine to predict sentiment phrases. They achieved 80% accuracy with F-measures.

Zhang Xia et al. (2009) proposed a new approach for sentiment classification based on granule network. The research was mainly focused on segmentation and feature selection for sentiment. The authors performed classification based on rule mining by granule network. Ahmed Abbasi et al. (2011) proposed a feature relation network (FRN) method for sentiment classification. The task is to improve the selection of text features for enhanced sentiment classification. FRN was implemented with the use syntactic relations and semantic information between n-grams. It was showed that FRN outperforms univariate, multivariate, and hybrid feature selection methods. ZHANG Wei et al. (2010) proposed a sentence-level sentiment classification method based on syntax tree pruning and tree kernel. It first uses convolution kernel of SVM to obtain structured information. Second, the adjectives-based and sentiment words based strategies were applied into the syntax tree pruning. In (Xin Wang, & Guohong Fu, 2010), the authors used morphemes as the basic tokens for sentence-level sentiment classification. The method was implemented by applying the morphological analysis, acquired morphemes-level sentiment information, and the combination of sentiment phrases and their polarity scores.

Peifeng Li et al. (2011) proposed a dependency tree based approach for sentiment classification. This method was implemented by preprocessing, converting all dependency relations to the dependency tree, pruning strategy to the dependency tree, and adding the category information to use the SVM classifier. In (Mostafa Karamibekr, & Ali A. Ghorbani, 2012), a verb-oriented sentiment classification method was proposed for social domains. The authors employed an English dictionary and WordNet to extract sentiment terms from a sentence. They formulated a sentiment model to find the relations between document, sentence, and opinion by applying general algorithms. Their results showed that the verb-oriented approach outperforms the classification 10% higher than the Bag of Words. Chihli Hung et al., (2013) improved the performance of Word of Mouth sentiment classification by reevaluating the objective words in SentiWordNet. The sentiment reevaluation module was implemented in four steps namely, finding sentiment orientation and values for words and sentences, negation processing, measuring the relevance of object words and associated sentiment sentences, and adjusting sentiments. Xiao Sun et al. (2014) proposed a deep belief network model (DBN) with extended multi-modality features for sentiment classification in microblogs. In this model, DBN is composed of several layers of Restricted Boltzmann Machine (RBM). The RBM initializes the neural network. A classification RBM (ClassRBM) layer was stacked on top of RBM. This layer achieves the final sentiment classification. The results proved that the deep learning method on sentiment classification outperforms the surface learning methods such as NB, SVM. etc.

Yanghui Rao et al. (2014) proposed a multi-label supervised topic model (MSTM) and sentiment latent topic model (SLTM) to associate latent topics with emotion readers. MSTM is the extension of the supervised topic model to generate a set of topics from words. SLTM generates topics from social emotions. These models were applied to sentiment classification. The authors have shown that MSTM and SLTM are more stable than the baseline ETM, SWAT, and ET. In (Bingwei Liu et al., 2013), the authors analyzed the scalability of Naïve Bayes Classifier (NBC) for sentiment classification in large datasets. They improved the accuracy of NBC by increasing the data sizes. Felipe Bravo-Marquez et al. (2014) proposed a novel approach for sentiment classification based on meta-level features. This approach was implemented in the combination of existing lexical resources and sentiment analysis methods to address the different dimensions of opinions such as subjectivity and polarity. The authors suggested that the classification result varies from one dataset to another. The performance of the system significantly improved on the combination of different sentiment dimensions.

Semi-Supervised Sentiment Learning

Semi-supervised learning is the part of supervised learning methods. This system learns from a small amount of labeled data and a large amount of labeled data. Various semi-supervised sentiment learning methods are discussed as follows: In (Mohammad Sadegh Hajmohammadi, Roliana Ibrahim, & Ali Selamat, 2014), a bi-view semi-supervised active learning model was proposed to reduce the human labeling effort for cross-lingual sentiment classification. In this model, unlabelled training data is enriched through the manual and automatic labeling from the target language. The authors represented labeled and unlabelled data in the source and target languages to create different views. They incorporated the unlabelled data from the target language into the active learning process by using co-training and co-testing algorithms. A density measure applied to avoid selecting outlier examples from unlabelled data as well as to increase the manual labeling in the co-testing algorithm. This method was employed to coss-lingual sentiment classification in three book reviews. The authors proved that the proposed model outperforms in all datasets. Shenghua Liu et al., (2015) proposed a semi-supervised topic-adaptive sentiment classification (TASC) model to minimize the loss to adapt unlabelled data and features. TASC learning algorithm mainly updates the topic-adaptive features, adaptive unlabelled data, and collaborative training for the dynamic tweets on a topic. The authors proved TASC algorithm outperforms than supervised and ensemble classifiers.

In Kyoungok Kim and Jaewook Lee (2014), the authors proposed a novel semi-supervised laplacian eigenmaps (SS-LE) to remove the redundant features. This method enabled the visualization of documents in low dimensional space for text analytics. They performed experiments on multi-domain review data set with respect to sentiment classification and visualization. SS-LE produced a better similarity in the visualization. Nádia Félix Felipe da Silva et al., (2016) proposed a semi-supervised learning framework by combining unsupervised information and unlabeled data from the constructed similarity matrix, with a classifier. A Self-training algorithm C³E-SL was used for a better tweet sentiment classification. The results proved that the proposed approach outperformed than the Self-training, Co-training, a Lexicon-based method, and a stand-alone SVM method. In (Jonathan Ortigosa-Hernandez et al., 2012), a semi-supervised multi-dimensional classification paradigm for sentiment analysis was proposed to build more accurate classifiers. This method divides the training dataset into labeled and unlabelled data. The authors built multi-dimensional Bayesian network classifier to join the different variables. They suggested that the proposed method can be improved in several ways.

In Shusen Zhou, Qingcai Chen, and Xiaolong Wang (2013), the authors proposed novel semi-supervised active learning methods (called Active Deep Network (AND) and Information ADN) to address the problem of sentiment classification based on insufficient labeled data. In this method, ADN was constructed by Restricted Boltzmann machines (RBM) with labeled and unlabeled reviews. The constructed ADN was fine-tuned by the gradient-descent method. Then the authors applied active learning method to identify labeled and unlabeled reviews in order to train ADN and combined the information density with ADN. They proved that ADN and IADN outperform than the existing semi-supervised learning and deep learning methods. Shusen Zhou et. al. (2014) proposed the fuzzy deep belief networks (FDBN) and an active FDBN for semi-supervised sentiment classification. First, the authors trained FDBN on labeled and unlabeled reviews in the training dataset and designed a fuzzy membership for each class of reviews on learning FDBN. Second, FDBN was constructed based on the fuzzy membership function and DBN. Then the authors applied the supervised learning method to improve the performance of the FDBN and handling sentiment data. They proved that the active FDBN gets the best result than the FDBN.

Unsupervised Sentiment Learning

Unsupervised sentiment learning is the machined learned based approach. This method learns hidden structure from unlabeled training data. Various unsupervised learning methods are discussed as follows: In Shi Feng et al. (2011), the authors proposed an integrated graph-based model for clustering sentiments in Chinese blogs. They implemented this model by the graph-based representation and clustering algorithm based on graph similarity. For example, consider a document D with title "abcd" and text "aefg". Here, a, b, c, d, e, f, and g are represented as seven different words in the document D. These seven nodes are represented as nodes and their relationships are edges. In this model, the blog search result – items are segmented and extracted sentiment words using sentiment lexicons, and represented as multi-graphs. It is modeled as SoB-graph. Each sentence in the blog search result items is modeled as a subgraph of SoB graph. Then the BSR sentiment clustering method was proposed to form a new SoB graph, measured sentiment similarity between SoB-graphs. Milagros Fernández-Gavilanes et al. (2016) proposed an unsupervised dependency parsing-based text classification method to predict sentiment in online resources such as posts, reviews, tweets, etc. The authors derived sentiment lexicons by using a semiautomatic polarity expansion algorithm. This method improved the accuracy of the proposed system in specific application domains. William B. Claster et al., (2010) proposed a multi-knowledge based approach for modeling movie sentiment based on Self-Organizing maps (SOM) and movie knowledge in multi-dimensional space. The authors weighted features in frequency matrix for clustering words instead of comments in movie datasets. They presented 20-dimensional space to locate movies based on SOM. Then they developed a visual model for expressing sentiment vocabulary in test data. Their results improved the prior filtering of comments by using the sensitive filter, extending and refining sentiment lexicon, and stemming algorithm.

Tonghui Li et al. (2012) proposed a new unsupervised and domain independent approach for sentiment classification. In this method, 5,000 reviews from different domains chosen as a training set, the reviews are not labeled. The proposed approach was implemented in three phases. First, the opinion words and their semantic orientation value are extracted using Latent Semantic Analysis (LSA) to create sentiment vocabulary list. Second, the document sentiment orientation score (DSOS) for each document is calculated based on syntax analysis method. Finally, the sentiment classification was performed to produce the vocabulary list with the appropriate value. In Suge Wang et al. (2012), the authors proposed a sentiment clustering method based on feature reduction algorithm. They extracted sentences from reviews for constituting sentences set for each product object and applied the feature reduction algorithm based on discernibility matrix to reduce high dimension and missing data. Finally, each product rate is aggregated by employing the k-means clustering algorithm. Their results showed that 41.38% reduced runtime and 15.69% reduced sparsity. Gang Li et al., (2010) introduced a new clustering-based approach for sentiment analysis. They built this approach based on k-means clustering algorithm by employing three strategies namely, TF-IDF weighting, voting mechanism, and term score. TF-IDF weighting scheme improves the accuracy. A voting mechanism extracts the clustering result. Term score enhances the clustering result. The authors suggested that the performance of the proposed approach is the most balanced, and it is more suitable for real applications.

Dionisios N. Sotiropoulos et al. (2014) proposed an entropic measure-based clustering approach by combining topic modeling and sentiment analysis algorithms. This approach extends low-level features such as words, phrases or sentences. The proposed approach was designed with sequences of seven steps namely, data collection & data preparation, corpus separation, VMS-based corpus vectorization, sentiment classification, topic modeling, sentiment per topic, semantic factors identification. An entropic-measure based clustering algorithm forms semantically coherent clusters on topically cluster centroids. In the semantic factors identification phase, the network infrastructure, product portfolio, distribution channel, support/customer service, sponsored event, and advertisement are identified to associate with different topics and their corresponding cluster. In Zheng Lin et al. (2016), the authors mentioned that existing cross-lingual topics models are not suitable for sentiment analysis. To overcome this problem, they proposed an unsupervised cross-lingual topic model framework for sentiment classification. In this framework, Cross-Lingual LDA (CLLDA) model was used to detect topics without sentiments. The existing Joint Sentiment/Topic Model (JST) and Aspect and Sentiment Unification Model (ASUM) were incorporated into CLLDA to capture aspects with sentiments. Moreover, the authors presented two unsupervised cross-lingual joint aspect/sentiment models (CLJST and CLASUM) for sentiment classification at aspect level in a target language.

LEXICON-BASED APPROACH

The lexicon-based sentiment approach is able to learn sentiment lexical phrases, chunks, etc. This approach is mainly focused on vocabulary. Various lexicon-based approaches are discussed as follows: In (Isa Maks, & Piek Vossen, 2012), a lexicon model was introduced for the description of verbs, nouns, and adjectives in opinion mining. This model consists of a categorization of semantic classes (nouns, verbs) and complementation patterns (actor's attitude, speaker/writer's attitude, everybody's attitude). The model described the detailed subjectivity relations that exist between different actors in a sentence expressing separate attitudes for each actor. Farhan Hassan Khan et al. (2016) proposed a semi-supervised subjective feature weighting and an intelligent model selection called SWIMS for sentiment analysis. A SWIM determines the feature weight based on SentiWordNet. They employed SVM to learn feature weights, and an intelligent model selection approach to enhance the performance of the system. Sungrae Park et al. (2015) proposed an extraction of a sentiment lexicon with active learning on a specific domain. The authors presented a simple probabilistic algorithm using Bayesian estimation to extract a sentiment lexicon from document-level annotations, and an active learning technique applied to minimize annotation effort. They suggested that the proposed method achieves the best F1 scores than the baseline methods, and it is more suitable to n-gram cases.

Sheng Huang et al. (2014) proposed a novel automatic construction of domain-specific sentiment lexicon based on constrained label propagation. The authors implemented this strategy into six steps. First, the sentiment terms are extracted by using the chunk dependency information and generic sentiment lexicon. Second, the sentiment seeds are extracted from domain reviews. Third, an association similarity graph is constructed to propagate sentiment polarity from sentiment seeds. Fourth, the constraint relations are defined and extracted between sentiment terms. Fifth, the constraint propagation is applied to the entire collection of contextual and morphological constraints between sentiment terms. Finally, a collection of pairwise constraints and their associated score values are obtained. The authors pointed out that the proposed strategy does not require any human effort to apply in other domains. In (Songbo Tan, & Qiong Wu, 2011), a random walk algorithm for automatic construction of domain-oriented sentiment lexicon was proposed by utilizing sentiment words and document from source domain and destination domain. This approach employed four relations namely, word to word relationship, word to document relationship, a document to document relationship, and document to word relationship in a unified framework. The framework consists of two phases such as graph-building and iterative reinforcement. In the graph-building phase, the proposed approach builds four graphs by including labeled data from source domain and unlabeled data from target domain or destination domain. In the iterative reinforcement phase, the proposed approach computes word and document sentiment scores based on the graphs. The authors conducted experiments on various domain-specific sentiment lexicons and proved that the proposed approach improves the accuracy for identifying sentiment polarity words.

In A. Moreo et al. (2012), a lexicon-based Comments-oriented New Sentiment Analyzer (LCN-SA) was proposed to deal with the user's tendency, detection of the target user opinions, and design of a linguistic knowledge lexicon with low cost-adaptability. The authors designed the proposed system in three stages. First, the knowledge preparation module is employed by filtering stage to remove noisy comments, PoS to improve the performance of stemmer, sentence splitter to separate sentences. Second, opinion focus detection module is applied to detect lexicon by interpretation context. Moreover, the disambiguation analysis and frequency analysis are applied to tackle with the focus co-reference and to discard low-referenced focuses in the comments. Third, a sentiment analysis algorithm is composed by expression labeling, tuples extraction, and tuples clustering and filtering. In Yan

Dang, Yulei Zhang, and Hsinchun Chen (2010), a lexicon-enhanced method for sentiment classification was proposed by combining machine learning and semantic orientation approach. The authors designed this method in three steps namely, data acquisition, feature generation, and classification and evaluation. First, the online product reviews are obtained by using the spidering programs. Second, the features, content-free, and content-specific are generated from machine learning approach and sentiment features from the semantic orientation approach. Third, a support vector machine is used as a classifier to measure the performance of the system. The authors achieved comparable classification accuracy with Blitzer's multidomain sentiment data set.

Pierluca Sangiorgi et al. (2013) presented an unsupervised data-driven cross-lingual method for creating a sentiment lexicon. The proposed method is implemented by an automatic review extraction, combined entropy TF-IDF scoring, and cross-lingual intersection. The authors tested this method over seven selected games and applications in four different languages and validated using SentiWordNet. In (Pedro Miguel Dias Cardoso, & Anindya Roy, 2016), the authors presented a novel approach for automatic sentiment lexicon creation using continuous latent space and neural networks. They trained two multilayer perceptron (MLP) systems using manually annotated corpus (SynthesioLex and EmoLex) to predict sentiment polarity and sentiment prediction for each word. The words are mapped into a continuous latent space to serve as input to MLP. The authors also studied a regression system to create features in a continuous sentiment space. Dehong Gao et al., (2014) introduced bilingual word graph label propagation to automatically create sentiment lexicons on the target languages. A bilingual word graph is used to represent the intra-language relations and inter-language relations. The authors used both synonym and antonym to build the intra-language relations, and the word alignment information derived from building the inter-language relation from bilingual parallel sentences. Their results showed that the proposed approach outperformed than the existing approaches.

ENSEMBLE LEARNING METHODS

An ensemble learning methods are trained on multiple learners instead of a single learner on the training data. This learning method used for three main reasons namely, statistical, computational, and representational. The variance and bias can be reduced by combining multiple classifiers [59]. The general ensemble learning method is shown in Figure 3. For example, consider a tweet for ensemble learning *"I'm in a happy mood today, I go to beach"* If the classifier 1 calculates a positive score = 0.98 and negative score = 0.02, classifier 2 calculates a positive score = 0.42 and negative score = 0.58, and classifier 3 calculates a positive score = 0.96

Figure 3. An ensemble learning method

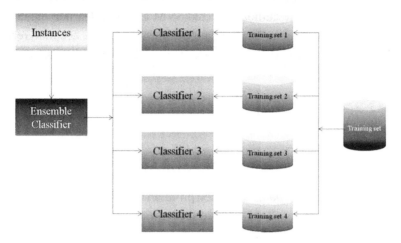

and negative score = 0.04, Then the average positive and negative score is 0.73 and 0.21(Nádia F.F. da Silva et al., 2014). In Nádia F.F. da Silva et al. (2014), an approach for sentiment analysis is proposed to automatically classify the sentiment using classifier ensembles and lexicons. The classifier ensembles are formed by Random Forest, Support Vector Machines, Multinomial Naïve Bayes, and Logistic Regression to classify unseen data. The authors employed a bag-of-words and feature hashing techniques to represent features, preprocessing to remove retweets, stop words, links, URLs, mentions and punctuation, and stemming to minimize sparsity.

Aytug Onan et al. (2016), the authors proposed a multiobjective weighted voting ensemble classifier based on differential evolution algorithm to enhance the predictive performance of sentiment classification. First, the authors trained the combined algorithms namely, Naive Bayes, Support Vector Machine, Logistic Regression, Bayesian Logistic Regression, and LDA to predict the output classes. Second, the weights are adjusted based on precision and recall values of predicted output class. Third, the weights are adjusted for each classifier and for each output class. Fourth, the classification algorithms trained on this new data. Finally, the voting mechanism is applied to predict each output class.

In Gang Wang et al. (2015, https://en.wikipedia.org/), the authors discussed that the random subspace method is an ensemble learning method. It reduces the correlation between observed data in the training process on randomly selected sub-datasets instead of the entire datasets. The random subspace method has been used in decision trees, random forests, support vector machines, etc. Gang Wang et al. (2015) proposed POS based random subspace method for sentiment classification. They used the content lexicon subspace rate and function lexicon subspace rate parameters to construct random sub-datasets. These control the accuracy and the diversity of base learners. They also trained the base learners on different sub-datasets to learn a pattern in the model. The authors selected SVM as a base learner and compared the results with many machine learning algorithms. The more accurate result was achieved by POS-RS method. The base learners $\{C_i(x), 1 \leq i \leq k\}$ are aggregated by the majority voting rule as expressed by the following equation.

$$C^*(x) = \mathrm{sgn}\left\{\sum_i C_i(x) - \frac{k-1}{2}\right\}$$

Rui Xia et al., (2013) proposed the feature ensemble plus sample selection (SS-FE) approach to address domain adaptation problem in sentiment classification. The authors improved SS-FE results by considering both labeling adaptation and instance adaptation. The changes in labeling function are modeled by labeling adaptation i.e. one feature might be expressing positive in the source domain and negative in the target domain. An instance adaptation models the change of vocabulary or word frequency from the source domain to target domain. The authors also employed a principal component analysis (PCA-SS) method to select a subset of source domains that close to the target domain, and a singular value decomposition (SVD) algorithm to extract latent concepts in the target domain. Dongmei Zhang et al., (2015) proposed a method for unbalanced sentiment classification by combining unbalanced classification method and ensemble learning technique. In this ensemble learning framework, the training set is generated in three steps namely, under-sampling, re-sampling, and random feature selection. Then the proposed ensemble learning method is applied to the training set. The authors enhanced the performance of the proposed method than the existing methods such as Bagging, Adaboost, Random Subspace, Random Forest, etc. In (Yun Wan, & Dr. Qigang Gao, 2015), the authors proposed an ensemble sentiment learning strategy to analyze customer sentiment in airline services. They compared the performance of different sentiment learning approaches and developed an ensemble approach to improving the sentiment classification performance. The proposed ensemble approach includes Naive Bayes, SVM, Bayesian Network, C4.5 Decision tree and Random Forest algorithms.

HYBRID APPROACH

A hybrid approach is composed of a larger part of the system. This approach allows more flexibility in modeling the system. Various hybrid approaches are discussed as follows: Farhan Hassan Khan et al. (2014) presented a twitter opinion mining framework using hybrid classification scheme to improve the classification accuracy, data sparsity, and sarcasm. The proposed method developed into three stages namely, data acquisition, pre-processing, classification, and evaluation. First, the publically available data is obtained from Twitter using Twitter streaming API and Twitter4J library. Second, the obtained raw tweets are preprocessed to refine data in terms of abbreviations, lemmatization, correction, and stop words removal. Third, the polarity classification algorithm is applied to classify twitter feeds on the basis of enhanced emotion classifier, improved polarity classifier, and SentiWordNet classifier. In this hybrid classification algorithm, the refined tweets serve as input to enhanced emotion classifier. If the tweet is classified as neutral, then the refined tweets are classified using improved polarity classifier. If the tweet is classified as neutral in this algorithm, then tweets are classified using SentiWordNet Classifier. The authors showed that the performance of proposed system achieves 85.3%.

Orestes Appel et al., (2016) presented a hybrid approach to the sentiment analysis problem at the sentence level. This new method employed by using five key components sentiment\opinion lexicon, semantic rules, fuzzy sets approach to sentiment analysis, the hybrid approach and its process, and sentiment enrichment. The hybrid method calculates sentiment polarity and its intensity in sentences based on hybrid standard classification and hybrid advanced classification processes. The authors performed an experiment on three different datasets and compared the result with Naive Bayes and Maximum Entropy methods. Their result revealed that presented the hybrid approach outperform than above-mentioned algorithms.

EXTENSIONS OF CLASSIFICATION AND CLUSTERING

Anna Jurek et al. (2015) proposed a new feature construction method using TF-IDF and an extended space forest ensemble method for sentiment classification. This method selects words from different data sets directly in the whole set. The authors have taken the advantage of TF-IDF to choose distinguishable unigram from positive and negative documents. They applied statistical methods to analyze the effectiveness of proposed system. Luis Trindade et al. (2014) proposed an extension of the gap-weighted soft matching factored sequence kernel for sentiment classification to make a strong distinction between a single feature and all features. Each word, PoS, and sentiment are represented as tridimensional for each sentence. The authors performed the proposed task on subjectivity and polarity classification.

APPLICATIONS

The most common applications of Bigdata sentiment analysis in the areas of consumer voice for searching products, companies and their brands, online advertising, financial markets and services, news, on-line commerce, opinion poll, voting advice applications, politicians positions, real-world events monitoring in articles and tweets, legal matters, policy or government regulation proposals, business decision making, intelligent transportation system, airline services, educational developments, urban planning (Justin B. Hollander et al., 2016), and operational improvements of organizations.

SOFTWARE TOOLS

There are many software tools that provide methods for Bigdata sentiment classification and clustering. The software tools are Hadoop, MongoDB, Talend Open Studio, FICO Bigdata, Skytree server, Pentaho, Cambridge semantics, Alteryx, CISCO Bigdata, Cloudera Enterprise Bigdata, Intel Bigdata, Vmware Bigdata, IBM Bigdata analytics, Teradata Bigdata, Tableau Desktop and server, Dell Bigdata, Oracle Bigdata, Talend, Viscovery SOMiner, HPCC Systems Bigdata, Pivotal Bigdata, Amazon Web Service, Microsoft Bigdata, HP Bigdata, Splunk, COGSA, Semantria, Daniel Soper Sentiment Analyzer, MarkLogic, SAP inMemory, Meltwater, Google Alerts, Werfamous sentiment analyzer, Sentiment140, Twitrratr, SAS sentiment analysis tool, Trackur, Hootsuite, Opentext sentiment analysis, UberVu, Statsoft sentiment analysis, Twendz, Social mention, HappyGrumpy, Sentiment viz, TweetFeel, Streamcrab, Clarabridge dictionary sentiment analysis, Opinion crawl, Emotions, Twazzup, They say, LIWC, SentiStrengh, SentiWordNet, SenticNet, Happiness Index, NetOwl Extractor, NICTA, TweetDeck, Get Cloud Cherry, SSIX, SumAll, The research bazaar, Dirt Deigital and TweetReach.

CONCLUSION

In this chapter, the authors discussed various methods and approaches of sentiment mining for Bigdata classification and clustering. First, the *machine learning-based approaches* are discussed as supervised, semi-supervised and unsupervised methods. *Supervised sentiment learning methods* perform common classification problem by using labeled training data. It includes Naive Bayes method, maximum entropy method, support vector machine, stochastic gradient descent method, n-gram based character language model, cross-domain sentiment classification, ranked WordNet graph, structured microblog sentiment classification, a multi-label classification based approach, BBS based sentiment classification, a fuzzy conceptualization model, supervised term weighting method, feature relation network based sentiment classification, a verb-oriented approach, meta-level sentiment models for big data, emotion topic model, syntax tree pruning and tree kernel based sentiment classification, morphemes based sentiment classification, joint sentiment – topic model, a dependency tree based approach, improved word-of-mouth sentiment classification, and a deep belief network based sentiment classification. *Semi-supervised sentiment learning methods* are a class of supervised learning and it makes use of labeled and unlabeled training data. It includes Semi-supervised dimensionality reduction, topic-adaptive sentiment classification (TASC), multi-dimensional classification, active deep learning method, and fuzzy deep belief networks. *Unsupervised sentiment learning methods* perform clustering problems. It includes clustering sentiment based on graph similarity, unsupervised artificial neural networks, unsupervised multi-class sentiment learning, an entropic measure based clustering, and unsupervised cross-lingual topic model.

Second, the following *lexicon based approaches* are discussed: Domain specific sentiment lexicon with active learning, domain-specific sentiment lexicon based on label propagation, a random walk algorithm for domain-specific sentiment lexicon, lexicon-based comments-oriented news sentiment analyzer system, a lexicon-enhanced method, context – aware sentiment lexicon, a lexicon model for deep sentiment analysis, Unsupervised data-driven cross-lingual method, Sentiment Lexicon Creation using Continuous Latent Space and Neural Networks, and a bilingual word graph label propagation. These approaches infer the sentiment on the ground of polarity word. Third, the following *ensemble-based approaches* are discussed: an approach for sentiment analysis using classifier ensembles and lexicons, a multiobjective weighted voting ensemble classifier based on differential evolution algorithm, random subspace method, feature ensemble plus sample selection (SS-FE) approach, and an unbalanced sentiment classification using ensemble learning. These approaches perform multiple learning algorithms for better performance. Fourth, hybrid approaches, extensions of clustering and classification, applications of sentiment analysis on Bigdata, and software tools are discussed. In future work, the authors intended to implement all the methods empirically using different data sets and different software tools for performance measure, visualization, and comparison in terms of Big Data classification and clustering.

REFERENCES

Abbasi, A., France, S., Zhang, Z., & Chen, H. (2011). Selecting Attributes for Sentiment Classification Using Feature Relation Networks. *IEEE Transactions on Knowledge and Data Engineering*, 23(3), 447–462. doi:10.1109/TKDE.2010.110

Alsaffar, A., & Omar, N. (2014). Study on Feature Selection and Machine Learning Algorithms For Malay Sentiment Classification. *IEEE International Conference on Information Technology and Multimedia (ICIMU)*, 270-275. doi:10.1109/ICIMU.2014.7066643

Appel, Chiclana, Carter, & Fujita. (2016). A hybrid approach to the sentiment analysis problem at the sentence level. *Knowledge-Based Systems*, 1-15.

Bello-Orgaz, G., Jung, J. J., & Camacho, D. (2016). Social big data: Recent achievements and new challenges. *Information Fusion*, 28, 45–59. doi:10.1016/j.inffus.2015.08.005

Bottou, L. (2012). Stochastic Gradient Descent Tricks. *Neural Networks, Tricks of the Trade, Reloaded, Springer*, 7700, 430–445.

Bravo-Marquez, F., Mendoza, M., & Poblete, B. (2014). Meta-level sentiment models for big social data analysis. *Knowledge-Based Systems*, 69, 86–99. doi:10.1016/j.knosys.2014.05.016

Claster, W. B., Dinh, Q. H., & Shanmuganathan, S. (2010). Unsupervised Artificial Neural Nets for Modeling Movie Sentiment. *Second International Conference on Computational Intelligence, Communication Systems and Networks*, 349-353. doi:10.1109/CICSyN.2010.23

da Silva, N. F. F., Hruschka, E. R., & Hruschka, E. R. Jr. (2014). Tweet sentiment analysis with classifier ensembles. *Decision Support Systems*, 66, 170–179. doi:10.1016/j.dss.2014.07.003

Dang, Y., Zhang, Y., & Chen, H. (2010). A Lexicon-Enhanced Method for Sentiment Classification: An Experiment on Online Product Reviews. *IEEE Intelligent Systems*, 25(4), 46–53. doi:10.1109/MIS.2009.105

Deng, Z.-H., Luo, K.-H., & Yu, H.-L. (2014). A study of supervised term weighting scheme for sentiment analysis. *Expert Systems with Applications*, 41(7), 3506–3513. doi:10.1016/j.eswa.2013.10.056

Dionisios, N., Sotiropoulos, C. D., Kounavis, P. K., & Giaglis, G. M. (2014). What drives social sentiment? An entropic measure-based clustering approach towards identifying factors that influence social sentiment polarity. *The 5th International Conference on Information, Intelligence, Systems and Applications*, 361 – 373.

Feldman, R. (2013). Techniques and applications for sentiment analysis. *Communications of the ACM*, *56*(4), 82–89. doi:10.1145/2436256.2436274

Felipe da Silva, N. F., Coletta, L. F. S., Hruschka, E. R., & Hruschka, E. R. Jr. (2016). Using unsupervised information to improve semi-supervised tweet sentiment classification. *Information Sciences*, *355*, 348–365. doi:10.1016/j.ins.2016.02.002

Feng, S., Pang, J., Wang, D., Yu, G., Yang, F., & Xu, D. (2011). A novel approach for clustering sentiments in Chinese blogs based on graph similarity. *Computers & Mathematics with Applications (Oxford, England)*, *62*(7), 2770–2778. doi:10.1016/j.camwa.2011.07.043

Fernández-Gavilanes, M., Álvarez-López, T., Juncal-Martínez, J., Costa-Montenegro, E., & González-Castaño, F. J. (2016). Unsupervised method for sentiment analysis in online texts. *Expert Systems with Applications*, *58*, 57–75. doi:10.1016/j.eswa.2016.03.031

Franco-Salvador, M., Cruz, F. L., Troyano, J. A., & Rosso, P. (2015). Cross-domain polarity classification using a knowledge-enhanced meta-classifier. *Knowledge-Based Systems*, *86*, 46–56. doi:10.1016/j.knosys.2015.05.020

Gao, D., Wei, F., Li, W., Liu, X., & Zhou, M. (2014). Cross-lingual Sentiment Lexicon Learning with Bilingual Word Graph Label Propagation. Association for Computational Linguistics.

Hajmohammadi, M. S., Ibrahim, R., & Selamat, A. (2014). Bi-view semi-supervised active learning for cross-lingual sentiment classification. *Information Processing & Management*, *50*(5), 718–732. doi:10.1016/j.ipm.2014.03.005

Hollander, J. B., Graves, E., Renski, H., Foster-Karim, C., Wiley, A., & Das, D. (2016). *A (Short) History of Social Media Sentiment Analysis*. Urban Social Listening. doi:10.1057/978-1-137-59491-4_2

Huang, S., Niu, Z., & Shi, C. (2014). Automatic construction of domain-specific sentiment lexicon based on constrained label propagation. *Knowledge-Based Systems*, *56*, 191–200. doi:10.1016/j.knosys.2013.11.009

Huang, W., Zhao, Y., Yang, S., & Lu, Y. (2008). Analysis of the user behavior and opinion classification based on the BBS. *Applied Mathematics and Computation, 205*(2), 668–676. doi:10.1016/j.amc.2008.01.038

Hung, C., & Lin, H.-K. (2013). Using Objective Words in SentiWordNet to Improve Word-ofMouth Sentiment Classification. *IEEE Intelligent Systems, Volume, 28*(2), 47–54. doi:10.1109/MIS.2013.1

Jurek, Mulvenna, & Bi. (2015). Improved lexicon-based sentiment analysis for social media analytics. *Security Informatics*, 4-9.

Karamibekr, M., & Ghorbani, A. A. (2012). Verb Oriented Sentiment Classification. *IEEE/WIC/ACM International Conferences on Web Intelligence and Intelligent Agent Technology*, 327-331.

Khan, F. H., Bashir, S., & Qamar, U. (2014). TOM: Twitter opinion mining framework using hybrid classification scheme. *Decision Support Systems, 57*, 245–257. doi:10.1016/j.dss.2013.09.004

Khan, F. H., Qamar, U., & Bashir, S. (2016). SWIMS: Semi-supervised subjective feature weighting and intelligent model selection for sentiment analysis. *Knowledge-Based Systems, 100*, 97–111. doi:10.1016/j.knosys.2016.02.011

Kim, K., & Lee, J. (2014). Sentiment visualization and classification via semi-supervised nonlinear dimensionality reduction. *Pattern Recognition, 47*(2), 758–768. doi:10.1016/j.patcog.2013.07.022

Li, Xiao, & Xue. (2012). An unsupervised Approach for sentiment classification. *IEEE symposium on Robotics and Applications (ISRA)*, 638-640.

Li, G., & Liu, F. (2010). A Clustering-based Approach on Sentiment Analysis. *International Conference on Intelligent Systems and Knowledge Engineering (ISKE)*, 331-337.

Li, P., Zhu, Q., & Zhang, W. (2011). A Dependency Tree Based Approach for Sentence-level Classification. *12th ACIS International Conference on Software Engineering, Artificial Intelligence, Networking and Parallel/Distributed Computing*, 166-171. doi:10.1109/SNPD.2011.20

Li, S.-T., & Tsai, F.-C. (2013). A fuzzy conceptualization model for text mining with application in opinion polarity classification. *Knowledge-Based Systems, 39*, 23–33. doi:10.1016/j.knosys.2012.10.005

Lin, Z., Jin, X., Xu, X., Wang, Y., Cheng, X., Wang, W., & Meng, D. (2016). An Unsupervised Cross-Lingual Topic Model Framework for Sentiment Classification. *IEEE/ACM Transactions On Audio, Speech, And Language Processing, 24*(3).

Liu, B., Blasch, E., Chen, Y., Shen, D., & Chen, G. (2013). Scalable Sentiment Classification for Big Data Analysis Using Na¨ ıve Bayes Classifier. *IEEE International Conference on Big Data*, 99-104.

Liu, S., Cheng, X., Li, F., & Li, F. (2015). TASC:Topic-Adaptive Sentiment Classification on Dynamic Tweets. *IEEE Transactions on Knowledge and Data Engineering, 27*(6), 1696–1709. doi:10.1109/TKDE.2014.2382600

Liu, S. M., & Chen, J.-H. (2015). A multi-label classification based approach for sentiment classification. *Expert Systems with Applications, 42*(3), 1083–1093. doi:10.1016/j.eswa.2014.08.036

Maks, I., & Vossen, P. (2012). A lexicon model for deep sentiment analysis and opinion mining applications. *Decision Support Systems, 53*(4), 680–688. doi:10.1016/j.dss.2012.05.025

Montejo-Ráez, A., Martínez-Cámara, E., Martín-Valdivia, M. T., & Urena-López, L. A. (2014). Ranked WordNet graph for Sentiment Polarity Classification in Twitter. *Computer Speech & Language, 28*(1), 93–107. doi:10.1016/j.csl.2013.04.001

Moreo, A., Romero, M., Castro, J. L., & Zurita, J. M. (2012). Lexicon-based Comments-oriented News Sentiment Analyzer system. *Expert Systems with Applications, 39*(10), 9166–9180. doi:10.1016/j.eswa.2012.02.057

Onan, A., Korukoglu, S., & Bulut, H. (2016). A multiobjective weighted voting ensemble classifier based on differential evolution algorithm for text sentiment classification. *Expert Systems with Applications, 62*, 1–16. doi:10.1016/j.eswa.2016.06.005

Ortigosa-Hernandez, J., Rodrıguez, J. D., Alzate, L., Lucania, M., Inza, I., & Lozano, J. A. (2012). Approaching Sentiment Analysis by using semi-supervised learning of multi-dimensional classifiers. *Neurocomputing, 92*, 98–115. doi:10.1016/j.neucom.2012.01.030

Pan, S. J., Ni, X., Sun, J.-T., Yang, Q., & Chen, Z. (2010). Cross-Domain Sentiment Classification via Spectral Feature Alignment. *WWW, 2010*(April), 26–30.

Park, S., Lee, W., & Moon, I.-C. (2015). Efficient extraction of domain specific sentiment lexicon with active learning. *Pattern Recognition Letters, 56*, 38–44. doi:10.1016/j.patrec.2015.01.004

Pedro, M. D. C., & Roy, A. (2016). Sentiment Lexicon Creation using Continuous Latent Space and Neural Networks. *Proceedings of NAACL-HLT, 2016*, 37–42.

Peng, T.-C., & Shih, C.-C. (2010). An Unsupervised Snippet-based Sentiment Classification Method for Chinese Unknown Phrases without using Reference Word Pairs. *IEEE/WIC/ACM International Conference on Web Intelligence and Intelligent Agent Technology*. 243-248. doi:10.1109/WI-IAT.2010.229

Rao, Y., Li, Q., Mao, X., & Wenyin, L. (2014). Sentiment topic models for social emotion mining. *Information Sciences, 266*, 90–100. doi:10.1016/j.ins.2013.12.059

Sangiorgi, P., Augello, A., & Pilato, G. (2013). An unsupervised data-driven cross-lingual method for building high precision sentiment lexicons. *IEEE Seventh International Conference on Semantic Computing*. 184-190. doi:10.1109/ICSC.2013.40

Sun, X., Li, C., Xu, W., & Ren, F. (2014), Chinese Microblog Sentiment Classification Based on Deep Belief Nets with Extended Multi-modality Features. *IEEE International Conference on Data Mining Workshop*, 928-935. doi:10.1109/ICDMW.2014.101

Tan, S., & Wu, Q. (2011). A random walk algorithm for automatic construction of domain-oriented sentiment lexicon. *Expert Systems with Applications, 38*(10), 12094–12100. doi:10.1016/j.eswa.2011.02.105

Trindade, Wang, Blackburn, & Philip. (2014). Taylor. Enhanced Factored Sequence Kernel for Sentiment Classification. *IEEE/WIC/ACM International Joint Conferences on Web Intelligence (WI) and Intelligent Agent Technologies (IAT)*, 519-525.

Tripathy, A., Agrawal, A., & Rath, S. K. (2016). Classification of sentiment reviews using n-gram machine learning approach. *Expert Systems with Applications, 57*, 117–126. doi:10.1016/j.eswa.2016.03.028

Wan & Gao. (2015). An Ensemble Sentiment Classification System of Twitter Data for Airline Services Analysis. *IEEE 15th International Conference on Data Mining Workshops*, 1318-1325.

Wang, G., Zhang, Z., Sun, J., Yang, S., & Larson, C. A. (2015). POS-RS: A Random Subspace method for sentiment classification based on part-of-speech analysis. *Information Processing & Management, 51*(4), 458–479. doi:10.1016/j.ipm.2014.09.004

Wang, S., Yin, X., Zhang, J., Li, R., & Lv, Y. (2012). Sentiment Clustering of Product Object Based on Feature Reduction. *9th International Conference on Fuzzy Systems and Knowledge Discovery (FSKD 2012)*, 742-746. doi:10.1109/FSKD.2012.6234203

Wang, X., & Fu, G. (2010). Chinese Sentence-Level Sentiment Classification Based on Sentiment Morphemes. *International Conference on Asian Language Processing*, 203-206. doi:10.1109/IALP.2010.21

Wu, F., Huang, Y., & Song, Y. (2016). Structured microblog sentiment classification via social context regularization. *Neurocomputing*, *175*, 599–609. doi:10.1016/j.neucom.2015.10.101

Xia, R., Zong, C., Hu, X., & Cambria, E. (2013). Feature Ensemble Plus Sample Selection: Domain Adaptation for Sentiment Classification. *IEEE Intelligent Systems*, *28*(3), 10–18. doi:10.1109/MIS.2013.27

Xia, R., Zong, C., & Li, S. (2011). Ensemble of feature sets and classification algorithms for sentiment classification. *Information Sciences*, *181*(6), 1138–1152. doi:10.1016/j.ins.2010.11.023

Ye, Zhang, & Law. (2014). Sentiment classification of online reviews to travel destinations by supervised machine learning approaches. *Expert Systems with Applications*, *36*, 6527–6535.

Zhang, , Li, , & Zhu, . (2010). Sentiment Classification Based on Syntax Tree Pruning and Tree Kernel. *Seventh Web Information Systems and Applications Conference*, 101-105.

Zhang, C., Zuo, W., Peng, T., & He, F. (2008). Sentiment Classification for Chinese Reviews Using Machine Learning Methods Based on String Kernel. *Third International Conference on Convergence and Hybrid Information Technology*. doi:10.1109/ICCIT.2008.51

Zhang, D., Ma, J., Yi, J., Niu, X., & Xu, X. (2015). An Ensemble Method for Unbalanced Sentiment Classification. *IEEE 11th International Conference on Natural Computation (ICNC)*, 440-445.

Zhang, Wang, Xu, & Yin. (2009). Chinese Text Sentiment Classification based on Granule Network. GRC '09. *IEEE International Conference on Granular Computing*. 775 – 778.

Zhou, S., Chen, Q., & Wang, X. (2013). Active deep learning method for semi-supervised sentiment classification. *Neurocomputing*, *120*, 536–546. doi:10.1016/j.neucom.2013.04.017

Zhou, S., Chen, Q., & Wang, X. (2014). Fuzzy deep belief networks for semi-supervised sentiment classification. *Neurocomputing*, *131*, 312–322. doi:10.1016/j.neucom.2013.10.011

Chapter 3
Data Compaction Techniques

R. Raj Kumar
RGMCET, India

P. Viswanath
IIITS Chittoor, India

C. Shoba Bindu
JNTUA, India

ABSTRACT

A large dataset is not preferable as it increases computational burden on the methods operating over it. Given the Large dataset, it is always interesting that whether one can generate smaller dataset which is a subset or a set (cardinality should be less when compare to original dataset) of extracted patterns from that large dataset. The patterns in the subset are representatives of the patterns in the original dataset. The subset (set) of representing patterns forms the Prototype set. Forming Prototype set is broadly categorized into two types. 1) Prototype set which is a proper subset of original dataset. 2) Prototype set which contains patterns extracted by using the patterns in the original dataset. This process of reducing the training set can also be done with the features of the training set. The authors discuss the reduction of the datasets in the both directions. These methods are well known as Data Compaction Techniques.

INTRODUCTION

The large datasets are always increases computational burden on the methods (algorithms) operating over them. In pattern recognition and its allied fields it is always interesting to generate smaller dataset which is a representative of the original

DOI: 10.4018/978-1-5225-2805-0.ch003

set. A dataset can be represented using a set of attributes or features and patterns or objects. The reduction of the original set can be achieved in both directions *i.e.* reducing the number of patterns and reducing the number of features. Reducing the number of patterns is called Prototype selection or Prototype generation. Reducing the number of features is called Feature Selection or Feature Extraction.

Forming Prototype set is basically categorized into two types.

- Prototype set which is a proper subset of original dataset.
- Prototype set which contains patterns extracted by using the patterns in the original training set.

Given the large dataset in which patterns are represented by large number of features, it is efficient to select a set of features which can best describe the dataset. Like prototype set discussed above, selection of feature set also basically divided into two categories.

- Feature set which is a proper subset of set of features in the original dataset.
- Feature set which contains features extracted from the features of the original dataset.

Both the methods attract the researchers of Big Data, Pattern Recognition and its allied fields.

This chapter is organized as follows. In the section Data Compression using Prototype selection methods the novel methods that are used for Prototype selection were presented. Nearest Neighbour rule is used for computing the Prototype set. The section Data Compaction using Feature selection, some of the important methods which are useful for reducing the data using based on feature selection were discussed. The next section presents how we can combine the methods present in the previous two sections so as to reduce the data both vertically and horizontally. Each section is strengthened by giving suitable examples and experimental results over datasets which are widely used in Machine Learning and its allied fields. The section conclusion and future enhancement gives the future scope for the researchers related to this area.

The last section presents brief summary of the chapter.

Data Compaction Using Prototype Selection

Usage of the representative dataset in place of the original dataset reduces the input data size. Some of the Prototype Selection methods are discussed in this section. A Prototype is a representation of the original pattern. For example, a mean pattern can act as a Prototype of a set of patterns. For example, consider the following data set of two dimensional patterns.

D={(2,4),(2,6),(6,4),(8,8),(6,6)}

The mean of the above patterns is $\left(\dfrac{2+2+6+8+6}{2}, \dfrac{4+6+4+8+6}{2} \right) =$ (12, 14).

Like mean, there are techniques to find the representative patterns which otherwise called Prototype Selection or Prototype Generation methods.

If the Prototype set contains the actual patterns of the training set (However the size of Prototype set is less compare to the original set) then it is called *Prototype selection*. Instead if the Prototype set contains the patterns which are generated using the patterns of the data set, then it is called *Prototype Generation*. Both Prototype selection and Prototype generation are two familiar methods in reducing the given data set. The authors focussed on the Prototype selection methods.

Condensed Nearest Neighbour (CNN) Method

Condensed Nearest Neighbour begins with the pattern selected from the training set which forms the initial condensed set. Then each pattern in the training set is classified using the condensed set. If a pattern in the training set is misclassified, it is included in the condensed set. After one pass through the training set iteration is carried out. This iterative process is carried out till there are no misclassified patterns. The final condensed set has two properties.

- It is a subset of original training set.
- It ensures 100% accuracy over the training set which is the source for deriving the condensed set.

Let S be the given training set and S (CNN) is the new condensed set formed by applying Condensed nearest neighbor rule. The algorithm is outlined as shown in *Algorithm 1*.

Algorithm 1. Condensed nearest neighbor algorithm

```
Step 1 Initially S (CNN) = { }.
Step 2 S (CNN) = 1ˢᵗsample in S.
Step 3 Classify S using S (CNN) using Nearest Neighbor rule.
Step 4 for each sample in S do
Step 5 a) if it is correctly classified then ignores it.
Step 6 b) if it is incorrectly classified, then add it to S
(CNN)
Step 7 Repeat step 3-6 till there are no new samples added to S
(CNN) i.e.
Step 8 S (CNN) ᵢ= S (CNN) ᵢ₋₁ where i is the iteration number.
Step 9 Output S (CNN) as condensed set over S.
```

Table 1. Example data set

No	A	B	Class
X_1	1	1	NO
X_2	1	2	NO
X_3	2	1	NO
X_4	2	2	NO
X_5	5	1	YES
X_6	5	2	YES
X_7	6	1	YES
X_8	6	2	YES

Numeric Example

Consider an Example data set as shown in Table 1. It has two features A and B along with the Class label information present in the last column. It is an example of binary class data where each sample is classified into one of the two classes present 'YES' or 'NO'. Let X_i refers the ith sample in the data set i.e. X_2 means the second pattern (1, 2).

The distance measure used to find the distance between the patterns is Euclidean distance and the rule followed is Nearest Neighbor rule. Let us understand the rule first before computing Prototype set S for the data set shown in Table 1 using CNN.

Advantages: The advantages of CNN method are:

1. The set formed by CNN is a condensed set i.e. it shows 100% accuracy over which it has built.
2. It is a subset of the original training set.

Disadvantages: The disadvantages of CNN method are:

1. It is order dependent. The set of patterns chosen are based on the first pattern selected initially in the set.
2. It scans the training set multiple times.

Nearest Neighbour Method

Nearest Neighbour classification (NNC) is a popularly known classification method in pattern recognition. NNC is simple to use and easy to understand. For a test pattern 'q', NNC or 1-NNC finds the nearest neighbour in the reference set and assigns the class label of this nearest neighbour to the test pattern. When the patterns are large (cardinality of the data set approaches to infinity) it can be shown that the error rate of 1-NNC is twice the Bayes' error rate. The nearest neighbour classifiers uses some or all of the patterns in the training set to classify the given query pattern.

Let there are 'n' training patterns, $(X_1, Y1), (X_2, Y2)... (X_n, Y_n)$ where X_i is of dimension d and Y_i is the class label of the ith pattern. Let us try to understand the 1-NN procedure using a concrete example. But, before that it is meaningful to understand the notion of nearest in NN. The nearest is based on the notion of distance and the most distance metric used in machine learning is *Euclidean Distance*. The Euclidean Distance D between two patterns a and b is given by the following:

$$D = \sqrt{\sum_{i=1}^{d} \left(a_i - b_i \right)^2}$$

For example, the distance between $(2,3)$ and $(1,4)$ is given by $\sqrt{(2-1)^2 + (3-4)^2}$ $= \sqrt{2} = 1.411$. Here d=2.

The 1-NN neighbour method is illustrated by using the Figure 1. In the Figure there are two classes present. The patterns belong to class 1 is represented by filled circles and the patterns that are belong to class 2 is represented with the symbol filled diamond. The query pattern is represented by using '*'. Now the problem is to determine the class label of this query pattern. Using Nearest neighbour one has to compute all the distances present between the query pattern and all the patterns belongs to class 1 and class 2. From the Figure it is obvious that '* 'belongs to class 1(filled circle) as the nearest neighbour pattern of '*' belongs to class 1.

Figure 1. Example showing the working of 1-NN

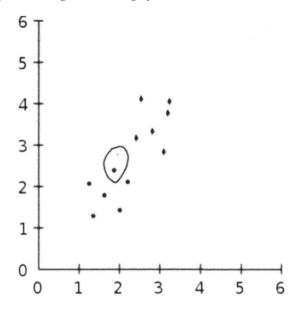

Advantages: The advantages of the NNC method are:

1. Simple and easy to understand.
2. The error rate of NNC is twice the Bayes' error rate.

Disadvantages: The disadvantages of NNC method are:

1. This method requires large memory space as it has to store the entire training set i.e. it faces space complexity problem.
2. It compares each and every pattern in the training set to classify a pattern. Hence it needs large computation time i.e. it faces time complexity problem.
3. The outliers affect the performance of NNC.
4. The curse of dimensionality problem exists in NNC.

Example

Let the training set consist of the following three dimensional points. The first two dimensions represent the features and the third dimension is class label.

Let there are two classes present. The patterns belong to either class 1 or class 2.

$$X_1 = (1.0, 1.0, X_2 = (1.0, 2.0, 1) \; X_3 = (2.0, 1.0, 1) \; X_4 = (2.0, 2.0, 1) \quad \quad 1)$$

X_5= (5.0, 5.0,X_6= (5.0, 6.0, 2) X_7= (6.0, 5.0, 2) X_8= (6.0, 6.0, 2)   2)

Let the query pattern q= (3.0, 3.0) for which we need to compute the class label. Following the 1-NN procedure, we find the distances between q and all the patterns i.e. X_1, X2...X_8.

$$D (q, X1) = \sqrt{(3-1)^2 + (3-1)^2} = \sqrt{2^2 + 2^2} = \sqrt{8}$$

similarly,

$$d_2 = \sqrt{5}, d_3 = \sqrt{5}, d_4 = \sqrt{2}, d_5 = \sqrt{8}\ d_6= \sqrt{13}, d_7= \sqrt{13}, d_8 = \sqrt{19}$$

So, the nearest neighbour for q is X_4 as it is very close to q. This infers the class label 1 for q saying that q belongs to class 1.

Now let us compute the prototype set S based on CNN method over the data set present in Table 1.

The Euclidean distances between the patterns of Table 1 are present in Table 2.

The first pattern X_1 forms the initial condensed set S. So S={X_1}. Using S, the dataset in Table1 is classified. During the first iteration, the patterns X_1, X_2, X_3, and X4 are ignored as they classify using S. The pattern X_5 is added to S because it is misclassified by S. The patterns X_6, X_7 and $X_8$are ignored as they classify using S. After the end of the first iteration, S={X_1, X_5}. Then the second iteration is carried out. During the second iteration new patterns are not added to S because all the patterns in the dataset are classified. At this stage, the algorithm is terminated with set S={X_1, X_5}, the final condensed prototype set. Now the Prototype Set S can be used instead of original set for classifying the patterns. The reduction rate achieved

Table 2. Euclidean distance between patterns of Table 1

NO.	X_1	X_2	X_3	X_4	X_5	X_6	X_7	X_8
X_1	0	1	1	1.414	4	4.12	5	5.09
X_2	1	0	1.414	1	4.12	4	5.09	5
X_3	1	1.414	0	1	3	3.16	4	4.12
X_4	1.414	1	1	0	3.16	3	4.12	4
X_5	4	4.12	3	3.16	0	1	1	1.414
X_6	4.12	4	3.16	3	1	0	1.414	1
X_7	5	5.09	4	4.12	1	1.414	0	1
X_8	5	5.09	4	4.12	1	1.414	0	1

in this case is $\dfrac{6}{8}$ = 0.75 or 75%. That's Researchers are interested always finding alternate and suitable set instead of original set. These types of techniques like CNN and other methods which are going to be discussed in the subsequent sections are helpful in the fields where data compaction techniques are needed especially like *Big Data and Big Data Classification.*

Other Class Nearest Neighbour (OCNN) Method

This method is based on the intuitive notion of retaining patterns that are near to decision boundary. It is obvious that the patterns which are near decision boundary plays very important role in the classification of a process. The boundary patterns are computed by using Other Class Nearest Neighbour (OCNN) method.

Let S be the given training set. S (OCNN) is the set formed after applying the OCNN method. OCNN (X_i) is the set of nearest neighbours for pattern X_i from other classes which can be computed by using k-nn rule. The method is outlined in algorithm 2. Consider the example training set shown in Figure 2. Two classes are present in the Figure 2. The positive class tuples are represented by '+' and negative class tuples are represented by '×'. For example, if a query pattern '*' lies on the left side of the boundary decision, then it is classified as '+' class otherwise '-' class. That means the patterns that are near to decision boundary are enough for classification. The other samples can be removed from the training set. This is the central idea of OCNN method. In the example present in the Figure 2, two patterns from '×' class and two patterns from '+' class near to decision boundary are typical patterns when compared to other training patterns.

This can be found by using the Other Class Nearest Neighbours algorithm (OCNN) discussed in Algorithm 2.

Advantages: The advantages of OCNN method are:

1. It is order independent i.e. the reduced set formed by OCNN method is independent of the patterns initially selected.
2. It does not require multiple scans of training data.

Disadvantages: The disadvantages of OCNN method are:

1. It has the time complexity $O(n^2)$
2. The reduced set does not have consistency property.

Figure 2. Working of OCNN

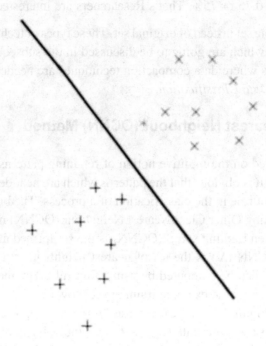

Algorithm 2. Other class nearest neighbour algorithm

```
1 Initially Set S=∅.
2 for each Xᵢ present in S
3 do
4 Find Sᵢ= OCNN (Xᵢ) using k-nn rule.
5 S = S ∪ S ᵢ.
6 end for
7 S (OCNN) =S;
8 output S (OCNN).
```

An Example

The algorithms are illustrated with the example dataset shown in Table 1. The Euclidean distances between the patterns are present in the Table 2.

The S_{Xi}=OCNN (X_i) where $i = 1, 2 \ldots 8$ obtained as follows. Consider k=2.

S_{X1}=OCNN(X_1) ={X_5, X6} S_{X2}=OCNN(X_2) ={X_5, X_6}

Table 3. Prototype set chosen by OCNN on Table 1

No.	A	B	Class
X3	2	1	NO
X4	2	2	NO
X5	5	1	YES
X6	5	2	YES

$S_{X3}=OCNN(X_3)=\{X_5, X6\}$ $S_{X4=}OCNN(X_4)=\{X_5, X_6\}$

$S_{X5}=OCNN(X_5)=\{X_4, X3\}$ $S_{X6}=OCNN(X_6)=\{X_4, X3\}$ $S_{X7}=OCNN(X_7)=\{X_4, X_3\}$ $S_{X8}=OCNN(X_8)=\{X_4, X_3\}$

The final prototype set S is computed by the union of all S_{Xi}. For this example, $S=S_{X1}\cup S_{X2}\cup S_{X3}\cup S_{X4}\cup S_{X5}\cup S_{X6}\cup S_{X7}\cup S_{X8}$. Hence, we get $S=\{X_5, X_6, X_4, X_3\}$ shown in Table 3.

Let us build the prototype set S based on the method CNN shown in Algorithm 1.

The first pattern X_1 forms the initial condensed set S. So $S=\{X_1\}$. Using S, the dataset in Table1 is classified. During the first iteration, the patterns X_1, X_2, X_3, and X_4 are ignored as they classify using S. The pattern X_5 is added to S because it is misclassified by S. The patterns X_6, X_7, X_8 are ignored as they classify using S. After the end of the first iteration, $S=\{X_1, X5\}$. Then the second iteration is carried out. During the second iteration new patterns are not added to S because all the patterns in the dataset are classified. At this stage, the algorithm is terminated with set $S=\{X_1, X_5\}$, the final condensed prototype set.

Modified Condensed Nearest Neighbour Method (MCNN)

In this algorithm, prototype set is built in an incremental manner. A typical pattern is selected from each class and it is kept in the set. This is considered as initial prototype set to begin with. The training set patterns are classified by using this prototype set. From the misclassified samples in the training set, a representative pattern is computed from each class and is added to the prototype set. Now again the training set is classified with the prototype set. This process is an iterative process and repeated till there are no misclassified samples present in the training set. Now the final typical pattern set is the desired prototype set. It is a subset of original training set and ensures consistency over the training set. In a class of patterns, the pattern which is near to centroid may be selected as typical pattern.

Algorithm 3. Modified condensed nearest neighbor algorithm

Step 1: Initially S (MCNN) = { }.
Step 2: S (MCNN) = {a pattern selected from each class in the training set}
Step 3: Classify S using S (MCNN) by 1-NN rule.
　　　　　Divide S into two sets as S_c and S_m
　　　　a. S_c = {Set of correctly classified samples}
　　　　b. S_m = {Set of incorrectly classified samples}
Step 4: From Set S_m select the pattern P_i where P_i represents a

Prototype for class i. $P = \left\{ \bigcup\limits_{i=1}^{c} P_i \right\}$ where c is the no. of

classes present in S.
Step 5: S (MCNN) = S (MCNN) $\bigcup P$.
Step 6: Use S (MCNN) to classify S.
Step 7: Repeat Step 3-6 till there are no misclassified samples from S or S (MCNN) $_i$ = S (MCNN) $_{i+1}$ i.e. there are no new samples added to S (MCNN). Here i is the iteration number.
Step 8: Stop the process and Output S (MCNN).

Let S be the given training set and S (MCNN) is the new condensed set formed by applying Modified Condensed nearest neighbor rule. The algorithm is outlined as shown in *Algorithm 3*.

Example: Let us understand how MCNN works. Consider the data set in Table 1 except X_8 is changed to (9, 2, YES) and the pattern $X_9 = (2.5, 2.5, YES)$ is appended. This change is done in order to understand the working of MCNN. Now the distances from X_8 to the remaining patterns are given below.

$d_{18} = 8.06$; $d_{28} = 8$; $d_{38} = 7.07$; $d_{48} = 7$; $d_{58} = 4.12$; $d_{68} = 4$; $d_{78} = 3.16$; $d_{88} = 0$; $d_{19} = 2.12$; $d_{89} = 9.19$;

Let X_1 and X8 are the randomly selected patterns.

So S (MCNN) = $\{X_1, X_8\}$. In the first iteration, patterns X_1, X2, X3, X4, X_6, X_7 and X_8 are correctly classified. Patterns X_5 and X_9 are wrongly classified.

Then $S_m = \{X_5, X_9\}$. Now a representative pattern should be selected. Let the representative pattern should be the pattern that is closest to the mean of the misclassified patterns.

The mean of the patterns X_5, X_9 is (3.75, 1.75). Both the patterns are at equal distance from this mean pattern. So either X_5 or X_9 can be included. Let X_5 is selected.

Figure 3. Working of MCNN

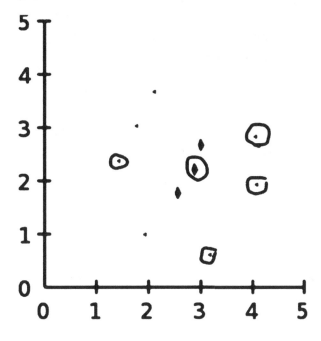

Figure 4. Working of CNN

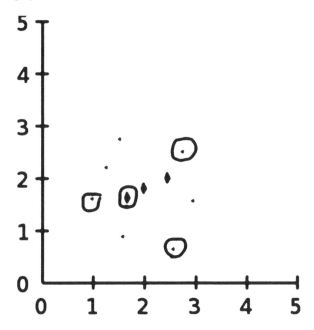

Then S (MCNN) = $\{X_1, X_8, X_5\}$. Now the second iteration is carried out. In the second iteration all the patterns are classified correctly. Hence the process stops and the output is the condensed modified condensed set $\{X_1, X_8,$ and $X_5\}$.The MCNN also obeys the same properties as CNN.

The diagrammatic representation of MCNN is show in Figure 3. There two class patterns present in the Figure. The patterns circled are the selected patterns by execution of MCNN over them.

The diagrammatic representations of CNN for the same patterns are shown in Figure 4. The patterns circled are the patterns selected by execution of CNN over them.

Advantages: The advantages of MCNN are:

1. It is order independent.
2. It has the consistency property.

Disadvantages: The disadvantage of MCNN is it requires multiple scans of data set.

Experimentation

In this section, the data sets used for the experiments are discussed. The methods CNN and OCNN are applied on the 5 data sets. All the data sets are taken from UCI Machine Learning Repository except Optical Character Recognition (OCR). The information about the data sets is shown in Table 4. It shows about the name of the data sets, number of training and testing patterns, no of features and also no of classes.

Table 4. Description of data sets

Data Set	Number of Training Patterns	Number of Testing Patterns	Number of Features	Number of Classes
Wine	120	57	13	3
Thyroid	144	71	5	3
Iris	99	51	4	3
Balance	416	209	4	3
Optical.digit.rec	3823	1797	64	10
OCR	6670	3333	192	10
Liver	230	155	6	2
Pima	512	256	8	2

The methods are applied on the popular data sets. The accuracies obtained on the data sets are shown in Table 5.

- **Accuracy:** Accuracy is a key component in evaluating performance of classifier. It is estimated based on the test set. The test set has the patterns which do not belong to training set or learning set. But both the training examples and test examples must be *i.i.d* (independently identically drawn) from the same distribution. Once the training set builds the classifier then it is tested for accuracy on the test set. The accuracy is computed as follows;

N_c =Number of test patterns that were correctly classified.
N_m=Number of test patterns that were incorrectly classified.

Now the classification Accuracy: $CA = \dfrac{N_c}{N_c + N_m}$

For example, let there are 100 patterns in a test set. Let the classifier classifies 85 patterns correctly and remaining were incorrectly classified.

So Nc = 85; N_m = 15.

$$CA = \frac{85}{85 + 15} = \frac{85}{100} = 0.85$$

The CA often expressed in terms of % *i.e.,* 85%.

Table 5. Accuracy obtained over data sets

Data Set	OCNN		MCNN		CNN		All Prototypes	
	# of Prototypes	Accuracy %	# of Prototypes	Accuracy %	# of Prototypes	Accuracy %	# of Prototypes	Accuracy %
OCR	1650	90.15	1527	88.0	1580	87.04	6670	**92.0**
Wine	45	94.74	14	94.74	27	94.74	120	94.74
Iris	22	**98.33**	10	92.16	16	96.08	99	94.12
Thyroid	38	92.10	18	**95.77**	16	91.55	144	94.37
Liver	154	**73.03**	136	72.17	150	64.35	230	63.48
Pima	329	**76.78**	250	67.97	266	65.23	512	69.14
Balance	214	74.64	157	74.64	143	71.77	416	**77.03**
OptdigitRec	622	96.55	325	94.32	305	96.38	3823	**98.00**

The misclassification rate or Error of the classifier can also be found using CA. Misclassification rate or Error of the classifier $= 1 - CA$

Hence, Error $= 1 - 0.85 = 0.15$ or 15%

In Table 5, the accuracies and the no of prototypes obtained by OCNN, MCNN and CNN are given. These results are evident enough to say that OCNN method is competing with CNN and MCNN methods and it is showing good accuracy. The methods are implemented on 'DELL OPTIPLEX740 n' model having Intel core 2 DUO 2.2 Giga Hz processor with 1GB DDR 2 RAM capacity.

On Iris, Liver and Pima data sets OCNN performed well than other methods. On OCR, Iris, Liver, Pima and

Optical Digit Recognition datasets OCNN is performing better than MCNN method as well as CNN method. The method which got the best accuracy is shown in bold case.

All the methods reduced the number of prototypes considerably and achieved good reduction rate. The number of patterns reduced and the reduction rate is shown in the Table 6.

- **Reduction Rate:** The reduction rate is also another important criterion to evaluate the classifier performance. The reduction rate indicates how many no of patterns a classifier can able to reduce from the original training data set without sacrificing its performance over the test set. It can be computed as:

Table 6. Reduction achieved by OCNN, MCNN, and CNN

Data Set	Training Set Size	OCNN		MCNN		CNN	
		# of Prototypes Reduced	Reduction Rate	# of Prototypes Reduced	Reduction Rate	# of Prototypes Reduced	Reduction Rate
OCR	6670	5020	0.75	5143	0.77	5090	0.76
Wine	120	99	0.68	130	0.90	117	0.81
Iris	99	77	0.77	89	0.89	83	0.83
Thyroid	144	106	0.73	126	0.87	128	0.88
Liver	230	76	0.33	94	0.40	80	0.34
Pima	512	183	0.35	262	0.51	246	0.48
Balance	416	202	0.48	259	0.62	273	0.65
OptdigitRec	3823	3201	0.83	3498	0.91	3518	0.92

Let N= Number of patterns in training set.

N_r= Number of patterns removed by the method.

Then the reduction rate of the method is RR $= \dfrac{N_r}{N}$

For example out of 100 patterns if 80 patterns are removed by the method then its reduction rate is $\dfrac{80}{100}$ =0.80. Oftenly the reduction rate is also expressed in terms of % i.e. 80%.

Contribution to Big Data

The size of the data is often the most important component in retrieving information from the BIG data. The big data has peta bytes of data from which the analysts has to draw the conclusions. The central theme of data compression techniques are to save the time of the analyst even when minimal resources are present. To get an idea of this consider the following example situation.

- **Example:** For example, assume that patient's data set is present where it contains information about the patients like patient id, name, age, gender, food habits, Blood pressure, sugar level, skin color, plasma level etc. To analyze whether the patient has a chance of getting heart attack after 10 or 15 years; this data has to be analyzed. A domain expert can understand that the feature B.P and Sugar level are important features for analyzing the heart attack disease rather than other features. This means the other features can be irrelevant so that they can be excluded from the data set. But actually every time an expert is not available at all the time. So there should be a way of removing the redundant and irrelevant features. Feature extraction or Feature selection does this on the data sets.

The word big data is relative and subjective with respect to the context used and one of the good definitions given as follows

Big Data

Data that needs a huge amount of time to analyze, to store and to process and take a decision.

An important benefit of data compression techniques is to save time and computing resources by enabling the user to deal with larger datasets within minimal resources available at hand. The key point of this process is to reduce the data without making it statistically indistinguishable from the original data, or at least to preserve the characteristics of the original dataset in the reduced representation at a desired level of accuracy. Because of the huge amounts of data involved, data reduction processes become the critical element of the Big data analysis. Reducing big data also remains a challenging task that the straightforward approach working well for small data, but might end up with impractical computation times for big data. Hence, the phase of software and architecture design together is crucial in the process of developing data reduction algorithm for processing big data.

One interesting question that will arise is *"How are the methods discussed in this section are helpful to BIG DATA?"* The answer is simple and straight: For example, observe the reduction rates achieved by the methods in Table 6. The data sets are reduced considerably. This has very profound influence especially in the case of large data sets like OCR and Opt. digit. Rec data sets where the data is reduced by 75% and 85% approximately by all the methods. That means these methods also takes proportionally less time to classify a new data item when compare to the original training set. This is very helpful in case of Big Data and the classification problem in Big Data. One can use any of the above methods according to their interest and appropriate method can be chosen.

Data Compaction Using Feature Selection

Feature selection methods reduce the dimensionality of the given dataset. Deciding the feature set that describes the dataset well is always catches the interest of the researchers. The data sets may contain large number of features (dimensions or attributes), some of which are irrelevant to the classification process. Some features might be redundant features. For example, if the classification task is to classify the person with Obesity or Not, based on his personal data which has the information about his Name, Age, Contact No, Blood Pressure, Waist Size, Cholesterol level. The features containing the person's Blood Pressure and Contact No are irrelevant. A domain expert may pick the useful features. But this process is inopportune in case of inadequacy of expert and when the data behaviour is unknown. This is time consuming in case of large numbered featured data sets. Moreover we need manual intervention. Feature Selection or Feature Subset Selection is the process of selecting a subset of existing features without using any transformation.

Hence in Machine Learning, Patter Recognition and allied fields dimensionality reduction is the topic of research over years. Dimensionality Reduction can be done in two ways:

Figure 5. Steps feature selection or extraction

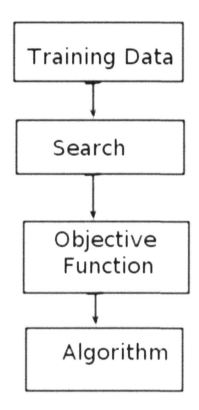

1. Feature Selection.
2. Feature Extraction.

Feature Selection or Feature Subset Selection is the process of selecting a subset of existing features without using any transformation. Feature Extraction projects the existing features onto a lower dimensional space with the help of transformations. Linear Discriminant Analysis (LDA) and Principal Component Analysis (PCA) are the good examples for Feature extraction methods. In this section, Both Feature Extraction and Feature Selection methods are discussed.

The steps in Feature Selection is shown in Figure 5.

Feature Extraction Methods

This section discusses Principal Component Analysis (PCA), Linear Discriminant Analysis (LDA) popular Feature extraction methods.

Principal Component Analysis

Linear Discriminant Analysis (LDA) and Principal Component Analysis (PCA) are linear transformation methods. They are related to each other. In PCA, we are interested to find the directions of the component that maximize the variance in the given dataset, where as in LDA, we are additionally interested to find the directions that maximize the discrimination power between the different classes present in the dataset.

In other words, Using PCA, we are projecting the entire set of data (Class labels are not taken into account) onto a different subspace. But in LDA we are trying to find the suitable subspace that separates the classes present in the dataset. Frankly speaking, in PCA we find the axes where the most of the data is spread over where as in LDA we additionally consider the class labels too. In a single work PCA treats the whole dataset belongs to one class but LDA considers the different labels of the dataset.

The PCA approach is listed in the following steps:

- Consider the d-dimensional data set samples ignoring class labels.
- Compute the mean vector. (i.e. mean of every dimension has to be computed).
- Compute the scatter matrix.
- Compute the eigenvectors and the corresponding Eigen values: $e_1, e_2 ... e_n \wedge \lambda_1, \lambda_2, ... \lambda_n$.
- Sort the eigenvectors by the decreasing order of their corresponding Eigen values and select c eigenvectors with largest Eigen values and form matrix $W_{d \times c}$.
- Use the matrix W to transform the patterns on to the new subspace. This can be done by applying the following mathematical equation:

$$Y = W^T \times X$$

where X is a d×1 dimensional vector representing a sample from the data set and Y is the transformed c×1 subspace sample.

The PCA approach is shown in the Figure 6.

Linear Discriminant Analysis

LDA is a Dimensionality reduction technique used in machine learning. It is also one of the pre-processing techniques. LDA extracts the good features and project

Figure 6. Principal component analysis

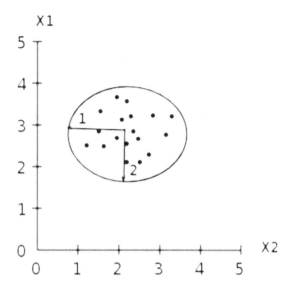

the dataset onto a lower dimensional space with good-class separability. It is similar to Principal Component Analysis but in addition to finding the ×Component axes that maximize the variance of data, we are additionally interested in the axes that maximize the separation between the classes. The LDA process is carried out as follows:

- Compute the mean vectors for the different classes from the dataset.
- Compute the in-between-class scatter matrix S_b and within-class-scatter matrix S_w:

$$S_w = \sum_{i=1}^{c} s_i$$

where i=1, 2... c i.e., c is number of classes and S_i is scatter matrix of class i:

$$S_i = \sum_{x \in D_i} (x - m_i)(x - m_i)^t$$

where m_i is the mean of class i:

$$m_i = \frac{1}{n_i} \sum_{x \in D_i} x$$

where D_i is the data set of class i. The in-between-class scatter matrices can be computed as:

$$S_b = \sum_{i=1}^{c} (m_i - m)(m_i - m)^t$$

The objective function is:

$$J(V) = \frac{\left| V^t S_b V \right|}{\left| V^t S_w V \right|}$$

where V is the projection matrix to the subspace of dimensionality k=c-1 at most (c is the no of classes). This can be converted to General Eigen value problem:

$$S_b V = \lambda S_w V$$

Figure 7. Linear discriminant analysis

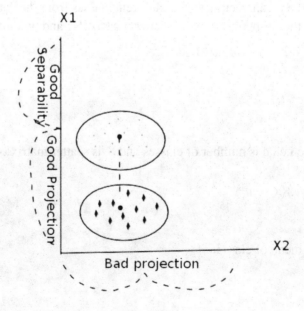

$$\lambda V = S_w^{-1} S_b V$$

Let $V_1, V_2 ... V_{c-1}$ be the corresponding Eigen vectors. The projection matrix V is of order d × k used to project the data onto subspace of dimension k (k ≤ d) is given by the Eigen vectors corresponding to the largest k Eigen values. V projects the dataset to subspace at most c-1 where c is no of classes using the following computation:

$$Y = V^t X$$

where Y is the pattern projected of order k × 1 and X is of order d × 1.

The LDA approach can be represented in the Figure 7.

Feature Selection Methods

The formal definition of Feature Subset Selection is given below.

- **Feature Subset Selection:** Let F be the feature set i.e. $F = \{F_i \vee i = 1, 2, ... N\}$, Find a subset Z= $\left\{F_{i1} F_{i2} ... F_{ij}\right\}$ with M < N which optimizes an objective function J(Y).Choosing objective function is categorized into two groups.
- **Filter Approach:** The objective function evaluates feature subsets by their information content, typically interclass distance, statistical dependence or information theoretic measures.
- **Wrapper Approach:** The objective function is a pattern classifier, which evaluates feature subsets by their predictive accuracy (recognition rate on test data) by statistical resampling or cross validation.

Sequential Forward Selection (SFS)

Sequential Forward selection (SFS) is a feature selection algorithm which selects the subset of features based on objective function J (.). It aims to find the best subset of features from the given original set of features. The process of SFS is carried as follows.

1. Start with the empty Set.
2. Add a feature X to J(Y+X) (that better optimizes J (.)) where Y is a subset of features that have been already selected.
3. SFS process may be terminated when the objective function reaches to threshold value or We can choose required number of features in the subset of features M,

Algorithm 4. Sequential forward selection algorithm

Step 1: Initially set $Y_0 = \varnothing$
Step 2: Select the next best feature $x^+ = argmax\Big[J(Y_i + x)\Big]$
Step 3: Update $Y_{i+1} = Y_i + x^+; i = i + 1$
Step 4: Go to step 2.

Figure 8. Sequential forward selection

Empty feature set

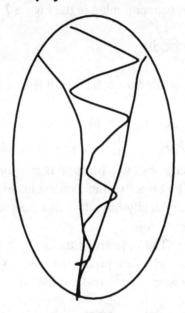

Full feature set

i.e. M<N where N is the total number of features in the dataset by maximizing J(.).J (.) should be a non-monotonic function.

SFS is outlined in Algorithm 4.
The SFS process is shown in the Figure 8.

- **Advantages:** The main advantage of SFS method is it is the simple greedy search algorithm. It works well when there is smaller number of features.

Algorithm 5.

Step 1: Initially set $Y_O = X$. Where X *is* the set of features.

Step 2: Select the bad feature that has to be removed

$$x^- = argmax\Big[J(Y_i - x)\Big]$$

Step 3: Update $Y_{i+1} = Y_i - x^-; i = i + 1$

Step 4: Go to step 2.

Figure 9. Sequential backward selection

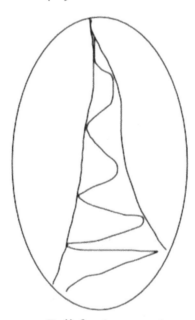

Empty feature set

Full feature set

- **Limitation:** The main disadvantage of SFS is it is unable to remove the features which may become useless after the addition of other features.

Sequential Backward Selection (SBS)

SBS starts from the full set of features and sequentially removes a feature say x that results minimum decrease in the value of objective function J(Y-x). J(.) is a non-monotonic function. The steps followed by SBS algorithm is given in Algorithm 5.

The SBS is shown in the Figure 9.

- **Advantages:** The main advantage of SBS is it works well when there is large number of features in the set.
- **Limitation:** The main limitation of SBS is once a feature is removed then it's not possible to reevaluate the useful ness of it and we cannot add it again.

Combination of SFS and SBS

This is parallel implementation of SFS and SBS method:

- SFS starts with empty set.
- BFS starts with full feature set as discussed in the previous sections.

But proper care has to be taken to ensure the convergence of solution. One has to ensure that:

- Features already selected by SFS should not be removed by SBS.
- Features already deleted by SBS should not be selected by SFS.

That means, before deleting any feature SBS has to check whether that feature is selected by SFS or not. SFS works in the same manner. This type of search is also called Bidirectional search.

Data Compaction Using Prototype Selection and Feature Selection

The dataset size can be reduced both in cardinality and dimensionality using Prototype Selection and Feature Selection methods respectively. It is always enlightening for researchers to examine Feature Selection followed by Prototype Selection or Prototype selection followed by Feature Selection would have any impact on the classification accuracy. There are two choices now:

- Applying feature selection method followed by prototype selection method.
- Applying prototype selection method followed by feature selection method.

In this section, LDA, SFS followed by OCNN and CNN (Feature selection followed by Prototype selection) and OCNN and CNN followed by LDA, SFS (Prototype selection followed by Feature selection) are discussed. These methods are the examples for reducing the data set both cardinality and dimensionality. First any one

Table 7. Accuracy over thyroid dataset

k	LDA+CNN		LDA+OCNN	
	No of Prototypes	Accuracy %	No of Prototypes	Accuracy %
3	14	89.61	19	90.00
5	14	80.51	19	85.71
7	14	75.32	19	87.32
9	14	85.60	19	88.66
11	14	77.91	19	86.51
		85.14±3.71		87.61±3.13

Table 8. Accuracy over thyroid dataset

k	CNN+LDA		OCNN+LDA	
	No of Prototypes	Accuracy %	No of Prototypes	Accuracy %
3	24	19.73	43	69.73
5	24	19.73	43	65.78
7	24	67.10	43	67.10
9	24	67.10	43	67.10
11	24	67.10	43	67.10
		48.15±21.20		67.36±1.28

Table 9. Accuracy over iris dataset

k	LDA+CNN		LDA+OCNN	
	No of Prototypes	Accuracy %	No of Prototypes	Accuracy %
3	29	78.33	35	53.33
5	29	58.33	35	60.00
7	29	58.33	35	58.33
9	29	68.33	35	59.16
		64.99±9.42		57.22±2.23

Table 10. Accuracy over iris dataset

k	CNN+LDA		OCNN+LDA	
	No of Prototypes	Accuracy %	No of Prototypes	Accuracy %
3	22	75.00	38	81.66
5	22	68.33	38	73.33
7	22	68.33	38	78.33
9	22	68.33	38	78.33
11	22	68.33	38	78.33
		70.55±3.14		77.77±3.42

Table 11. Accuracy over wine dataset

k	LDA+CNN		LDA+OCNN	
	No of Prototypes	Accuracy %	No of Prototypes	Accuracy %
3	59	60.93	68	65.62
5	59	64.03	68	59.37
7	59	56.25	68	60.93
9	59	62.76	68	62.49
11	59	58.59	68	63.27
		60.51±3.14		62.33±2.36

Table 12. Accuracy over wine dataset

k	CNN+LDA		OCNN+LDA	
	No of Prototypes	Accuracy %	No of Prototypes	Accuracy %
3	22	25.86	60	29.31
5	22	27.56	60	25.86
7	22	25.86	60	43.10
9	22	24.13	60	44.82
11	22	25.86	60	43.33
		25.85±1.09		37.28±8.01

Table 13. Accuracy over balance dataset

k	LDA+CNN		LDA+OCNN	
	No of Prototypes	Accuracy %	No of Prototypes	Accuracy %
3	103	79.80	102	78.84
5	103	82.69	102	84.43
7	103	82.21	102	83.65
9	103	81.24	102	81.24
11	103	81.00	102	81.48
		81.38±1.15		81.92±2.20

Table 14. Accuracy over balance dataset

k	CNN+LDA		OCNN+LDA	
	No of Prototypes	Accuracy %	No of Prototypes	Accuracy %
3	143	60.00	163	62.85
5	143	61.90	163	63.81
7	143	60.95	163	57.14
9	143	58.57	163	58.09
11	143	56.19	163	56.19
		59.52±2.23		59.61±3.47

of the feature selection methods (either LDA or SFS) is applied on the dataset. Then the dataset is reduced dimensionally. After this, any one of the prototype selection method (either CNN or OCNN) is applied over the reduced set. Now, the dataset is reduced in cardinality. LDA+CNN or SFS+OCNN refer to first applying LDA or SFS following CNN or OCNN. Similarly, this process can be done in vice versa *i.e.* First reducing the dataset in cardinality follows reducing it in dimensionality.

The results obtained over thyroid data set are given in Table 7 and Table 8.

The results obtained over Iris Dataset are presented in Table 9 and Table 10.

The results obtained over Wine Dataset are presented in Table 11 and Table 12.

The results obtained over Balance Dataset are presented in Table 13 and Table 14.

The results obtained over Opt.digit.rec Dataset are presented in Table 15 and Table 16.

The experiments are repeated over Thyroid, Iris and Pima with the feature selection method SFS. The results obtained over Thyroid dataset are shown in Table 17 and Table 18.

The results obtained over Iris dataset are presented in Table 19 and Table 20.

Table 15. Accuracy over opt.digit.rec dataset

k	LDA+CNN		LDA+OCNN	
	No of Prototypes	Accuracy %	No of Prototypes	Accuracy %
3	1537	62.49	2463	65.71
5	1537	71.16	2463	71.16
7	1537	72.46	2463	72.46
9	1537	73.14	2463	73.14
11	1537	66.82	2463	66.82
		69.24±4.49		69.85±3.37

Table 16. Accuracy over opt.digit.rec dataset

k	CNN+LDA		OCNN+LDA	
	No of Prototypes	Accuracy %	No of Prototypes	Accuracy %
3	1514	63.14	2313	62.36
5	1514	61.83	2313	61.93
7	1514	58.09	2313	56.29
9	1514	54.52	2313	57.24
11	1514	56.88	2313	56.59
		58.89±3.55		58.88±3.00

Table 17. Accuracy over thyroid

k	SFS+CNN			SFS+OCNN		
	# of Prototypes	# of Features Reduced	Accuracy %	# of Prototypes	# of Features Reduced	Accuracy %
3	24	1	82.10	43	1	87.27
5	24	1	84.44	45	1	86.45
7	24	1	86.22	48	1	87.22
9	24	1	85.54	46	1	86.88
			84.57±1.58			86.95±0.37

The results obtained over Pima dataset are presented in Table 21 and Table 22.

Table 18. Accuracy over thyroid

k	CNN+SFS			OCNN+SFS		
	# of Prototypes	# of Features Reduced	Accuracy %	# of Prototypes	# of Features Reduced	Accuracy %
3	28	2	81.57	46	1	89.47
5	28	2	83.34	48	1	88.47
7	28	2	84.42	45	1	89.32
9	28	2	85.79	47	1	88.52
			83.78±1.78			89.01±0.45

Table 19. Accuracy over iris

k	SFS+CNN			SFS+OCNN		
	# of Prototypes	# of Features Reduced	Accuracy %	# of Prototypes	# of Features Reduced	Accuracy %
3	23	1	76.33	31	2	78.83
5	23	1	75.45	35	2	76.43
7	23	1	76.67	33	2	77.88
9	23	1	75.65	38	2	79.55
			76.04±0.60			78.14±1.33

Table 20. Accuracy over iris

k	CNN+SFS			OCNN+SFS		
	# of Prototypes	# of Features Reduced	Accuracy %	# of Prototypes	# of Features Reduced	Accuracy %
3	21	1	76.84	33	1	80.48
5	21	1	77.53	35	1	81.22
7	21	1	74.55	36	1	79.67
9	21	1	78.87	39	1	81.77
			76.94±1.80			80.78±0.91

Conclusion and Future Enhancement

This chapter explores different Data Compaction techniques. There are different variations of the Nearest Neighbour methods are presented. Each method has its own advantages and disadvantages. Any method can be used to reduce the size of the

Table 21. Accuracy over pima

k	SFS+CNN			SFS+OCNN		
	# of Prototypes	# of Features Reduced	Accuracy %	# of Prototypes	# of Features Reduced	Accuracy %
3	301	2	57.52	350	2	58.92
5	301	2	58.32	358	2	59.45
7	301	2	57.22	360	2	60.42
9	301	2	59.32	368	2	61.88
			58.09±0.60			60.16±1.29

Table 22. Accuracy over pima

k	CNN+SFS			OCNN+SFS		
	# of Prototypes	# of Features Reduced	Accuracy %	# of Prototypes	# of Features Reduced	Accuracy %
3	266	2	61.11	365	3	63.09
5	266	2	60.21	371	3	62.67
7	266	2	62.23	368	3	63.32
9	266	2	62.88	378	3	65.52
			61.60±1.18			63.65±1.27

training set size. If the issue is with cardinality then the methods like CNN, MCNN or OCNN which are data compaction techniques using Prototype selection can be used. If the issue is with dimensionality of the data set then the methods PCA or LDA can be preferable. If it is a classification problem prefer LDA otherwise PCA.

If the issue is with both the cardinality and dimensionality of the data set, then the methods any of the methods CNN, MCNN or OCNN can be combined with the methods PCA or LDA. Again if it's a classification problem prefer LDA instead of PCA. This is known as Data Compaction using Prototype selection and Feature selection. The effectiveness and usefulness of prototype selection and feature selection methods were elucidated. Experiments have been carried out and results are expatiated. These methods are helpful to the researchers where there is necessity of reducing the data size.

The future directions in this area are the researches can find the mathematical proof of the prototype selection methods presented. The directions can be further extended as CNN or MCNN can be modified as they require single scan of the data set and OCNN algorithm can be modified as it exhibits consistency property and one can reduce its time complexity.

FURTHER READINGS

The nearest neighbor algorithm is explained well by Cover and Hart (1967). Patrick and Fischer (1970) proposed the *k*NN algorithm. The m*k*NN algorithm is proposed byDudani (1976) while the fuzzy *k*NN algorithm is described by Jozwick(1983). More number of papers were published on finding the efficient nearest neighbor algorithm.

The condensed nearest neighbor algorithm was one of the earliest methods of prototype selection and proposed by Hart (1968). In 2005, Viswanath, Murthy and Bhatnagar proposed an efficient NN classifier, called overlap pattern nearest neighbor (OLP-NNC) which is based on overlap pattern graph (OLPgraph). In this paper, they built OLP-graph incrementally by scanning the training set only once and OLP-NNC works with OLP-graph. In 2007, Suresh babu and Viswanath proposed the generalized weighted k-nearest Leader Classifier method which finds the relative importance of prototypes called weighting of prototypes and this weight is used in classification process.In 2011, Viswanath and Sarma proposed an improvement to the k-Nearest Neighbor Mean Classifier (k-NNMC), finds k nearest neighbor class-wise. Classification process is carried out with these mean patterns. In 2014, Raj kumar, Viswanath and Bindu proposed anew prototype selection method for nearest neighbor classification called Other Class NearestNeighbor (OCNN) which is based on the retaining samples that are near to decision boundary and which are crucial in the classification task. Considerable numbers of papers were published on reducing the cardinality of training set but Less number of papers were published on reducing the training set size in both i.e., cardinality and dimensionality. In 1999, Kuncheva and Jain proposed genetic algorithm based method for simultaneous editing and feature selection. In 2001, Kuncheva extended the paper for reducing the computational demands of nearest neighbor classifier. In this paper Incremental Hill Climbing (IHC), and Stochastic Hill Climbing SHC)methods were used to reduce the training set in both directions. In 2013, TR Babu, MNMurthy and SV subrahmanya published book on Data Compression Schemes for Mining Large Datasets.

REFERENCES

Babu, V. S., & Viswanath, P. (2007, December). Weighted k-nearest leader classifier for large data sets. In *International Conference on Pattern Recognition and Machine Intelligence* (pp. 17-24). Springer Berlin Heidelberg. doi:10.1007/978-3-540-77046-6_3

Berkhin, P. (2006). A survey of clustering data mining techniques. In *Grouping multidimensional data* (pp. 25–71). Springer Berlin Heidelberg. doi:10.1007/3-540-28349-8_2

Blake, C., & Merz, C. J. (1998). *{UCI} Repository of machine learning databases*. Academic Press.

Bratko, A., Cormack, G. V., Filipič, B., Lynam, T. R., & Zupan, B. (2006). Spam filtering using statistical data compression models. *Journal of Machine Learning Research*, 7(Dec), 2673–2698.

Chen, Z., Wen, Y., Cao, J., Zheng, W., Chang, J., Wu, Y., & Peng, G. et al. (2015). A survey of bitmap index compression algorithms for big data. *Tsinghua Science and Technology*, 20(1), 100–115. doi:10.1109/TST.2015.7040519

Cover, T., & Hart, P. (1967). Nearest neighbor pattern classification. *IEEE Transactions on Information Theory*, 13(1), 21–27. doi:10.1109/TIT.1967.1053964

Devi, V. S., & Murty, M. N. (2002). An incremental prototype set building technique. *Pattern Recognition*, 35(2), 505–513. doi:10.1016/S0031-3203(00)00184-9

Duda, R. O., Hart, P. E., & Stork, D. G. (2012). *Pattern classification*. John Wiley & Sons.

Fan, W., & Bifet, A. (2013). Mining big data: current status, and forecast to the future. *ACM SIGKDD Explorations Newsletter, 14*(2), 1-5.

Izenman, A. J. (2008). Modern multivariate statistical techniques. *Regression, Classification and Manifold Learning*.

Jain, A., & Zongker, D. (1997). Feature selection: Evaluation, application, and small sample performance. *IEEE Transactions on Pattern Analysis and Machine Intelligence*, 19(2), 153–158. doi:10.1109/34.574797

Kumar, R. R., Viswanath, P., & Bindu, C. S. (2016). An Approach to Reduce the Computational Burden of Nearest Neighbor Classifier. *Procedia Computer Science*, 85, 588–597. doi:10.1016/j.procs.2016.05.225

Kumar, R. R., Viswanath, P., & Bindu, C. S. (2016, February). Nearest Neighbor Classifiers: Reducing the Computational Demands. In *Advanced Computing (IACC), 2016 IEEE 6th International Conference on* (pp. 45-50). IEEE.

Kumar, R. R., Viswanath, P., & Bindu, C. S. (2017). A Cascaded Method to Reduce the Computational Burden of Nearest Neighbor Classifier. In *Proceedings of the First International Conference on Computational Intelligence and Informatics* (pp. 275-288). Springer Singapore. doi:10.1007/978-981-10-2471-9_27

Kuncheva, L. I. (2001). *Reducing the computational demand of the nearest neighbor classifier*. Academic Press.

Kuncheva, L. I., & Jain, L. C. (1999). Nearest neighbor classifier: Simultaneous editing and feature selection. *Pattern Recognition Letters*, *20*(11), 1149–1156. doi:10.1016/S0167-8655(99)00082-3

Pu, I. M. (2005). *Fundamental data compression*. Butterworth-Heinemann.

Raschka, S. (2014). *About feature scaling and normalization*. Academic Press.

Salomon, D. (2004). *Data compression: the complete reference*. Springer Science & Business Media.

Salomon, D., & Motta, G. (2010). *Handbook of data compression*. Springer Science & Business Media. doi:10.1007/978-1-84882-903-9

Sayood, K. (2012). *Introduction to data compression*. Newnes.

Song, Y., Zhou, G., & Zhu, Y. (2013). Present status and challenges of big data processing in smart grid. *Power System Technology*, *37*(4), 927–935.

Suarjaya, I. M. A. D. (2012). *A new algorithm for data compression optimization*. arXiv preprint arXiv:1209.1045

Swonger, C. W. (1972). *Sample set condensation for a condensed nearest neighbor decision rule for pattern recognition*. Academic Press.

Tomek, I. (1976). Two modifications of CNN. *IEEE Transactions on Systems, Man, and Cybernetics*, *6*(11), 769–772. doi:10.1109/TSMC.1976.4309452

Verleysen, M., & François, D. (2005, June). The curse of dimensionality in data mining and time series prediction. In *International Work-Conference on Artificial Neural Networks* (pp. 758–770). Springer Berlin Heidelberg. doi:10.1007/11494669_93

Viswanath, P., Murty, N., & Bhatnagar, S. (2005). Overlap pattern synthesis with an efficient nearest neighbor classifier. *Pattern Recognition*, *38*(8), 1187–1195. doi:10.1016/j.patcog.2004.10.007

Viswanath, P., & Sarma, T. H. (2011, September). An improvement to k-nearest neighbor classifier. In Recent Advances in Intelligent Computational Systems (RAICS), 2011 IEEE (pp. 227-231). IEEE. doi:10.1109/RAICS.2011.6069307

Zongker, D., & Jain, A. (1996, August). Algorithms for feature selection: An evaluation. In *Pattern Recognition, 1996. Proceedings of the 13th International Conference on* (*Vol. 2*, pp. 18-22). IEEE.

KEY TERMS AND DEFINITIONS

Cardinality: The number of patterns present in data set. It must be always positive integer.

Data Compaction: The reduced form of data after applying an algorithm.

Features: Features are the attributes that are used to describe the patterns.

Patterns: The objects present in the data set which gives information about an entity.

Prototypes: The representative patterns present in the reduced data set. A prototype can be one of the patterns present in original set or it is derived from two or three patterns.

Reduction Rate: The ratio between the no of patterns in the reduced data set to the no of patterns in the original set.

Test Set: The set over which the performance of classifier is estimated.

Training Set: The set which is used for building a classifier.

Chapter 4
Methodologies and Technologies to Retrieve Information From Text Sources

Anu Singha
South Asian University, India

Phub Namgay
Sherubtse College, Royal University of Bhutan, Bhutan

ABSTRACT

A tool which algorithmically traces the effectiveness of the text files would be helpful in determining whether the text file have all the characteristic of important concepts. Every text source is build up on key phrases, and these paramount phrases follow a certain grammatical linguistic pattern widely used. An enormous amount of information can be derived from these key concepts for the further analysis such as their dispersion, relationship among the concepts etc. The relationship among the key concepts can be used to draw a concept graphs. So, this chapter presents a detailed methodologies and technologies which evaluate the effectiveness of the extracted information from text files.

INTRODUCTION

Before the advent of internet, text files formed the only source to get the content knowledge. Text files are read as a part of academics for a university student or for leisure, who fancy reading. With the rise of modern technology, paper based text files is being replaced by electronic version and is easily available online. Though

DOI: 10.4018/978-1-5225-2805-0.ch004

the readers embrace comfort and portability provided by electronic version of the text files, paper based text files are still popular. Unlike decades back, text files in any field of study is readily available now. With the demand for text files rising, the qualities of the text files are compromised. With the rate reading habits on decline, impatient readers hardly spent some time to evaluate the content of the file. A technique to analyze the effectiveness by evaluating the text files in detail will be of great importance. This ultimately would help the readers in finding the text file most suitable to his / her needs and comprehension capability.

A tool which algorithmically traces the effectiveness the text files would be helpful in determining whether the text file have all the characteristic of a good source. Every file is build up on key concepts, and these key concepts form the foundation of a good source. The text sources that contain concepts that share some common properties and semantically related are more lucid and intelligible than those text sources which contain many unrelated concepts. These paramount phrases follow a certain grammatical linguistic pattern widely used. An enormous amount of information can be derived from these key concepts for the further analysis such as their dispersion across the file, relationship among the concepts, etc. Such analysis will help in better assessment of the text file. The relationship among the key concepts can be used to draw a concept graphs. Since we live in an increasingly visual society, pictorial representation of the key concepts as a graph would help the readers in easily judging the text source and their content.

The goal of this chapter is to confer the methodologies on the key concepts retrieval from the text files. The authors investigate the techniques for examining the key concepts in the text files. This chapter also presents some of the different tools used in natural language processing. Their uses and implementation methods are explicitly discussed. The key concepts in our context correspond to the terminological noun phrases. These extracted set of phrases can be further analyzed to check the credibility of the text file in conveying the required set of information to the readers. It is based on the intuition that a source which contains right set of related key concepts is more beneficial and comprehensible. The set of key concept which form the cornerstone of a text file can be further used to draw concept graphs. The noun phrases from the candidate set of extracted phrases form the nodes of the graph and the relationship that exists between the nodes can be denoted by a link between the concept pairs. The 'in' degree and 'out' degree of each vertex of the graph i.e., the noun phrases can be used to determine the most important key concepts. Such representation of the source in a visual form helps readers in easily judging and grasping the key concepts. This ultimately serves as a preface to the text files and reduces the cognitive burden of the readers.

BACKGROUND

An extensive study on how information technology can be used to improve education system is carried out by IBM (IBM, 2005). The report identified lack of language clarity, incoherent concepts and inadequacy of information provided as a major problem in the text files used as a part of academics.

There are many websites aimed to enrich learning experience; for example: *notemonk.com. notemonk.com* allows users to download text files, ask questions on the topic of the file, and annotate them for quick reference. The members are also invited to contribute videos that can be viewed by many other readers (Agarwal, Gollapudi, Kenthapadi, Srivastaya & Velu, 2010). The problems with this video sharing are that though many of the videos have relevance to the text files, their quality are varied. This variance creates a comprehension burden to the user in relating the insight of the document with the video content. It is important that these supplementary files is authoritative, must be contextually related and is linked as close to where the abstract concepts needs deep elaboration.

Related works includes efforts by the book authors to make videos covering the key concepts of the text source. These videos are available to readers via online or for free distribution. *Education-Portal.com* provides links to free video lectures from several universities. However, it is individual student's initiative to find the most relevant and comprehensible text files to support their knowledge. Though providing free videos and lectures are embraced by people, the difference in socio-economic and cultural differences has posed a real difficulty in understanding the context. The difference in language, pronunciation, and the accent of the speakers and the difficulty to relate the examples and illustration are some of the problems faced today.

Today, text files on any field of study are readily available. The rise of technology has made the availability of text sources in different versions; electronic or paper based. An ideal file on the desired field is hard to get. The quality of a text file is determined by several factors. The important concepts form the backbone of a good text source. The widely accepted view of a good file is that the text file should present concepts in a coherent manner and provide sufficient coverage on important concepts. Though the readily availability of text files is boon to the enthusiastic readers, many files today suffer from two major problems i.e. the poor clarity of the languages used and incoherent presentation of concepts and inadequacy of information provided.

TECHNOLOGIES USED IN THE EXTRACTION OF TEXT INFORMATION

The field of data mining has produced technologies that can perform computational task without human intervention. These technologies has helped people who spend their entire life studying in the areas of data mining such as text mining, image mining, etc., in discovering new information from a rough set of inputs. Today, data mining technologies teach computers skills that human possess and even perform task beyond human endeavors. The task performed by these technologies in text mining process includes information extraction, topic tracking, clustering, concept linkage, information visualization, etc. The following sections discuss technologies used in the extraction of text information.

Part-of-Speech (POS) Tagger

A Stanford part-of-speech (POS) Tagger is a piece of software that reads the contents of the user specified input file (line by line or every sentence) in some language. The tagger assigns a unique part of speech to each word in a line or sentence (such as noun, verb, adjective, etc.), by processing the entire line or sentence. This software is a Java based wrapper over Stanford's Natural Language Processing (NLP) POS Tagger (Toutanova, Klein, Manning & Singer, 2003). Stanford POS tagger can be used in any application that deals with natural language text to analyze words / tokens and classify them into different part of speech categories as in Table 1 (Taylor, Marcus, & Santorini, 2003).

The libraries (such as *Stanford-postagger.jar*) lets the user "tag" the words, that is, the "tagger" gets a noun, a verb, etc., for each word and then assigns the result to the word. To do this, the tagger loads a "trained" file that contains the necessary information for the tagger to tag the line or sentence. The "trained" file is called a model and has an extension ".tagger". There are several trained models provided by Stanford natural language processing (NLP) group for different languages (such as *left3words-wsj-0-18.tagger* for English language).

JavaCC

JavaCC is a widely used tool for lexical and parser component generation which follows regular expression and BackusNaur Form (BNF) notation syntax for Lex and parser specifications. Creating a parser needs an iterative step. Unlike YACC (Yet Another Compiler Compiler), JavaCC generates top down parser for LL type grammars. LR parsing (left recursion) is not possible in JavaCC. JavaCC creates LL parsers for context free grammars (a context free grammar contains production

Table 1. Penn TreeBank POS tag set

Tag	Meaning	Tag	Meaning
1. CC	Coordinating conjunction e.g. and, but, or,...	25. TO	To
2. CD	Cardinal Number	26. UH	Interjection e.g. uh, well, yes, my,...
3. DT	Determiner	27. VB	Verb, Base form
4. EX	Existential there	28. VBD	Verb, Past tense
5. FW	Foreign Word	29. VBG	Verb, Ground or present participle
6. IN	Preposition or subordinating participle conjunction	30. VBN	Verb, past participle
7. JJ	Adjective	31. VBP	Verb, non-3rd person singular present
8. JJR	Adjective, Comparative	32. VBZ	Verb, 3rd person singular present
9. JJS	Adjective, Superlative	33. WDT	Wh-determiner e.g. which
10. LS	List Item Marker	34. WP	Wh-pronoun e.g. what, who, whom,...
11. MD	Modal e.g. can, could, might, may,...	35. WP$	Possessive wh-pronoun
12. NN	Noun, Singular or Mass	36. WRB	Wh-adverb e.g. how, where, why
13. NNP	Proper Noun, Singular	37. #	Pound sign
14. NNPS	Proper Noun, Plural	38. $	Dollar sign
15. NNS	Noun, Plural	39. .	Sentence-final punctuation
16. PDT	Predeterminer e.g. all, both,...	40.,	Comma
17. POS	Possessive Ending e.g. Nouns ending in 's	41.:	Colon, Semi-colon
18. PRP	Personal Pronoun e.g. I, me, you, he,...	42. (	Left bracket character
19. PRP$	Possessive Pronoun e.g. my, your, mine	43.)	Right bracket character
20. RB	Adverb	44. "	Straight double quote
21. RBR	Adverb, Comparative	45. '	Leftopen single quote
22. RBS	Adverb, Superlative	46. "	Leftopen double quote
23. RP	Particle	47. '	Rightclose single quote
24. SYM	Symbol	48. "	Rightclose double quote

rules in the format NT→T, where NT is a non-terminals and T is a combination of terminals and or non-terminals). An LL parser parses the input from left to right, and creates the leftmost derivation of a sentence when compared to the LR parser where the right most derivation of a sentence is created. These kinds of parser use next tokens to take the parsing decisions without any back tracing (LookAhead), so LL parsers are not much complicated, and hence popularly used even if they are fairly restrictive.

WordNet Lexical Database

WordNet lexical database is designed to establish the connections between four types of Parts of Speech (POS) - noun, verb, adjective, and adverb. Information in WordNet is organized around a logical grouping called *synsets*. This smallest unit in WordNet represents a specific meaning in a word. A word form can be a single word or compound words connected by underscores (referred to as collocations). Synsets includes the word, its explanation, and its synonyms. The specific meaning of one word under one type of POS is called a *sense*. Each sense of a word is in a different synset.

Synsets are equivalent to senses = structures containing sets of terms with synonymous meanings. Each synset is associated with a gloss that defines the concept it represents. *For example, the words night, nighttime and dark constitute a single synset that has the following gloss: the time after sunset and before sunrise while it is dark outside.* Synsets are connected to one another through the explicit semantic relations. Some of these relations (hypernym, hyponym for nouns and hypernym and troponym for verbs) constitute *is-a-kind-of* (holonymy) and *is-a-part-of* (meronymy for nouns) hierarchies.

For example, tree is a kind of plant, tree is a hyponym of plant and plant is a hypernym of tree. Analogously, trunk is a part of a tree and we have that trunk as a meronym of tree and tree is a holonym of trunk. For one word and one type of POS, if there is more than one sense, WordNet organizes them in the order of the most frequently used to the least frequently used (Semcor).

1. **JWNL-Java WordNet Library:** Java WordNet Library (JWNL) is a Java application programming interface (API) for accessing the WordNet dictionary. JWNL makes it, for example possible to look up words in WordNet, get their different senses, and find related words through one of a number of relations. It also provides functionality beyond data access, such as relationship discovery and morphological processing.

   a. **Java WordNet Library Configuration:** A Java WordNet Library properties file is an XML file that can be validated using the included Document Type Definition (DTD) or XML Schema Definition (XSD). Basically, the properties file allows the library user to specify three properties:

i.   **Dictionary Class:** This defines the class used to interface with the dictionary. JWNL comes with three dictionary classes - MapBackedDictionary, FileBackedDictionary, and DatabaseBacked-Dictionary. Exactly 1 dictionary tag is required in a properties file. If there is more than one, the first one will be used.

```
<dictionary class="[dictionary class name]">...parameters </
dictionary>
```

ii.   **Version:** Gives information on the version of WordNet being interfaced with. Exactly 1 version tag is required in a properties file.

```
<version publisher="[publisher]" number="[version number]"
language="[language]" country="[country]"/>
```

iii.   **Resources:** A resource file contains mapping between keys and text used in the program. Typically, this text is error or status messages. Resource files are used so that a program can be used with different (spoken) languages without having to modify the code.

```
<resource class="[resource file path]"/> Example: <resource
class="Princeton- Resource"/>
```

In the top-level tag, the language and country can be specified to resolve the resources.

For example: *<jwnl-properties language="en" country="us"> ...properties </jwnl-properties>* tells the program to print all messages in American English (a resource file containing these messages has to be present, of course). The dictionary and dictionary element factory allows the library user to provide parameters. Parameters are of the form:

```
<param name="[param name]" value="[param value]"> ..nested
parameters </param>
```

Parameters are provided to the install method of the class. Parameters can be nested. For example:

```
<param name="file-manager" value="net.didion.jwnl.dictionary.
file-manager. FileManagerImpl">
<param name="file-type" value="net.didion.jwnl.princeton.file.
PrincetonRandom-AccessDictionaryFile">
```

Microsoft Web N-Gram Services

Microsoft Web N-gram Services is a corpus which allows materials from the body, title and anchor text to be available separately. Microsoft Web N-gram services is a cross platform XML web services (Brants, Torsten & Franz, 2006) that is freely and readily accessible by users through the Internet. Microsoft Web N-gram corpus is based on the web documents indexed by a commercial web search engine, Bing service in the EN US market. The URLs in the En US market visited by Bing are at the order of hundreds of billions, though the spam and other low quality web pages are actively excluded using Bing's proprietary algorithms. The various streams of the web documents are then downloaded, parsed and tokenized by Bing, in which processed text is lower-cased with the punctuation marks removed. However, no stemming, spelling corrections or inflections are performed.

Microsoft Web N-gram provides open-vocabulary, smoothed back-off N-gram models for the three text streams using the CALM algorithm (Wang, Thrasher, Viegas, Li & Hsu, 2010) that dynamically adapts the N-gram models as web documents are crawled. The design of CALM ensures that new N-grams are incorporated into the models as soon as they are encountered in the crawling and become statistically significant. The models are therefore kept up-to-date with the web contents. CALM is also designed to make sure that duplicated contents will not have outsize impacts in biasing the N-gram statistics. This property is useful as Bing's crawler visits URLs in parallel and on the web many URLs are pointing to the same contents. Currently, the maximum order of the N-gram available is 5.

Microsoft Web N-Gram Service provides access to petabytes of data via public beta web N-gram Services. These services are hosted on a cloud based platform, highly useful in areas related to language processing, speech and web-search. It also provides access to specific content types like the document body, title and anchor texts and supports smoothed models. A user token issued by Microsoft Research is needed to access the Microsoft N-gram services. The web N-gram services can be invoked via SOAP or REST requests.

1. **N-gram:** An N-gram is a contiguous sequence of N-terms from a given sequence of text or speech. An N-gram of length 1 is called a unigram, of size 2 a bigram and of size 3 a trigram. N-grams of lengths 4 or more are called as four-grams, five-grams and so on. They can be used to predict the next item in a sequence based on statistics collected from the text corpus.

2. **SOAP – Simple Object Access Protocol:** SOAP (Simple Object Access Protocol) is a simple XML - based protocol to let applications exchange information over HTTP. SOAP is a way for a program running in one kind of operating system (such as Windows) to communicate with a program in the

same or another kind of an operating system (such as Linux) or same by using Hypertext Transfer Protocol (HTTP) and Extensible Markup Language (XML) as the mechanisms for information exchange. Since Web protocols are installed and available for use by all major operating system platforms, HTTP and XML provide an already at-hand solution to the problem of how programs running under different operating systems in a network can communicate with each other. SOAP specifies exactly how to encode an HTTP header and an XML file so that a program in one computer can call a program in another computer and pass it information. It also specifies how the called program can return a response (Sivaram, 2005).

SOAP was developed by Microsoft, DevelopMentor, and Userland Software and has been proposed as a standard interface to the Internet Engineering Task Force (IETF). SOAP shares similarity with Internet Inter-ORB Protocol (IIOP), a protocol that is part of the Common

Object Request Broker Architecture (CORBA).

3. **REST – Representational State Transfer:** REST (representational state transfer) is an approach for getting information content from a Web site by reading a designated Web page that contains an Extensible Markup Language (XML) file which describes and includes the desired content. For example, REST could be used by an online publisher to make syndicated content available. Periodically, the publisher would prepare and activate a Web page that includes content and XML statements that described the content. Subscribers would need only to know the URL (Uniform Resource Locator) for the page where the XML file was located, read it with a Web browser, interpret the content data using the XML information, and reformat and use it appropriately (perhaps in some form of online publication).

As described in a dissertation by Roy Fielding (Fielding, 2000), REST is an "architectural style" that basically exploits the existing technology and protocols of the Web, including HTTP (Hypertext Transfer Protocol) and XML. REST is simpler to use than the well-known SOAP (Simple Object Access Protocol) approach, which requires writing or using a provided server program (to serve data) and a client program (to request data). SOAP, however, offers potentially more capability.

JWPL: Java Wikipedia Library

Java Wikipedia Library is a free, Java-based application programming interface that allows access to all information in Wikipedia. The high-performance Wikipedia

API provides structured access to information nuggets like redirects, categories, articles and link structure. To further analyze the contents of a Wikipedia page, JWPL contains a Mediawiki Markup parser. The parser can also be used stand-alone with other texts using MediaWiki markup. The core feature of JWPL includes: fast and efficient access to Wikipedia, Parser for the MediaWiki syntax and Language independent.

JWPL contains tools like JWPLDataMachine and Wikipedia Revision Toolkit. JWPLDataMachine can be used to create JWPL dumps and Wikipedia Revision Toolkit consists of two tools - the TimeMachine and the RevisionMachine. The TimeMachine tools is for reconstructing past states of Wikipedia and the RevisionMachine tools offers efficient access to all article while storing the revisions in a dedicated storage format.

Wikipedia Dump

Wikipedia is a multilingual, web-based, freely available encyclopedia. Given that Wikipedia is an ultimate online encyclopedia, it is a widely used resource for reference today. Apart from being available online, the Wikipedia data is provided for download. Wikipedia offers free copies of all available content to interested users. These databases can be used for mirroring, personal use, informal backups, and offline use or database queries (such as for Wikipedia: Maintenance). Articles in Wikipedia form a heavily interlinked knowledge base, enriched with a category system emerging from collaborative tagging, which constitutes a thesaurus (Voss, 2006). Wikipedia thus contains a rich body of lexical semantic information. This includes knowledge about named entities, domain specific terms or domain specific word senses. Additionally, the redirect system of Wikipedia articles can be used as a dictionary for synonyms, spelling variations and abbreviations.

1.   **Ways to Process and Use English Wikipedia Dump:** The largest free data-set available on the internet is the full dump of the English Wikipedia. Crawling of the web can be avoided by running an own server using publicly available Wikipedia database dumps. The server we discussing in this chapter is the freely available WAMP server. The data-set in its uncompressed form is enormous. The sheer size of this data-set poses some serious challenge to analyze the data and load into the database. *Wiki-media.org* provides public dumps of Wikipedia's content for archival/backup purposes, offline use, academic research, etc. Before downloading the Wikipedia dump, reading carefully about the time and space scale information is essential. There are

a number of versions that are "friendlier" in size and content, which can be customized for scalability by using or not using images, talk pages, etc.

The Wikipedia dump files which consist of SQL files for handling the dump data are imported into a database. Then, sophisticated indexing offered by the database that guarantees nearly constant retrieval time for each article is used. This approach is superior to web server based retrieval, as it only involves querying the database and directly delivering the results to the application. Another important benefit is that the database schema explicitly represents information about an article's links or categories, which is only implicitly encoded in the HTML structure (Mller, Zesch & Gurevych, 2008).

All databases are dumped via 3 groups of processes which run simultaneously. The largest database, en_wiki is dumped periodically once a month. A second set of 'large' wiki's runs in a continuous loop with the aim of getting dumps for those twice a month; the rest are dumped thrice a month, also on a rolling basis. Failures in the dumping process are generally dealt with by rerunning the portion of the dump that failed. Larger databases such as *jawiki*, *dewiki*, and *frwiki* takes a long time to run, especially when compressing the full edit history or creating split stub dumps.

The Java Wikipedia Library performs the following:

1. It takes a dump of all the contents of Wikipedia in a specific language.
2. It parses the dump into a set of articles.
3. It parses each article and recognizes links from page to page and additional meta-data attached to each page (in particular, its categories).
4. It stores the resulting information into a relational database (MySQL) with appropriate indexes.
5. It exposes the resulting graph data model through a convenient Java API.

English Wikipedia dump is parsed into a graph representation that can be efficiently queried through the Java Wikipedia Library API. The task is carried out using the following Java Archive files:

1. de.tudarmstadt.ukp.wikipedia.api-0.9.1-jar-with-dependencies.jar and
2. de.tudarmstadt.ukp.wikipedia.datamachine-0.9.1-jar-with-dependencies.jar

The Wikipedia dump which consist of three files - *Pages Articles xml*, *Page Link Sql* and *Category links sql* file are required for successful implementation. The following set of code parses the Wikipedia dump and creates a set of text files that captures the graph structure of Wikipedia:

```
public class enwiki{
public static void main(String[] args){
org.apache.log4j.BasicConfigurator.configure();
String args1[] = {[LANGUAGE][MAIN_CATEGORY_NAME]
[DISAMBIGUATION_CATEGORY_NAME][SOURCE_DIRECTORY]
};
```

1. **LANGUAGE:** A language string matching one the JWPL Languages.
2. **MAIN_CATEGORY_NAME:** The name of the main (top) category of the Wikipedia category hierarchy.
3. **DISAMBIGUATION_CATEGORY_NAME:** The name of the category that contains the disambiguation categories.
4. **SOURCE_DIRECTORY:** The path to the directory containing the source files.

The design of the object-oriented programming interface is centered on the objects: WIKIPEDIA, PAGE, and CATEGORY (Mller, Zesch & Gurevych, 2008). The WIKIPEDIA object is used to establish the connection with the database, and to retrieve PAGE and CATEGORY objects. JWPL supports retrieval by keywords or via a query interface that allows for wild-card matches as well as retrieving subsets of articles or categories depending on parameters like the number of tokens in an article or the number of in-going links. The WIKIPEDIA object also allows iterating over articles, categories, redirects, and disambiguation pages.

A PAGE object represents either a normal Wikipedia article, a redirect to an article, or a disambiguation page. Each PAGE object provides access to the article text (with markup information or as plain text), the assigned categories, the in-going and outgoing article links, as well as all redirects that link to the article.

CATEGORY objects represent Wikipedia categories and allow access to the articles within this category. As categories in Wikipedia form a thesaurus, a CATEGORY object also provides means to retrieve parent and child categories, as well as siblings and all recursively collected descendants.

The execution of the two Java Archive file i.e., *de.tudarmstadt.ukp.wikipedia. api-0.9.1-jar-with-dependencies.jar* and *de.tudarmstadt.ukp.wikipedia.datamachine-0.9.1-jar-with-dependencies.jar* creates 11 text files which serves as input to the tables in the database. These 11 text files are Category, category_inlinks, category_outlinks, category_pages, MetaData, Page, page_categories, page_inlinks, page_outlinks, page_redirects, and PageMapLine. The content of the text files are imported into the local database created for Wikipedia dump. After successfully importing the data into the database, it is ready to be used with the JWPL core API. When connecting for the first time to a newly imported database, indexes are created. This takes some time depending on the server used and the size of the Wikipedia dump.

The schema of the Wikipedia dump database is as follows:

1. Category (id, pageId, name)
2. Category_inlinks (id, inLinks)
3. Category_outlinks (id, outLinks)
4. Category_pages (id, pages)
5. Metadata (id, language, disambiguationCategory, mainCategory, nrofPages, nrofRedirects, nrofDisambiguationPages, nrofCategories)
6. Page (id, pageId, name, text, isDisambiguation)
7. Pagemapline (id, name, pageID, stem, lemma)
8. Page_category (id, pages)
9. Page_inlinks (id, inLinks)
10. Page_outlinks (id, outLinks)
11. Page_redirects (id, redirects)

The Table 2 gives a visual overview of the 11 tables in the English Wikiepdia dump database dated February 04, 2013.

iText Library for PDF Document

iText is a programmatic tool for creating, splitting and manipulating portable document format (PDF) files dynamically in Java. Java does not have default application programming interface (API) to handle PDF files. It is a free open source library, distributed under the Affero General Public License. iText is an ideal library for developers looking to add bookmarks, page numbers, watermarks, barcodes, etc. (Lowagie, 2010).

RCaller: Calling R From Java

RCaller is a Java open source library for calling R commands and scripts from Java without Java Native Interface (JNI). RCaller is used by several users who are interested in both R and Java. It includes functionality for plot handling, histogram drawing and something useful. It sends text scripts to the R interpreter and converts the results to XML using the R package Ruinversal or rJava. After this, the XML document is parsed to convert those results to Java matrices and arrays. Finally, user can handle the results from Java.

Table 2. Tables in the Wikipedia dump database

Table	Rows	Type	Size	Comments	
Category	962,288	MyISAM	99.4 MiB	Creation:	Feb 18, 2013 at 01.55 AM
				Last Update:	Mar 05, 2013 at 05.19 PM
				Last check:	Mar 05, 2013 at 05.20 PM
Category_inlinks	2,414,381	MyISAM	128.8 MiB	Creation:	Feb 18, 2013 at 01.56 AM
				Last Update:	Mar 05, 2013 at 05.22 PM
				Last check:	Mar 05, 2013 at 05.22 PM
Category_outlinks	2,414,381	MyISAM	128.8 MiB	Creation:	Feb 18, 2013 at 01.56 AM
				Last Update:	Mar 05, 2013 at 05.23 PM
				Last check:	Mar 05, 2013 at 05.23 PM
Category_pages	25,617,031	MyISAM	1.3 GiB	Creation:	Feb 18, 2013 at 01.56 AM
				Last Update:	Mar 05, 2013 at 05.24 PM
				Last check:	Mar 05, 2013 at 05.28 PM
Metadata	1	MyISAM	2.1 KiB	Creation:	Feb 18, 2013 at 01.55 AM
				Last Update:	Mar 05, 2013 at 05.32 PM
Page	330,845	MyISAM	4 GiB	Creation:	Feb 18, 2013 at 01.55 AM
				Last Update:	Mar 05, 2013 at 05.39 PM
				Last check:	Mar 05, 2013 at 05.42 PM
Pagemapline	10,005,486	MyISAM	1.3 GiB	Creation:	Mar 06, 2013 at 12.29 PM
				Last Update:	Mar 06, 2013 at 01.37 PM
Page_category	25,617,031	MyISAM	1.3 GiB	Creation:	Feb 18, 2013 at 01.56 AM
				Last Update:	Mar 05, 2013 at 07.04 PM
				Last check:	Mar 05, 2013 at 07.07 PM
Page_inlinks	252,047,753	MyISAM	13.1 GiB	Creation:	Mar 06, 2013 at 01.37 PM
				Last Update:	Mar 06, 2013 at 02.55 PM
				Last check:	Mar 06, 2013 at 02.55 PM
Page_outlinks	252,047,753	MyISAM	13.1 GiB	Creation:	Feb 18, 2013 at 01.57 AM
				Last Update:	Mar 05, 2013 at 11.51 PM
				Last check:	Mar 06, 2013 at 12.45 AM
Page_redirects	5,785,308	MyISAM	430.7 MiB	Creation:	Feb 18, 2013 at 01.58 AM
				Last Update:	Mar 06, 2013 at 12.54 AM
				Last check:	Mar 06, 2013 at 12.55 AM
11 Tables	577,242,258	--	35 GiB	--	

METHODOLOGIES: TO ANALYZE THE EXTRACTION INFORMATION

The following sections discuss methodologies used to analyze the extracted text information.

Key Concepts

The basic approach adopted in this chapter is the identification/extraction of key concepts/information in the text file and inferring the relationship between the concepts. Back-of-the-file index (Mulvancy, 2005) is an important source to obtain the concept phrases in a text file. Not all text files have back-of-the-file index. The algorithms on extracting the key phrases/information from a text source can guide the task. Many approaches are adopted to carry out the task of identifying the concept phrases. The candidate set of key concepts are formed using the grammatical linguistic pattern is based on the part of speech associated with each word in a sentence (Agarwal, Gollapudi, Kannan & Kenthapadi, 2012). In the implementation of methods of the algorithms, the authors recommended the linguistic pattern:

$$P_1 = A*N^+ \tag{1}$$

proposed in the paper (Agarwal, Gollapudi, Kenthapadi, Srivastaya & Velu, 2010). A and N represents Adjective and Noun in the sentence respectively. * represents zero or more terms and + represents one or more terms. Presently, there are two popular linguistic patterns widely used in natural language processing community.

$$P_2 = C*N \tag{2}$$

where

$C = (A|N)$ and | represents OR.

$$P_3 = (C*NP)^?(C*N) \tag{3}$$

where P represents prepositions in the sentence and $?$ matches 0 or 1 occurrence of preceding expression. The three existing grammatical patterns are compared by studying the overlap of the key concepts with the Wikipedia page titles. The articles title in Wikipedia constitutes a bunch of concepts. An overlap concept is used to determine the effectiveness of the grammatical linguistic patterns. Overlap is defined as the fraction of generated phrases that match exactly with the Wikipedia page title.

Only multi-word phrases are used in determining the overlap value as Wikipedia pages with canonical single titles typically corresponds to a broad concept (Agarwal, Gollapudi, Kenthapadi, Srivastaya & Velu, 2010). From an experiment, comparison of linguistic patterns across different subjects carried out in paper (Agarwal, Gollapudi, Kenthapadi, Srivastaya & Velu, 2010), the authors concluded that with respect to overlap irrespective of subject area, pattern P_2 outperform pattern P_3. They also observed that pattern P_1 performs better than pattern P_2 although slightly. With P_1 as pattern of interest, the authors are typically interested in phrases containing noun, adjectives and sometimes prepositions. In literature, concepts rarely contain other parts of speech such as verbs, adverbs and conjunctions (Agarwal, Gollapudi, Kannan & Kenthapadi, 2012).

Following task are carried out to correctly determine the key concept phrases:

Step 1: Perform the part of speech tagging.
Step 2: Select a grammatical linguistic pattern and detect the terminological noun phrases.
Step 3: Correct the errors made by POS tagger using WordNet lexical database.
Step 4: Prune the undesirable phrases form the candidate set using Microsoft Web N-gram Services.

Following subsections are discussed details about the above steps:

1. **Tagging the Words With Part of Speech:** Every sentence in a text file considered is tagged using the Stanford POS Tagger. To implement the functionality of the tagger, the Java archive library *Stanford-postagger.jar* is used. This library contains all the required java classes to perform the task of tagging, i.e., for each word, the tagger gets unique part of speech and then assigns the result to the word. The tag set used by Stanford POS tagger is Penn TreeBank tag set as shown in the Table 1. Following example demonstrates the process of tagging the words in a sentence. Consider a following piece of sentence:

This page is about South Asian University

The Stanford POS Tagger returns the tagged output:

```
This/DT page/NN is/VBZ about/IN South/NNP Asian/NNP University/
NNP
```

In the above example, it is clear that the POS Tagger breaks the sentence into words and assigns a unique part of speech. The input to Stanford POS Tagger may contain poorly formed words. For such sentences, the assigned part-of-speech tags may be incorrect.

2. **Formation of the Terminological Noun Phrases:** With the tagging of the words in a text file completed in step 1, next a candidate set of key concepts is formed using a grammatical linguistic pattern. The pattern P_1 in Eq. 1 is used to extract the noun phrases from the output of step 1. The concepts of interest in our context are concepts containing nouns and adjectives. The regular expression of the pattern is implemented in java using JavaCC parser generator and lexical analyzer. The set of extracted noun phrases consist of maximum pattern matches. For example, in a sentence, "The experiment with Swadeshi gave Mahatma Gandhi important ideas about using cloth as a symbolic weapon against British rule", mentioned as an example in paper (Agarwal, Gollapudi, Kannan & Kenthapadi, 2012) for evaluating the patterns, due to the arbitrary order of adjectives and nouns, the linguistic pattern P_2 in Eq. 2 returns the result "Mahatma Gandhi important ideas". On the other hand, pattern P_1 returns the result "Mahatma Gandhi" and "important ideas". The latter pattern satisfies the notion of maximum pattern matches. Clearly, pattern P_1 gives a more promising result. Here some of examples of extracted noun phrases using linguistic pattern $P_1 = A*N^+$:

```
scientific/JJ psychology/NN
emotional/JJ responses/NNS
Captain/NNP Kirk/NNP
humans/NNS
```

3. **Correction of Tagging Error using WordNet:** Stanford POS tagger makes mistakes on sentences containing ill-formed and unknown words. The reason is POS tagger is aggressive and it returns part-of-speech tags for unknown words and always returns a unique assignment for each sentences. Lexical database software, WordNet is used to correct the errors. WordNet is used to determine the part of speech (noun, adjective, verb, and adverb) for the noun phrases. However, WordNet fails to recognize the words which are not in its lexical database. WordNet therefore is used as a validation and error-correction tool. Tags assigned by Stanford POS tagger are checked with the WordNet assignment for consistency. A phrase is said to have disagreement if for some word *w* in the phrase, WordNet recognizes *w* and returns one or more part of

speech tags and the part-of-speech tags assigned by the Stanford POS tagger is not among the part-of-speech tag assigned by the WordNet.

In the process of correcting the tagging disagreement between POS Tagger and WordNet, first the extracted noun phrase is checked for its existence in the WordNet lexical database. If the noun phrase is a valid word, the noun phrase is stored for further analysis. If the noun phrase doesn't exist in the WordNet lexical database, the noun phrase is split into combination of words. These set of words is checked for its existence in the lexical database. If it exists, the tagging procedure and the consistency with POS tagger are checked. If there is an inconsistency in tagging and the Stanford POS tagging is among the tagging returned by WordNet, the tags are uniquely corrected. The correction is carried out only if the linguistic pattern is satisfied with the correction procedure. However, sometimes WordNet may return more than one part of speech for the tokens. If the part of speech assigned by POS Tagger is not among the part of speech assigned by WordNet, a disagreement is said to exist. In such case, the noun phrase cannot be uniquely corrected and it is dropped from the candidate set. Such exclusion helps in reducing the workload in carrying out further analysis.

For example, consider the following noun phrase: "*causeless emotional conditions*". The POS tagging for the noun phrase is: "*causeless/JJ emotional/JJ conditions/NNS*". This noun phrases is first checked for its existence in the WordNet lexical database. If it does exist as collocation, the WordNet tagging corresponding to the phrase is returned. If it does not exist, the noun phrase is further split into phrases as in the following example:

First the noun phrase is split in a pattern of 2:1. Splitting is done with a condition that all the noun phrases which are split into further sub phrases must exist in the WordNet lexical database.

```
causeless emotional
conditions
```

These two noun phrases are checked for its existence in the WordNet lexical database. Since it does not exist, a new pattern 1:2 is formed as follows:

```
causeless
emotional conditions
```

With all the splitting procedures returning a noun phrase which does not exist in WordNet database, the multi-word noun phrases is finally split into individual noun phrases as follows:

<u>causeless</u>   <u>emotional</u>   <u>conditions</u>

The part of speech returned by WordNet for the tokenized noun phrases is:

```
causeless/[POS: adjective]
emotional/[POS: adjective]
conditions/[POS: Noun][POS: Verb]
```

The set of sub-phrases obtained is checked for disagreement with POS tagging. If the noun phrases exist in the WordNet lexical database and there is no disagreement in tagging, the noun phrase is checked with its match with the linguistic pattern.

4.   **Pruning Using Microsoft Web N-Gram Services:** The WordNet corrected phrases in step 3 is likely to contain common knowledge phrases as well as malformed phrases. To check whether the noun phrases falls into these categories, we could obtained the log probability of occurrence of these noun phrases on the web using the Microsoft web N-gram services. Common knowledge phrases have significant presence while malformed noun phrase has fewer occurrences on the web. Some log probability scores of the noun phrases are listed in Table 3.

After obtaining the probability score for each phrase, scores distribution across noun phrases over the entire text file is computed. The pruning is performed based on the distribution to remove undesirable phrases. The undesirable phrases include the common knowledge and malformed phrases. Microsoft Web N-gram Services provides the probability of occurrence of a given phrases over three corpora; bodies

Table 3. Log probability scores of the noun phrases

manhood	-6.153736
emotional arousal	-7.760618
temperature	-4.240634
feedback	-3.74289346
responsibility	-4.21962261
evolution	-4.457664
soundtrack	-4.986339
Questionnaire	-5.00994968
heart rate	-5.507678
minimal cognitive analysis	-12.5402021

of web pages, title of pages, and anchor texts for web pages. Compared to title or body, in paper (Agarwal, Gollapudi, Kenthapadi, Srivastaya & Velu, 2010) the authors concluded that anchor provides a stronger signal. This is because anchor text represents how the web authors describe the target page concisely. Microsoft Web N-Gram services currently provide two services for the community, Lookup and Generate (Microsoft, 2011). Lookup allows the user to look up the probability of words, and Generate allows users to get a list of words for which user has probability data. Lookup service includes the method: getModel, GetProbability, getProbabilities, getConditionalProbability and getConditionalProbabilities. Basically the methods GetModel and GetProability are used in most implementations. Following Tables 4 and 5(Microsoft, 2011) shows overview of these two methods:

Given the distribution D of N-gram log probability scores of the candidate noun phrases across the entire text file of a chapter from a textbook, a parameterized statistical boundaries is computed.

Let Q_1 denote the first quartile, that is Q_1 satisfies $\Pr_{x \in D}(x \leq Q_1) = 0.25$. Similarly, let Q_3 denote the third quartile, that is, Q_3 satisfies $\Pr_{x \in D}(x \leq Q_3) = 0.75$. The inter-quartile range, $IQR = Q_3 - Q_1$ is a measure of mid-spread of the distribution. A non-negative pruning parameters t_1 and t_2 is used to define fences on both ends of the distribution as in the following equation:

$$LF(t_1) = Q_1 - t_1.IQR \qquad (4)$$

Table 4. GetModels( ) method of Microsoft web n-grams services

Method	String [] GetModels()
Description	Get a list of currently supported N-Gram models
Arguments	None
Returns	The return value is an array of URNs, one for each model supported by this service. Uniform Resource Names (URNs) are resource identiers with the specic requirements for enabling location independent identication of a resource, as well as longevity of reference. URNs are part of the larger Uniform Resource Identier (URI) family [RFC3305] with the specic goal of providing persistent naming of resources. Unlike a URL, URN has persistent signicance i.e., the owner of the URN can expect someone else (or a program) will always be able to nd the resource. The URN follows the following form: urn:ngram:model-name:version:order For example, urn:ngram:bing-body:jun09:3 corresponds to a trigram (order=3) model named bing-body, version jun09 (i.e. June 2009).

Table 5. GetProbability() method of Microsoft web n-grams services

Method	float GetProbability (string authorizationToken, string modelUrn, string phrase)
Description	Find the joint probability of the words in a phrase in the specified model.
Arguments	authorizationToken modelUrn phrase

Arguments	authorizationToken modelUrn phrase	- It is a token of hexadecimal digit provided by Microsoft after agreeing with the Terms of Use of Microsoft Web N-gram Services. - The token serves as the Globally Unique Identier(GUID). - One of the URNs returned by GetModels(). - A string containing a sequence of words for which to compute the probability. The words should be separated by spaces.
Returns	The base-10 log of the joint probability of the word sequence. For instance, if you have an order m model and the following word sequence: $w_1, w_2, ..., w_n$ The return value is the log of the following: $P(w_1)P(w_2|w_1)...P(w_n|w_{n-m+1}...w_{n-1})$ Notes: - The token h $<$ s $>$ represents the beginning of a phrase. - Punctuation is generally ignored.	

$$UF(t_2) = Q_3 - t_2.IQR \qquad (5)$$

The noun phrases whose log probability scores are not within the fences are pruned. Noun phrases with low scores below the fence LF (t_1) are likely to be malformed and those with scores above the upper fence UF (t_2) are likely to be of common knowledge (Agarwal, Gollapudi, Kannan & Kenthapadi, 2012). The pruning parameters are selected based on the distribution of the log probability scores around the mean.

Graphical Representation of the Key Concepts

For graphical representation of key concepts we are recommending to use *Gephi* tool, which is an open-source network analysis and visualization software package. Successfully extracting the set of key concepts using the Microsoft Web N-gram services after performing the final pruning process, further analysis is carried out to determine the relationships between the key concepts and their influence over a text file. A straight forward approach to derive the relationship between key concepts is to manually label the concept pairs. Otherwise, an authoritative structured external source of concepts that also contains relationships between them (e.g. Wikipedia). Determine the set V of nodes corresponding to key concept phrases, say in C that match an article title from the external source. To infer the relationship between the concepts, a concept C_i *(i = 1, 2, 3,...)* is considered to be related to other concepts C_j *(j = 1, 2, 3,...)* if Wikipedia articles corresponding to C_i has links to the Wikipedia articles corresponding to C_j. Let W denote the set of all links in the external source, define as

$$E = \{(v_1, v_2) | v_1, v_2 \in V \wedge (v_1, v_2) \in W\} \tag{6}$$

Then the directed graph G = (V, E) induced by the links in W, thereby obtaining a concept graph that encapsulates the relationship between the key concepts. Compute the directed graph G = (V, E) thus induced by the links in W. The graph in Figure 1 illustrates an overview of key concept graph (Namgay & Singha, 2016).

Figure 1. Key concept graph of the noun phrases

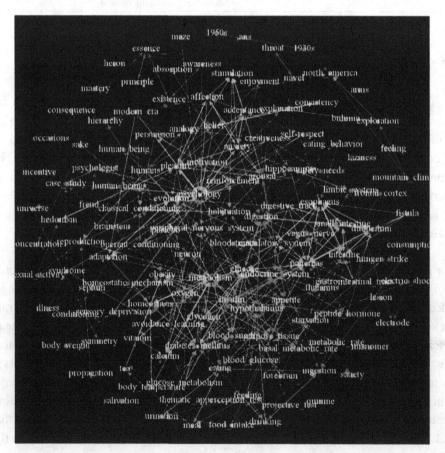

Evaluating a Textbook Chapter Based on Dispersion of Key Concepts

The decision model for identifying poorly written file is based on the notion of dispersion of key concepts across the text file. A text file that discussed concepts related to each other is more lucid and comprehensible than one that discussed many unrelated concepts. Let V represent the set of key concepts, *rel* be a binary relation that determines whether a concept in V is related to another concept in V, that is *rel(x,y)* is true if concept x is related to concept y and false otherwise. Dispersion of a chapter is defined as the fraction of ordered key concept pairs that are not related:

$$Dispersion = \frac{|\{(x,y) \mid x,y \in V \wedge x \neq y \in rel(x,y)\}|}{|V|(|V|-1)} \qquad (7)$$

In the process of calculating the dispersion of the key concepts, the isolated nodes are omitted i.e., noun phrases which have 0 in-link and out-link. Dispersion takes value between 0 and 1, with 0 corresponding to a section where all key concepts are mutually related and 1 corresponding to a section with mutually unrelated concepts.

CONCLUSION

In this chapter, we have presented detailed methodologies and technologies which evaluate the effectiveness of the extracted information from text files. The linguistic patterns adopted i.e., P_1, P_2, P_3 are used throughout the natural language processing (NLP) community due to the superior advantages over the other patterns (Agarwal, Gollapudi, Kannan & Kenthapadi, 2012). Such detailed description enhances the understanding about the technology which is of great help. We can successfully extract the key concepts from the Stanford part-of-speech (POS) tagged text files. The key concepts set consist of noun phrases which exactly matches the grammatical linguistic patterns. These set of noun phrases is likely to have inconsistent tagging. These disagreements in tagging are corrected using the WordNet lexical database. Such correction in tagging resulted in eliminating some noun phrases from the candidate set which were discovered by virtue of their match with the linguistic patterns. The eliminated noun phrases do not contribute any value to the analysis of text files. The pruning process employed further extracted a set of meaningful noun phrases. These noun phrases are used in the detailed analysis to conclude useful information. The pruning process also helped in the improvement of overlap value of the key concepts from a respective text file. We hypothetically assume that these set of key concepts obtained with pruning is free of malformed and common knowledge phrases. In the process of obtaining the pruning phrases, the authoritative structured external source used is the Wikipedia dump dated February 04, 2013.

The key concepts obtained are mapped with other concepts which share common relationship and use it to infer the relationship between the concepts in a text file. These relationships among the concepts are used to draw a concept graph of all the key concepts. Since we live in an increasingly visual society, pictorial representation of the key concepts as a graph helps in easily judging the text files and its content. The calculation of the dispersion value from the concept graph conveys that text file which contains related concepts results in lower dispersion of concepts. Such text files are ideal for study and it lowers the comprehension burden.

Though key concepts form the cornerstone of a good text file, ability to figure out the key concepts has been a big hurdle and troubling task. Recognizing the importance of key concepts, we conclude that devising such methodologies, technologies, and the linguistic patterns to extract the key concepts from a text file and evaluate the text file based on key concepts is of immense importance.

REFERENCES

Agrawal, R., Gollapudi, S., Kannan, A., & Kenthapadi, K. (2012). Data mining for improving textbooks. *SIGKDD Explor. Newsl, 13*(2).

Agrawal, R., Gollapudi, S., Kenthapadi, K., Srivastava, N., & Velu, R. (2010). Enriching textbooks through data mining. *Proceedings of the First ACM Symposium on Computing for Development*. doi:10.1145/1926180.1926204

Brants, Thorsten, & Franz. (2006). *Web 1t 5-gram version 1*. Academic Press.

Fielding, A. T. (2000). *Architectural Styles and the Design of Network-based Software Architectures*. Irvine, CA: University of California.

IBM. (2005). *Improving india's education system through information technology*. IBM.

Lowagie, B. (2010). iText in Action (2nd ed.). Manning Publications.

Microsoft. (2011). Retrieved October 11, 2013, from http://web-ngram.research.microsoft.com/info/

Mller, C., Zesch, T., & Gurevych, I. (2008). Extracting lexical semantic knowledge from wikipedia and wiktionary. In *Proceedings of the Sixth International Conference on Language Resources and Evaluation (LREC'08)*. European Language Resources Association (ELRA).

Mulvancy, N. (2005). *Indexing books*. Chicago: University of Chicago Press. doi:10.7208/chicago/9780226550176.001.0001

Namgay, P., & Singha, A. (2016). Evaluation and Analysis of Grammatical Linguistic Pattern over Social Science and Technology Textbooks. In *Proceedings of the Sixth International Conference on Advances in Computing & Communications (ICACC'16)* (*vol. 93*, pp. 521-532). Procedia Computer Science. doi:10.1016/j.procs.2016.07.247

Sivaram, D. (2005). *Soap-simple object access protocol*. Academic Press.

Taylor, A., Marcus, M., & Santorini, B. (2003). *The Penn Treebank: An overview*. Academic Press.

Toutanova, K., Klein, D., Manning, C. D., & Singer, Y. (2003). Feature-rich part-of-speech tagging with a cyclic dependency network. In *Proceedings of the 2003 Conference of the North American Chapter of the Association for Computational Linguistics on Human Language Technology* (Vol. 1) Association for Computational Linguistics. doi:10.3115/1073445.1073478

Voss, J. (2006). *Collaborative thesaurus tagging the Wikipedia way*. Academic Press.

Wang, K., Thrasher, C., Viegas, E., Li, X., & Hsu, B. (2010). An overview of microsoft web n-gram corpus and applications. In *Proceedings of the NAACL HLT 2010 Demonstration Session*, (pp. 45-48). Association for Computational Linguistics.

Chapter 5
Twitter Data Analysis

Chitrakala S
Anna University, India

ABSTRACT

Analyzing Social network data using Big Data Tools and techniques promises to provide information that could be of use in recommendation systems, personalized service and many other applications. A few of the analytics that do this include sentiment analysis, trending topic analysis, topic modeling, information diffusion modeling, provenance determination and social influence study. Twitter Data Analysis involves analyzing data specifically obtained from Twitter, both tweets and the topology. There are three major classifications on the type of analysis being performed such as Content based, Network based and Hybrid analysis. Trending Topic Analysis in the context of Content based static data analysis and Influence Maximization in the context of Hybrid analysis on data streams using the power of Big Data Analytics are discussed. A novel solution to Trending Topic analysis to generate topic evolved, conflict-free sequential sub summaries and influence maximization to handle streaming data are explained with experimental results.

INTRODUCTION TO TWITTER DATA ANALYSIS

One of the outcomes of the popularity of online social networks is the development of a new field, social network analysis (SNA). This field studies not just the structure of social network but also the behavior of the people who belong to it. One social network that has become popular for analysis is Twitter. Tweets based on a specific topic of interest, once extracted can be analyzed and the results obtained can be used in many applications. Twitter Data Analysis has gained popularity due to few notable reasons. First, obtaining information from Twitter makes it possible for

DOI: 10.4018/978-1-5225-2805-0.ch005

vendors to provide personalized solutions to their customers. Second, unlike other social networks, most accounts of Twitter are public, making it possible to obtain the necessary data. Also, the limitation on the number of characters ensures that the amount of time required to process a single tweet is typically rather small.

Analysis performed on Twitter data can be broadly classified into three categories: Content Based, Network Based and Hybrid Analysis. Techniques which rely solely on the tweets/text produced are named as Content based analysis, whereas techniques that rely on the network structure are called Network based analysis. A combination of both text and structure based analysis is termed as Hybrid analysis. The following sections expose the readers to techniques/methodologies in Twitter Data Analysis and its significance.

Overview

In this chapter, it is intended to show how analytical techniques namely Trending Topic Analysis and Influence Maximization can be utilized to study and mine significant information from a social network such as Twitter. Also, to illustrate their applications in real life business value use cases. It is believed that these illustrations would trigger ideas for researchers in various fields.

Firstly, a study on Trending Topic Analysis technique which is a content based static data analysis is emphasized accounting to the urging need of a complete analyzed summary of the topic under interest, presented in a topic evolved manner.

Secondly a study on Influence maximization technique which is a hybrid data analysis is discussed. It is important as it provides a way to find a small set of users, thus reducing the cost of promoting a product or campaign while simultaneously maximizing the spread of word about them. Distinguishing and critical aspect of the proposed Influence Maximization methodology is that it follows a Big Data approach enhancing its significance many folds.

Motivation

It is evident over the recent years that Twitter has grown from a vague invention to become a mainstream medium for dissemination of messages and the public discussion of news and events. The rapid proliferation of Twitter posts presents a big obstacle for efficient information acquisition. It is impossible for a user to get an overview of important topics on Twitter by reading all tweets every day. In addition, because of information redundancy and the informal writing style, it is time consuming to find useful information about a topic from a huge number of tweets. The tremendous volume of tweets suggests summarization as the key to facilitating the requirements of topic exploration, navigation, and search from hundreds of thousands of tweets. Specifically, a summary that provides representative information of topics with no redundancy and well-written sentences would be preferred.

Furthermore, Analysis of topics is truly strengthened by performing a sentiment classification but summarization applications lack this component and as a result produce conflicting summaries. Sentiment classifiers always dedicate themselves to a specific domain or topic. Namely, a classifier trained on sentiment data from one topic often performs poorly on test data from another. Most of the recent applications for sentiment analysis deal with a single topic under interest. But this is not the case when handling Twitter data since topics discussed in Twitter are very diverse and unpredictable. Another concern regarding sentiment classification is if carried out as a supervised approach it will incur heavy manual effort in annotation. The proposed Trending Topic Analyzer addresses these issues and combines both the flavored twitter summarization and as well topic based sentiment classification paving way to an appropriate solution. This Trending Topic Analysis system is of great value to communication experts where they use Twitter data to measure the pulse of public opinion and generate business intelligence.

The study of social influence is very important today. An influential person's endorsement could be the difference between success and failure for a product or campaign. For a promoter, identifying such influential users is crucial. This would provide them with a cost efficient way of promoting their products. No doubt, social media has no dearth of such information.

Technology and Tools Available

An overview of tools available focusing the issues in Content based and Hybrid Twitter data analysis is discussed below.

In the context of tools for Content based analysis, there are quite a few applications which alleviates the problem of generating crisp and topic evolved summaries. For example, many applications have evolved from Twitter (serving as their clients), namely "*echofon*" (www.echofon.com), "*whatthetrend*" (whatthetrend.com), which provide services to explain why the term becomes a trending topic or to give a short description of the topic. These systems generally track the topics in Twitter and use existing tweets or encourage users to edit a new tweet to explain the topics.

"*whatthetrend*" encourages users to edit explanatory tweets about topics. It ranks the submitted explanatory tweets by readers' agreements. These explanatory tweets can be regarded as tiny summaries about the topic, providing a good way to help users understand the topic. However, a short summary can only sketch the topic in a simple way. Some researchers attempt to aggregate several explanations into one long summary using traditional summarization approaches, but it still loses much useful information, such as the change of twitters' focus and the temporal information. A well generated traditional summary can reflect the overall picture of topic, but performs poorly in summarizing these temporal changes of the crowd's focus in Twitter. Note that the focus of tweets changes much more frequently than that of the traditional mainstream media.

Another such readily available application namely "Summary Card" caters a full-width prominent image alongside a tweet. It is designed with the motive to give the reader a rich photo experience.

SONDY (2016)(Social Network Dynamics) is an open source tool that is built specifically for performing event detection and influence analysis. It requires the use of two files, a network file to provide the structure of the network and a messages file which will contain the actual tweets. The tool can additionally perform certain pre-processing steps such as stemming and tokenization on the messages file.

In addition to such tools, certain big data frameworks also lend themselves for use in analyzing Twitter data. While Apache Hadoop and Apache Spark can be used for speeding up the computations that need to be done, Apache Storm is more suited to streaming applications.

Applications

The applications of twitter data analysis are many. It can be helpful in any use case where a personalized experience is to be presented to the end user. The most common of this is the recommendation system. Books, movies, products and many more can be recommended to users of twitter based on the sentiment expressed in their tweets.

Trending topic analysis can also be used in conjunction with sentiment analysis to determine the rise and fall in popularity of products and ideas. Its significance also spans across multiple uses cases such as a source of content preparation for Content Marketing,archival of past significant trends which could be used in domains such as Journalism andPolitics, sensing public views to analyze their political allegiance and civic engagement etc.

Mining the network structure can provide valuable information about the flow of information. This can help determine the best ways to promote a product or service. A study of provenance can even determine the source of any piece of information. This means, the source of rumors or erroneous information can be determined and dealt with the source. Community detection is also a very common analysis that is performed to group similar people together based not only on physical locality, but also a number of other features.

Other applications include question answering, expert finding, security, spam and advertisement detection, opinion mining, behavior analysis, churn analysis and disaster management. The applications are really only limited by the developer's imagination.

Challenges

While analyzing data on Twitter has some very interesting and useful applications, there are still some key challenges that are to be addressed. These challenges are described briefly here.

The information obtained from Twitter may often be biased and as a result may not be able to provide an accurate view of the real world. This could be due to the fact that a large section of people are not active on Twitter or because information retrieval was not performed properly.

According to Twitter's terms of service, a dataset consisting of Tweets cannot be shared. However, it is admissible to share the list of IDs so that the dataset is reconstructed. Over time, some tweets may go missing due to it being deleted or the account being deactivated or an account that was previously public being made private. If the dataset consists of tweets that cannot be obtained due to any of the above reasons, it will not be possible to reproduce the dataset completely. This means that a benchmark dataset does not exist for such applications making comparisons of similar work much more difficult.

Another problem with data collection is the large number of spam messages and irrelevant tweets within the network. No matter how carefully the parameters are set, it may yet be difficult to obtain a dataset that does not contain these unnecessary tweets.

A research challenge that goes hand in hand with twitter data analysis is the closed world assumption. When performing any type of analysis, an assumption is made that the user is influenced by people and their actions within the network. External sources are ignored, leading to errors in the final predicted results. Another challenge arises from the dynamic nature of the online social networks. Most existing solutions assume that the structure of the network is static. Provisions have to be made to add and remove links within the network.

RESEARCH BACKGROUND

Text summarization is typically split into two groups: extractive summarization and abstractive Summarization. In that there are two main approaches are used namely structure based approach (Approaches using prior knowledge), semantic based approach (Approaches using NLP generation). Structured primarily based approach encodes most vital data from the document(s) through psychological feature schemas like templates, extraction rules and alternative structures like tree, ontology, lead and body, rule, graph based structure. In semantic based technique, linguistics illustration of document(s) is employed to feed into natural language generation (NLG) system. This technique specialize in identifying noun phrases and verb phrases by using the following methods namely multi-model semantic method, Information item based method, semantic graph based method and semantic text representation model for processing of linguistic data.

The popularity of micro-blogging services, such as Twitter has caught increasing attention from worldwide researchers. There exist some pioneering researches made in Twitter summarization and as well on Sentiment Classification which forms the two building blocks for the proposed Content based Twitter Data Analysis approach.

Focusing on Twitter Summarization first, it is evident from few of the following researches that each of them lacks certain attributes that forms a major component of Trending Topic Analyser. Highlights and set-back of each approach are discussed.

G.Maneet all (2014) proposed an approach of Phrase Reinforcement algorithm combined with Word Sense Disambiguation and Textual Entailment techniques for generating one line summary. Phrase Reinforcement algorithm aimed at constructing a graph which helps in identifying the most commonly occurring phrases for a central topic by simply searching for the most weighted set of paths through the graph. This methodology lacked temporal nature of summaries and created coherence issues in the summary generated.

Similarly work made by Wen et al(2014) and O'Conor et al(2010) also lack temporal nature in summaries generated. Wen et al (2014) accomplished Summarization using a non-parametric Bayesian model applied to Hidden Markov Models. A novel observation model was designed to allow ranking based on selected predictive characteristics of individual tweets. Major focus was to investigate the possibility of using a temporal probabilistic data model known as Hierarchical Dirichlet Process Hidden Markov Model (HDP-HMM) to process a stream of tweets pertaining to a single subject and cluster the tweets into groups or rankings based on the value of the individual tweets.But Summaries generated did not project the temporal nature. O'Conor et al (2010) explained Twitter topics by presenting a simple list of messages. An exploratory search application for Twitter called TweetMotif grouped messages by frequent significant terms and result set's subtopics facilitated navigation and drilldown through a faceted search interface. The topic extraction system was based on syntactic filtering, language modeling, near-duplicate detection, and set cover heuristics. But the system lacked temporal aspect in summaries generated and topic development was not observed.

Twitter data is known to be diverse in nature. Therefore the quality of summaries would be better when there are techniques incorporating such tweet specific features. One such work is cited below. Lui et al (2011)proposed a Concept Based optimization framework for topic Summarization using Integer Linear Programming. Target data comprised of original and normalized tweets along with web content relevant to the topic. The focus was not on developing new summarization systems but rather utilizing and integrating diverse text sources to generate more informative summaries. But, another driving factor called "topic evolvement" is very critical when it comes in handling trending topics. To understand a trending topic completely, the entire topic development need to be known which also includes another research area called sub topic detection. Lui et al work lacked series of sub events identification to show topic evolving process.

A work by Gao et al (2014) generated sequential summaries on a topic using Stream and Semantic based approaches. Though this technique was able to incorporate the temporal aspect and topic evolving aspect, it fell short of readability of summaries generated. System failed to capture the opinion expressed in the data thus leading to conflicting summaries. Kar et al(2016) proposed a Twitter-Network (TN) topic model that jointly build network in Bayesian nonparametric method. Hierarchical Poisson-Dirichlet processes (PDP) is utilized by the TN topic model and for building social network a Gaussian process random function model is used. TN topic model also interprets hash tag analysis, authors' interests, automatic topic labeling author recommendation and hashtag suggestion. Luyi et al(2016) semantically find and visualize the trendy topics examined on Twitter for a particular duration of time. A pooling schema correlated to meaningful contexts is proposed for a tweet that makes LDA based methods work properly.

Next, study on few of the researches made in Sentiment classification relevant to data analysis is discussed. One of the major issues of Sentiment classification using machine learning approaches is the need for labeled training data. But unfortunately, Twitter dataset lack labeled data which often poses a huge effort in manual annotation. On that note, Rui et al (2013) used supervised algorithms namely Naïve Bayes Classifier and Support Vector Machine Classifier for sentiment classification to investigate whether and how Twitter WOM affects movie sales. Contributions included measuring the impacts of WOM from people with different degrees of connectivity in a social network. But as mentioned earlier, this kind of system incurred heavy labor work in labeling the huge training data set.

Twitter data diversity also causes trouble in training a universal classifier. Some works have been done for cross domain sentiment analysis for review datasets like in(2010), Pan et al used Spectral Feature Alignment algorithm (SFA) for classifying sentiment polarity, for bridging the gap between the domains and to align domain-specific words from different domains into unified clusters. System significantly outperformed previous approaches to cross-domain sentiment classification but unfortunately it could not be applied for twitter dataset. Solution to this issue would be to reach out in search of techniques that function based on the content of the relevant data which is also called Topic based sentiment classification. One such work addressing this issue was done by Lui et al(2015) where they performed semi supervised multi class model for topic adaptive sentiment classification. The classifier was initially built using common features which did not adapt well for cross domains. Semi supervised learning was used to adaptively learn the build a topic adaptive classifier. But the system needed topic labeled data in order to apply the respective classifier model. Obtaining labeled data poses a major constraint which in turn reduces the adaptability of this system to any kind of data to be analysed.

As Twitter Summarization and Sentiment Classification were discussed in the previous sections, rest of the research background details figure out about the techniques in Information Diffusion and Influence Maximization.

The earliest information diffusion models were built not for social networks, but for real world networks. When this was extended into the world of online social networks, two prominent models emerged: the independent cascade model and the linear threshold model. A survey of some of the most recent advances in information diffusion modeling is presented below.

Time and the network structure were identified as the key components of an information diffusion modeling system. Guille et al (2012) proposed an asynchronous information diffusion model called T-BaSIC (Time Based Asynchronous Independent Cascades) where the various parameters considered are functions of time.

Jiang et al (2014)on the other hand, focused on the network structure and proposed a graphical evolutionary game theoretic framework to model and understand the information diffusion process in online social networks. Based on whether the users have in depth knowledge of other users in the network, the diffusion process had been divided into type dependent or type independent.

It didn't escape the attention of the research community that both of these parameters must be studied in conjunction. Taxidou (2013) studied the process of information diffusion in real time from both a structural and temporal view point. The role of different users in the dissemination of information in the underlying social network was also studied. Wang, et al (2012) proposed a partial differential equation to model both the temporal and topological dynamics of diffusion of information that is injected into the network. But topology is considered only in terms of distance from the source.

The main drawback to these systems is that they failed to acknowledge the role played by the topic in the information dissemination process. The time delay in propagation has also not been modeled accurately in most existing works.

Soon, simply modeling the diffusion process became insufficient. The next step was to maximize the information flow. This is also a problem that is not exclusive to online social networks. A few interesting contributions to this problem are noted below.

Liu et al (2014) attempted to solve the influence maximization problem by running the solution on a GPU in order to speed up the calculation. A novel approach called the Bottom Up Traversal Algorithm (BUTA) was introduced which builds a tree using a subset of the network and the traverses it from the bottom up, all the while combining nodes whose influence can be calculated independent of each other.

Song et al (2015) acknowledge that even the best approximations of the greedy algorithm are time consuming. The solution provided is to divide the network into communities and run the algorithm on each of these communities in parallel.

While the two mentioned earlier, aimed at a faster solution, Liu et al(2014), in their paper defined an all new version of the problem called the time constrained influence maximization problem and also prove that it is NP hard, sub modular and monotonic. The authors acknowledged the fact that in the real world, people were more likely to require a solution to the time constrained problem and not the conventional problem. The idea of influence spreading paths is introduced in order to solve the problem.

While each system attempts to reduce the running time and had varying degrees of success, they are still not capable of providing a near real time solution. Almost all research in the arena is geared towards reducing the run time.

TWITTER DATA EXTRACTION

The need to work on a well known data set is a known issue when it comes to working on Twitter data. Twitter's terms of service prevent users from making uniquely identifiable information public. Depending on what's best suited, data from Twitter can be extracted using the REST API or the Streaming API. To make accessing these APIs much simpler, packages are available online for both Java and Python. These packages are often well documented and easy to use. In this section, an overview of the two APIs is presented.

Extraction via REST API

The Twitter REST API (2016) provides programmaticaccess with which one can read or write twitter data, i.e. using REST API users can search for historic tweets, read user profile information and post tweets. The word REST stands for Representational State Transfer. REST API identifies twitter users andapplications using an authentication protocol termed OAuth. Responses from the API are inJSON format. API rate limits are either per user based or per application based where thesearch limit is 180 queries per 15 minute window. Some of REST APIs are Search API, GET API and POST API. Search API functions similar to but not exactly like the Search feature in Twitter. It focuses more on relevance than on completeness. GET and POST API- functions along with several attribute statuses, followers, friends, direct messages etc.

Extraction via Streaming API

There are two major limitations in collecting data using the REST API. One is the rate limit that is imposed and the second is the timeliness of the data fetched. In order to help fetch data in real time, the Streaming API (2016) was introduced. This API also returns the data in JSON format. There are three different types of streams available, namely, the user stream, site stream and public stream.

The user stream fetches all the data from a single user. A single application can only connect to a limited number of user streams regardless of the IP from which the stream is being accessed. Site stream makes it possible to process events generated by multiple users who have provided OAuth access to the application. At the time of writing, this feature is in a close beta stage. The public stream is the most suitable for data mining applications. It enables the application to fetch events based on a particular keyword or from a set of users.

Care must be taken while processing streaming data. The stream must be consumed as quickly as possible. A delay could cause the connection to be severed. The system must also be capable of handling duplicates. On receiving a 420 status code, if a client doesn't implement a back off strategy but attempts to connect repeatedly, it may be rate limited.

A final option available to programmers is Fire hose, Using Firehose guarantees that all the tweets in the public domain are fetched and as a result can come in handy for security applications. Access to Firehose comes at a cost.

TRENDING TOPIC ANALYSIS

Content based static twitter-data analysis is achieved via the proposed Trending Topic Analysis approach. It is evident in recent years that Twitter collects millions of tweets every day serving as a rich information delivering platform. However, users especially the new usersmight find it difficult to understand the trending topics in Twitter when confronted with overwhelming and unorganized tweets.

There have been attempts in past to provide a short snippet to summarize a topic but, this does not scale up to user's expectation as it does not provide any analyzed summary. The proposed Trending Topic Analysis model analyses trending topics by performing Topic adaptive sentiment classification thereby summarizing public

Figure 1. Trending topic analyser

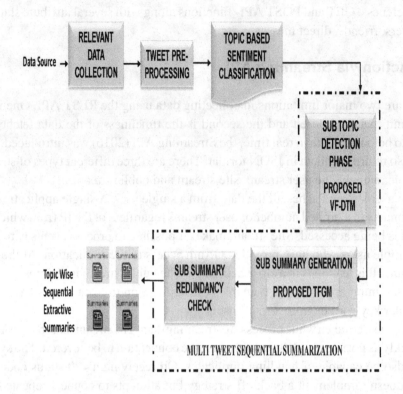

views on selected trending topics and generates extractive sub summaries of topics over the time period. Figure 1 depicts the overall flow of the model.

Different from the traditional summarization task, conflicting summary generation could be avoided with sentiment classification sorting the data into separate sentiment corpus. Stream-based followed by semantic-based approach of detecting sub topic in the corpus help generate short sub-summary for each subtopic under the trending topic. For Semantic based approach a new model called Volume fed Foreground DTM (VF-DTM) is proposed which distils the noisy content and extracts the foreground tweets from the corpus and then builds the intended model on it. Finally summary generation is accomplished using a graph based algorithm named TFGM by incorporating the proposed salient features of a tweet nature for better relevancy of tweets selected. Rest of this section details about various phases involved in Trending Topic Analysis Model.

Relevant Data Collection

Twitter API enables extraction of region wise trends. Relevant data collection is performed by extracting trending topics using a specific region's "WOEID" which uniquely identifies any region in the world. Extracted trends will be analyzed to confirm to the requirement that the topic involves several sub topics hidden in it. Extracted trending topics will be stored in the database for topic based tweet collection.

Pre-Processing

Once the relevant tweet/data set is ready, few pre-processing steps are to be carried out before using the data for the required content analysis. Necessary pre-processing such as URL removal, Slang Word Replacement, Non English Tweet Filter, Stemmer and Stop Word Removal are performed to prepare the target useable data. Along with the pre-processing phase, the proposed system also handles other language tweet translation which is essential to prevent discarding of public opinion about the trending topic.

Topic Based Adaptive Classification

Topic based sentiment classification is inspired by the method proposed by Liu et al. in [8] for labeling the corpus with their corresponding sentiments. Topic based sentiment feature extraction involved in this system creates a significant impact in the performance of sentiment classification task. Tweets have a special nature unlike normal English sentences like @ symbol used to refer to a user, emoticons expressed in the tweets, etc. Incorporating such features while performing feature extraction will enhance the overall process. Features extracted could be classified into two broad categories namely Common Features and Tweet Specific Features. With the extracted features, classifier model is built based on each topic without exhaustively labeling the training set. Support Vector Machine is used as the classifier to perform the semi supervised classification task. The classifier model is built using a collaborative training approach where the unlabeled data and the features extracted will be iteratively augmented with the initial labeled set.

Multi Tweet Sequential Summarization

Multi Tweet Sequential Summarization aims to generate a serial of chronologically related sub-summaries for a given topic while retaining the order of information presentation and each sub-summary attempts to concentrate on one theme or subtopic. The sequential summary, made up by the chronologically ordered sub-summaries, shall provide the entire development of the topic or the full view of the topic. The proposed framework uses a two-step process for generating a sequential summarization namely: Sub Topic Detection and Sub Summary Generation. Sub topic detects the hidden details about a given topic which are detected using a Volume based approach followed by a modified Semantic based approach termed Foreground DTM. In addition to these two phases of work, Redundancy checking is also performed to ensure that the produced sub summaries are novel.

Tweet stream that is collected may contain many irrelevant data which may tamper the quality of the extractive summary generated. This raises a need to clean and extract only the relevant corpus. Noisy and irrelevant tweets given a trending topic is handled by a bi-level process of executing Volume based approach (V) and the output from the previous step i.e. the tweet set collected will be fed into the novel topic modeling approach thus termed as Volume fed Foreground Dynamic Topic Modeling (VF-DTM). This overall process forms the first step of sequential summarization. Figure 2 shows the process of VF-DTM where the input is from Volume based approach.

Unlike LDA, DTM regards the topics evolve over time and supposes that the data is divided by a special time interval. The tweets in each time interval are modeled by K-component topic model, and the subtopic associated with the time t interval evolves from the subtopic associated with the time interval t-1. Initially, the entire corpus is spilt presenting background/noisy and foreground data separately. This step greatly accounts to analysis only on relevant data by striking away noisy content. Further process of the model is adapted as in (2014), where word distribution and tweet distribution are computed. Before generating the sequential summary for the semantic-based approach, first need to sort the subtopics detected from VF-DTM

Figure 2. Foreground-dynamic topic modeling

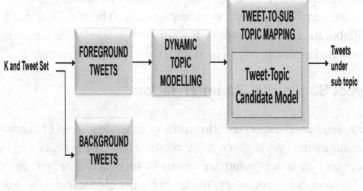

according to their temporal information. Particularly, Reason candidate model (2014) is used to output the relationships between tweets and subtopics to assign each tweet to the subtopic that it most likely belongs to. Most probable tweets will be associated to each sub topic by the extracting the word distribution only from the foreground set and not the background set. This process is applicable for mining topics for specific set of data collection. The tweets being assigned signify that they best represent the topic under consideration.

As mentioned earlier, second step in generating sequential summarization is Sub summary generation termed as Tweet Feature Graph Model (TFGM). Each tweet is limited to 140 characters which poses a challenge to extract most significant tweets from the corpus mixed with noisy data. Various graph based tweet selection proved to be more efficient than other form of approaches as in (2015). In this work, a graph based approach is employed to select the highly scored tweets as candidates for extractive summary to be generated. Initially the tweets will be represented as a tweet vector. Cosine similarity between tweets in the corpus is calculated as in equation (1). Then, weights of each edge which incorporates special nature of tweets namely: Retweet number and Followers count are computed as in equation (2). Finally, transition probability values are calculated and hence the salience score for each tweet will be generated. Figure 3 shows the process flow of Tweet Feature Graph Model.

The weights of the edges in the graph $w(i,j)$ are calculated as in equation (1) where sim calculates the similarity between tweets in the corpus and salient feature of tweet a_j is computed using equation (2) where $retw(j)$ is the retweet count and $foll(j)$ is the followers count.

$$w(i,j) = \frac{sim\left(\vec{t_i}, \vec{t_j}\right)}{\sum_j sim\left(\vec{t_i}, \vec{t_j}\right)} \frac{a_j}{a_{j'}} \qquad (1)$$

Figure 3. Tweet feature graph model

137

$$a\left(j\right) = retw\left(j\right).foll\left(j\right) \tag{2}$$

The transition probability $p(i,j)$ in equation (3) is sufficiently different from $p(j,i)$ because of the different normalization factor in the denominator.

$$p(i,j) = \begin{cases} \dfrac{w(i,j)}{\Sigma_j w(i,j)} & \text{if } \sum_j w(i,j) \neq 0 \\ 0 & \text{otherwise} \end{cases} \tag{3}$$

Finally, the salience score for each tweet will be calculated according to equation (4) where s_i is the salience score of the ith vertex, λ is the damping factor and V is the number of tweets for summarization.

$$s_i = \lambda.\Sigma_{j \neq 1} s_j.p(i,j) + (1-\lambda).1 / |V| \tag{4}$$

Whether a tweet is selected as a representative depends on two factors: its *salience score* and its *similarity* to the already selected tweets. Specifically, a tweet is chosen if it is the candidate with the greatest salience score and its similarity to any selected tweet is below a threshold. No matter whether the most salient candidate is chosen or not, it will be removed from the candidate. This selection process repeats until M tweets are chosen or the candidate set is empty.

System generated sequential summaries are evaluated majorly from the following two aspects:

1.   Coverage

Coverage measures the overlap between the system generated summaries and human generated summaries as per equation (5) given below.

$$\text{Coverage}\left(N - gram\right) =$$

$$\frac{1}{|D^H|} \cdot \sum_{d_i \in D^H} \frac{1}{w_{ij}} \frac{\sum_{d_j \in D^S} \sum_{N-gram \in d_i^H, d_j^S} \sum Count_{match}\left(N - gram\right)}{\sum_{d_j \in D^S} \sum_{N-gram \in d_j^S} \sum Count\left(N - gram\right)}$$

$$where, \ w_{ij} = \begin{cases} \left| j - i \right| + 1, j \neq i \\ 1 \qquad\quad , j = i \end{cases} \tag{5}$$

In equation (5), i and j denotes the index of sub summaries in both system generated D^S and human generated summaries D^H. w_{ij} is the penalty coefficient to discount mismatches in sub-summaries.

2. Novelty

Novelty measures the average information increment in any two successive summaries that is being generated as per equation (6). In addition, Cosine Similarity also is used to evaluate sub topic segmentation performance of the proposed approach as per equation (7).

$$Novelty = \frac{1}{\left| D \right| - 1} \sum_{i>1} \left(I_{d_i} - I_{d_i, d_{i-1}} \right) \tag{6}$$

$$where, Information \ in \ sub \ summary = I_{d_i} = \sum_{w \in d_i} I_w$$

$$Overlapped \ Information = I_{d_i, d_{i-1}} = \sum_{w \in d_i \cap d_{i-1}} I_w$$

$\left| D \right|$ in equation (6) is the number of sub summaries under study.

$$\cos \left(X, Y \right) = \frac{\sum_i x_i y_i}{\sqrt{\sum_i \left(x_i^2 \right)} \sqrt{\sum_i \left(y_i^2 \right)}} \tag{7}$$

In equation (7) $X \ and \ Y$ denotes any two tweets respectively. Table 1 shows the comparative results of the system in terms of Coverage and Novelty.

Table 1 show that the first trending topic performs better that the second topic accounting to the fact that the former had more number of hidden sub topics in it. As mentioned earlier sub topic segmentation performance is evaluated using Cosine similarity and the results are shown in Table 2.

Table 1. Comparison with baseline systems

Trending Topic	Metric	Heuristic-Baseline	Human Generated	Proposed Trending Topic Analysis Model
#YakubMemon	Coverage	2.15	4.20	3.55
	Novelty	2.26	4.95	4.10
#Black Day For Indian Democracy	Coverage	2.10	4.05	3.42
	Novelty	2.13	4.90	4.00

Table 2. Cosine similarity for sub topic segmentation

Sub-Topic Detection Models	Cosine Similarity
Heuristic Baseline	0.841
LDA	0.688
OPAD	0.693
DTM	0.677
Proposed VF-DTM	0.6585

Heuristic value is adapted as in Gao et al (2014) for comparison with the various sub topic detection models. Average of cosine similarity between adjacent subtopics was computed as an indicator of segmentation performance and *"the lower similarity means the better performance"*. As seen in Table 2, performance of Volume based approach i.e. Offline Peak Area Detection in sub topic segmentation proves that detecting topic merely based on volume will affect the segmentation performance leading to unidentified topics in the corpus. DTM uses semantic approach and not merely volume but the performance of proposed (VF- DTM) system is still better than standalone DTM due to the reason that the model building process is not interrupted with noisy content .Therefore distilling noise and further proceeding with building the required model has proved to be an efficient choice.

INFORMATION DIFFUSION: A BIG DATA APPROACH

The study of information diffusion has two major components, both of which fall squarely under the category of hybrid analysis techniques as per the classification explained earlier. They are information diffusion modeling and influence maximization. Information diffusion modeling deals with determining the path that a piece of information will take while spreading through the network. It passively studies the network and determines who will and will not spread the information. Influence maximization, on the other hand, is a more active process. Here, the network is observed and influence of various users is studied in order to determine the set of users most likely to maximize information spread. Influence maximization dictates the source of the information by picking the most suitable candidates.

A solution is discussed for each of these problems. What makes these solutions interesting is the fact that they take into account the dynamic nature of the network and updates are made to the structure as time progresses. Before getting to these specific solutions, some basic pre-processing steps are explained. Following this, the results obtained by these techniques are discussed. Network 1, 2 and 3 have 10000, 20000 and 30000 users respectively. For each of these networks, the corresponding numbers of tweets collected are around 3 millions, 7 millions and 1.2 billions correspondingly. The tweets obtained with an average data size of 10GB are stored for duration of 60 days.

Pre-Processing

Since hybrid techniques deal with both the content as well as the topology, both the tweets as well as the network topology must be pre-processed. Text pre-processing for Twitter data typically involves short hand removal, punctuation removal, stop word removal, stemming and language check. Most of these are self-explanatory but language check is worth a brief discussion. Language check is performed to ensure that the tweet is in the desired language. For English, this can be done by comparing the words against a dictionary (which can be constructed using a trie). Tweets that do not belong to the target language may be discarded. But if a large percentage of the relevant tweets extracted are of language other than that being processed, translations techniques may be considered.

Two other major analyses that can be considered as a text pre-processing technique for information diffusion are sentiment analysis and topic modeling. The sentiment analyser used can be anything from a simple classifier to a much more complex system that is dynamic and robust. In this implementation, the sentiment analyser is a perceptron with a linear basis function. This classifier is seen to work well for sentiment analysis with an accuracy of about 86%. There are other implementations which are capable of providing better results. These systems were not chosen due to their high complexity and the emphasis is on the diffusion modeling process and not the sentiment analyser.

Topic Identification pertaining to Machine Learning and Natural Language Processing is a type statistical model that is used for discovering the abstract "topics" occurring through a collection of documents. They are broadly classified in two categories namely: 1) Static Topic Identification and 2) Dynamic Topic Identification.

Static topic Identification also referred to as probabilistic topic models, discovers the hidden text of latent semantic structures from a large collections of unstructured documents. They have been extensively used to detect instructive structures in data such as genetic information, images, and networks. Dynamic topic Identification analyze the evolution of (unobserved) topics in a collection of documents over time. Eg: Latent Dirichlet Allocation (LDA) sees to that, the order of words in a document and order of documents in a corpus are unconsciously interchangeable.LDA follows multinomial distribution for a set of terms and derives documents of each group from a set of topics that evolved from a set of the previous time slice. Thus, for each word of each document, a topic is drawn from Dynamic Topic Identification and a term is subsequently drawn from the multinomial distribution corresponding to that topic.

The most commonly used technique used for topic modeling is the Latent Dirichlet Allocation (LDA). LDA works even well for a static data set but not entirely practical for performing on data set that is being built from a data stream. In order to solve this problem, a streaming version of this algorithm has been proposed and tested by Hoffman et al. (2010) The system makes use of variational Bayes to ensure that the calculation of topic happens in a timely manner.

The second half of this section deals with pre-processing the network topology. The network topology must first be built from the list of followers that is obtained from Twitter. Links in Twitter are unidirectional. This means that parallel edges are possible but must be of opposite directions. The most suitable way to store this kind of data is in a graph database such as neo4j or allegrograph. Other options include saving the edges as ordered pairs with the first element indicating the origin of the edge and the second indicating the destination.

In order to speed up the computation in the later stages of this system, the edges can be stored along with weights that indicate the likeliness of information passing between the two users. In cases where the assumption is made that the network is static, this would be the best option. But in the case where the information is streamed in real time, it is not as simple. There would of course be a decrease in running time but it won't be as evident as in the case of a static dataset. This is because each time a user leaves or enters the network or a new edge is introduced, the values will have to be recalculated. If the changes in the topology are not as rare as they are assumed to be, too much time will be spent on this recalculation. If such a scenario is anticipated, the weights can be recalculated only as and when required.

Information Diffusion Modeling

Once pre-processing is completed, the process of modeling begins. There are a number of techniques that are available to accomplish this, each with their own strengths and drawbacks. The choice of the modeling technique is based purely on the

Figure 4. Information diffusion modelling

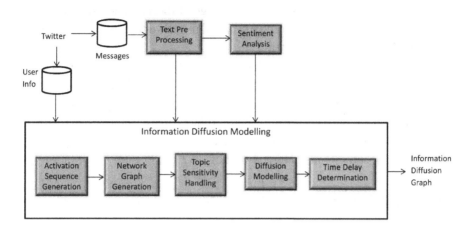

end requirements. Instead in this section, the main emphasis will be on augmenting any one of these models with topic sensitivity. Figure 4 provides an outline of the stages in the information diffusion modeling process. The specific technique that has been used in drawing the conclusions derived in this chapter is the evolutionary game theoretic approach.

Introducing topic sensitivity is a concept that's easy enough to understand. A model is said to be topic sensitive when the result generated by it varies depending on the topic of interest. In the case of information diffusion modeling, the users who forward the information and hence the path that the information flows via will be different when the query term belongs to a different topic.

There may be any number of topics present in the tweets that are collected. But this number has to be decided upon by the designer. Following this, the utility of forwarding the information for each node for the given topic must be determined. There are two ways in which this can be accomplished. The simplest is by performing topic modeling on the tweets and then using the percentage of tweets generated, liked and retweet by each user in that specific topic in order to determine the utility of forwarding. In this approach, the topic to be selected would be the one that the query term is most likely to belong to.

The second and more computationally intensive technique would be to determine the topic at runtime. The reason why this works out better is because we can never be sure of how many topics are present and also a single tweet may contain information pertaining to more than one topic. In fact, LDA assumes that a sentence is made up of a mixture of topics. In this technique, the term coupling between the query term and every other word in the set of tweets collected. The words that are highly coupled with the query term are first selected and then tweets that contain the query term and any of these highly coupled words are selected. These tweets are assumed to belong to the topic of interest. The percentage of these tweets belonging to each user is determined to be their relevance score. This relevance score can then be used to determine the utility in forwarding.

At its simplest form, the value obtained at the end of either of these approaches can be directly used as the utility of forwarding. While this might not be entirely accurate, the results produced are quite close to the actual diffusion process. The actual extent of diffusion is determined by studying diffusion processes for the topic of interest in the network. This value is then compared with the results provided by the mode. The accuracy thus obtained is shown in Table 3.

Influence Maximization on Streams

The influence maximization problem aims to select a subset of 'k' users such that the information diffused by these 'k' users is to the maximum extent possible.

Existing solutions to the influence maximization problem are time consuming. While the aim is to find a near optimal solution, the primary focus is on lowering the running time of the algorithm. There are many ways to accomplish this. One is by optimizing the algorithm to run in parallel on infrastructure such as Hadoop or GPUs. With proper algorithm design, the running time can be cut down drastically. A second option would be to find a way to reduce the possible candidates. However, this candidate set must be chosen with care so as to ensure that the users who are supposed to be included in the final solution are present in this candidate set as well. It is a combination of the two that will be used in the solution detailed here. Figure 5 outlines the various steps involved in this technique.

In order to reduce the size of the candidate set, sampling is done on the entire data set, biased towards nodes which are capable of maximizing the information spread. The odds of such nodes are increased; all the nodes in the network are first ranked based on their influence. Then, a random sampling is done on this list to determine which 'n' nodes make the cut. The size of 'n' should be sufficiently large. If the value selected is too small, the final result may not have as many nodes are required by the user. Finally, the greedy algorithm is run in parallel to select the final subset of users who can maximize the information diffusion.

Table 3. Accuracy

Network	Network 1	Network 2	Network 3
Accuracy	0.76	0.78	0.75

Figure 5. Influence maximization

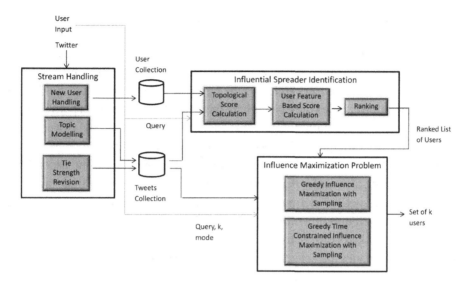

The first point that has to be discussed is the ranking of users based on influence. As mentioned earlier, the system is topic sensitive which means that topic information must be saved from the tweets. This information will be used as a feature while ranking the users. There have been a large number of techniques proposed, each with their own set of features. When the source of information is a social network like Twitter, two types of features must be considered, viz, topological features and user features. Topological features can include the k core, in and out degree. On the other hand, number of retweets, replies and mentions, location, verification status and interest in the topic can be considered as user features. It is important to take both types of features into consideration. If the features considered are not sufficient, the results obtained will be skewed.

The second and probably the most important component of the system is the utility function used. In this particular problem, the utility function determines the contribution of a given node to the information spread. This value is often determined iteratively by calculating the utility of all nodes influenced by the given node and so on using Monte Carlo simulations. This is a time consuming process. One extra consideration that exists while handling Twitter data is the possibility of information flow between two nodes which do not have an explicit link between them. This is a very likely scenario because of the retweet feature. In addition, tweets from public profiles are easily searchable. This could especially be the case when the tweet pertains to a trending topic. The utility function used here is given in the equation (8).

$$Utility = \sum_{y} \left(\alpha \, nPaths \, x \, f + \left(1 - \alpha\right) r_{xy} \right) \qquad (8)$$

'r_{xy}' is the similarity between the users, calculated using Pearson's correlation coefficient between the interests of each pair of users, x and y. 'nPaths' is the number of paths between the two users and 'f' is the frequency of communication. The first half of the equation handles the cases where there is a direct or indirect path between the two nodes. This typically implies that the user is influenced by a tweet that's visible on his/ her timeline, either because the user is following the tweeting user or is following someone who has retweeted that particular tweet. The second half pertains to finding a tweet by performing a search on a keyword or trending topic. The advantage to such a function is that it doesn't have to be calculated iteratively, thus reducing the running time of the entire system.

Finally, the ranked list is sampled and the greedy approach is applied on these sample sets. The nodes are selected in such a way that the overlap is minimized and information spread is maximized.

As mentioned earlier, the running time of the system as well as its ability to provide a solution that is very close to the optimal solution are important. The system has been tested on a cluster of 4 quad core multithreaded machines running the Ubuntu operating system. Hadoop is used as the cluster manager. The running time of the system with and without the above discussed features is shown in Table 4.

The closeness of the obtained solution to the optimal solution is measured by the size of overlap of the solution provided by the system and the optimal solution. This metric is suitable since the order of the elements in the list does not matter. All that matters is that the same set of elements is selected. The larger the size of

Table 4. Running time

Approach	Greedy	Greedy With Sampling	Greedy With MR	Greedy With MR and Sampling
Running Time	271 s	255 s	153 s	129 s

Table 5. Size of overlap

K	Size of Overlap
5	4
10	8
15	13

overlap, the more accurate the system is. The sizes of overlap obtained for different values of k are shown in Table 5.

DISCUSSIONS

While these approaches show promising results, there are still a number of elements that are to be considered, each of which could lead to a potential rise in accuracy. Some of these aspects are discussed with respect to both systems.

Research Directions in Trending Topic Analysis

The system can be further drilled down to enhance by normalizing the selected significant tweets for better understanding. Other forms of texts or for example from relevant newspapers could be used to improve the readability of summary generated. For further increasing the accuracy of the classifier, NLP techniques such as negation handling and Word Sense Disambiguation could be considered while handling tweets.

Another research path is that the system can be modeled to generate abstractive summaries of the topic which also contributes to the readability of the summary. Once plunged into generation of abstractive summaries, the system can be further extended to deal with Voice to Text Generation of MOM (Minutes of Meeting) based on the agenda of the meeting. Building of such an application assures a strong industrial impact.

Research Directions in Information Diffusion

In this system, the diffusion process of a keyword can be determined only if the word exists in the set that is identified in the initial stages of the system. It is necessary to devise other techniques that can take advantage of dictionary knowledge and make it possible to determine the diffusion process even for keywords that do not belong to this set.

An interesting way to better the results of the information diffusion system is by studying other features so that the likelihood of information passage is modeled more accurately. A possible extension is to make it possible to decide the location or demographic region within which the users are to be selected. This could be utilized in cases where a promotion or topic is important to certain locations only.

In addition, the size of the sample, when selecting nodes to test whether they belong to the solution set, is fixed. A technique to determine the most suitable sample size could be introduced. This would ensure that the required numbers of users are selected and the sample size is no larger than absolutely necessary.

REFERENCES

Chen, Y., Zhang, X., Li, Z., & Ng, J. P. (2015). Search engine reinforced semi-supervised classification and graph-based summarization of microblogs. *Neurocomputing, 152*, 274–286. doi:10.1016/j.neucom.2014.10.068

Developers, T. (n.d.a). *REST APIs | Twitter Developers*. Retrieved on June 30, 2016 from https://dev.twitter.com/rest/public

Developers, T. (n.d.b). *The Streaming APIs |Twitter Developers*. Retrieved on June 30, 2016, from https://dev.twitter.com/streaming/overview

Gao, D., Li, W., Cai, X., Zhang, R., & Ouyang, Y. (2014). Sequential summarization: A full view of twitter trending topics. *IEEE/ACM Transactions on Audio, Speech, and Language Processing, 22*(2), 293-302.

Guille, A., & Hacid, H. (2012) A predictive model for the temporal dynamics of information diffusion in online social networks. *Proceedings of the 21st international conference on World Wide Web*. doi:10.1145/2187980.2188254

Guille, A. (n.d.). *SONDY*. Retrieved June 30, 2016, from https://github.com/AdrienGuille/SONDY

Hoffman, M., Blei, D., & Bach, F. (2010). On-line learning for latent Dirichlet allocation. *Neural Information Processing Systems*.

Jiang, C., Chen, Y., & Liu, K. R. (2014). Evolutionary dynamics of information diffusion over social networks. *IEEE Transactions on Signal Processing, 62*(17), 4573–4586. doi:10.1109/TSP.2014.2339799

Lim, K. W., Chen, C., & Buntine, W. (2016). *Twitter-Network Topic Model: A Full Bayesian Treatment for Social Network and Text Modeling. NIPS 2013 Topic Models: Computation* (pp. 1–5). Application, and Evaluation.

Liu, B., Cong, G., Zeng, Y., Xu, D., & Chee, Y. M. (2014). Influence spreading path and its application to the time constrained social influence maximization problem and beyond. *IEEE Transactions on Knowledge and Data Engineering, 26*(8), 1904–1917. doi:10.1109/TKDE.2013.106

Liu, F., Liu, Y., & Weng, F. (2011, June). Why is sxsw trending?: exploring multiple text sources for twitter topic summarization. In *Proceedings of the Workshop on Languages in Social Media* (pp. 66-75). Association for Computational Linguistics.

Liu, S., Cheng, X., Li, F., & Li, F. (2015). TASC: Topic-adaptive sentiment classification on dynamic tweets. *IEEE Transactions on Knowledge and Data Engineering, 27*(6), 1696–1709. doi:10.1109/TKDE.2014.2382600

Liu, X., Li, M., Li, S., Peng, S., Liao, X., & Lu, X. (2014). IMGPU: GPU-accelerated influence maximization in large-scale social networks. *IEEE Transactions on Parallel and Distributed Systems, 25*(1), 136–145. doi:10.1109/TPDS.2013.41

Mane, M. G., & Kulkarni, M. A. (2015). Twitter Event Summarization Using Phrase Reinforcement Algorithm and NLP Features. In Proceedings of International Journal of Advanced Research in Computer and Communication Engineering (vol. 4.5 pp. 427-430). doi:10.17148/IJARCCE.2015.45157

O'Connor, B., Krieger, M., & Ahn, D. (2010, May). TweetMotif: Exploratory Search and Topic Summarization for Twitter. *Proceedings of the Fourth International AAAI Conference on Weblogs and Social Media*, 384-385.

Pan, S. J., Ni, X., Sun, J. T., Yang, Q., & Chen, Z. (2010, April). Cross-domain sentiment classification via spectral feature alignment. In *Proceedings of the 19th international conference on World wide web* (pp. 751-760). ACM. doi:10.1145/1772690.1772767

Rui, H., Liu, Y., & Whinston, A. (2013). Whose and what chatter matters? The effect of tweets on movie sales. *Decision Support Systems, 55*(4), 863–870. doi:10.1016/j.dss.2012.12.022

Song, G., Zhou, X., Wang, Y., & Xie, K. (2015). Influence maximization on large-scale mobile social network: A divide-and-conquer method. *IEEE Transactions on Parallel and Distributed Systems, 26*(5), 1379–1392. doi:10.1109/TPDS.2014.2320515

Tan, S., Li, Y., Sun, H., Guan, Z., Yan, X., Bu, J., & He, X. (2014). Interpreting the public sentiment variations on twitter. *IEEE Transactions on Knowledge and Data Engineering, 26*(5), 1158–1170. doi:10.1109/TKDE.2013.116

Taxidou, I., & Fischer, P. (2013). Realtime analysis of information diffusion in social media. *Proceedings of the VLDB Endowment, 6*(12), 1416–1421. doi:10.14778/2536274.2536328

Wang, F., Wang, H., & Xu, K. (2012). Diffusive logistic model towards predicting information diffusion in online social networks. *2012 32nd International Conference on Distributed Computing Systems Workshops*. IEEE. doi:10.1109/ICDCSW.2012.16

Wei, W., & Zou, L. (2016). LDA-TM: A two-step approach to twitter topic data clustering. *Proceedings of the 2016 IEEE International Conference on Cloud Computing and Big Data Analysis*, 342-347. doi:10.1109/ICCCBDA.2016.7529581

Wen, D., & Marshall, G. (2014, December). Automatic twitter topic summarization. In *Computational Science and Engineering (CSE), 2014 IEEE 17th International Conference on* (pp. 207-212). doi:10.1109/CSE.2014.69

KEY TERMS AND DEFINITIONS

Biased Sampling: Biased sampling is a technique in which the probability with which an item is selected to be a part of the sample set is not equal That is, the sampling strategy is biased towards items with certain desirable characteristics.

Influence Maximization Problem: Given an integer k and a network, a set of k users must be found such that the information flow in the network is maximized. This implies that the k users chosen are not only influential but also have minimal overlap in the set of users they influence.

Sequential Summarization: Sequential Summarization aims to generate a serial of chronologically related sub-summaries for a given topic while retaining the order of information presentation and each sub-summary attempts to concentrate on one theme or subtopic. The sequential summary, made up by the chronologically ordered sub-summaries, shall provide the entire development of the topic, or the full view of the topic.

Sub-Topic Detection: Each topic may contain several hidden latent topics which would be revealed only by a process termed Sub Topic Detection. This process contributes to the sequential nature of summarization approach produced in form of topic evolved sub summaries. This chapter also details about the advancements made to the existing sub topic detection models.

Tie Strength: Tie strength is defined as a (probably linear) combination of the amount of time, emotional intensity, the intimacy and the reciprocal services which characterize the tie. In the context of information diffusion, the stronger the tie between two users, the more likely information is to pass between them.

Topic Adaptive Sentiment Classification: Topic-adaptive sentiment classification model starts with a classifier built on common features and mixed labelled data from various topics. It later refines towards topic based text and non-text features. A combined and adaptive classifier finally performs the sentiment classification.

Trending Topic Analysis: Trending Topic Analysis system provides a deep analysis via topic adaptive sentiment classification and multi tweet sequential summarization, which aims to provide a serial of chronologically, ordered short sub-summaries for a trending topic in order to provide a complete story about the development of the topic while retaining the order of information presentation.

Twitter Trending Topics: Twitter trending topics are the sensational topics discussed or tweeted by more number of users at the moment. These hashtag driven topics help in capturing interesting news/updates about popular topics at a particular time. It is populated for each user based on his/her social network and location.

Chapter 6
Use of Social Network Analysis in Telecommunication Domain

Sushruta Mishra
KIIT University, India

Hrudaya Kumar Tripathy
KIIT University, India

Brojo Kishore Mishra
C. V. Raman College of Engineering, India

Monalisa Mishra
C. V. Raman College of Engineering, India

Bijayalaxmi Panda
BPUT Rourkela, India

ABSTRACT

Social network analysis (SNA) is the analysis of social communication through network and graph theory. In our chapter the application of SNA has been explored in telecommunication domain. Telecom data consist of Customer data and Call Detail Data (CDR). The proposed work, considers the attributes of call detail data and customer data as different relationship types to model our Multi-relational Telecommunication social network. Typical work on social network analysis includes the discovery of group of customers who shares similar properties. A new challenge is the mining of hidden communities on such heterogeneous social networks, to group the customers as churners and non-churners in Telecommunication social network. After the analysis of the available data we constructed a Weights Multi-relational Social Network, in which each relation carry a different weight, representing how close two customers are with one another. The centrality measures depict the intensity of the customer closeness, hence we can determine the customer who influence the other customer to churn.

DOI: 10.4018/978-1-5225-2805-0.ch006

INTRODUCTION

The process of defining social communication by the help of network and graph theory is known as Social Network Analysis (SNA).(Otte et al, 2002). The network structure is characterized in terms of actors, people or things associated by ties or links. Social network analysis is described by different social media networks, collaboration graphs, kinship. (Pinheiro, 2011; D'Andrea et al 2009). The representation of network is done through a diagram called sociograms where nodes are represented as points and links as lines. A social network can be established between person, groups or organizations. It indicates the ways in which they are connected through various social familiarities ranging from casual acquaintance to close familiar bonds (Hanneman and Riddle, 2005). Different scenarios can be modeled in social networks such as email traffic, disease transmission, criminal activity etc. The co-ordination and flow between people, groups, organizations, or other resources information sharing is analyzed by Social network analysis. People in the network represented as nodes and groups, while the links show relationships or flows between the nodes. A mathematical or graphical analysis of human relationship can be established by Social network analysis. This method is also used as Organizational Network Analysis by Management consultants for business clients. Social structure of the organization is described by groupings. As a whole the behavior of the network is explained by number, size, and connections between sub-groupings in a network. (Hanneman and Riddle, 2005). Some of the features of sub-group structure can define the behavior of the network by solving following questions. How fast will things move across the actors in the network? Will conflicts most likely involve multiple groups, or two factions? To what extent do the sub-groups and social structures overlap one another? The basic approaches for collecting data are questionnaires, interviews, observations, and some other secondary sources. (Breiger 2004).

A sample example of SNA is represented in Figure 1. Social network research understands individuals within their social context, acknowledging the influence of relationships with others on one's behavior. Hence, social networks can promote innovation processes and expand opportunities for learning. Despite the consensus regarding the value of social network approaches, there is a lack of empirical investigations in innovation and futures studies that use Social Network Analysis (SNA). In most cases, the scientific literature uses the concept of social networks metaphorically, ignoring the chances presented by SNA methods. At the same time, conventional empirical research in innovation and futures studies often disregards relational information. Hence, analyses of statistical data on structural and individual levels are treated as separately. Activities that are expected to have impacts on

Figure 1. Illustration of a social network diagram

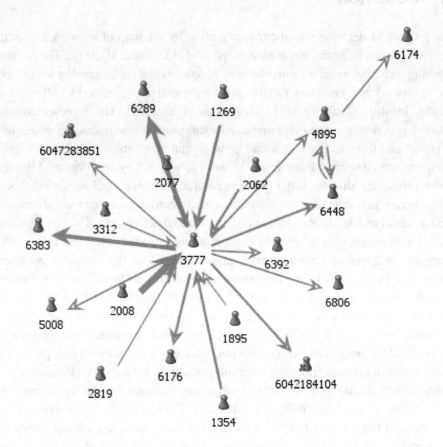

future developments are usually modeled as isolated individual or group behavior, on the one hand, or as the characteristics of structural issues, on the other hand. SNA provides us with empirical tools that capture the social context and help to better understand how innovations are implemented and diffused and why social change takes place. Network approaches explicitly challenge the difference between deduction and induction and highlight the relevance of relationships. Individuals both shape and are shaped by the social context in which they interact. By applying techniques of SNA, actor-centered and structuralist reductions are avoided. Instead, SNA emphasizes the mutual influence of structure and social connections. In order to better understand and model developments in innovation and futures research, relational data inherent to the social network perspective is needed.

Evolution of Social Network Analysis

A summary of the development of social network analysis has been mentioned in the book by Linton Freeman. (Freeman and Linton 2006). In the late 1800s, Tonnies argued that social groups can exist as personal and direct social ties that either link individuals who share values and belief or impersonal, formal, and instrumental social links. Durkheim gave a non-individualistic explanation of social facts arguing that social phenomena arise when interacting individuals constitute a reality that can no longer be accounted for in terms of the properties of individual actors. In the 1930s, J.L. Moreno pioneered the systematic recording and analysis of social interaction in small groups, especially classrooms and work groups (sociometry), while a Harvard group led by W. Lloyd Warner and Elton Mayo explored interpersonal relations at work. In 1940, A.R. Radcliffe-Brown's presidential address to British anthropologists urged the systematic study of networks. However, it took about 15 years before this call was followed-up systematically.Social network analysis developed with the kinship studies of Elizabeth Bott in England in the 1950s and the urbanization studies of the University of Manchester group of anthropologists investigating community networks in southern Africa, India and the United Kingdom.In the 1960s-1970s, a growing number of scholars worked to combine the different tracks and traditions. One group was centered around Harrison White and his students at the Harvard University Department of Social Relations. Also independently active in the Harvard Social Relations department at the time were Charles Tilly, who focused on networks in political and community sociology and social movements, and Stanley Milgram, who developed the "six degrees of separation" thesis.(Wellman, n.d.) Significant independent work was also done by scholars of University of California interested in mathematical applications, centered around Linton Freeman. In terms of theory, it critiqued methodological individualism and group-based analyses, arguing that seeing the world as social networks offered more analytic leverage. (Granovetter, 2007).

Social Network Analysis Process

The SNA process involves:

- Gathering information regarding relationships in a specified group or network of people.
- Defining the target group of network.
- Data collection about specific needs and problems can be done by interview of managers.
- Detecting and explaining scope and aim of analysis.
- Identifying the required level of reporting.

- Formation of questions and solutions.
- Development of questionnaire and survey method.
- Detection of network by interviewing personnel.
- Implementing and constructing actions to bring about.
- Mapping the network manually or by using software tools designed tools for the specific purposes.
- Creating a base for the analysis of data from the survey resources.
- Using this base for increasing social connections and information flows within the group or network.
- For the required changes actions are to be designed and implemented.
- Mapping the network within specific time period.

SNA Performance Measures

Connections

- **Homophily:** The ties between similar and dissimilar actors. Similar actors mean equality in gender, age, occupation, educational achievement, status, values or any other common characteristic (Pherson, 2001).
- **Multiplexity:** The number of content-forms contained in a tie (Podolny and Barron, 1997) For example, two people who are friends and also work together would have a multiplexity of 2 (Kilduff and Tsai, 2003). Multiplexity has been associated with relationship strength.
- **Mutuality/Reciprocity:** The level of actor's friendship or other communication. (Kadushin 2012).
- **Network Closure:** Forthe completeness of relational structure an individual's assumption of network closure (i.e. that their friends are also friends) is called transitivity. (Flnynn, 2010).
- **Propinquity:** To have more ties with others the tendency of actors is that they are geographically close to others. (Kadushin, 2012).

Distributions

- **Bridge:** An actor whose connection is weak fills a structural hole, providing the only link between two individuals or groups. It also includes the shortest route when a longer one is unfeasible due to a high risk of message distortion or delivery failure. (Granovetter, 1973).
- **Centrality:** Centrality refers to a group of metrics that aim to quantify the "importance" or "influence" (in a variety of senses) of a particular node (or group) within a network. (Hansen, et al, 2010; Liu et al, 2011; Hanneman

et al 2011, Tsyetovat 2011). Examples of common methods of measuring "centrality" include betweenness centrality, (Tsyetovat et al 2011). closeness centrality, eigenvector centrality, alpha centrality, and degree centrality. (Opsahl 2010).

- **Density:** The ratio of direct link in a network related to the total number possible. (Department of Army n.d.; Xu et al, 2010).
- **Distance:** For connecting two particular actors the minimum link is known as distance.
- **Structural Holes:** The absence of links among two parts of a network. Defining and exploring a structural hole can initiate entrepreneur a competitive advantage. This concept was developed by sociologist Ronald Burt, and is sometimes referred to as an alternate conception of social capital.
- **Tie Strength:** Explained by the association of time, emotional factor, depth of closeness and mutuality. (Department of Army, n.d.). Strong ties are associated with homophily, propinquity and transitivity, while weak ties are associated with bridges.

Segmentation

- **Cliques:** Groups are defined as 'cliques' if each individual is directly associated to every other individual, 'social circles' if there is less stringency of direct contact, which is imprecise, or as structurally cohesive blocks if precision is wanted.(Moody-White, 2003).
- **Clustering Coefficient:** A measure of the likelihood that two associates of a node are associates. A higher clustering coefficient indicates a higher 'cliquishness'. (Hanneman et al, 2011).
- **Cohesion:** The degree to which people are linked directly to each other by cohesive bonds. Structural cohesion refers to the minimum number of members who, if removed from a group, would disconnect the group. (Pattillo, 2011; Liben-Nowell et al, 2003).

Features of Social Network Analysis

Some important features of social networks are size, density, degree, reachability, distance, diameter, geodesic distance. Some other complex properties that may be used in social network analysis are described as follows (Hanneman and Riddle, 2005).

Maximum Flow

The concepts of connectivity of two actors, asks the number of actors in the surroundings of a resource indicates the ways to a target. If I want to send a message to you, and another person to whom I can send the same for retransmission, there are several ways how the message will reach the destination. Similarly, more people to whom I can send my message, each of them has one or more ways of resending my message to you, and then my association will be strong. This "flow" concept suggests that my tie is not stronger than the weakest link in the chain of ties, where weakness means a lack of alternatives.

Hubbell and Katz Cohesion

The maximum flow concept is targeted on the duplication of links between pairs of actors - kind of a "strength of the weakest link" parameter. Another approach, we need to consider the strength of all ties as predicting the link. If we are willing to know how much two actors may interact with one another, or share some common features, the complete range of their links should probably be considered. Although we need to involve every link between two actors, it may not create a great deal of sense to consider a path of length 10 as important as a path of length 1. The Hubbell and Katz methodology count the total links among actors, both sending and receiving links for directed data. Each link, however, is associated with a weight, according to its length.

Taylor's Influence

The Hubbell and Katz approach may create more sense while implemented on symmetric data; due to less focus on the directions of links. If we have special interest on the influence of one actor on another on a directed graph, the Taylor approach provides an interesting measure. This measure, uses all links, and implements a weaker approach. Rather than standardizing on the whole resulting matrix, however, a different approach is adopted. The column marginals for each actor are subtracted from the row marginal, and the result is then normalized. Converted into English, we look at the balance among each individual's sending links and their receiving links. Positive values then reflect a preponderance of sending over receiving to the other actor of the pair -or a balance of influence between the two.

Centrality and Power

All sociologists state that power is a basic feature of social structures. There are very few agreements regarding the concept of power, and the method which explain and analyze its causes and consequences. Table I describe some of the important features that social network analysis has developed to know what is power, and the closely related concept of centrality.

Benefits of Social Networking Analysis

After social relationships and knowledge flows become visible, they can be evaluated, compared and measured. Results of the SNA can then be applied by individuals, departments or organizations to:

- Identify who the persons who are playing central roles (thought leaders, knowledge brokers, information managers, etc.);
- Identify bottlenecks and those who are isolated;
- Spot opportunities for improving knowledge flows;
- Target those areas where better knowledge sharing will have the most impact;
- Raise awareness of the significance of informal networks.

ANALYSIS OF SOCIAL NETWORK IN TELECOM SECTOR

Social Network Analysis (SNA) defines a set of research techniques to identify a group of people sharing common system configuration based on the basis of their relationship with actors. This approach has now become a powerful tool to study on networks in various areas like Banking, Telecommunication, Web applications, Physics and Social Science. Social network analysis (SNA) is the methodical analysis of social networks. Social network analysis views social relationships in terms of network theory, consisting of *nodes* (representing individual actors within the network) and *ties* (which represent relationships between the individuals). These networks are often depicted in a social network diagram, where nodes are represented as points and ties are represented as lines.

Relationships in a network can either be directional or nondirectional. In a directional relationship, one person is the initiator (or source of the relationship) while the other is the receiver (or destination of the relationship). For example, in the diagram above, node 1269 is the source while node 3777 is the destination. Relationships can also be described as dichotomous or valued. A dichotomous relationship is one where the only information that exists is whether or not a relationship exists between two people, where as in a valued relationship, a weight indicating the strength of the relationship is also available. Analyzing huge amount of data manually in telecom industries becomes very difficult. Hence the SNA procedures were applied for Churn Prediction in Telecom data. The fundamentals of social network analysis include building of a multi-relational telecom social network and defining the core metrics for identification of churners in telecom social network. In multi relational social network different relations are extracted that exist in the network. Every relationship can be graphed using customers' data and the call details of telecommunication [24]. These companies handle huge amount of data including customer data, network data and call detail data. Call detail data gives information about the calls that traverse through the telecommunication networks, network data, which describes the state of the hardware and software components in the network, and customer data, which describes the telecommunication customers. Manual handling of such huge amount of data is too difficult but not impossible. The proposed work describes about the main applications of data mining in telecommunication environment: churn management by using Multi-relational Social Network.

In telecommunication social networks, two customers having social relationships are linked to each other. The connection is made on the basis of call frequency, voice call duration etc. exchanged during a certain time interval. Establishment of relationships involves different types of association and communication which makes these networks more complex. To design a Multi-Relational Telecommunication Social Network, attributes of call detail data and customer data are required as different relationship types. A Weights Multi-Relational Social Network was made after proper analysis of data where each relation carried a different weight, indicating the closeness between two customers.

Previously, the churn was considered as an issue in most of the industrial sectors. It refers to the rate of loss of customers from a company's customer's base in general. Much attention is given to churn as churning customers' yields in revenue loss. Churn is considered as a major problem in business areas like telecom and broadcast services and also it is regarded as a critical issue other businesses like online games, online social networks and discussion sites. It is better for the companies to identify the churn in its primary stages because it is easier and cheaper to retain a customer than to win him. If the risk could be estimated early, then different marketing departments can provide the customers with proper incentives preventing them from leaving. Indirectly the churn refers to the full or partial lacuna in a customer. When a subscriber moves from one carrier to another, it is said to have churned. (Hwang et al, n.d.) Churn rate is ratio of the total gross number of subscribers leaving the service in a period and the average total customers in the period. In the telecom company, the churn rate is the degree of threat and unpredictability in the marketplace and will be cited in the company's yearly report. The major problem in management is to know who are the subscribers and their reasons for leaving the company. Therefore, it becomes more difficult to forecast which customers would leave the company, and frame cost effective incentives to satisfy the likely churners to stay back. Mostly, the telecommunication social network mining methods acknowledge only homogeneous social Networks. In real sense, almost all the social networks posses' different kinds of relationships among customers. Deriving the different relations present in the network is a problem in Multi-relational Social Network. Each of the relation can be represented using graph. Instead of studying about other relations, it is better to focus on a relation whose information is required. Hence, for better results positive social relations must be taken into account for churn prediction in telecommunication networks.

Although these networks give many benefits to users by facilitating communication between them and the exchange of any kind of information in real time, this social networks represents a serious threat to the privacy rights and their data protection or to third parts related to them (family, friends, etc.) because the data they dump on the social networks (contact information, photographs, videos, etc.) are accessible in a public and global way. Likewise, there are many marketing firms that use the data published on social networks to make surveys and statistics about various products. In some cases, even these companies have nothing to do with social networks are allowed to send questionnaires to users for commercial use. The vast amount of information related to a user in the social network represents a risk to his safety and privacy if we consider the possible use of the data by unauthorized third parts to misappropriate our identity. Therefore, it is necessary to create globally applicable rules able to respond to global problems which due to its nature usually pose this kind of networks.

Social Media Influence on the Telecom Industry

1. Real-Time Monitoring of Social Web

Assume, if you are using a T-Mobile and AT&T decided to project a new data plan just few minutes before, then the fastest way to track about that is through the social media. Social media *monitoring* is therefore a necessary tool to gather information about your brands, competitors' strategies, and product advertisements. In this way, you will be able to track your competitors' actions in real-time and react accordingly giving a tough competition.

2. Identifying and Focusing on Tailored Audiences

Social media never allows any customer to get diverted towards its competitor. It always keeps updated information about every customer. Telecom companies know how to involve their customers with them in a timely manner and to keep them away from their competitors. With the help of company's social media, the telecom brands can target their influential customers and attract them by providing special incentives. After pervasive filtering, social media allows telecom companies to develop a wide range of campaigns designed to target a large scope of people while covering an entire community.

3. Building a Strategy for Communication That Reflects

Customers are required to be updated periodically about new proposals, tenders and special events. Keeping interaction with the customers on social media, *the* companies can very well understand their needs and to what they are looking for. They can be attended faster than any other type of traditional communication like phone, mail or website. If the competitors will acknowledge the social media for promoting themselves openly, then they might catch this opportunity to interact with them on a personal basis. The social media always allows the telecom brands to interact in a bidirectional way. Instead of just forecasting the messages, telecom brands can contact with their audience personally to identify their problems which actually play a vital role in retaining the customers. In contrary to address the audience just to seek attention, telecom brands can listen to their problems minutely and build a healthy relationship with them.

4. Reforming Interactions and Assuring Correct Information

Telecom companies are frequently engaged with numerous interactions with the customers over a time period. One of the tools of social media management has a built-in CRM system which helps to track the previous conversations providing a detailed overview. This combination reforms future interactions and helps to track the good profile customers to interact with them on a personal basis. Further, the social media teams should immediately comply suitable information to the customers by giving access with different links or websites. Hence, this would help in providing an up-to-date method to yield important information.

5. Customer Care: A Tweet Away

Nowadays the people are not waiting or standing in a queue at their local telecom outlets for any support and service. If any customer has a simple query, then he or she can simply tweet to their service provider and can quickly seek help within a short time. It completely depends upon the telecom companies to catch this opportunity and immediately acknowledge with adequate information. The telecom outlets can gain similar experience by making personal interactions with the customers and satisfying them by providing correct information upon inquiry.

6. Telecom Industries Benefitting From Social Analytics

Social analytics support companies in analyzing their brand values among the customers. This type of analysis would help in businesses by determining the areas of customer satisfaction or customer obligation for any product if they have. It also gives feedback about the advertisements done for marketing thus helping the companies to know their users requirement. In this paper, the social media is considered as a source for data analytics in the telecom sector. One of the finest ways to develop a healthy relationship with the Telecom industry is the social media which gets continually involved in price conflicts. If we are provided with a medium that would help to communicate with the consumers directly, then it would help in supporting them ceaselessly through online channels. But sorrowfully this is not the case. The telecom industries in some aspects could not even meet the basic requirements of customers; they only concentrate on the strategies for their brand popularity. A study has been done about the leading players like Bharti Airtel, Reliance Communication, Idea Cellular, Vodafone India, Tata Docomo, Uninor, Aircel, MTS and Loop, their presence on Social Media and individual support services is compared.

7. The Kind of Queries Brands Get

The customers have a lot of questions and grievances about the services and products of different telecom brands. Generally their questions include tariff plans and add-on services. The grievances of the customers are basically on network and billing issues. The Airtel receives the highest number of queries from the customers on its Twitter and Facebook accounts that is around 40 a day. The other brands does not get so many complaints in a day and if they do, the customers are directed to a toll free number, email address or a website. Even if the simple queries are diverted, this can easily be handled by the representatives. When a user wants to inquire about the latest offers, the Docomo provides a web link instead of looking into the link themselves and providing a solution.

8. How Often They Respond and Their Response Time

Most brands do not respond on Facebook and only some respond on Twitter. Aircel and MTS have even closed their page for user posting. The comments section of every brand on my list is brimming with conversation that is damaging the brand reputation and the brands simply do not care. A huge list of complaints against Idea Celullar has gone unanswered on Facebook. The response time of the brands on Facebook is an average of 2 days. While Airtel is the fastest at 4 hours, Uninor takes up to 3 days. This is a lot of time for a medium like Social Media where response time is one of the most important metrics to measure success. A very casual attitude comes across among all telecom brands while analyzing their customer support strategy. On Twitter, again Airtel responds the fastest within an average time of 8 hours while Uninor takes over 2 days.

SOCIAL NETWORK ANALYSIS IN CHURN PREDICTION OF TELECOM DATA

The proposed work, considers the attributes of call detail data and customer data as different relationship types to model our Multi-relational Telecommunication social network. After the analysis of the available data Weights Multi-relational Social Network was constructed, in which each relation carries a different weight, representing how close two customers are with one another. Typical work on social network analysis includes the discovery of group of customers who shares similar properties. This is known as community mining. Most algorithms for community mining assume that there is only one social network, representing a relatively homogenous relationship. In reality there exist multiple, heterogeneous social networks, representing various relationships. A new challenge is the mining of hidden communities on such heterogeneous social networks, to group the customers as churners and non-churners in Telecommunication social network.

Methodology

Telecommunication social networks are social networks where two customers are considered as connected if they have social relationships. The social relationship is based on the duration of voice calls; call frequency and age that are exchanged during a certain period. These networks are more complex as their relationships involve different types of collaboration or interaction. Thus Telecommunication Social Networks can be a kind of Multi-Relational social Networks. The attributes of call detail data and customer data are considered as different relationship types to model Multi-relational Telecommunication social network. After the analysis of the available data Weighted Multi-relational Social Network, has been constructed, in which each relation caries a different weight, representing how close two customers are with one another.

Data Analysis

Telecom data consist of Customer data and Call Detail Data (CDR). Customer data consist of attributes like customer name, Address, age, Customer ID, sex, and Call Details Records (CDR), is a data record produced by a telephone exchange, it contains the fields such as Calling number, Called number, Call type (Outgoing / Incoming),Service used (Voice/SMS/Etc.),Call start time, Call end time, Duration, Cell ID, Call sequence Number, Switch number or ID. The 32,000 records are considered while analysis and contains detailed information about voice calls, SMS, value added calls of users. During pre-processing we excluded the service numbers so that number of nodes in Telecom Social Networks can be reduced. The attributes that are considered while construction of multi-relational telecom Social Networks are customer name, age from customer data and calling number, called number, duration from CDR.

Representing Social Network Data

Conventional data consist of rectangular array of measurements. The rows of arrays are the cases, subjects, or observations. The columns consist of scores (quantitative or quality) on attributes, variables, or measures. Social network data consist of a square array of measurements. The rows of array are the cases, subjects, or observations. The column of the array is the same set of cases, subjects, or observations. Each cell of the array describes the relationship between actors. The most common method of representing the social network data is by using matrices. The common form of matrix in social network analysis is a square matrix. The most common matrix is binary in which cells of a matrix is filled with either 0 or 1. The relationship used here is friendship, that is if the two customer is connected then the cell is filled with 1, otherwise it is filled with 0.This method of representing the social data is called adjacency matrix. The adjacency matrix is extremely useful to conduct various formal analysis of network, in particular it tells us how many paths of length 1 there are from each actor to each other actor. In general, it can be shown that the powers of the adjacency matrix give the number of walks of length n from each actor to each other actor.

Construction of Weighted Multi-Relational Telecom Social Network Model

The term network has different meaning in different disciplines. In the data mining disciplines social network is defined as a set of actors (or agents, or nodes, or points, or vertices) and one or more relationships (or links, or edges, or ties) between pairs of actors. Network that represent a single type of relation among the actors are called simplex, while those that represent more than one kind of relation are called multiplex. Multiplex relations are analyzed using different networks, one for each relation type. Each tie or relation may be directed, or undirected that represents co-occurrence, co-presence, or a bonded-tie between the pair of actors. Directed ties are represented with arrows, and bonded tie relations are represented with line segments. Directed ties may be reciprocated (A links to B and B links to A) such ties can be represented with a double-headed arrow. The ties may have different values, that is binary values representing presence or absence of a tie, signed values representing a negative tie, a positive tie, or no tie, ordinal values representing whether the tie is strongest, next strongest, and numerically valued measured on an interval or ratio scale. The Multi-Relational Social Network constructed for Telecom data by

Figure 2. Multi-relational telecom social network

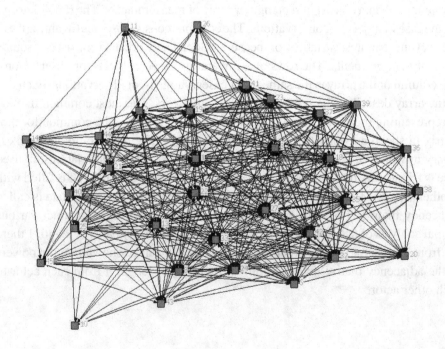

considering the multiple relations as friendship, age and frequency of call, volume of call as ties between the customers is given below Figure 2.

Centrality Measures

The centrality of a node in a network is a measure of its structural importance that is, how important a person is within a social network. There are three approaches to calculate the centrality of a node: based on degree, on closeness, and on betweenness. Degree approaches are based on the idea that having more ties means being more important. Finally, when using betweenness approaches, it is being in between many other actors what makes an actor central. These three approaches describe the locations of nodes in terms of how close they are to the "centre" of the action in a network. A central actor, presumably, has a stronger influence on other network members (i.e. central positions tend to be powerful positions). Thus, measures of centrality are often interpreted as measures of power. Actors who have many ties with other actors may be in an advantageous position. Having many ties may mean having alternative ways of satisfying needs, it may mean having access to more resources, and it may also mean acting frequently as a third-party or deal maker in exchanges among others. With directed data, however, it is important to distinguish between in-degree centrality and out-degree centrality. That is, many other actors seek to direct ties towards them, and this may be an indicator of importance. Actors with unusually high out-degree may be able to influence many others, or make many others aware of their views. Thus, actors with high out-degree centrality are often called influential actors. Closeness centrality using geodesic distance is the reciprocal of the sum of geodesic distances to all other vertices in the graph. These scores can be normalized dividing by the maximum value. Another way of thinking about how close an actor A is to all others is to calculate the proportion of other actors that A can reach in one step, two steps, three steps, etc. (or, alternatively, the proportion of nodes that reach A in n steps).

We calculated a single index for each node by summing up the proportion of other nodes reached (for the first time) at a given distance, appropriately weighted (e.g. 1 for nodes at distance 1, ½ for nodes at distance 2…). These scores can be then normalized dividing by the maximum value, if this is considered appropriate. The idea behind between's centrality is that the customer who is between the two customers is considered as powerful customer as he is able to control the flow of information, resources, between them. Nodes with high betweenness are often called key- players. Betweenness centrality using only shortest paths is the nodes that occur on many shortest paths between other nodes have higher betweenness than those that do not. The betweenness of a node A is the fraction of all the possible shortest paths between any two nodes in the network (excluding A) that pass through A.

Table 1. Centrality metrics for telecom social network

Id	Degree Centrality	Betweenness Centrality	Closeness Centrality	Harmonic Closeness	Total Centrality	Endogenous	Exogenous
1	31	9.553	31.000	31.000	62.000	31.000	31.000
2	27	4.745	35.000	29.000	49.000	24.000	25.000
3	28	4.644	34.000	29.500	49.000	23.000	26.000
6	25	2.328	37.000	28.000	47.000	23.000	24.000
8	26	2.515	36.000	28.500	45.000	22.000	23.000
10	9	0.000	53.000	20.000	11.000	9.000	2.000
11	12	0.259	50.000	21.000	15.000	8.000	7.0000
14	19	1.554	43.000	25.000	50.000	22.000	28.000
19	28	5.045	34.000	29.500	30.000	11.000	19.000
20	19	0.520	43.000	25.000	47.000	24.000	23.000
21	25	3.090	37.000	28.000	48.000	23.000	25.000
22	30	7.378	32.000	30.500	29.000	14.000	15.000
23	28	4.764	34.000	29.500	38.000	25.000	13.000
24	29	5.895	33.000	30.000	58.000	28.000	30.000
26	14	0.270	48.000	22.500	47.000	23.000	24.000
27	29	6.438	33.000	30.000	46.000	18.000	28.000
32	26	2.578	36.000	28.500	36.000	19.000	17.000
33	29	5.895	33.000	30.000	21.000	14.000	7.000
36	21	0.567	41.000	26.000	50.000	21.000	29.000
37	26	2.903	36.000	28.500	48.000	22.000	26.000
38	20	0.354	42.000	25.500	54.000	25.000	29.000
39	25	3.143	37.000	28.000	44.000	18.000	26.000
41	26	3.824	36.000	28.500	33.000	16.000	17.000
43	20	1.940	42.000	25.500	46.0000	23.000	23.000
44	27	6.891	35.000	29.000	37.000	19.000	18.000
45	16	0.442	46.000	23.500	34.000	25.000	9.000

Centrality measures for the nodes are given in Table 1. The structural property of the Telecom Social Network of size 32000 nodes has been realized in the research work. For illustration purpose 26 nodes has taken. Figure 3 shows distribution of degree centrality, betweenness centrality, closeness centrality, harmonic centrality and total centrality of the nodes. It has the values range between 9-31, 0.000-9.553.,

Figure 3. Centrality distribution

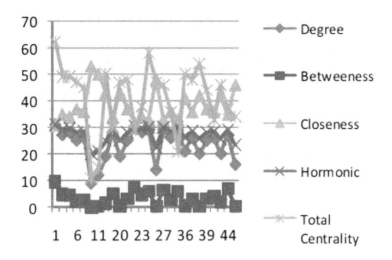

31.000 – 53.000, 20.000-31.000 and 11.000-62.000 respectively. Endogenous refers to out-degree and exogenous refers to in-degree of the nodes. Hence showing they are closely connected to each other. These measures show the intensity of the influence of the customer to churn other customers in the network. By this measures we can found out the more influenced customers in the network and by providing the more services for those customers, we can retain them.

SOCIAL NETWORK ANALYSIS IN SMS PATTERN BEHAVIOR OF CUSTOMERS

In the recent years, Short Message Service (SMS) has emerged as one of the very popular means of communications. The trends indicate that the volume of SMS traffic is further expected to grow exponentially in the next few years. However, in spite of SMS volume increasing manifold, the operators' margins have not increased significantly, probably due to a mismatch between carrier competition and consumer expectation. The highly competitive mobile telecom market drives the service providers to continually rethink, and work out schemes that not only offer better incentives to their customers, but also maximize the revenue generated. This invokes a need of thorough analysis of the SMS behavior of the users, and realizes recommendations to increase both utilization of network resource as well as revenue of the operators.In this section, we investigate how the social interaction of the customers can be utilized to achieve this goal. An SMS network could be

Table 2. Some statistics of the CDR data, and TTSL telecom network

MSCs	100
A2P SMSCs	2
P2P SMSCs	3
STPs	4
ITPs	4
Number of Cells	8000
Average SMS Volume	88 million/day
Voice/SMS Traffic	2
Buffer Length at SMSC	0.6 million
Channels at SMSC	30 (E1 TDD Link)
Message Delivery Attempts (MDAs)	4000/sec

visualized as an overlay of social network on the underlying telecommunication infrastructure. The degree of connectivity of users, base stations, mobile switching center (MSC) with other users, base stations and mobile switching center (MSC) is a reflection of social behavior. Hence, to better understand the traffic or rather network usage patterns, it is important to analyze this abstract social network. In this paper, we represent these social interactions in form of an SMS graph (graphs induced by people exchanging messages). Towards this, we analyze Call Detail Records (CDR), generated at the Short Message Service Center (SMSC), of SMS transactions from one of the largest telecom operators in India. To protect users' privacy the telecom operator had anonymized the data. Some information available in the CDR is originating User ID (an anonymous identification for a user), originating MSC, destination User ID, time of sending and delivering the message, and status of delivery. Some of the data statistics are listed in Table 2.

System Architecture

In this section, we briefly describe the representative cellular system architecture followed by the SMS call flow. A simplified architecture of a cellular system has been depicted in Figure 4. The concerned telecom operator's network consists of 100 Mobile Switching Centers (MSC) throughout the country.Each of these MSCs is connected to the two Signal Transfer Points (STPs). The STPs are connected to Internet Transfer Points (ITP) in a mesh topology by SS-7 links. The total traffic is equally divided between the two ITPs. The function of ITPs is to equally divide the incoming traffic onto outgoing links which gets connected to the SMSC. There are total five SMSCs in this network, however, only three are used for Person to Person (P2P) traffic, and the rest two are used for Application to Person (A2P) traffic. The two ITPs routes the incoming P2P traffic to the three P2P SMSCs in a Round Robin fashion. SMSC is the most important element in the SMS network; it operates on a store and forward mechanism, and is solely responsible for delivering SMS messages. When a user sends an SMS, it first goes to the base-station in the user's cell, and from there is forwarded to the MSC. The MSC forward messages as andwhen they arrive, and may queue them for systematic forwarding, however no processing is done at MSC. From MSC, the SMS reaches the SMSC, via STP-ITP mesh network. As an SMS arrives at the SMSC, it goes to the end of the arrival queue, and a Call Detail Record (CDR) is generated. While serving a particular SMS, the SMSC queries the HLR to locate the destination MSC and then delivers the messagedirectly to the destination MSC. After this, it is the MSC's responsibility to deliver the message to the mobile station. After success delivery, another CDR is generated at the SMSC.If the HLR/VLR is not able to locate the mobile station then the SMS is queued in waiting. When the mobile comes online, this information is updated in HLR/VLR which then sends this information to SMSC, which in turn tries to deliver the SMS. Such pending SMSs will be queued for a maximum duration of one day, and then deleted.

Figure 4. Simplified architecture of the discussed SMS cellular network

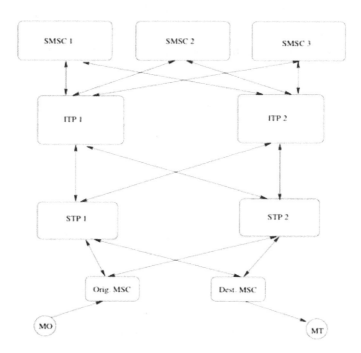

Figure 5. Visualization of social interaction in SMS transactions

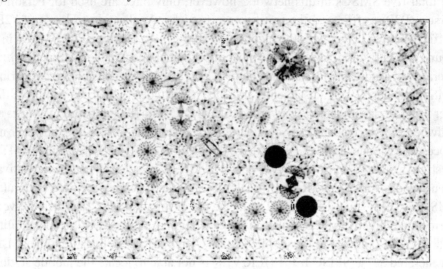

SMS Social Graph

Using the CDR data, we have generated an SMS Social Graph for visualization of various clusters and groups. This sample SMS Graph, depicted in Figure 5, highlights many small components. This graph has been generated using data of around 16 hours of Monday. In order to capture the cluster formation, we created a base-user-pool with 10,000 users, randomly picked from the entire user-set, and then plotted the graph by taking only those transactions into account, in which atleast one of the users fell in the base-user-pool. In the graph, red edges represent lost messages. Such data can be used for network planning. For example, if many red edges correspond to SMS between a certain pair of MSCs, this pair can be investigated for performance bottlenecks. Furthermore, this graph may also be used to identify a large group of users, which can be used for tariff planning.

EMPIRICAL ANALYSIS OF SMS GRAPHS

In this section, we analyze various structural properties of the SMS graphs.

Degree Distribution

The degree of a node in a graph is the number of connections or edges the node has to other nodes. The degree distribution P(d) of a graph is defined to be the fraction of

Figure 6. The message in-degree distribution

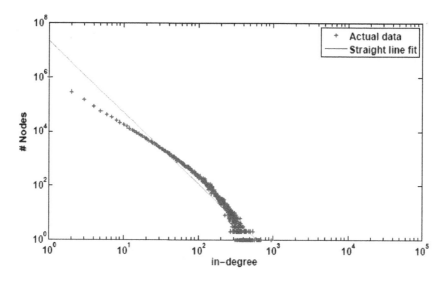

Figure 7. The edges in-degree distribution

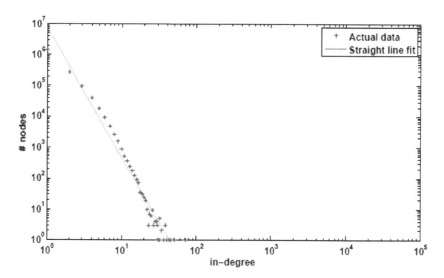

Figure 8. The message out-degree distribution

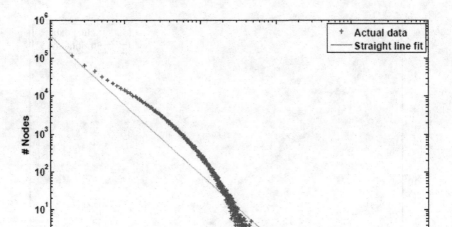

nodes in the network with degree d. Thus if there are total n nodes in graph, and nd of them have degree d, then P(d) = nd=n. degree associated with the total number of incoming or outgoing messages, which we call the message degree. In Figure 6 and Figure 7, we report the behavior of the indegree distributions for message in-degree, and edge in-degree respectively. All graphs are plotted in log-log scale with the degree on the X-axis, and the number of nodes/users on the Y-axis. The distribution in the figures demonstrates power law behavior with exponents 3.02 and 4.22 for message, and edge in-degree respectively. Similarly, out-degree distributions are depicted in Figure 8 and Figure 9, for message and edge out-degree respectively. The power law exponents for the two graphs are 1.55 and 1.03. Note that there are a significant number of nodes having a very high out-degree. The users having very high values of out-degrees in terms of edges can be considered as spammers/outliers.

Figure 9. The edges out-degree distribution

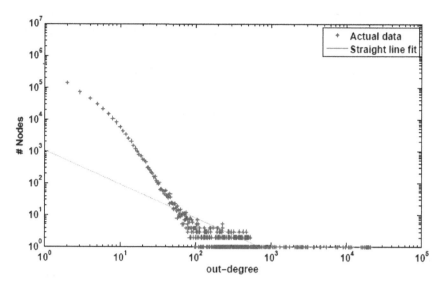

Clusters and Connected Components

Telecom service providers may use the information on clusters or connected components, including strongly connected components and cliques, to identify various user groups within an SMS graph/network. The general observation is that the number of components of smaller size is larger. From the figure, and data in Table 2, following important observations can be made:

- 70% of the components are that of size two, which means that maximum user communication takes place in isolated pairs.
- The second important observation is that the number of users who communicate in isolated pairs is nearly equal to the number of users in the largest connected component, which may be worthy of further investigation.

Table 3. Distribution of connected components

Total number of components	213042
Number of components of size 2	150267
Size of the largest component	472838
Value of power-law exponent	1.51

Table 4. Cliques data

Clique size	Number of cliques
3	23602
4	1116
5	65
6	3

Cliques

A clique, in an undirected graph, is defined as a sub-graph in which there exists an edge between every pair of nodes. From our analysis, relevant data is provided in the Table 3. In our analysis, no clique of size greater than 6 was observed. Furthermore, the observation made after the removal of outliers was almost the same. There was slight decrease in the number of cliques of size 3 (difference of less than 30). The number of cliques of size 4, 5, 6, and 7 were found to be exactly same, thus it indicates that the spammers do not have a significant impact on the distribution of cliques.

CONCLUSION

In reality the social networks are heterogeneous in nature, the accuracy of the churning model can be increased by considering the multiple relationship between the customer while construction of the telecom social network. In this work, we use attributes of call detail data and customer data as different relationship types to model our Multi-relational Telecommunication social network. After the analysis of the available data we constructed a Weights Multi-relational Social Network, in which each relation carry a different weight, representing how close two customers are with one another. The centrality measures depicts the intensity of the customer closeness, hence we can found the customer who influence the other customer to churn.Our second study comprises analysis of various structural properties of the SMS graph, including the in-degree distribution, out degree distribution, connected components and cliques. From the study on connected components, we show that almost 70% of the components are of size two, i.e., maximum user communication takes place in isolated pairs. One of the possible uses of the degree distribution is to develop a traffic plan which benefits the users as well as the service providers. Information Dissemination is another possible application of connected and strongly connected components. In a commercial network, the service providers would like to exploit the social networking aspects, and try to achieve maximum spread of information from minimum resources using underlying social dynamics.

REFERENCES

Breiger. (2004). *The Analysis of Social Networks*. Sage Publications Ltd.

D'Andrea, A. (2009). An Overview of Methods for Virtual Social Network Analysis. In *Computational Social Network Analysis: Trends, Tools and Research Advances* (p. 8). Springer.

Department of the Army. (n.d.). Social Network Analysis. *Field Manual 3-24: Counterinsurgency (PDF). Headquarters*, (pp. B–11 – B–12). Author.

Flynn, , Reagans, R. E., & Guillory, L. (2010). Do you two know each other? Transitivity, homophily, and the need for (network) closure. *Journal of Personality and Social Psychology*, *99*(5), 855–869. doi:10.1037/a0020961 PMID:20954787

Freeman & Linton. (2006). *The Development of Social Network Analysis Vancouver*. Empirical Press.

Granovetter, M. (2007). Introduction for the French Reader. *Sociologica*, *2*, 1–8.

Granovetter. (1973). The strength of weak ties. *American Journal of Sociology, 78*, 1360–1380.

Hanneman, . (2011). *Concepts and Measures for Basic Network Analysis. In The Sage Handbook of Social Network Analysis* (pp. 364–367). SAGE.

Hanneman, . (2011). *Concepts and Measures for Basic Network Analysis. In The Sage Handbook of Social Network Analysis* (pp. 346–347). SAGE.

Hanneman, A., & Riddle, M. (2005). *Introduction to social network methods*. Online at http://www.faculty.ucr.edu/ hanneman/nettext/

Hansen, D. (2010). *Analyzing Social Media Networks with NodeXL*. Morgan Kaufmann.

Hwang. (n.d.). *An ltv model and customer segmentation based on customer value: a case*. Academic Press.

Kadushin. (2012). *Understanding social networks: Theories, concepts, and findings*. Oxford, UK: Oxford University Press.

Kilduff & Tsai. (2003). *Social networks and organisations*. Sage Publications.

Liben-Nowell & Kleinberg. (2003). The Link Prediction problem for social networks. Proceedings of the Twelfth International Conference on Information and Knowledge Management, 556-559.

Liu, B. (2011). *Web Data Mining: Exploring Hyperlinks, Contents, and Usage Data.* Springer. doi:10.1007/978-3-642-19460-3

Moody, , & White, D. R. (2003). Structural Cohesion and Embeddedness: A Hierarchical Concept of Social Groups. *American Sociological Review, 68*(1), 103–127. doi:10.2307/3088904

Moody-White. (2003). In *Wikipedia.* Retrieved from https://en.wikipedia.org/wiki/Structural_cohesion

Opsahl, , Agneessens, F., & Skvoretz, J. (2010). Node centrality in weighted networks: Generalizing degree and shortest paths. *Social Networks, 32*(3), 245–251. doi:10.1016/j.socnet.2010.03.006

Otte, E., & Rousseau, R. (2002). Social network analysis: A powerful strategy, also for the information sciences. *Journal of Information Science, 28*(6), 441–453. doi:10.1177/016555150202800601

Pattillo, J. (2011). Clique relaxation models in social network analysis. In Handbook of Optimization in Complex Networks: Communication and Social Networks. Springer.

Pherson, . (2001). Birds of a feather: Homophily in social networks. *Annual Review of Sociology, 27*(1), 415–444. doi:10.1146/annurev.soc.27.1.415

Pinheiro, C. A. R. (2011). *Social Network Analysis in Telecommunications.* John Wiley & Sons.

Podolny, J. M., & Baron, J. N. (1997). Resources and relationships: Social networks and mobility in the workplace. *American Sociological Review, 62*(5), 673–693. doi:10.2307/2657354

Tsvetovat, . (2011). *Social Network Analysis for Startups: Finding Connections on the Social Web.* O'Reilly.

Wasserman, . (1994). *Social Networks Analysis: Methods and Applications.* Cambridge, UK: Cambridge University Press. doi:10.1017/CBO9780511815478

Wellman, B. (n.d.). *The Networked Individual.* Retrieved from http://www.semioticon.com/semiotix/semiotix14/sem-14-05.html

Xu, G. (2010). *Web Mining and Social Networking: Techniques and Applications.* Springer.

Chapter 7
A Review on Spatial Big Data Analytics and Visualization

Bangaru Kamatchi Seethapathy
VIT University, India

Parvathi R
VIT University, India

ABSTRACT

Spatial dataset, which is becoming nontraditional due to the increase in usage of social media sensor networks, gaming and many other new emerging technologies and applications. The wide variety of sensors are used in solving real time problems like natural calamities, traffic analysis, analyzing climatic conditions and the usage of GPS, GPRS in mobile phones all together creates huge amount of spatial data which really exceeds the traditional spatial data analytics platform and become spatial big data .Spatial big data provide new demanding situations for their size, analysis, and exploration. This chapter discusses about the analysis of spatial data and how it gets descriptive manipulation, so that one can understand how multi variant variables get interact with each other along with the different visualization tools which make the understanding of spatial data easier.

INTRODUCTION

The data generation becomes easier in these modern days, for example taxi booking which stores the traveler location and the frequent routes travelled by the user and much more information. Handling of those huge data and making it more productive become the most difficult task. Thus "big data" comes into the picture, the data

DOI: 10.4018/978-1-5225-2805-0.ch007

which is bigger in both size and complexity can be analyzed and processed using different big data methodologies. The sources of big data are originating from different fields like social networks, sensor information, messaging system and much more. One of the most interesting things about big, data is that it can handle unstructured data which means that data which is not in pre-defined manner example photos, videos, voice recordings, etc. Interpreting such unstructured data shows big data as a new door of innovation and one among such unstructured data is the spatial data. Spatial data is the information or data that distinguishes the geographic area of elements and limits on Earth, such as natural or built components, seas, and many more. Spatial information is normally put away as directions and topology, and is information that can be mapped. Spatial information is regularly gotten to, control or broke down through Geographic Information Systems (GIS) (Aji, Wang, Vo et al., 2013) . Large percentage of data produced all over the world have the spatial component According to the recent survey, 80% of data is geographic which indicates the importance of handling geospatial big data especially societal applications like disaster management, disease surveillance, transportation monitoring and critical infrastructure but there are a huge number of constraints.Big data is characterized by the following(Chen & Zhang, 2014)

- **Volume:** Petabyte archives for remotely sensed imagery data, ever increasing volume of real-time sensor observations and location-based social media data, vast amount of VGI data, etc.., as well as the continuous increase of these data, raise not only data storage issues but also a massive analysis issue.
- **Variety:** Map data, imagery, data, geotagged text data, structured and unstructured data, raster and vector data, all these different types of data – many with complex structures – calls for more efficient models, structures, indexes and data management strategies and technologies.
- **Velocity:** Imagery data with frequent revisits at high resolution, continuous streaming of sensor observations, Internet of Things (IoT), real-time GNSS trajectory and social media data all require matching the speed of data generation and the speed of data processing to meet demand.
- **Veracity:** Much of geospatial big data are from unverified sources with low or unknown accuracy, level of accuracy varies depending on data sources, raising issues on quality assessment of source data and how to ''statistically'' improve the quality of analysis results.
- **Visualization:** Provides valuable procedures, to impose human thinking into the big data analysis. Visualizations help analysts identifying patterns (such as outliers and clusters), leading to new hypotheses as well as efficient ways to partition the data for further computational analysis. Visualizations

also help end users to better grasp and communicate dominant patterns and relationships that emerge from the big data analysis.

- **Visibility:** The emergence of cloud computing and cloud storage has made it possible to now efficiently access and process geospatial big data in ways that was not previously possible. Cloud technology is still evolving and once issues such as data provenance – historical metadata – are resolved, big data and the cloud would be mutually dependent and reinforcing technologies.

DATA COLLECTION

The Geo spatial data has several different forms which fall under three different categories: vector data, raster data and graph data. The following Figure 1 shows the representation of three different data. Vector data use X and Y directions to characterize the areas of focus, lines, and zones (polygons) that compare to guide components, for example, fire hydrants, trails, and bundles. Accordingly, vector information have a tendency to characterize focuses and edges of elements. Vector data are superb for catching and putting away spatial subtle elements, while raster data are appropriate for catching, putting away, and breaking down information, for example, height, temperature, soil pH, and so on that fluctuate consistently from area to area. Raster data, then again, utilize a framework of square ranges to characterize where components are found. These squares, additionally called pixels, cells, and networks, commonly are of uniform size, and their size decides the point of interest that can be kept up in the dataset. Since raster data speak to square ranges, they portray insides as opposed to limits similar to the case with vector data. The raster data are being provided by digital map services, e.g., Google Earth. Raster information arrangers additionally are utilized to store aeronautical and satellite imagery. Data for the most part shows up as street systems. Here, an edge speaks to a road fragment, and a hub speaks to a crossing point or a milestone. The directions of the vehicles out and about system are spoken to by arrangements of road fragments (edges). With the headways of sensor and correspondence advances, new wellsprings of geospatial enormous data are developing. To begin with, sensors (or sensor systems) turn out to be more predominant in nowadays. The illustrations are circle identifiers for recognizing movement in roads, electrical matrices, natural sensors for measuring air quality, etc. These sensors are normally associated through wired or remote correspondences and structure sensor systems. Second, cell phones turn out to be practically universal in nowadays. Advanced cells can be utilized in following the directions of people effortlessly. Particularly, since the limit of batteries and the effectiveness of utilization processors have enhanced altogether, it gets to be conceivable to record the area of a man as often as possible.

Figure 1. vector, raster and graph data

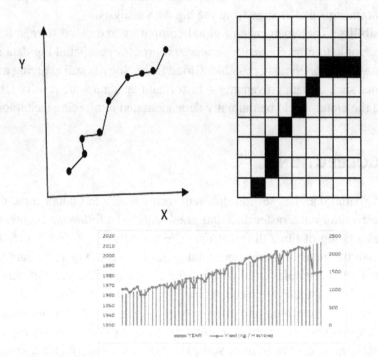

GEO-SPATIAL DATA AS BIG DATA

The data creation which becomes enormous due to the increase of various other gadgets and advancement in technologies. Each and every field need a data analytics in order to do make better decisions or to make more profit or to get the best opinion out of it. The social media, which never fails to create tons and tons of data everyday, out of this the spatial data which is created at the rate of terabytes. Due to the creation of such huge data the data mining activity which is getting hyperactive by various data mining approaches and algorithms. The remote sensing data which seems to be one of the special case in spatial data analysis. The data collected from the space via satellites and meteorological data detected by the sensors to determine land and sea perceptions are making handling spatial data a huge one. The investigations of such substantial data display their own difficulties, despite the fact that with exceedingly capable processors and rapid data access conceivable shortly. Geospatial Data has always been Big Data. Now Big Data Analytics for geospatial data is available to allow users to analyze massive volumes of geospatial data. Petabyte archives for remotely sensed Geo data were being planned in the 1980s, and growth has met expectations. Add to this the ever increasing volume and reliability of real time sensor observations, the need for high performance, big data analytics for modeling and simulation of geospatially enabled content is greater than ever. Workstations capable of fast geometric processing of vector Geo data brought a revolution in GIS. Now big processing through cloud computing and analytics can make greater sense of data and deliver the promised value of imagery and all other types of geospatial information. Cloud initiatives have accelerated lightweight client access to powerful processing services hosted in remote locations. The recent ESA/ESRIN "Big Data from Space" event addressed challenges posed by policies for dissemination, data search, sharing, transfer, mining, analysis, fusion and visualization.

HADOOP FRAMEWORK FOR SPATIAL DATA ANALYSIS

The Hadoop framework which is created by the google and later it was received by the Apache Foundation. The framework which is categorized into two, first one is Hadoop Distributed File System (HDFS) and the next one is MapReduce. Former will help in putting away the data and the latter will do handling of those data It is a dispersed data handling system. It is fit for overseeing extensive volume data proficiently, utilizing an expansive number of production equipment as Nodes shaping a Hadoop cluster The divide and conquer rule which is the major concept hidden behind the concept of this framework where the data get split into small clusters and then processed. The function of the mapper is to create the key-value pair, the key value pair gets generated once the mapper reads the data and change it into the key value pair. Next the reducer phase begins, here the process of shuffling occurs where the key-value pairs have transformed into key-multiple value pairs(Bhosale & Adekar, 2014). The Figure 2 shows the Hadoop framework where the input file will be split into name node and data node.Namenode which contains the metadata which means contain information about the data. and further processing will be carried out in the data node.

This Hadoop structure is further reached out by Smart and RESQUE. A run of the mill database needs a list keeping in mind the end goal to accomplish quick question preparing. The R-Tree based lists aggregate close-by substances and speak to them utilizing their base bouncing rectangle. It can be inherent three-stages, in the first stage each of close information is separated by their magnitude properties. Secondly Hadoop framework produces a lower level R-Trees from the data which is already partitioned. Finally, in the last stage, the converted lower level R-Trees are joined together to frame an ample R-Tree record of the data. This can be demonstrated which shows how the MapReduce model tackled taking after too common place and delegate spatial data handling issues quickly and effectively first one is Processing advanced flying symbolism and calculation and putting away picture

Figure 2. Hadoop framework

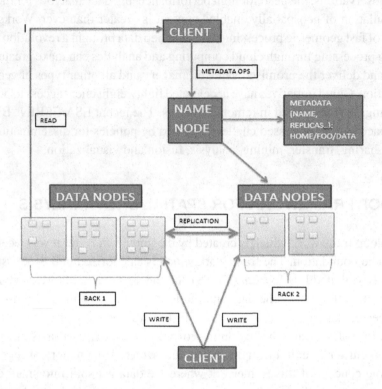

quality attributes as metadata and the next one is the substantial scale development of R-Trees, a famous indexing component for spatial hunt inquery preparing also tools like Radoop is used to run distributed process in Hadoop (Prekopcsák, Makrai, Henk & Gaspar-Papanek, 2011)

Spatial Hadoop

As the name indicates it is specially designed framework to handle the spatial data. For this spatial Hadoop three different prototypes are introduced (Eldway, 2014b) (i) Parallel-Second (ii) MD-HBase (iii) Hadoop-GIS. Here in the primary one Hadoop is made to act as a distributed task scheduler and is mainly for handling spatial database parallelly, the next one extends HBase to support multi-dimensional indexes and is mainly to handle non-relation databases. The final one extends the Hive, which is a data warehouse infrastructure and is mainly to handle self-join and range queries(Bação, 2006). Whoever the Integration of Hadoop becomes the major downside. The query processing which is the main concentration, hence it has built-in Hadoop, which is made possible by adding spatial constructs in the core. The two main features of spatial data which paves way for more research and development is that Map reduce components and spatial indexes which provides more options like R, R+ tree and grid file.. Basic Operations of the SpatialHadoop are: range query,knn and spatial join.

Figure 3 shows the spatial Hadoop architecture.The SpatialHadoop's core consists of the following four layers:

- **Language Layers:** High level language for understanding spatial data analysis for layman.
- **Storage Layers:** It has two layers .The global index allotments information crosswise over hubs in the group while local index sorts out information productively inside every hub.
- **MapReduce Layers:** To have the capacity to handle spatially recorded documents, SpatialHadoop presents two new segments in the MapReduce layer, to be specific, SpatialFileSplitter and SpatialRecordReader, that endeavors the worldwide and nearby records, individually, for effective information access.
- **Operations Layers:** These contain various spatial operations (range query, kNN and spatial join) executed utilizing the aforementioned records and new segments in the MapReduce layer.

Spatial Hadoop has three different types of data type polygon, rectangle and points which store the spatial information in the form of shapes represented in two dimensional x, y coordinates.Based on this shape different geographic features like agricultural lands, water bodies, roads and many more can be analyzed. For example, to extract the details of agriculture lands spatial Hadoop will be more useful. consider the scenario to differentiate agriculture land on and off side of the river for this initially map reduce will run for the particular data which is selected by

Figure 3. Spatial Hadoop architecture

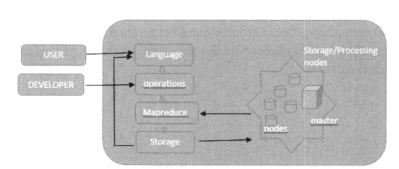

producing a key value pair it generates an image to get visualized then range query operation can be performed by mentioning the corner points (x and y coordinates) mostly the agriculture lands will be in polygon or rectangle in representation by providing such query the lands will be extracted. To find the nearest neighbour information can query will be used. The most interesting part of spatial operation is the spatial join operation in which to join agriculture land with the river to find out which agricultural lands are on the side of the river.

APACHE MAHOUT

The word mahout implies elephant driver in Hindi. Apache Mahout is a venture of the Apache Software Foundation to create free usage of conveying or generally adaptable machine learning calculations concentrated principally in the zones of collaborative filtering, clustering and classification. it doesn't confine commitments to Hadoop-based usage. Commitments that keep running on a solitary hub or on a non-Hadoop group are additionally invited A large portion of the usage utilize the Apache Hadoop platform. Mahout likewise gives Java libraries to basic math operations (concentrated on direct variable based math and insights) and primitive Java accumulations. Mahout is a work in advancement; the quantity of actualized calculations has developed quickly, yet different calculations are as yet absent. While Mahout's center calculations for collaborative filtering, clustering and classification are executed with respect to top of Apache Hadoop utilizing the guide/decrease worldwide, For instance, the "Taste" cooperative sifting recommender part of Mahout was initially a different venture and can run remain solitary without Hadoop Apache Mahout has taken after three describing qualities: It has an Open source machine learning library, has a Java library, Scalable when the accumulation of information to be handled develops expansiveIn any case, it doesn't give a UI or a prepackaged server or an installer. A portion of the systems and calculations Mahout incorporates are still a work in progress or in a trial stage. Three center capacities are accessible, viz. recommender motors (community oriented sifting), grouping, and arrangement. Hadoop actualizes Mahout with MapReduce worldview. It does the accompanying: bring about partitioning, the identification and recuperation from individual machine disappointments, data exchanges between hub machines, accomplishes capacity of the info information.

VISUALIZATION

Data visualization is the presentation of data in a pictorial or graphical organization(Wang, Wang & Alexander, 2015). It empowers chiefs to see investigation exhibited outwardly, so they can get a handle on troublesome ideas or recognize new examples (Sucharitha, Subash, & Prakash, 2014). With intuitive visualization, one can make the idea a stride further by utilizing innovation to bore down into diagrams and charts for more detail, intelligently changing what data you see and how it's prepared. In light of the way the human mind forms data, utilizing diagrams or charts to imagine a lot of complex data is simpler than poring over spreadsheets or reports. Data representation is a brisk, simple approach to pass on ideas in an all inclusive way – and you can explore different avenues regarding diverse situations by making slight modification.Emerging different visualization technique apart from traditional one like star-cordinate based visualization (Chen, 2014) model producing optimal results.Data representation can likewise:

- Recognize regions that need consideration or change.
- Clear up which variables impact client conduct.
- Help you comprehend which items to place where.
- Anticipate sales volumes.
- Helps in human pattern recognition. (Donalek, Djorgovski, Cioc et al., 2014)

Visualization of big data, with differing qualities and heterogeneity (organized, semi-organized, and unstructured) is a major issue since the emergence of social network to visualize the association between users (Kim, Ji & Park, 2014). Pace is the sought element of the enormous data examination. Outlining another visualization instrument with proficient indexing is difficult in big data. Distributed computing, web based technologies (Fox & Hendler, 2011) progressed graphical UI can be converged with the huge data for the better administration of huge data adaptability There are also following problems for big data visualization:

- **Visual Noise:** Most of the objects in dataset are too relative to each other. Users cannot divide them as separate objects on the screen.
- **Information Loss:** Reduction of visible data sets can be used, but leads to information loss.
- **Large Image Perception:** Data visualization methods are not only limited by aspect ratio and resolution of device, but also by physical perception limits.
- **High Rate of Image Change:** Users observe data and cannot react to the number of data change or its intensity on display.

- **High Performance Requirements:** It can be hardly noticed in static visualization because of lower visualization speed requirements--high performance requirement.

BIGDATA VISUALIZATION METHODS

This passage contains huge information representation technique depiction. Every portrayal contains contentions for technique arrangement to one of the enormous information classes. We expect the accompanying information criteria:

1. Large information volume;
2. Data assortment;
3. Data flow.

Treemaps

Treemaps are perfect for showing a lot of hierarchically organized (tree-organized) information (Gorodov & Gubarev, 2013). Figure 4 shows the representation of trauma. The space in the representation is part up into rectangles that are measured and requested by a quantitative variable. The levels in the chain of command of the trauma are visualized as rectangles containing different rectangles. Every arrangement of rectangles on the same level in the order speaks to a segment or an expression in an information table. Every individual rectangle on a level in the chain of command speaks to a class in a segment. For instance, a rectangle speaking to a landmass may contain a few rectangles speaking to nations in that mainland. Every rectangle speaking to a nation may thusly contain rectangles speaking to urban areas in these nations. You can make a treemap pecking order straightforwardly in the representation, or utilize an effectively characterized chain of command.

Since the technique depends on shapes, volume estimation, figured from one or more information components, each adjustment in information is trailed by aggregate repaint of the entire picture for the at the present unmistakable level of the chain of command. Changes on more elevated amounts don't require, the picture repainting on the grounds that the data it contains is not unmistakable for an expert.

The visualization procured by this technique can just show two information variables. The first is the component utilized for a shape volume count. What's more, the second is a color, utilized for gathering the shapes. Likewise, figures utilized for volume estimation must be exhibited by processable information sorts, so the paradigm information assortment is not met. What's more, the last rule likewise

Figure 4. Tree map

Benefits	Percentages (%)
Improved decision-making	77
Better ad-hoc data analysis	43
Improved collaboration/information sharing	41
Provide self-service capabilities to end users	36
Increased return on investment (ROI)	34
Time savings	20
Reduced burden on IT	15

can't be fulfilled, on the grounds that Treemap just shows data representation at one minute in time.

Points of interest:

1. Hierarchical gathering unmistakably demonstrates data relations
2. Extreme anomalies are promptly noticeable utilizing unique shading

Drawbacks:

1. Data must be hierarchical and, considerably more, TreeMaps are better to analyze data sets where there is no less than one imperative quantitative measurement with wide varieties
2. Not appropriate for inspecting recorded patterns and time designs
3. the variable utilized for size count can't have negative qualities

Circle Packing

Circle packing is an adjustment to anticipate ample amounts of hierarchically structured data. Inspired by tramps and Grokker, Wang et al. developed this blueprint algorithm for timberline structures: Tangent circles represent brother nodes at the aforementioned level; to anticipate the hierarchy, all children of a bulge are arranged into that bulge (and appropriately actuate its size). The sharing of a leaf-node can represent an approximate property, such as book size. An advantage of this algorithm is the acceptable overview of ample abstract sets and the bright representation

As a space-filling technique, circle Packing visualizes advice as spatial extension. The algorithm on which it is based is accompanying to the algebraic botheration with the aforementioned name .It places any bulk of brother nodes, represented by circles, in an adjustment that has a top body and retains an arched appearance approximating a circle as the bulk of nodes grows. Due to this property, a set of brother nodes can consistently be arranged into its (also circle-shaped) ancestor node.

Compared to that of treemaps, a decision generated by this address is - while possibly a bit beneath space-efficient - easier to appreciate visually while it retains the adeptness to (theoretically) affectation all hierarchies at once. This, of course, requires an apt user interface to calmly zoom into the anatomy if that is appropriate to see the blade nodes in detail.example of circle packing is represented in the following Figure 5 which has the various districts with the information of annual rainfall and annual temperature.

Sunburst

A Sunburst decision is an adorable space-filling decision address for announcement timberline like structures. Sunburst which can also be called as multilevel pie chart visualization. There are added space-filling decision methods that use added be held encodings for anecdotic hierarchies. For example, the Treemap is a space-filling decision that uses "containment" to appearance "parent-child" relationships. There are a brace of attenuate changes that can advance the way the advice is announced by this visualization. The "classic" Sunburst decision uses accumbent labels for big names. One band-aid for this is to circle labels in a way that they're not occluded. A simple yet important affair to do if alternating labels are to circle the labels in a way that they're consistently adverse up Data object are placed around a circle and linked by curves based on the rate of their relativeness. The different line width or color saturation usually is used as a measurement of object relativeness. Also a method usually provides interactions, making unnecessary links invisible and highlighting selected one. So, this method underlines direct relation between multiple objects and shows how relative it is. As for typical use-cases for that method, there are the following examples: product transfer diagram between cities, relations between buying product in different shops, and so forth.The following Figure 6 will show the illustration of sun burst.

Circular Network Diagram

This method allows us to represent aggregated data as a set of arcs between analyzed data objects, so that the analyst can get quantitative information about relations between objects. The following Figure 7 will provide the overall visualization of circular network diagrams. This method can be applied to large data volumes, placing data objects by circle radius and varying ark area of objects. Also, there can be additional information, shown near an arc, which can be provided from

Figure 5. Circle Packing

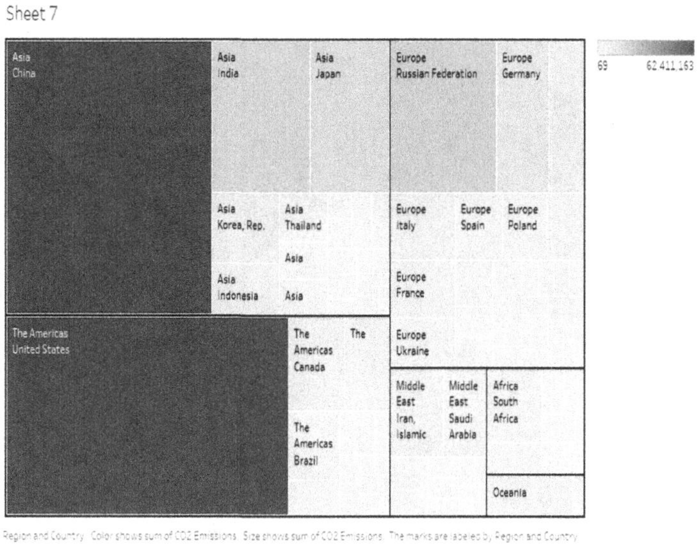

Sheet 7

Asia China	Asia India	Asia Japan	Europe Russian Federation	Europe Germany

Region and Country. Color shows sum of CO2 Emissions. Size shows sum of CO2 Emissions. The marks are labeled by Region and Country.

69   62,411,163

Figure 6. Sun burst

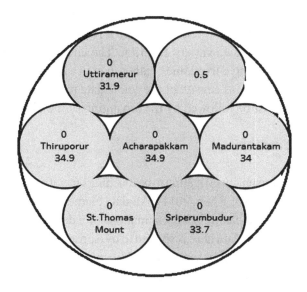

other factors of data objects. And it is necessary to add that there is no limitation in using only one factor per diagram, we can always put different factors of objects and make relations between them. It can be difficult to percept and understand, but in some cases, this approach will produce the analyst with enough information to

Figure 7 Circular network diagram

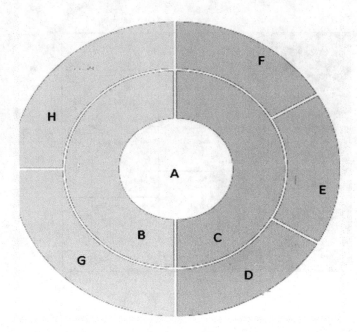

change the direction of his research or to make a final decision. That property of circular diagram satisfies data variety criterion. The circular form encourages eye movement to proceed along curved lines, rather than in a zigzag fashion in a square or rectangular figure. And, as a result of the whole data representation, every single change in the data must be followed by the repainting of the diagram.

Parallel Coordinates

This strategy permits visual investigation to be reaching out with various data elements for various articles (Khan & Khan, 2011). All data elements to be examined are put on one of the pivot, and the comparing estimations of a data article in relative scale are put on the other. Every data item is spoken to by a progression of connected cross lines, demonstrating its place in setting of different articles. This strategy permits us to utilize just a thick line on the screen to speak to individual data item and this methodology permits it to meet the principal basis—extensive data volumes. One augmentation of standard 2D parallel directions is the multi relational 3D parallel directions. Here, the cut are put, similarly isolated, on a circle with a center hub in the inside. A data thing is again shown as a progression of line sections crossing all cuts.This pivot design has the favorable position that all pairwise connections between the center variable in the inside and every external variable can be explored at the same time.

Streamgraph

Streamgraph is a sort of a stacked territory chart, which is dislodged around a focal pivot, bringing about streaming and natural shape. This strategy demonstrates the patterns for various arrangements of occasions, the amount of its events, its relative rates, thus one. Along these lines, there can be an arrangement of comparative occasions, appeared through the course of events in the picture. The technique has the twin objectives: to indicate numerous individual time arrangement, while additionally passing on their entirety. Since the statures of the individual layers signify the tallness of the general court, it is conceivable to fulfill both objectives without a moment's delay. In the meantime, this includes certain exchange offs. There can be no spaces between the layers, since this would bend their total. As an outcome of having no spaces between layers, changes in a center layer will essentially bring about squirms in the various encompassing layers, squirms which have nothing to do with the fundamental data of those influenced time arrangement .The following figure shows the annual rainfall of state tamilnadu in india from 1961 to 2003.

CONCLUSION

In this chapter, the big data approach of handling spatial data is discussed along with the visualization technique. The Hadoop framework which provides various ways to handle the spatial data and also the map reduce framework which is explained here paves way to the emergence of different algorithms for handling the spatial data which acts as the base.The spatial Hadoop and apache mahout environment are becoming more and more curious and lot of researches getting emerged in it. When coming to visualization, whatever is done should get a shape and a view which is only possible through the visualization tools. The tools discussed here also did not reach its heights and further researches are carried out and most user friendly visualization tools has to be created in order to view the results of big data and also one of the open challenge of Hadoop framework is security in handling the spatial data.

REFERENCES

Aji, A., Wang, F., Vo, H., Lee, R., Liu, Q., Zhang, X., & Saltz, J. (2013). Hadoop GIS: A high performance spatial data warehousing system over mapreduce. *Proceedings of the VLDB Endowment*, 6(11), 1009–1020. doi:10.14778/2536222.2536227 PMID:24187650

Bação, F. L. (2006). *Geospatial Data Mining. ISEGI.* New University of Lisbon.

Bhosale, H. S., & Gadekar, D. P. (2014). A review paper on big data and hadoop. International Journal of Scientific and Research Publications, 756.

Cary, A., Sun, Z., Hristidis, V., & Rishe, N. (2009, June). Experiences on processing spatial data with mapreduce. In *International Conference on Scientific and Statistical Database Management* (pp. 302-319). Springer Berlin Heidelberg. doi:10.1007/978-3-642-02279-1_24

Chen, C. P., & Zhang, C. Y. (2014). Data-intensive applications, challenges, techniques and technologies: A survey on Big Data. *Information Sciences*, 275, 314–347. doi:10.1016/j.ins.2014.01.015

Chen, K. (2014). Optimizing star-coordinate visualization models for effective interactive cluster exploration on big data. *Intelligent Data Analysis*, 18(2), 117–136.

Donalek, C., Djorgovski, S. G., Cioc, A., Wang, A., Zhang, J., Lawler, E., … Davidoff, S. (2014, October). Immersive and collaborative data visualization using virtual reality platforms. In *Big Data (Big Data), 2014 IEEE International Conference on* (pp. 609-614). IEEE. doi:10.1109/BigData.2014.7004282

Eldawy, A. (2014, June). SpatialHadoop: towards flexible and scalable spatial processing using mapreduce. In *Proceedings of the 2014 SIGMOD PhD symposium* (pp. 46-50). ACM. doi:10.1145/2602622.2602625

Eldawy, A., & Mokbel, M. F. (2013). A demonstration of SpatialHadoop: An efficient mapreduce framework for spatial data. *Proceedings of the VLDB Endowment*, 6(12), 1230–1233. doi:10.14778/2536274.2536283

Eldawy, A., & Mokbel, M. F. (2014, March). Pigeon: A spatial mapreduce language. In *2014 IEEE 30th International Conference on Data Engineering* (pp. 1242-1245). IEEE. doi:10.1109/ICDE.2014.6816751

Fox, P., & Hendler, J. (2011). Changing the equation on scientific data visualization. *Science*, 331(6018), 705–708. doi:10.1126/science.1197654 PMID:21311008

Gorodov, E. Y. E., & Gubarev, V. V. E. (2013). Analytical review of data visualization methods in application to big data. *Journal of Electrical and Computer Engineering*, *2013*, 22. doi:10.1155/2013/969458

Khan, M., & Khan, S. S. (2011). Data and information visualization methods, and interactive mechanisms: A survey. *International Journal of Computers and Applications*, *34*(1), 1–14.

Kim, Y. I., Ji, Y. K., & Park, S. (2014). Social network visualization method using inherence relationship of user based on cloud. *International Journal of Multimedia and Ubiquitous Engineering*, *9*(4), 13–20. doi:10.14257/ijmue.2014.9.4.02

Prekopcsák, Z., Makrai, G., Henk, T., & Gaspar-Papanek, C. (2011, June). Radoop: Analyzing big data with rapidminer and hadoop. *Proceedings of the 2nd RapidMiner community meeting and conference (RCOMM 2011)*, 865-874.

Sucharitha, V., Subash, S. R., & Prakash, P. (2014). Visualization of big data: Its tools and challenges. *International Journal of Applied Engineering Research*, *9*(18), 5277–5290.

Wang, L., Wang, G., & Alexander, C. A. (2015). Big data and visualization: Methods, challenges and technology progress. *Digital Technologies*, *1*(1), 33–38.

KEY TERMS AND DEFINITIONS

BASE: The elasticity of storage and server resources is at the crux of BASE paradigm. BASE databases use strategies to have Consistency, Atomicity and Partition tolerance "eventually". BASE does not flout CAP theorem but works around it. In case of BASE Availability and scalability gets highest priorities Consistency is and Weak. Base is simple and fast. In an asynchronous model, when no clocks are available, it is impossible to provide consistent data, even allowing stale data to be returned when messages are lost. However, in partially synchronous models it is possible to achieve a practical compromise between consistency and availability.

Map: produce a list of (*key*, *value*) pairs from the input structured as a key(k) value(v) pair of a different type i.e. (k1, v1) → list (k2, v2) The "reducer" is applicable to some or all values related to identifying the intermediate key to come up with output key-value pairs.

MapReduce: It is quite easy to use programming model that supports parallel design since it is very scalable and works in a distributed way. It is also helpful for huge data processing, large scale searching and data analysis within the cloud. It provides related abstraction by a process of "mapper" and "reducer". The "mapper" is applicable to each input key-value pair trying to come up with an associated absolute range of intermediate key-value pairs(Eldawy& Mokbel, 2013, 2014a; Cary, Sun, Hristidis, & Rishe, 2009).

Reduce: produce a list of values from an input that consists of a *key* and a list of *values* associated with that key i.e. (k2, list (v2)) → list (v2) MapReduce is having adequate capability to support many real and global algorithms and tasks. It can divide the input data, schedule the execution of programs over a set of machines and handle machine failures. MapReduce can also handle the inter-machine communication.

APPENDIX

Map/Reduce:

- Programming model from Lisp and other functional languages
- Many problems can be phrased this way
- Easy to distribute across nodes
- Nice retry/failure semantics

MapReduce provides:

- Automatic parallelization and distribution
- Fault tolerance
- I/O scheduling
- Monitoring & status updates

The limitations of MapReduce are:

- Extremely rigid data flow
- Constantly hacked in Join, Union, Split
- Common operations must be coded by user
- Semantics hidden inside map-reduce functions, Difficult to maintain, extend, and optimize

Chapter 8
A Survey on Overlapping Communities in Large-Scale Social Networks

S Rao Chintalapudi
JNTUK, India

H. M. Krishna Prasad M
JNTUK, India

ABSTRACT

Social network analysis is one of the emerging research areas in the modern world. Social networks can be adapted to all the sectors by using graph theory concepts such as transportation networks, collaboration networks, and biological networks and so on. The most important property of social networks is community, collection of nodes with dense connections inside and sparse connections at outside. Community detection is similar to clustering analysis and has many applications in the real-time world such as recommendation systems, target marketing and so on. Community detection algorithms are broadly classified into two categories. One is disjoint community detection algorithms and the other is overlapping community detection algorithms. This chapter reviews overlapping community detection algorithms with their strengths and limitations. To evaluate these algorithms, a popular synthetic network generator, i.e., LFR benchmark generator and the new extended quality measures are discussed in detail.

DOI: 10.4018/978-1-5225-2805-0.ch008

1. INTRODUCTION

With the advent of internet, websites and social networks generate large amount of data. Social Network Analysis (Aggarwal 2014) (Reza et al., 2014) is a traditional research area that faces the challenge of big data in the recent years. As social networks are getting more popular, analyzing such networks has become one of the most important issues in various areas. In the era of big data, the amount of available data is growing unprecedentedly. Thus, data analysis techniques need very scalable approaches that can cope with huge network datasets. The significance of big data has attracted the concern of governments, companies and scientific institutions. The voluminous data available in social network sites and web like Facebook, Twitter, Instagram, Linkedin, Weibo, World Wide Web and Wikipedia can be treated as bi data. This data can be represented as a graph/ Network, where nodes denote persons or pages, while edges represent the relationship between persons or pages. This relationship represents following in Twitter, friendship in Facebook, professional connections in LinkedIn, hyperlinks in WWW. This data may constitute several communities based interactions between people or entities. The members of community have some common interests such as movies, travel, photography, music, novels … etc and hence, they tend to interact more frequently within the community than the outside. Finding Communities in social networks is similar to Graph clustering problem, hence, it can also be called as Big graph clustering with respect to larger networks.

The basic objective of the chapter is to answer the following three questions in detail.

1.   What is community detection?
2.   How can we detect overlapping communities?
3.   How can we evaluate detected overlapping communities?

This chapter is organized as follows. Section 2 discusses about the preliminaries of community detection. The several popular overlapping community detection algorithms with their strengths, limitations are discussed in section 3. In section 4, the synthetic networks and real world networks with their quality measures such as Overlapping Normalized Mutual Information (ONMI), Omega index, F-Score, Overlap Modularity that can be used for evaluating overlapping community detection algorithms were discussed. Finally, conclusions and the future research directions were discussed in section 5.

2. PRELIMINARIES

Given an undirected and unweighted graph $G(V,E)$ representing a social network, where $V = \{v1, v2, \ldots, vn\}$ is the non-empty set of vertices representing actors and $E = \{(i,j) | v_i, v_j \in V$ is the set of edges representing relationships among them. The cardinality of vertex set (|V|) and edge set (|E|) are n, m respectively. Let v_i and v_j be two vertices from V, if $e(v_i, v_j)$ belongs to E then v_i and v_j are neighbors. The objective of the community detection problem is to partition the vertex set into C disjoint subsets in a way that place densely connected nodes in the same community. Here C can be given as input parameter or determined by the algorithm itself.

Community detection is similar to clustering in the context of social networks. It is one of the most fundamental problems in social network analysis.

It is a method that identifies the groups of nodes in such a way that nodes in each group are densely connected inside and sparsely connected to the outside. A densely connected component in the network means that a subgraph that has more number of links between nodes, whereas sparsely connected component has less number of links between nodes. Communities are also called as modules, groups, clusters and cohesive subgraphs. The detection of Communities has found wide range of applications like tracking group dynamics in social networks, tracking functional units in neural networks, categorizing web pages for search engines, simplifying visualization of complex networks, finding customers with similar interests, predicting protein function in biological networks, analyzing gene networks, analyzing scientific collaboration networks, link prediction in recommender systems, Target marketing and so on. The real-world network before social network analysis and after social network analysis is shown in Figure 1 and Figure 2.

Communities are broadly categorized into two types based on their nature namely, disjoint communities and overlapping communities. In disjoint communities, each node in the network is a member of single community. They are also called as non-overlapping communities. A sample network with two disjoint communities is shown in Figure 3 and each color represents one community.

Each node in the network can be a member of multiple communities such communities are called as overlapping communities. Overlap is the one of the general characteristics of the social networks in the real world, in which a person may belong to more than one social group such as family, friends… etc. Identifying overlapping community structures is hard in real social networks. It is an NP-hard problem because there are several possibilities to form communities. Overlapping communities are also called as soft communities. Figure 4 represent a sample network with two overlapped communities, where node 5 is shared between two communities {1,2,3,4,5} and {5,6,7,8}. A list of popular disjoint community detection algorithms and overlapping community detection algorithms are shown in Figure 5.

Figure 1. Real world network before social network analysis

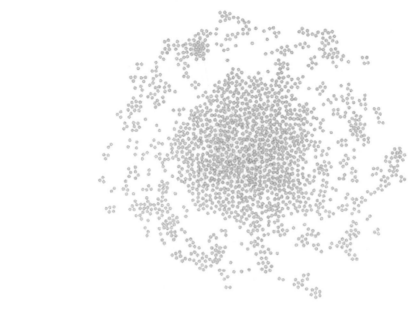

Figure 2. Real world network after social network analysis

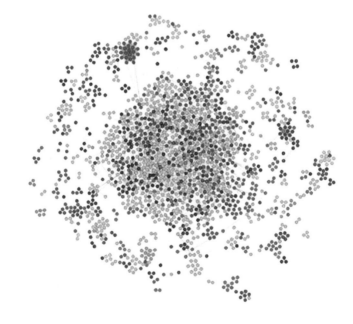

Figure 3. Sample network with two disjoint communities (green, red)

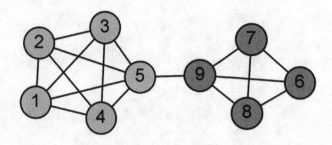

Figure 4. Sample network with two overlapped communities (green, red) where node 5 is an overlapped node between two communities

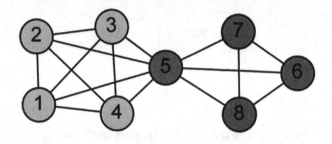

Figure 5. Community detection algorithms

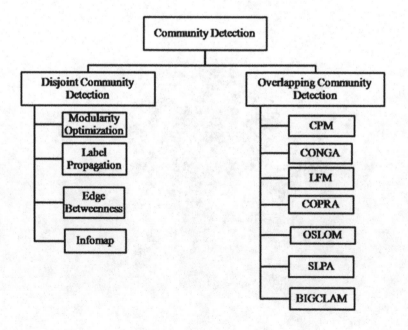

3. OVERLAPPING COMMUNITY DETECTION ALGORITHMS

In this section, authors reviewed several overlapping community detection algorithms in large scale social networks (Xie et al., 2013) (Harenberg et al., 2014) (Chakraborty 2015). The algorithms studied in this chapter and their characteristics are listed in Table 1. The time complexities listed in the Table 1 are for the worst case scenario.

3.1. Clique Percolation Method (CPM)

One of the most popular method for finding overlapping communities is Clique percolation Method (CPM) proposed by (Palla et al., 2005). It is based on the assumption that a community consists of fully connected subgraphs i.e., Cliques. This method detects overlapping communities by searching for each such subgraph for adjacent cliques that share with it at least certain number of nodes. Given parameter k, the algorithm starts by identifying all cliques of size k. Then a new graph is constructed where all cliques are denoted as nodes and cliques that share k-1 members are connected using edges. Communities are then identified by reporting the connected components of this new graph. A node can be a part of multiple k-cliques at the same time; hence, overlapping communities can be formed. This algorithm is suitable for only networks with densely connected components but it is a computationally intensive approach. CFinder is an implementation of CPM, whose time complexity is polynomial for some applications. However, it fails to terminate in many large social networks and also the communities discovered by CFinder are usually of low quality. This is like a pattern matching algorithm rather than community detection because it is aimed to find particular structure in the network.

Table 1. Overlapping Community Detection Algorithms and characteristics

Algorithm	Network Type	Disjoint Communities	Overlapping Communities	Time Complexity	Implementation	Year
CPM	Undirected	No	Yes	*exponential*	C++	2005
CONGA	Undirected	No	Yes	$O(m^3)$	Java	2007
CONGO	Undirected	No	Yes	$O(nlogn)$	Java	2008
LFM	Undirected	No	Yes	$O(n^2)$	C++	2009
COPRA	Undirected	No	Yes	$O(vmlog(vm/n))$	Java	2010
OSLOM	Directed & Undirected	No	Yes	$O(n^2)$	C++	2011
SLPA	Directed & Undirected	Yes	Yes	$O(tm)$	Java	2012
BIGCLAM	Undirected	Yes	Yes	$O(kn^2)$	C++	2013

3.2. Cluster Overlap Newman Girvan Algorithm (CONGA)

Cluster Overlap Newman Girvan Algorithm (CONGA) (Gregory 2007) is an extension of Girvan and Newman's divisive clustering algorithm that finds overlapping communities and it allows a node to split into multiple communities based on split betweenness. Initially, edge betweenness of edges and split betweenness of nodes are calculated. Then an edge with maximum edge betweenness is removed or a node with maximum split betweenness is split. After completion of this step, recalculate edge betweenness and split betweenness. Repeat the above process until all edges are considered. The calculation of edge betweenness and split betweenness are computationally expensive for large networks. CONGA Optimized (CONGO) (Gregory 2008) is a refined version of CONGA, in which local betweenness is used to optimize the runtime of the algorithm.

3.3. Lancichenetti and Fortunato Method (LFM)

LFM (Lancichinetti et al., 2009) starts with a random seed node and expands community until the fitness function is maximal. The fitness function used in this algorithm is as in Eq. (1).

$$f(c) = \frac{k_{in}^c}{\left(k_{in}^c + k_{out}^c\right)^\alpha} \tag{1}$$

where k_{in}^c and k_{out}^c are the total number inner and outer links of the community c, and α is the resolution parameter that controls the community size. Once a community is found, the algorithm selects another node that is not yet assigned to any other community. This method is significantly depends on resolution parameter (α) of the fitness function. The time complexity of this algorithm for a fixed α-value is $O(n_c s^2)$ approximately, where n_c is number of communities and s is average size of the communities. The worst-case time complexity of this algorithm is $O(n^2)$.

3.4. Community Overlap Propagation Algorithm (COPRA)

Community Overlap Propagation Algorithm (COPRA) (Gregory 2010) is an extension of label propagation that allows a node can be a member of v communities, where v is supplied by the user. Each node is associated with belonging coefficient as in Eq. (2) for indicating strength of community membership. The parameter v controls the maximum number of communities that a node can associate. The time complexity of this algorithm is $O(vm \log(vm / n))$ per iteration. This method produces small size communities for majority of the networks

$$b_t\left(c, x\right) = \frac{\sum_{y \in N(x)} b_{t-1}\left(c, y\right)}{\left|N(x)\right|} \qquad (2)$$

where x is a node, c is a community identifier and t represents an iteration number. Each propagation step updates node labels to the union of its neighbors and normalizes the sum of belonging coefficients of all neighbors. It is a non deterministic algorithm, so there is a scope to improve determinacy.

3.5. Order Statistics Local Optimization Method (OSLOM)

Order Statistics Local Optimization Method (OSLOM) (Lancichinetti et al., 2011) checks the statistical significance of a community with respect to a global null model during community expansion. It uses local optimization of fitness function. This algorithm consists of three phases. In the first phase, it identifies significant communities until convergence. In the next phase, the algorithm analyzes the resulting set of communities, trying to detect their internal structure and possible unions. In the final phase, the algorithm detects hierarchical structure of communities. Usually, this algorithm generates more number of singleton communities and outliers. In general, the worst-case time complexity of this algorithm is $O(n^2)$, while the actual time complexity is dependent on community structure in the given network.

3.6. Speaker-Listener Label Propagation Algorithm (SLPA)

Speaker-Listener Label Propagation Algorithm (Xie et al., 2011; Xie et al., 2012) is an extended version of Label Propagation Algorithm (LPA) that detects both disjoint and overlapping communities. This algorithm is developed based on speaker-listener interaction dynamic process. Initially, the memory of each node in the network is assigned with a unique label. That means each node can be considered as a different community. Next, a node is selected as a listener. Each neighbor of the listener randomly selects a label and sends the label to the listener. Neighbors of the Listener now play a role of speakers. Then the listener adds most popular label received to its memory. The above procedure can be repeated until upto maximum number of iterations (T), which is supplied as a parameter to the algorithm. Finally, the post processing based on the labels in the node memories and the threshold r is applied to produce the communities. In the post processing step, the algorithm converts memory of each node into a probability distribution of labels. If the probability of a particular label during the post processing step is less than a given threshold r, then the label is deleted. If a node contains multiple labels, then the node belongs to more than one community, called overlapping node. The smaller value of r produces more number of overlapping communities. If the threshold (r) is ≥ 0.5, then the algorithm produces only disjoint communities. The algorithm produces stable results when the iterations are greater than 20.

3.7. Cluster Affiliation Model for Big Networks (BIGCLAM)

Cluster Affiliation Model for Big Networks (BIGCLAM) (Yang et al., 2013) is an overlapping community detection algorithm that can process large networks with millions of nodes and edges. It is a model-based community detection algorithm that can detect densely overlapping, hierarchically nested as well as disjoint communities in the massive networks. It is based on the observation that overlaps of communities are more densely connected rather than the non-overlapping parts of communities. Non-negative matrix factorization is used to develop the model. The main concern of this algorithm is to choosing the number of communities.

4. EVALUATION CRITERIA FOR OVERLAPPING COMMUNITY DETECTION ALGORITHMS

The accuracy of the overlapping community detection algorithm can be evaluated in two ways. One is to test the algorithm on synthetic networks with ground truth information. The results can be quantified using Overlapping Normalized Mutual Information (ONMI), Omega index and F-Score. The second way of evaluating the algorithm is to test with real-world social networks. But the problem with these networks is that the required ground truth information is not available. So, one has to evaluate the algorithm without ground truth information. It can be possible with the quality metric called overlap modularity. Synthetic networks, the measures used to evaluate overlapping community detection algorithm with ground truth information such as ONMI, Omega Index, F-Score, some of the real-world networks and measure to evaluate algorithms without ground truth information i.e. overlapping modularity are discussed in the rest of the section.

4.1. Synthetic Networks

Random graphs are not sufficient for evaluating community detection algorithms in social networks because they do not have community structure. To study the behavior of the community detection algorithms, one need to have networks with similar properties of social networks such as community structure, power law distribution and so on. Such networks can be generated using LFR benchmark network generator (Lancichinetti et al., 2009). It can generate both networks with disjoint communities and networks with overlapped communities. The parameters used in generating LFR benchmark networks are number of nodes (N), average degree $\left(\bar{k}\right)$, mixing parameter $\left(\mu\right)$, maximum degree (k_{max}), exponents of the power law distribution (t_1, t_2), minimum community size (C_{min}), Maximum community size (C_{max}), number of overlapping nodes (O_n) and number of memberships of the overlapping nodes (O_m). The lower mixing parameter $\left(\mu\right)$ value generates highly modular communities in the network. To generate overlapping communities the values of the parameters O_m and O_n should be greater than one. The degree distribution of the network is controlled by power laws with exponents t_1 and t_2 respectively. These networks resemble real-world social networks in terms of degree distribution and clustering coefficient. Ground truth information for these networks is available, so one can apply the metrics such as ONMI, Omega Index and F-Score.

4.2. Overlapping Normalized Mutual Information (ONMI)

Normalized Mutual Information (NMI) is a concept of information theory and it can be used to measure the quality of community detection algorithm. This can be applicable for disjoint community detection algorithms only. Hence, the extended version of NMI proposed by (McDaid et al., 2013) is called Overlapping Normalized Mutual Information (ONMI), can used to evaluate overlapping community detection algorithms. It is defined based on two normalization inequalities, such as max(H(X),H(Y)) is denoted by ONMI$_{MAX}$ and 0.5*(H(X)+H(Y)) is denoted by ONMI$_{SUM}$. ONMI$_{MAX}$ and ONMI$_{SUM}$ can be calculated using Eq. (3) and Eq. (4) respectively. The range of ONMI$_{MAX}$ and ONMI$_{SUM}$ is also in between 0 and 1. If ONMI=1, t means the detected community structure is completely the same with the ground truth community structure. If ONMI=0, then the detected community structure is entirely different from the ground truth community structure. That is, the value of ONMI increases when the accuracy of the detected community structure is improved.

$$ONMI_{MAX} = \frac{I(X:Y)}{\max(H(X), H(Y))} \tag{3}$$

$$ONMI_{SUM} = \frac{I(X:Y)}{0.5 * (H(X) + H(Y))} \tag{4}$$

The mutual information I(X:Y) can be calculated as follows.

$$I(X:Y) = \frac{1}{2}\Big[H(X) - H(X \mid Y) + H(Y) - H(Y \mid X) \Big] \tag{5}$$

where X, Y are two covers, H(X) and H(Y) are the entropy of covers X and Y respectively, H(X|Y) and H(Y|X) are conditional entropies.

4.3. Omega Index

Another popular metric to evaluate overlapping community detection algorithm is Omega Index. It is an Overlapping version of Adjusted Rand Index. It is based on pairs of nodes in agreement in two covers. Let C_1, C_2 are two covers, the omega index can be defined as in Eq. (6)

$$\Omega(C_1, C_2) = \frac{\Omega_u(C_1, C_2) - \Omega_e(C_1, C_2)}{1 - \Omega_e(C_1, C_2)} \tag{6}$$

where $\Omega_u(C_1, C_2)$ represents unadjusted omega index, is the fraction of pairs that belong to same community in both C_1 and C_2.

$$\Omega_u(C_1, C_2) = \frac{1}{M}\sum_j \left| t_j(C_1) \cap t_j(C_2) \right| \tag{7}$$

where M represents the number of node pairs i.e. *n(n-1)/2* and $t_j(C)$ is the set of pairs of items that appear together in exactly j communities in a cover C.

$\Omega_e(C_1, C_2)$ is the expected omega index value in the null model and it can be computed as follows.

$$\Omega_e(C_1, C_2) = \frac{1}{M^2}\sum_j \left| t_j(C_1) \right| \cdot \left| t_j(C_2) \right| \tag{8}$$

The above definition of omega index is reduced to Adjusted Rand Index, if the network doesn't have overlapping communities. The range of omega index is 0 to 1, where 1 represents perfect matching. The higher values of omega index represent good similarity between detected and actual covers.

4.4. F-Score

F-score (Xie et al., 2013) is used to evaluate accuracy of overlapping nodes detection and it can be defined as the harmonic mean of precision and recall. The range for F-score is from 0 to 1, where 1 represents best case and 0 represents worst case and the value of F-score is higher when the accuracy of detecting overlapping nodes is higher. It can be computed using Eq. (9).

$$F = \frac{2 \times precision \times recall}{precision + recall} \tag{9}$$

where

$$recall = \frac{\#Correctly\_detected\_overlapping\_nodes}{\#actual\_overlapping\_nodes} \tag{10}$$

$$precision = \frac{\#Correctly\_detected\_overlapping\_nodes}{\#total\_detected\_overlapping\_nodes} \tag{11}$$

4.5. Real World Social Networks

The actual performance of the overlapping community detection algorithms can be observed when the algorithms are tested on real-world social networks such as Karate, Dolphins, Polbooks, football, Jazz, Netscience and Polblogs. These network datasets are acquired from Newman's personal web page (Newman 2015). The detailed summary of some of real world social networks are listed in (Table 2). The large collection of network datasets is also available in Stanford Large Network Dataset Collection (Leskovec et al., 2015). And the most of these networks does not have ground truth information so it is not possible to find accuracy of the algorithm using ONMI, Omega Index and F-score. Therefore, Overlap modularity proposed by (Nicosia et al., 2009) can be helpful in such situations. The ground truth of Dolphin

Table 2. Summary of real-world social networks

Dataset	Nodes	Edges	Description
Karate	34	78	Zachary's karate club
Sawmill	36	62	Sawmill Communication network
Dolphins	62	159	Dolphin social network
Lesmis	77	254	Co-appearances of characters in Les Miserables
Polbooks	105	441	Books about US Politics
Words	112	425	Adjectives and nouns
Football	115	613	American college football
Jazz	198	2742	Jazz musicians network
Netscience	379	914	Co-authorship Network
Metabolic	453	2025	Metabolic network of C. elegans
Email	1133	5451	Network of e-mail interchanges
Polblogs	1490	16718	Political blogs

social network and American football network is shown in Figure 6 and 7 and each color represent one community.

4.6. Overlap Modularity

It is a quality measure that evaluates overlapping community detection algorithms without ground truth information and it is based on belonging coefficients of links. It can be used as both evaluating and detecting overlapping communities in social networks. If $l=(i,j)$ is an edge that belongs to community c, then the belonging coefficient of l can be represented as a function of belonging coefficient of node i and node j to the community c.

$$\beta_{l,c} = F\left(\alpha_{ic}, \alpha_{jc}\right) \tag{12}$$

where $F\left(\alpha_{ic}, \alpha_{jc}\right)$ is an arbitrary function and can be taken as product or average or maximum of α_{ic} and α_{jc}. The expected belonging coefficient of any possible link $l(i,j)$ starting from a node into community c is an average of all possible belonging coefficients of l to community c.

Figure 6. Two communities found in dolphin social network

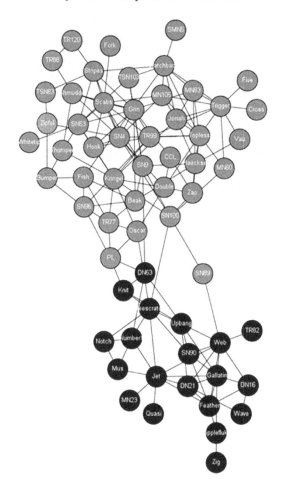

$$\beta^{out}_{l(i,j),c} = \frac{\sum\limits_{j \in V} F\left(\alpha_{ic}, \alpha_{jc}\right)}{|V|} \qquad (13)$$

Accordingly, the expected belonging coefficient of any link *l(i,j)* pointing to node j in community c is defined as:

$$\beta^{in}_{l(i,j),c} = \frac{\sum\limits_{j \in V} F\left(\alpha_{ic}, \alpha_{jc}\right)}{|V|} \qquad (14)$$

Figure 7. Eleven communities found in American college football network

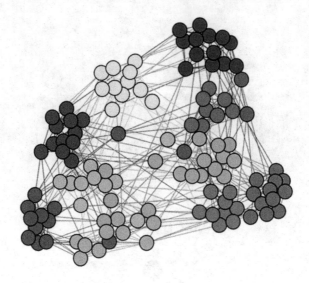

These belonging coefficients are used as weights for the probability of having a link starting at node i and pointing to node j. Therefore, modularity in the case of overlapped communities can be computed as in Eq. (15).

$$
Q_{ov} = \frac{1}{m} \sum_{c \in C} \sum_{i,j \in V} \left[\beta_{l(i,j),c} A_{i,j} - \frac{\beta_{l(i,j),c}^{out} k_i^{out} \beta_{l(i,j),c}^{in} k_j^{in}}{m} \right]
\tag{15}
$$

where k_i^{out}, k_j^{in} are the number of outgoing and incoming links of i and j respectively and m is the total number of edges. The overlap modularity is significantly dependent on the arbitrary function $F\left(\alpha_{ic}, \alpha_{jc}\right)$ The higher values of overlap modularity indicates good community detection algorithm. Usually, the modularity above 0.3 indicates good modular structures in the network.

5. CONCLUSION AND FUTURE RESEARCH DIRECTIONS

In this chapter, authors discussed overlapping community detection in social networks by answering three general questions (1) what is community detection, (2) How can we detect overlapping communities, and (3) How can we evaluate detected overlapping communities? Authors started with a description of communities and how they are formed. And also, types of communities in the social networks such as disjoint and overlapping communities were discussed. Later, authors reviewed several overlapping community detection algorithms with their strengths and limitations were discussed. Finally, authors presented evaluation criteria for overlapping community detection algorithms. The quality measures for overlapping communities such as ONMI, Omega Index, F-Score and Overlap Modularity were discussed in detail. Many of the real world networks does not contain ground truth information, in such cases how to generate benchmark networks and how to apply quality measures on those networks were also discussed.

Most of the research in community detection is done for unweighted and undirected networks only. Hence, there is a scope for future work in this area by developing algorithms for weighted and directed, attributed, bipartite networks. Scalability of the algorithm is also another research direction in this area because the number of nodes and edges in a real world social network are increasing rapidly. Moreover, social networks are dynamic in nature that means they evolve over time. Hence, community detection in dynamic networks is a challenging task for future work.

REFERENCES

Aggarwal, C. C. (2014). *Data Mining: The Textbook.* Springer International Publishing.

Chakraborty, T. (2015). Leveraging disjoint communities for detecting overlapping community structure. *Journal of Statistical Mechanics*, *2015*(5), P05017. doi:10.1088/1742-5468/2015/05/P05017

Gregory, S. (2007). An algorithm to find overlapping community structure in networks. In J. N. Kok, J. Koronacki, R. Lopez de Mantras, S. Matwin, D. Mladenic, & A. Skowron (Eds.), *PKDD 2007, LNAI* (Vol. 4702, pp. 91–102). Heidelberg, Germany: Springer. doi:10.1007/978-3-540-74976-9_12

Gregory, S. (2008). A fast algorithm to find overlapping communities in networks. In W. Daelemans (Ed.), *ECML PKDD 2008, LNAI* (Vol. 5212, pp. 408–423). Berlin: Springer. doi:10.1007/978-3-540-87479-9_45

Gregory, S. (2010). Finding overlapping communities in networks by label propagation. *New Journal of Physics*, *12*(10), 10301. doi:10.1088/1367-2630/12/10/103018

Harenberg, S., Bello, G., Gjeltema, L., Ranshous, S., Jitendra, H., Ramona, S., Padmanabhan, K., & Samatova, N. (2014). Community detection in large-scale networks: a survey and empirical evaluation. *WIREs Comput Stat, 6*, 426-439.

Lancichinetti, A., Fortunato, S., & Kertesz, J. (2009). Detecting the overlapping and hierarchical community structure of complex networks. *New Journal of Physics*, *11*(3), 033015. doi:10.1088/1367-2630/11/3/033015

Lancichinetti, A., Radicchi, F., Ramasco, J. J., & Fortunato, S. (2011). Finding statistically significant communities in networks. *PLoS ONE*, *6*(4), e18961. doi:10.1371/journal.pone.0018961 PMID:21559480

Leskovec, J., & Krevl, A. (2015). *SNAP Datasets: Stanford Large Network Dataset Collection*. Retrieved from http://snap.stanford.edu/data

McDaid, A. F., Greene, D., & Hurley, N. (2013). *Normalized Mutual Information to evaluate overlapping community finding algorithms*. CORR,abs/1110.2515

Newman, M. E. J. (2015). *Real world network datasets*. Retrieved from http://www-personal.umich.edu/~mejn/netdata/

Nicosia, V., Mangioni, G., Carchiolo, V., & Malgeri, M. (2009). Extending the definition of modularity to directed graphs with overlapping communities. *Journal of Statistical Mechanics*, *2009*(03), 03024. doi:10.1088/1742-5468/2009/03/P03024

Palla, G., Derenyi, I., Farkas, I., & Vicsek, T. (2005). Uncovering the overlapping community structure of complex networks in nature and society. *Nature*, *435*(7043), 814–818. doi:10.1038/nature03607 PMID:15944704

Reza, Z., Abbasi, M. A., & Liu, H. (2014). *Social Media Mining: An Introduction*. Cambridge University Press.

Xie, J., & Szymanski, B. K. (2012). Towards linear time overlapping community detection in social networks. *Proceedings of PAKDD Conf.* (pp. 25-36). doi:10.1007/978-3-642-30220-6_3

Xie, J., Szymanski, B. K., & Liu, X. (2011). SLPA: Uncovering Overlapping communities in Social Networks via A Speaker-listener Interaction Dynamic Process. *Proceedings of 11th IEEE International Conference on Data Mining Workshops (ICDM)* (pp. 344-349). IEEE. doi:10.1109/ICDMW.2011.154

Xie, J. R., Kelley, S., & Szymanski, B. K. (2013). Overlapping community detection in networks: The state of the art and comparative study. *ACM Computing Surveys*, *45*(4), 1–43. doi:10.1145/2501654.2501657

Yang, J., & Leskovec, J. (2013). Overlapping Community Detection at Scale: A Nonnegative Matrix Factorization Approach. *Proceedings of WSDM* (pp. 587-596). Rome, Italy: ACM. doi:10.1145/2433396.2433471

KEY TERMS AND DEFINITIONS

Community: It is a group of densely connected nodes within the group and sparsely connected to the rest of the network. It can also be called as modules, clusters, groups or cohesive subgraphs.

Community Detection: The method of finding group of nodes in such a way that the nodes in the group are densely connected and sparsely connected to the outside the group. It is also called as Graph clustering.

Cover: It is a set of communities detected for a network.

Disjoint Communities: Each node of the network is participated in only one community then such communities are called as Disjoint Communities. That means no two communities share a node in the network.

F-Score: It is the harmonic mean of precision and recall.

Normalized Mutual Information: It is an information theory concept to measure the quality of detected disjoint communities using ground truth information.

Overlapping Communities: Each node of the network is participated in more than one community then such communities are called as Overlapping Communities.

Overlapping Normalized Mutual Information: It is an extension of Normalized Mutual Information for evaluating overlapping community detection algorithms.

Precision: It is a fraction of the number of correctly detected overlapping nodes and the total number of detected overlapping nodes.

Recall: It is a fraction of the number of correctly detected overlapping nodes and the real number of overlapping nodes.

Social Network: It is a collection of nodes or actors with relationships among them.

Chapter 9
A Brief Study of Approaches to Text Feature Selection

Ravindra Babu Tallamaraju
Flipkart Internet Private Limited, India

Manas Kirti
Flipkart Internet Private Limited, India

ABSTRACT

With reducing cost of storage devices, increasing amounts of data is being stored and processed for extracting intelligence. Classification and clustering have been two major approaches in generating data abstraction. Over the last few years, text data is dominating the types of data shared and stored. Some of the sources of such datasets are mobile data, e-commerce, and wide-range of continuously expanding social-networking services. Within each of these sources, the nature of data differs drastically from formal language text to Twitter or SMS slangs thereby leading to the need for different ways of processing the data for making meaningful summarization. Such summaries could effectively be used for business advantage. Processing of such data requires identifying appropriate set of features both for efficiency and effectiveness. In the current Chapter, we propose to discuss approaches to text feature selection and make a comparative study.

1. INTRODUCTION

With the increasing ability to collect, store, and share data, there is a need to find efficient algorithms that provide insights on the data that have potential utility to business advantage in commercial organizations. Some contributors to these

DOI: 10.4018/978-1-5225-2805-0.ch009

datasets are related to mobile, social networking, content-sharing, search-engines, and e-commerce enterprises.

Data Mining algorithms help to generate abstractions from these datasets. Many definitions are in use for Data Mining. The generally accepted definition (Shapiro & Frawley, 1991; Chen, et al., 1996; Leskovec et al., 2014) is that *the data mining is a process of extraction of potentially useful and hitherto unknown information which is non-trivial, and hidden in the data.* Largeness of the dataset can broadly be characterized by the limitation of in-memory processing. With increasing volumes of datasets, large datasets are termed *massive datasets* or *big data*. Big data (Douglas, 2011) is defined by three V's: *volume, velocity* and *variety* of the data. In the current chapter, we refer to big data and large data equivalently. Some experts suggest additional V representing *value*.

Approaches to generating abstraction from large data as discussed in the works of Leskovec et al. (2014) and Babu et al(2013) are the following.

- Real time as well as batch processing through single, distributed or parallel computation depending on requirement and nature of resources
- Divide and conquer approaches in terms of patterns or features or both
- Operate in the compressed data domain

An important aspect while processing big data is the possibility of seeing random occurrences as meeting an experimental hypothesis. Benferroni principle as discussed in the work of Leskovec et al. (2014) suggests that if the expected number of occurrences when the data is assumed random is higher than actual number of real occurrences, the results are unlikely to be correct. Following are some of the salient characteristics of algorithms for big data abstraction.

- **Scalability:** Scalability (Bondi, 2000) refers to ability of a system to process growing volumes of data gracefully. The work formally defines attributes for a scalable system.
- **Limited Number of Database Scans:** Ability to generate an abstraction with a single or least number of database scans is necessary since multiple views of databases, like that of iterative algorithms, would become expensive in terms of computation time.
- **Data Reduction:** Working on the representative patterns of dataset, instead of working on the entire dataset. Prototypes can be generated using efficient unsupervised learning algorithms.

- **Dimensionality Reduction:** Reduce the dimensionality of the patterns by means of feature selection or extraction.
- **Divide and Conquer Approaches:** Divide and conquer techniques (Leskovec et al., 2014) such as Map-Reduce, hashing, shingling, etc.
- **Compressing Schemes for Data Mining:** Lossless and lossy compression to represent the data and working in the compressed domain without having to decompress for generating abstraction (Babu et al., 2013) would lead to efficient algorithms for big data systems.
- **Multiagent Systems:** Multiagent systems in agent-mining paradigm (Cao, 2009; Babu et al., 2013) is an important direction of dealing with big data. Such systems consist of intelligent agents that collaborate, interact proactively and reactively, and are capable of carrying out autonomous machine learning tasks. An integrating agent would provide aggregated summarization.
- **Deep Learning Approaches:** The above approaches focus on efficient use of resources. The deep learning or deep machine learning approaches are disruptive and important direction to process big data in generating effective abstractions. (Najafabadi et al., 2015; Li et al., 2015)

In the present work, we focus on feature selection for large datasets. We discuss general feature selection approaches, issues that are specific to text feature selection and experimental comparison of some text feature selection approaches on a common dataset.

The chapter is organized in the following manner. Section 2 contains formal classification of approaches to feature reduction. Section 3 contains a discussion on specific issues in text feature selection and a discussion on various terminology related to this topic. Experimental comparison of few indicative feature selection approaches is provided in Section 4. The work is summarized in Section 5 and further research directions are provided in Section 6. References are provided in the end.

2. APPROACHES TO FEATURE SELECTION

In this section, we initially define basic terms and discuss various approaches to feature selection.

For any machine learning tasks, pattern representation is primary. A pattern may be defined as a multi-dimensional data point, consisting of a number of attributes or measurements. The individual measurements are referred to as features. Pattern representation (Jain et al., 1999) involves identification of patterns, number of classes, number and nature of features that characterize the patterns. Feature selection (Jain et al., 1999; Chandrashekar & Sahin, 2014; Ferri et al., 1994) refers to the process of identifying most relevant and effective subset of the original features that help in obtaining best performance of a machine learning task that is compatible with the entire set of original features. Feature extraction (Jain et al., 1999) is the process of generating new features through a transformation of original set of features.

Selecting features from an original set of 'k' features by evaluating all the subsets of 2^k for a given dataset is NP-hard as number of features is large. This leads to the need for finding a near-optimal algorithm to select relevant features.

With reference to text domain, text feature selection or term selection is also referred to *as term space reduction* (Sebastiani, 2002). It is defined as an activity to select k' features out of original k features, where $k' << k$, that are used to represent the document meaningfully and improve the effectiveness of algorithms that are based on such data. The techniques used for scoring the features are referred to *Feature Evaluation Function (FEF)* (Yang & Pedersen, 1997). Associated to feature reduction is a measure known as *reduction factor* (Yang & Pedersen, 1997) which is given by $\rho = \dfrac{k - k'}{k}$.

2.1 Feature Relevance

Selection of relevant features by eliminating irrelevant and redundant ones is one of the primary tasks of feature selection (Kohavi & John, 1997; Blum & Langley, 1997; Li et al., 2015). Presence of irrelevant features leads to inaccurate abstraction of the dataset. Kohavi & John (1997) formally define and discuss the concepts of relevant and irrelevant features, strong and weak relevance, and, relevance and optimality. Some interesting examples in the work indicate that relevance does not imply optimality and vice versa. Blum & Langley (1997) elaborate the concept of *relevance* to a machine learning task. The work further goes on to define notions of relevance to a target, strong weak relevance to a sample or distribution, relevance to complexity measure and incremental usefulness. Together, both the works (Kohavi & John, 1997; Blum & Langley, 1997) provide insights on relevance vs. usefulness of features and various notions of relevance.

In the context of discovery of relevant features for text mining, it is important to note (Li et al., 2015) that useful features are available in both relevant and irrelevant text documents. For finding relevant features in relevant and irrelevant documents, the challenges include the following. For a topic, large patterns (group of features) are likely to be more relevant but they usually have low support. On the contrary, reducing the frequency leads to noisy pattern discovery. The work (Li et al., 2015) argues that conventional measures used in frequent pattern mining such as support and confidence are not suitable in relevant text feature discovery. Thus, the problem reduces to the ability to make use of discovered patterns to accurately evaluate weights of useful features in the training data. The work proposes a method which is based on measures such as absolute and relative term supports, and document ranking to decide on relevance. The experimental results obtained indicate better performance than Rocchio, Support Vector Machine (SVM) and BM25 (Manning et al., 2009)

Clustering based feature subset selection for high dimensional data is well studied (Parsons et al., 2004; Song et al., 2013). The approaches consist of clustering features according some criteria and the representative features that are related to target classes are considered to form feature subsets. Song et al. (2013) propose a fast clustering feature subset algorithm based on graph-theoretic (Jain et al., 1999) clustering methods, known as FAST. The work compares the proposed algorithm with five feature clustering algorithms on variety of datasets relating to image, text and microarray data. The authors demonstrate that they performed consistently well in terms of subset size, run time and classification accuracy.

Feature selection algorithms can broadly be classified into Filter, Wrapper and Embedded methods. The methods are used independently as well as in conjunction with each other. We discuss each of the approaches in the following sections.

2.2 Filter Methods

Filter methods order the features by means of a criterion. Features ranked in such a manner are chosen as *relevant features*. Based on ranking criteria, features above a chosen threshold are selected. These ranking methods are referred to as *filtering methods*, which are applied before carrying out a machine learning task to ensure that relevant features are retained. A number of feature relevance measures are defined in the works of Yang & Pedersen (1997), Li et al. (2015), Blum & Langley (1997), Forman (2003), Guyon & Elisseeff (2003), and Sebastiani (2002). We

Table 1. Symbols and Description

Sl. No.	Symbol	Description
1	n	No. of classes. Also used for degrees of freedom for $\chi 2$
2	k	No. of features
3	H(.)	Entropy
4	p(.)	Probability
5	w	Feature, word or term
6	Ci	ith Class

discuss few such measures below. Table-1 contains list and description of symbols used in the chapter.

2.2.1 Information Gain (IG)

Before defining *Information Gain*, we define few related terms (Cover & Thomas, 2006; Yang & Pedersen, 1997). *Entropy* is a measure of uncertainty of random variable or equivalently expected value of information content in a random variable. Given probability mass function of a discrete random variable, *X*, *entropy* is defined as,

$$H(X) = -\sum p(x)h(x) = -\sum p(x)\log_2 p(x) \tag{1}$$

Equivalently in terms of expectation, E,

$$H(X) = E\left\{\log\frac{1}{p(X)}\right\} \tag{2}$$

By virtue of base of 2 for the logarithm, units of h(x) are bits. It should also be noted here that *H(X)* depends on probabilities of *X* and not the actual values taken by *X*.

The *joint entropy, H(X,Y)* of a pair of discrete random variables *X* and *Y*, with *p(x,y)* representing the corresponding joint distribution is defined by,

$$H\left(X,Y\right) = -\Sigma\Sigma\, p\left(x,y\right)\log\left(p\left(x,y\right)\right) = -E\left(\log\left(X,Y\right)\right) \tag{3}$$

The *conditional entropy* is defined as,

$$H\left(Y\,/\,X\right) = \sum P\left(X\right)H\left(Y\,/\,X = x\right) = -E\left(p\left(\left(Y\,/\,x\right)\right)\right) \tag{4}$$

Consider a set of patterns that belongs to *n* classes, C_1, C_2, ... C_n. *Information Gain* measures the number of bits of information gained for classification by knowing that whether a feature *w* is present or absent in a document. It can be represented (Yang & Pedersen, 1997) as,

$$G(w) = -\sum_{i=1}^{n} p\left(C_i\right) \log p\left(C_i\right) + p\left(w\right) \sum_{i=1}^{n} p\left(C_i / w\right) \log\left(p\left(C_i / w\right)\right)$$
$$+ p\left(w^c\right) \sum_{i=1}^{n} p\left(C_i / w^c\right) \log\left(p\left(C_i / w^c\right)\right)$$

(5)

where, w^c indicates absence of the feature.

2.2.2 Mutual Information (MI)

Relative entropy or *Kullback-Leibler distance* (Cover & Thomas, 2006) between two probability mass functions, *p(x)* and *q(y)* of discrete random variables X and Y is defined as,

$$D(p,q) = \sum_{x \in X} p(x) \log \frac{p(x)}{q(x)} = E\left\{\log \frac{p(x)}{q(x)}\right\}$$

(6)

Relative entropy represents distance between two distributions, albeit it does not satisfy the triangular inequality.

Consider two random variables *X* and *Y* with joint and marginal probability mass functions as *p(x,y)*, *p(x)* and *p(y)*. The *Mutual Information, I(X;Y)* is defined as,

In terms of *entropy*, mutual information can be written as,

$$I(X,Y) = H(X) - H(X / Y) = H(X) + H(Y) - H(X,Y)$$

(7)

Information Gain is also referred to as *Expected Mutual Information*.

2.2.3 Gini Index

Gini index(GI) as discussed in the work by Uysal (2016) is considered global feature selection method. It is given as below.

$$GI(x) = \sum_{i=1}^{n} P\left(w / C_i\right)^2 P\left(C_i / w\right)^2$$

(8)

where $P(w/C_i)$ is the probability of term w given the presence of class C_i and $P(C/w)$ is the probability of class C_i given presence of term w.

2.2.4 χ^2 Statistic

The χ^2 statistic measures lack of independence between a feature, w and class C. It is compared with χ^2 value with '*n*' (with *n=1*) degrees of freedom to decide on independence. Consider 2×2 contingency table of feature w and class C. Define the following parameters.

A = Number of times w and C occur together
B = Number of times w and $\bar{C}$ occur
C = Number of times $\bar{w}$ and C occur
D = Number of times $\bar{w}$ and $\bar{C}$ occur

$$\chi^2(w,c) = \frac{N(AD - CB)^2}{(A+C)(B+D)(A+B)+(C+D)} \tag{9}$$

After computing individual χ^2 statistics between feature and class C, combined scores and category specific scores are as given below.

$$\chi^2_{avg}(w) = \sum_{i=1}^{n} P(C_i)\chi^2(w, C_i) \tag{10}$$

/(X^2_{max} (w) = max_{i=1}^{n}\{\chi^2(w,C_{i})\} \tag{11}

Since χ^2 is a normalized one, it can be compared across the features for the same class. But the score is not known to be reliable for low scores.

2.2.5 Odds Ratio

Given features $w_1, w_2, \ldots, w_p$ and classes $C_1, C_2, \ldots, C_n$, Odds Ratio (OR) (Sebastiani, 2002) for term w_q, and class C_i is defined as below.

$$OR(w_q, C_i) = \frac{P(w_q / C_i)\left(1 - P(w_q / \overline{C_i})\right)}{\left(1 - P(w_q / C_i)\right)P(w_q / \overline{C_i})} \tag{12}$$

2.2.6 Term Strength (TS)

Term strength (Yang & Pedersen, 1997; Wilbur & Sirotkin, 1992) helps in identifying term importance based on related documents. The documents with many common words are considered similar and related. It is computed through following steps.

- Consider a set of training documents
- Identify pair of similar documents as those whose cosine similarity is above a chosen threshold
- Term strength in a pair of related documents is given by the estimated conditional probability that the probability that it occurs in document y given that it occurred in document x.

2.2.7 Correlation

Pearson correlation criteria between q^{th} feature, x_q and a continuous outcome, Y detects linear relationship between feature and variable is given by

$$r_q = \frac{\text{cov}\left(x_q, Y\right)}{\sqrt{\text{var}\left(x_q\right)\text{var}\left(Y\right)}} \tag{13}$$

where cov() is the covariance between x_q and Y and var is the variance.

2.3 Wrapper Methods

Wrapper methods (Chandrashekar & Sahin (2014); Kohavi & John, 1997) identify a feature subset with the help of an induction algorithm that is treated as a black box. Sequential selection of search algorithms find a subset of features heuristically that maximizes an objective function such as classification performance. Some of the search algorithms that helps to achieve this objective are (a) branch and bound method (Narendra & Fukunaga, 1977), where the search systematically identifies higher number of features, (b) Genetic Algorithms (Goldberg, 1989) (c) particle swarm optimization and (d) sequential selection algorithms. We provide an overview of feature selection using genetic algorithms and sequential selection algorithms.

2.3.1 Feature Selection Using Genetic Algorithms

Genetic algorithms(GA) fall in the class of heuristic search algorithms. Genetic algorithms are randomized search methods that attempt to find a global minimum motivated by natural evolution. It makes use of genetic operators known as selection, cross-over and mutation. It simultaneously evaluates a population of potential solutions. For feature selection, a chromosome length equal to the initial set of features is considered. Each feature is associated with a binary value indicating presence (1) or absence (0) of the corresponding feature. The objective function is classification accuracy obtained by some chosen supervised learning algorithm. From generation to generation, highly fit individuals are retained to arrive at a near-global optimal feature subset. The parameters that needs to be chosen empirically are the probabilities of selection, cross-over and mutation. There are many variants of genetic algorithms, generic operators, termination criterion, problem encoding, quantization of parameters, etc. (Yang & Honavar, 1998; Oh et al., 2004; Chen et al., 2013)

2.3.2 Sequential Feature Selection Approaches

Sequential feature selection (Feri et al., 1994, Pudil et al., 1994, Chandrashekar & Sahin, 2014) refers to iterative approaches to feature selection. Different variants of sequential feature selection are given as below.

- **Sequential Feature Selection (SFS):** In SFS, one starts with an empty set and includes features one by one sequentially till the classification accuracy stops improving or required number of features is reached. The feature subset increases as we include additional features. The disadvantage of this method is that correlation between the features is not accounted for. Secondly, there is no backtracking step as the features are permanently included.
- **Sequential Backward Selection (SBS):** In this case, one starts with complete feature set and removes features one by one till decrease in performance is minimal.
- **Sequential Floating Forward Selection (SFFS):** The approach is similar to that of SFS. It includes a backtracking step. In addition to SFS step, it excludes one feature at every stage, and evaluates the performance. If the performance shows improvement, that excluded feature is removed otherwise it continues with SFS step. The process is terminated when required number of features is reached.
- **Adaptive Sequential Floating Forward Selection (ASFFS):** SFS and SFFS produce nested subsets as during SFS step two correlated features could

be included. Correlated features do not provide additional information. It attempts to reduce the redundant selected features by choosing two adaptive parameters that represent number of features that could be included or excluded based on the classification performance.

2.4 Embedded Methods

In wrapper methods, each time a feature subset is chosen, the feature set is evaluated based on performance of a learning machine. This is computationally expensive. Further they do not incorporate knowledge about specific structure of the classification function. Embedded methods integrate feature selection and the structure of classification function. Following is the broad structure of an embedded feature selection method (Lal et al., 2006; Stoppiglia, 2003; Guyon et al., 2003; Weston et al., 2000)

- Consider an objective function that measures the performance of a model returned by an algorithm
- Carry out sensitive analysis or compute gradient of the objective function when one feature is removed
- Rerun the algorithm
- Select features for removal/addition that would induce desired change in the objective function

Theoretical Framework: Lal et al. (Lal et al., 2006) provide a unifying theoretical framework for embedded feature selection methods. We provide a brief overview of the discussion. Consider a parameterized family of classification or regression functions. The objective is to find a vector of indicator variables that take values 0 or 1 indicating absence or presence of the feature respectively and a parameter set of the learning functions such that expected risk is minimized.

Wrapper methods minimize the risk by means of training on the given data with a feature subset defined by the indicator functions. The features are selected by measuring the performance of a trained classifier without depending on the structure of the learning function. If the optimizing function makes use of the learner and class of functions on which it operates, we refer to such methods as embedded methods. Some embedded methods directly evaluate subset of features without making use of model selection criterion. Depending on how the embedded methods solve the above two problems, they are broadly classified into the following.

- Approaches that include or exclude features iteratively in a greedy manner to approximate expected risk minimization. The features added in either through forward selection where one or more features are selected according to criteria, backward elimination where by starting with all features, one or more features are iteratively removed or nested methods where during an iteration features are added or removed. Many approaches (Guyon et al., 2003) are in use in ranking features in accordance with the influence on classifier.

- Approaches that generate scaling factors for features instead of indicator variables.
- If the learner and count function of non-zero features are convex, the problem reduces to minimization of a regularized function of the learner.

We discuss few specific approaches. They are usually referred to by their short forms in the literature. Hence they are listed by their abbreviated forms and the expansion is provided during the discussion.

2.4.1 LASSO

LASSO (Least Absolute Shrinkage and Selection Operator) is in the class of shrinkage methods (Friedman et al., 2001). It constructs linear model for features with L_1 penalty for regression coefficients resulting in shrinkage of many coefficients to zero. Through appropriate choice of thresholding, this is useful for feature selection

2.4.2 RFE

RFE (Recurrent Feature Elimination) (Lal et al., 2006) is in the broad class of backward feature elimination embedded algorithms. It aims at selecting features recursively by considering smaller set of features. An estimator (support vector machine) is trained to assign weights to initial set of features. Recursively, features with smaller weights are eliminated from the current set of features. The recursion can be stopped once a desired set of features is reached.

2.4.3 OBD

OBD (Optimal Brain Damage) (Lal et al., 2006) is a backward feature selection approach. It is a method to prune weights in Neural Networks. It identifies weights that could be eliminated in a trained neural network by computing a saliency measure which is a function of second derivative of weight and square of the weight. Thus, the weights which do not affect the training error are eliminated.

2.4.4 Grafting

Grafting (Lal et al., 2006) is a greedy forward feature selection algorithm that minimizes the objective function over enlarged feature set. The methods depend on the structure of the target linear function. The other forward selection embedded algorithms include LARS (Least Angle Regression) and Gram-Schmidt Orthogonalization

2.5 Other Approaches

A number of other interesting approaches include hybrid methods that integrate conventional feature selection methods to approaches such as genetic algorithms, fuzzy methods, and chaos theory (Gunal, 2011; Ebrahimpour & Eftekhari, 2017; Ghareb, et al., 2016; Chen, et al., 2013), structure regularization (Luo et al, 2017) artificial neural networks (Verikas & Bacauskienne, 2002), annealing (Barbu et al., 2017), game theory approach to feature selection (Nunzio & Orio, 2016) and global feature selection with the help of local and global feature selection scores (Uysal, 2016).

Gunal (2011) demonstrates that a hybrid feature selection approach, which is a combination of filter and wrapper feature selection methods is more effective than either one of the approaches for text classification. The filters are selected using document frequency, mutual information, chi-square and information gain. Genetic algorithms based feature selection is used as wrapper method. Ebrahimpour & Eftekhari (2017) propose a feature selection approach by an ensemble of ranking algorithms and an ensemble of similarity measures. The ensemble of ranking algorithms measure feature class relevancy. The ensemble of similarity measures help minimize feature-feature redundancy. The ensembles are integrated to hesitant fuzzy sets. This novel approach termed as Maximum Relevancy and Minimum Redundancy (MRMR) approach by using Hesitant Fuzzy Sets (HFS). MRMR-HFS is shown to be effective for high dimensional feature selection. Ghareb et al. (2016) propose hybrid feature selection algorithm. The work modifies the crossover and mutation operations from the conventional genetic algorithms operators which is discussed earlier in Section 2.3. The modifications take into account term and document frequencies of the terms (genes) for crossover and the mutation is based on the classifier performance of the parent chromosomes and feature importance. The method, termed as Extended Genetic Algorithm (EGA) is applied on six well-known filter feature selection methods thereby creating six different hybrid approaches. The work demonstrates that such hybrid approaches are more effective than filters-alone methods for dimensionality reduction. Chen et al. (2013) integrate chaos optimization to genetic algorithm, terming the method as Chaos Genetic Feature Selection optimization (CGFSO). It explores all subsets of given feature set. After completing the mutation step in generating next generation in conventional genetic algorithm, the logistic chaos mutation for population is carried out to generate new population of chromosomes. The update step to next generation passes through a decision based on comparison of fitness values between pre- and post- chaotic mutation step. The experiments carried out on the chosen dataset indicate better performance of CGFSO than SVM and GA.

Luo et al. (2017) propose adaptive unsupervised feature selection with structure regularization, acronymed ANFS. A desired feature subset is arrived at by locally linear embedded (LLE) adaptive reconstruction graph and selective matrix simultaneously. The approach is examined on various bench mark datasets and demonstrated that ANFS outperformed many of state of the art algorithms. Verikas and Bacauskienne (2002) use the feed forward neural network for feature selection (NNFS). The work compares the proposed method with five other methods such as NNFS based on elimination of input layer weights, the weights based feature saliency measure, NN output sensitivity based feature saliency measure, the fuzzy entropy and the discriminant analysis and demonstrates better performance on UCI bench mark datasets (Lichman, 2013). Although the approach is promising, the feature sets considered for demonstration are not large. Barbu et al. (2017) propose feature selection with annealing (FSA) algorithm. The work provides theoretical guarantees, selection of annealing parameters with respect to computation time, learning rate, and typical number of iterations needed. Experimental results are presented with simulated data, UCI bench mark data, face image key point detection, and ranking experiments. The work demonstrates applicability of FSA for different types of problems such as regression, classification and ranking. Nunzio and Orio (2016) apply game theory framework to select positive and negative features for a text classification task. The work discusses theoretical framework and shift of Nash equilibrium with respect to different strategies. It provides directions for practical implementation of their proposed work. Uysal (2016) achieves global feature selection by computing local feature selection scores and global feature selection metrics and iterating over the features till a representative subset is obtained. The work evaluates such selection using classification algorithms such as SVM, and Naive Bayes. With the help of micro-F1 and macro-F1 scores (Uysal, 2016), the work demonstrates on several benchmark datasets that such a global feature selection approaches achieves better scores than those obtained filter based feature metrics.

Few other algorithms include optimization based algorithms with sparsity induced penalties used for feature selection. They have theoretical guarantees as well. But for large number of features such algorithms are not scalable (Barbu et al., 2017). Boosting for feature selection is also effective. But with large feature set scenarios such as those in big data, boosting is not fast enough. (Barbu et al., 2017)

In summary, *filter methods* examine all features in identifying relevant feature set. It usually orders features by individual ranking or by nested subsets of features. The relevance is evaluated through statistical tests. They are robust against overfitting but may fail to select all useful features. *Wrapper methods* evaluate multiple feature subsets for their usefulness in arriving at an optimal representative feature set with the help of a learning machine. In this process it searches feature subsets. It uses cross validation for evaluation. The methods are prone to overfitting and need significant amount of computation time. *Embedded methods* are similar to wrapper methods. It evaluates usefulness of feature subsets. Search for such subsets is guided by learning and makes use of structure of a learning algorithm. It uses cross validation for evaluation. They are computationally less expensive and less prone to overfitting.

3. SPECIFIC ISSUES WITH PRACTICAL TEXT DATA PROCESS AND FEATURE REDUCTION

Most text data related to clustering and classification problems need to process huge amount of unique words or tokens. The relevant data depends on the nature of the problem. In the broad category of document classification and clustering, there are many problems that are encountered. We list a few practical problems that are predominantly related to e-commerce domain.

- Author classification of literary works (Stamatatos, 2009)
- E-mail classification as fraud or genuine (Sahami et al., 1998)
- Postal address normalization
- Address text classification (Babu et al., 2015)
- Short text classification (Sriram et al., 2010)
- Incomplete address classification
- Product review categorization as multi-label classification of positive, negative, actionable, non-actionable, assignment to which of the `k' subsystems of an Organization (Hu & Liu, 2004; Catal & Mehmet, 2017)
- Large scale catalogue data classification, where categories could contain thousands of product verticals and millions of products given a blob of text or description (Shen et al.,2012)
- Categorization of short text documents (Sriram, et al., 2010; Bhushan et al., 2017)
- Chat classification (Ptaszynski, et al., 2017)

It should be noted here that the list is not exhaustive. They are chosen to represent practical problem scenarios.

One needs to characterize the data well before embarking on to generating a relevant abstraction of the data. The text data related to each of the above problems provide different kind of challenges. For example, in case of author classification of documents, one would expect formal English documents that are grammatically sound. In public supplied documents such as reviews, and entered addresses, the data would contain a number of challenges as listed below.

- Unintended special characters while entering the data
- Deliberate special characters or repeat words, such *as NOT GOOD ** NOT GOOD ** NOT GOOD*
- Merged words or missing spaces, such as, *the product wasnot deliveredon time*
- Complete set of capital words to convey emphasis about liking or displeasure, such as *AAWWSSSOMMMEEE, WOWWWWW*
- Non-standard abbreviations leading to thousands of variants, such as *apts, aparts, aptts* to represent *'apartments'*
- Spell variations due to lack of literacy or carelessness. {*B'lore, Bangaloor, Bangaluru, Benguluru*} to represent *'Bangalore or Benguluru'*
- Incomplete sentences

Each of these datasets is challenging and require a domain specific modeling. Also, features that are necessary for appropriate machine learning problem are also different. One needs to choose a list of *stop words*, which are problem dependent. For example, parts of speech could be useful in classifying works generated by authors but not useful in user generated content or short text documents such as chats or twitter messages. In view of this, the list of words that needs to eliminated from raw data, referred to as, stop words becomes problem dependent. The words that do not *possibly help the classification in the context of problem objective* should be eliminated. Some related issues are whether to retain frequent terms (term-frequency, *tf*) and inverse document frequency (*idf*), product of *tf* and *idf*, exploiting or removing the letter case (lower or upper case or both), etc (Manning et al., 2009).

3.1 Need for Preprocessing

In the context of feature selection of numerical data, the problem relates to a tradeoff of effective representativeness vis-a-vis redundancy of features. In case of text related problems, before attempting to select features through formal approaches, it would be ideal to remove features that are unlikely to help the machine learning objective. Some associated preprocessing models that could be developed prior to resorting to feature selection methods are the following.

- Reducing data by removing features that occur below a term-frequency threshold
- Automated approaches to spell variant detection, and equivalent spell mapping (Babu et al., 2015)
- n-grams generation and assessment of its use against 1-gram
- Probabilistic separation of words
- Attribute relevance of a product
- Equivalent or similar words to represent a concept which helps in reducing the vocabulary through domain expertise or automated methods

For example, in address classification problem consisting of of about 5.6 million addresses in (Babu et al., 2015), such methods reduced the data set to 45% of its original size.

Thus it is important to subject text data to preprocessing before subjecting them to formal feature selection methods.

4. EXPERIMENTS ON FEATURE SELECTION

We demonstrate working of text feature selection using some representative filter, wrapper and embedded methods for a common dataset of address classification. In this section we describe data under consideration, and present experimental results.

4.1 Description of Dataset

The dataset consists of Bangalore addresses. The addresses belong to a delivery hub area of an e-Commerce Organization. They are registered addresses of users who purchase items online with the company. As mentioned earlier, the addresses contain the previously discussed challenges. They are resolved through multiple

Table 2. Sample Address Data

Sl. No.	Address
1	Honeywell Techologies ADARSH Prime projects, Devarabisanahalli, Cessna Business Park
2	1BMAIN, 1st Block, Koramangala, Jakkasandra Extn, KMG, 1ST block
3	A-Block, SLS Sunflower, bhoganahalli, Marathalli, Sarjapur ORR, Devarabisinahalli
4	Wipro Corporate Office, Doddakannelli, Sarjapurroad
5	Accenture, Pritechpark, SEZ, 7Block, Outer Ring Road, Bellandur village, Varthur Hobli, ECOSPACE

preprocessing models (Babu et al., 2015). A geographical area spanning over about 300 sq. km area is considered. It is subdivided into 24 subareas that represent 24 classes. The entire work of identifying subareas, and labeling the addresses belonging to these subareas is achieved through integration of domain knowledge of the field executives of the Organization. We consider a dataset consisting of 16,562 addresses belonging to 24 subareas. It consisted of about 49,683 words. The number of unique features after subjecting the data to preprocessing reduces to 7373.

Table 2 contains some sample addresses. In order to maintain privacy of the users, the names of the individuals and dwelling numbers are not presented. Following are some of the challenges found in this limited set of addresses.

- The contain spelling mistakes like that in Honewell *"Techologies"*
- Mix of upper and lower case letters
- Spelling variations for *Devarabisanahalli* and *Devarabisinahalli*
- Equivalent representations which effectively reduce the feature set such as {*ORR, Outer Ring Road*}, and {*KMG, Koramangala*}

A domain expert can identify the redundant information. Such data is unlikely to help classification. With massive datasets, manual identification of such patterns is impossible and also avoidable. For achieving automated processing, some of these issues could be sorted out by data understanding, integration of domain knowledge and development of innovative models for preprocessing.

Table 3. Results with Original Data

Experimental Data	No. of Classes	No. of Features	Classification Accuracy
Original dataset prior to feature selection and preprocessing	24	7373	90.08%

Table 4. Results with indicate experiments on feature selection

Sl. No.	Approach	No. of selected features	Classification Accuracy	Reduction factor
1	χ2	3000	90.48%	0.59
2	Lasso	2370	90.42%	0.68
3	RFE	2200	90.73%	0.70

4.2 Experiments and Results

We consider the above data. It is 24-category text classification problem. We carried out feature selection experiments with different multi-class classifiers with few sample approaches. We present all the results with SVM with squared hinge loss. The multi-class classification is carried out using with one vs. rest approach. Table 3 contains the results with original data.

The experiments are of indicative nature for feature selection using different methods. Table 4 contains the results. The original number of features is 7373. Feature selection using χ^2, Lasso and RFE are presented. RFE provided best values for classification accuracy and reduction factor. It may be recalled that reduction factor is defined as $(f - f')/f$, where f is the number of original features and f' is number of selected features.

Figure 1 contains classification accuracy for different number of features selected using χ^2 approach. Figure 2 provides classification accuracy for different number of features selected using RFE approach. It is interesting to note that all the methods

Figure 1. Feature Selection using Chi-square method

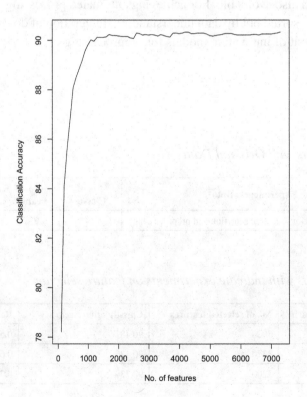

Figure 2. Feature Selection using RFE method

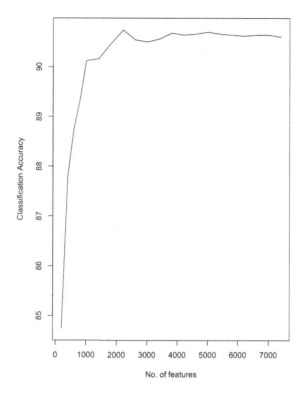

considered for experiments outperformed the classification with original dataset. Secondly, it achieved marginally higher accuracy with significantly less number of features with a reduction factor of 0.59 and above.

5. CONCLUSION

The work forms a brief study of feature selection algorithms. Relevant celebrated works that focused on different aspects of feature selection ranging from specific methods, feature selection metrics, theoretical frameworks, empirical studies, feature selection studies in relation to text mining, text categorization, similarity preserving, etc., are provided. We did not cover deep learning based approaches (Li et al., 2015; Najafabadi, et al., 2015) and feature selection with reference to topic models and their variants.

In the work, we defined the topics of big data and data mining, challenges with large data size and high dimensions and efficient approaches to generate abstraction from large datasets. We discuss various approaches to feature selection such as filter methods, wrapper methods and embedded methods along with relevant work carried out so far.

Filter methods are simple, fast and scalable. Based on a reference metric, variables are ranked to identify most representative features. They need not be combined with prediction. However, we use supervised learning to demonstrate their effectiveness. Further, filter methods can be seen as a preprocessing step before finding optimal feature set or weighting the feature set. Some of drawbacks of filter methods (Guyon & Elisseeff, 2003) include whether redundant variables help each other. Secondly, perfectly correlated variables do not provide any additional information to pattern characterization or classification. Further, by means of filter approaches when a feature is ranked low and eliminated, it may not always imply that the subsequent task like classification is not adversely affected by those eliminated variables.

Wrapper methods select the variables or features with the help of a learning machine by treating it as a black box. A number of approaches such as sequential feature selection variants, randomized search algorithms and branch and bound algorithms are used. It is generally found that wrapper methods require large amount of computation time which is compounded by high dimensionality of patterns. Sequential selection algorithms such as forward selection and backward elimination are known to be robust against over fitting and computationally fast.

Embedded methods integrate feature selection as part of training process and makes use of structure of learning algorithm as against wrapper methods which use learning algorithm as a black box. Embedded systems are likely to over fit. Each of these three approaches has its relative advantages and disadvantages.

We discussed practical issues in text feature selection problem in the context of e-commerce, informal text and short text categorization. In the chosen sample data related to e-commerce logistics problem of address classification, we note that in spite of reducing the feature set almost by half through preprocessing methods, chosen feature selection approaches significantly reduced the feature set while marginally improving the classification accuracy. The experiments are indicative of feature selection methods and do not cover entire spectrum of methods.

6. FURTHER RESEARCH DIRECTIONS

In order to process voluminous massive datasets, it is usual practice to scale up the machines to process such dataset. Such datasets are also characterized by feature sparseness and non-linear relationships among the features. We believe that notwithstanding the ability to process the data, it is necessary to carry out appropriate preprocessing and dimensionality reduction to generate meaningful and actionable abstractions. From this context, feature selection assumes significance in massive datasets. One interesting ongoing work is feature selection nuances in the presence of severe class imbalance. A motivating discussion that cites related works can be found in the work by Uysal (Uysal, 2016). This research direction acquires significance in view of the increasing datasets in real world applications are imbalanced such as those in fraud/spam detection and trust and safety. Subspace methods, multi-agent systems where each agent focusing on different aspect of feature subsets, hybrid feature selection approaches, deep learning based approaches focusing on necessary theoretical frameworks and empirical nuances are some of the other ongoing and future research directions.

REFERENCES

Babu, T. R., Chatterjee, A., Khandeparker, S., Subhash, A. V., & Gupta, A. (2015). Geographical address classification without using geolocation coordinates. *Proceedings of the 9th Workshop on Geographic Information Retrieval*, 8. doi:10.1145/2837689.2837696

Babu, T. R., Murty, M. N., & Subrahmanya, S. V. (2013). *Compression Schemes for Mining Large Datasets*. London: Springer-Verlag. doi:10.1007/978-1-4471-5607-9

Barbu, A., She, Y., Ding, L., & Gramajo, G. (2017). Feature Selection with Annealing for Computer Vision and Big Data Learning. *IEEE Transactions on Pattern Analysis and Machine Intelligence*, *39*(2), 272–286. doi:10.1109/TPAMI.2016.2544315 PMID:27019473

Bhushan, S. B., Danti, A., & Fernandes, S. L. (2017). A Novel Integer Representation-Based Approach for Classification of Text Documents. *Proceedings of the International Conference on Data Engineering and Communication Technology*, 557-564.

Blum, A. L., & Langley, P. (1997). Selection of relevant features and examples in machine learning. *Artificial Intelligence*, *97*(1), 245–271. doi:10.1016/S0004-3702(97)00063-5

Bondi, A. B. (2000). Characteristics of scalability and their impact on performance. *Proceedings of the 2nd international workshop on Software and performance,* 195-203. doi:10.1145/350391.350432

Cao, L. (Ed.). (2009). *Data mining and multi-agent integration*. Springer Science & Business Media. doi:10.1007/978-1-4419-0522-2

Catal, C., & Mehmet, N. (2017). A sentiment classification model based on multiple classifiers. *Applied Soft Computing*, *50*, 135–141. doi:10.1016/j.asoc.2016.11.022

Chandrashekar, G., & Ferat, S. (2014). A survey on feature selection methods. *Computers & Electrical Engineering*, *40*(1), 16–28. doi:10.1016/j.compeleceng.2013.11.024

Chen, H., Jiang, W., Li, C., & Li, R. (2013). A heuristic feature selection approach for text categorization by using chaos optimization and genetic algorithm. *Mathematical Problems in Engineering*, *2013*, 1–6. doi:10.1155/2013/524017

Chen, M. S., Jiawei, H., & Yu, P. S. (1996). Data Mining: An Overview from Database Perspective. *IEEE Transactions on Knowledge and Data Engineering*, *8*(6), 866–883. doi:10.1109/69.553155

Cover, T. M., & Thomas, J. A. (2006). *Elements of Information Theory*. John Wiley & Sons.

Douglas, L. (2011). *3D Data Management: Controlling Data Volume, Velocity and Variety*. Meta Group.

Ebrahimpour, M. K., & Eftekhari, M. (2017). Ensemble of feature selection methods: A hesitant fuzzy sets approach. *Applied Soft Computing*, *50*, 300–312. doi:10.1016/j.asoc.2016.11.021

Ferri, F., Pudil, P., Hatef, M., & Kittler, J. (1994). Comparative study of techniques for large-scale feature selection. *Pattern Recognition in Practice*, *4*, 403–413.

Forman, G. (2003). An extensive empirical study of feature selection metrics for text classification. *Journal of Machine Learning Research*, *3*, 1289–1305.

Friedman, J., Trevor, H., & Tibshirani, R. (2001). The elements of statistical learning (vol. 1). Springer.

Ghareb, A. S., Bakar, A. A., & Hamdan, A. R. (2016). Hybrid feature selection based on enhanced genetic algorithm for text categorization. *Expert Systems with Applications*, *49*, 31–47. doi:10.1016/j.eswa.2015.12.004

Goldberg, D. (1989). *Genetic Algorithms in search, optimization and machine learning*. Addison-Wesley.

Günal, S. (2012). Hybrid feature selection for text classification. *Turkish Journal of Electrical Engineering & Computer Sciences, 20*(Sup. 2), 1296-1311.

Guyon, I., & Elisseeff, A. (2003). An introduction to variable and feature selection. *Journal of Machine Learning Research*, *3*(Mar), 1157–1182.

Guyon, I., Weston, J., Barnhill, S., & Vapnik, V. (2003). Gene Selection for Cancer Classification using Support Vector Machines. *Journal of Machine Learning Research, 3*(March), 1439–1461.

Hu, M., & Liu, B. (2004, August). Mining and summarizing customer reviews. *Proceedings of the tenth ACM SIGKDD international conference on Knowledge discovery and data mining*, 168-177.

Jain, A. K., Murty, M.N., & Flynn, P.J. (1999). Data clustering: A Review. *ACM Computing Surveys (CSUR), 31*(3), 264-323.

Kohavi, R., & John, G. H. (1997). Wrappers for feature subset selection. *Artificial Intelligence, 97*(1), 273–324. doi:10.1016/S0004-3702(97)00043-X

Lal, T. N., Chapelle, O., Weston, J., & Elisseeff, A. (2006). Embedded methods. In *Feature extraction* (pp. 137–165). Springer Berlin Heidelberg. doi:10.1007/978-3-540-35488-8_6

Leskovec, J., Rajaraman, A., & Ullman, J. D. (2014). *Mining of massive datasets*. Cambridge University Press. doi:10.1017/CBO9781139924801

Li, Y., Algarni, A., Albathan, M., Shen, Y., & Bijaksana, M. A. (2015). Relevance feature discovery for text mining. *IEEE Transactions on Knowledge and Data Engineering, 27*(6), 1656–1669. doi:10.1109/TKDE.2014.2373357

Li, Y., Chen, C. Y., & Wasserman, W. W. (2015) Deep feature selection: Theory and application to identify enhancers and promoters. *International Conference on Research in Computational Molecular Biology*. Springer International Publishing. doi:10.1007/978-3-319-16706-0_20

Lichman, M. (2013). *UCI Machine Learning Repository*. Irvine, CA: University of California, School of Information and Computer Science.

Luo, M., Nie, F., Chang, X., Yang, Y., Hauptmann, A. G., & Zheng, Q. (2017). *Adaptive Unsupervised Feature Selection With Structure Regularization. IEEE Transactions on Neural Networks and Learning Systems*.

Manning, C. D., Raghavan, P., & Schutze, H. (2009). *An Introduction to Information Retrieval*. Cambridge University Press.

Najafabadi, M. M., Villanustre, F., Khoshgoftaar, T. M., Seliya, N., Wald, R., & Muharemagic, E. (2015). Deep learning applications and challenges in big data analytics. *Journal of Big Data, 2*(1), 1. doi:10.1186/s40537-014-0007-7

Narendra, P., & Fukunaga, K. (1977). A branch and bound algorithm for feature subset section. *IEEE Transactions on Computers*, *26*(9), 917–922. doi:10.1109/TC.1977.1674939

Nunzio, G. M. D., & Orio, N. (2016). A game theory approach to feature selection for text classification. *Proc. of 7th Italian Information Retrieval Workshop, 1653*.

Oh, I. S., Lee, J. S., & Moon, B. R. (2004). Hybrid genetic algorithms for feature selection. *IEEE Transactions on Pattern Analysis and Machine Intelligence*, *26*(11), 1424–1437. doi:10.1109/TPAMI.2004.105 PMID:15521491

Parsons, L., Ehtesham, H., & Liu, H. (2004). Subspace clustering for high dimensional data: A review. *ACM SIGKDD Explorations Newsletter*, *6*(1), 90–105. doi:10.1145/1007730.1007731

Ptaszynski, M., Masui, F., Rzepka, R., & Araki, K. (2017). *Subjective? Emotional? Emotive?: Language Combinatorics based Automatic Detection of Emotionally Loaded Sentences*. Academic Press.

Pudil, P., Novovicova, J., & Kittler, J. (1994). Floating search methods in feature selection. *Pattern Recognition Letters*, *15*(11), 1119–1125. doi:10.1016/0167-8655(94)90127-9

Sahami, M., Dumais, S., Heckerman, D., & Horvitz, E. (1998, July). A Bayesian approach to filtering junk e-mail. *Learning for Text Categorization: Papers from the 1998 Workshop, 62*, 98-105.

Sebastiani, F. (2002). Machine learning in automated text categorization. *ACM Computing Surveys*, *34*(1), 1–47. doi:10.1145/505282.505283

Shapiro, G. P., & Frawley, W. J. (1991). *Knowledge Discovery in Databases*. AAAI/MIT Press.

Shen, D., Ruvini, J. D., & Sarwar, B. (2012). Large-scale item categorization for e-commerce. *Proceedings of the 21st ACM international conference on Information and knowledge management, 595-604*.

Song, Q. (2013). A fast clustering-based feature subset selection algorithm for high-dimensional data. *IEEE Transactions on Knowledge and Data Engineering*, *25*(1), 1–14. doi:10.1109/TKDE.2011.181

Sriram, B., Fuhry, D., Demir, E., Ferhatosmanoglu, H., & Demirbas, M. (2010, July). Short text classification in twitter to improve information filtering. *Proceedings of the 33rd international ACM SIGIR conference on Research and development in information retrieval, 841-842*. doi:10.1145/1835449.1835643

Stamatatos, E. (2009). A survey of modern authorship attribution methods. *Journal of the American Society for Information Science and Technology*, *60*(3), 538–556. doi:10.1002/asi.21001

Stoppiglia, H., Dreyfus, G., Dubois, R., & Oussar, Y. (2003). Ranking a Random Feature for Variable and Feature Selection. *Journal of Machine Learning Research*, *3*, 1399–1414.

Uysal, A. K. (2016). An improved global feature selection scheme for text classification. *Expert Systems with Applications*, *43*, 82–92. doi:10.1016/j.eswa.2015.08.050

Verikas, A., & Bacauskiene, M. (2002). Feature selection with neural networks. *Pattern Recognition Letters*, *23*(11), 1323–1335. doi:10.1016/S0167-8655(02)00081-8

Weston, J., Mukherjee, S., Chapelle, O., Pontil, M., Poggio, T., & Vapnik, V. (2000). In S. A. Solla, T. K. Leen, & K.-R. Muller (Eds.), *Feature Selection for SVMs* (Vol. 12, pp. 526–532). Cambridge, MA: MIT Press.

Wilbur, J. W., & Sirotkin, K. (1992). The automatic identification of stop words. *Journal of Information Science*, *18*(1), 45–55. doi:10.1177/016555159201800106

Yang, J., & Honavar, V. (1998). Feature subset selection using a genetic algorithm. *Feature extraction, construction and selection. Springer US*, *1998*, 117–136.

Yang, Y., & Pedersen, J.O. (1997). A comparative study on feature selection in text categorization. *ICML*, *97*, 412-420.

APPENDIX

Related Concepts

The section contains a brief discussion on some related concepts to the activity for the sake of completeness.

Pattern and Feature

A *pattern* is an entity that can be named. Some examples of patterns are a handwritten digit, an image, a text document, an ECG, etc. A pattern is characterized by its attributes, measurements, or aspects, which are called *features*. Depending on nature of pattern, the feature vector can be of very high dimension. For example, in case of an image, every pixel can be considered as a feature. For a given a pattern recognition task, *pattern representation* is pivotal.

Curse of Dimensionality, Feature Selection and Feature Extraction

The goal of pattern recognition can be stated as recognition of patterns with the help of features. Depending on nature of learning process, they can be divided into *supervised* and *unsupervised* learning. Consider a case where the number of features representing a pattern is very large. Further, the number of values that a feature can assume a number of possible values. With high dimensional feature space leading a large volume of space, the available data (patterns) would become sparse. This leads to the concept called *curse of dimensionality*. Such scenarios are very common for text processing applications, where number of features (words or tokens) is very large making a classification or clustering task difficult. This leads to the need for a task for arriving at a subset of features, which is called *feature selection* or *feature subset selection*. Alternately, identify a process through which a new set of features is obtained by transforming the high dimensional input features to a low dimensional feature set, which is known as *feature extraction*. In both these tasks, appropriate feature set is arrived at such that the pattern representation continues to be valid. Such representation validity is ensured through classification task and its accuracy.

Address Data in E-Commerce Domain

In B2C (business to customer) e-commerce companies, customers order their interested products by registering their addresses. Such entered addresses offer a number of challenges to the e-commerce companies. Some of them are aggravated by non-availability of geo-location for every customer especially in some developing countries. This makes an automated operations of shipment delivery difficult. Some of the challenges are the following.

- **Incomplete Addresses:** The addresses are incomplete more often by oversight. It is inadequate for a shipment to be delivered.
- **Special Characters/Un-Intended Spaces:** While entering addresses, a number of special characters become part of addresses either created by interface and in-appropriate key strokes. Un-intended spaces or missing spaces make normal locality names appear different. For example, HSR Layout, could be written as HSRLayout making two different terms of same locality. If number of such terms is large, the combinations of such words, lead to more number of features.
- **Redundant Data:** Usually address entry while customer registration have suggested locations for entering data related to street, locality, city, state, zip-code, etc. Usually, it is found that the data that should have been entered at other locations get listed at first opportunity, leading to data redundancy, making a machine based inference difficult.
- **Additional Information:** Depending on nature of delivery location and nature of the customer, one provides additional data such as directions to delivery executive which makes the address very long and avoidable.
- **Spelling Variations:** Either inadvertently or due to lack of knowledge of customers, same locality or a term is spelled multiple ways. For example, one finds about 1000 variants for "apartments" in about 50,000 addresses. This makes vocabulary size or number of features very large.

Need for Preprocessing Prior to Optimal Feature Selection

Preprocessing of terms based on domain knowledge is an important prerequisite to application of feature selection algorithms. This significantly reduces the input set prior to applying relevancy and redundancy metrics.

Chapter 10
Biological Big Data Analysis and Visualization:
A Survey

Vignesh U
VIT University, India

Parvathi R
VIT University, India

ABSTRACT

The chapter deals with the big data in biology. The largest collection of biological data maintenance paves the way for big data analytics and big data mining due to its inefficiency in finding noisy and voluminous data from normal database management systems. This provides the domains such as bioinformatics, image informatics, clinical informatics, public health informatics, etc. for big data analytics to achieve better results with higher efficiency and accuracy in clustering, classification and association mining. The complexity measures of the health care data leads to EHR (Evidence-based HealthcaRe) technology for maintenance. EHR includes major challenges such as patient details in structured and unstructured format, medical image data mining, genome analysis and patient communications analysis through sensors – biomarkers, etc. The big biological data have many complications in their data management and maintenance especially after completing the latest genome sequencing technology, next generation sequencing which provides large data in zettabyte size.

DOI: 10.4018/978-1-5225-2805-0.ch010

INTRODUCTION

The chapter was initiated by requirement of higher and efficient methodologies to analyze big data in a faster manner. The deficiency has motivated us to investigate the problems in an existing technology and frame a feasible model for this big data analysis. On the other hand, there is a considerable interest in the development of new techniques using dynamic programming algorithms to work faster for bioinformatics methods. High throughput sequencing workflow systems provide easy and cost reduced perspective to genome sequencing with timely detection of functions, accurate and fast solutions for big data in bioinformatics. The table 1 shows the detailed view of the different workflow systems that can support high throughput sequencing technologies which includes a big data incorporated in it for analysis.

Bioinformatics is an interdisciplinary area that deals with the biology, computer and statistics. It involves the major aspects of genomics and proteomics with the genome sequencing, which are very sensitive in nature as representing the individual letter for a single nucleotide in case of DNA sequencing. Since 1970, the biological databases are digitized and their sensitivity factors with efficiency are maintained in a perfect manner but due to the vast amount of increasing data the maintenance aspect and extraction of information from gene expression becomes so complex,

Table 1. High Throughput Sequencing Workflow Systems

Name	Illumina	Solid	Requirements	GUI	CLI	Online	Cloud
Ergatis	yes	yes	Linux, MAC OS X, Windows	yes	no	yes	Yes
Galaxy	yes	yes	Linux, MAC OS X	yes	no	yes	yes
Genboree Workbench	yes	yes	Linux, MAC OS X, Windows	yes	no	yes	Yes
GenePattern	yes	yes	Linux, MAC OS X, Windows	yes	no	yes	No
GeneProf	yes	yes	Linux (it is not tested on Others yet)	yes	no	yes	No
Kepler (bioKepler)	yes	yes	Linux, MAC OS X, Windows; > 1 GB RAM, 2 GHz CPU	yes	no	no	No
KNIME	yes	-	Linux, MAC OS X, Windows	yes	yes	no	Yes
LONI Pipeline	yes	yes	Linux, MAC OS X, Windows	yes	yes	no	No
Moa	yes	yes	Linux	yes	yes	no	No
Tavaxy	yes	yes	Linux	yes	no	yes	Yes
Taverna	yes	yes	Linux, MAC OS X, Windows	yes	yes	no	yes
Yabi	-	-	Linux	yes	yes	yes	yes

thus the big data gives the better results for these problems in an accurate manner. The big data includes the analysis of following major characteristics, viz.

Scale of data – representing the high amount in size
Streaming data – maintaining the velocity for extraction process
Various data forms – variety in form of data included in database can also be easily analyzed
Uncertainty of data – Poor and inaccurate data can be identified

These characteristics are applied on the biological data to provide the information efficiently, accurately and in a faster manner by saving enormous time with big data concepts.

Big data is defined by the dimensions volume, variety, veracity, value and velocity. Most of big data management deals with the map reducing paradigm. In past two decades, data has tremendous growth day by day. Large amount of data is generated from various sources in structured form or unstructured form, which is difficult to analyze. The availability of tremendous data in volume paves the way for higher efficient analysis in an active interdisciplinary area like bioinformatics. In a survey, IBM indicates 2.5 Exabyte's (2003) and 2.72 zettabytes (2012-2015) created every day in social media, which is very hard to analyze. Other than these, the massive amount of data in genome analysis also difficult to handle. Most of these big data prefers Hadoop technology to process, which reads the raw sequence and produce the map to undergo sequence alignment, then identify the variants. The likelihood function plays major role in variant detection. The preliminary analysis is done using functional annotations. Protocols are used to deal with the raw variants. Although they are giving large volume of data, the interpretation of data doesn't take place here in the database. The bioinformatics area provides greater importance to the computational intelligence and analysis methodologies for the purpose of biological data study. The traditional model uses centric data processing with big data (4-5 Gbp) and it takes run time in days to complete the analysis. In these existing models, the aspects of analyzing image and base calling tools are to be already defined and they just incorporate them into it. The alignment algorithm has the presence of repeated known segment duplication and incomplete reference genome.

This chapter includes analysis, interpretation and visualization of big biological data produced by high throughput technologies such as next generation sequencing, microarray etc. The project is a framework for integrating new computational tools. NGS data are aligned by proposed alignment tool pairwise-multiple alignment tool. NGS data undergo assembly process with new proposed algorithm package gene assembler. A new machine learning approaches for resequenced genomes are included to detect polymorphism and structural variant. The resultant analyzed data are visualized using tabular and graphical method with inclusion of new packages of big data visualization using python language. The user will able to connect to the large high amounts of data dumped in the public databases like PDB, NCBI and from several other available online databases. In uploading a custom data, the two ways are practiced: First, uploading the data from local directory by specifying a file name. Secondly, for large files (>3GB) such as NGS data, uploading process can be performed through HTTP/FTP. Though there are various NGS platform offer parallel sequencing analysis, the enormous data is a fundamental problem for analyzing and managing. The proposed software is well suitable for managing the data in a local database providing the storage management of raw and processed sequenced data with newer schema and it integrates proposed algorithms with high performance computing, which occupies minimum amount of memory space for this huge data with good complexity measures. This model clearly states the process of interpretation analysis occurs on data. Data pre-processing involves alignment process to avoid the noisy and missing data. Web Interface provides access to the web to get a data for specific processes of comparison to maximize the project outcome. The model supports file formats such as FASTA, FASTAQ and ARFF to give efficient analysis on big biological data and it includes set of tools to handle all known variants and convert it to a feasible format. This model predicts the cancer diseases to which the given data belongs to. It can be of different types of cancer – skin cancer, breast cancer, anal cancer, brain tumor, bone cancer, bile duct cancer, cervical cancer, gall bladder cancer, kidney cancer and lung cancer. Thus, the main aspect of this software is to predict the cancer disease in a given big data. The model also supports all types of big biological data for analysis and it is not limited to the particular problem cancer. The general aspects of bioinformatics such as gene prediction, protein prediction, sequence analysis, clustering, biological filter and statistical methods to view the data in different manner. The project implementation will lead to a continuous improvement and optimization in performance to achieve better results. Visualization domain includes the statistical tool to deliver the report in user's format. These models are useful in a big data biomedical research to identify the type and specification of cancer patterns with all necessary technical needs.

The status of research in big volume of data for biological aspects such as Protein, DNA etc. has been increased from every nine months to one year. Since, the database contains trillion-fold updating annually and daily in the sequencing aspect, the illumine technology can faster the performance in their own way as their perceptions are considered to be 3GB/min for sequencing a genome. As a performance increases, this DNA or protein sequencing methodology can also be used for several other applications which relates the process of sequence methodology.

The identification of properties in a biological gene network analysis is a challenging factor. The method of regulating gene is to identify nuclear factors approving short DNA sequence motifs which occur in upstream of the promoter and encoded regions. This analysis gives a way by which the genes occurring in the same tissue with certain conditions are confirmed to share some of the common regulatory binding sites. This method of identifying motifs gives the necessary details about the tissue specified for their expression related control and signal control. In this way, the features of promoters are identified by the genome DNA and runtime characteristics of gene expression that are found in the process of identifying gene through start codon and stop codon. This codon identification can be performed by studying the methods of promoters and their analysis in a sequence, which acts as a major problem for sequence analysis in most of the cases. Hence, newly series methods are found for identifying and studying the regions of promoters. The functions of promoters can be retrieved from several databases such as PDB, which gives structured sequence, in which the regions are found through the 3D structure. Characterized promoters have been frequently mined from several online databases (annotated promoters in PubMed) or the "Eukaryotic Promoter Database" of the ISREC (EPD, http://www.epd.isb-sib.ch).

This chapter helps to create customized big data solutions keeping in mind the direct needs of biomedical research and to provide the manual aspects to desktop systems in an easy, faster and efficient manner. As of in the path of previous technologies does, big data also has its influence in the IT industry without any hiding techniques in it to the world. This big data not only has their influence in the industry but also makes the industry to move to the next level through which their businesses can be grown in an effective and efficient way. Although it has its advantage in business growth, Microsoft provides that managing big data is a major problem. The COE of Microsoft said that the big data helps in making decisions for the business and identifying the hot spots in the architecture very quickly. "Big data absolutely has the potential to change the way governments, organizations, and academic institutions conduct business and make discoveries, and it's likely to change how everyone lives their day-to-day lives," said Hauser. According to this quote the analysis, interpretation and visualization of big data needs lot to be improved than the existing models available, our work will fulfill all these aspects and gives the efficient result useful for the research and development in the area of biotechnology.

BIOINFORMATICS – BIG DATA

Bioinformatics and big data are much related together since the biological data have to be maintained for the interdisciplinary areas like bioinformatics analysis, interpretation, prediction and pattern recognition etc. the maintenance of this biological data are very tough for the database since the databases are available on public, their updating are done daily and also in an annually manner. This maintenance of large volume of data paves the need for big data in bioinformatics. Thus, the big data enters biological data with necessity of its function unavoidable. The functions involved in database includes pattern recognition, pattern matching, pattern analysis with different categories of biological data such as gene, genome, DNA, protein, RNA, SNP, SRA, probe, taxonomy etc. there are separate public databases are maintained for different biological data's such as structured proteins in databases like PDB, unstructured protein in NCBI like public databases, drug sequences are maintained in an drug bank database etc. the data warehouse are the major gateway for bioinformatics in an research aspects to get their input biological data and perform processes, add functionalities and upload to a public database again for the world reference.

NGS DATA ANALYSIS, INTERPRETATION AND VISUALIZATION

The process takes place in NGS is to unravel the ordered sequence of nucleic acids that group together to make DNA of the given sample. The big data from NGS becomes so big and the challenge of maintaining and analyzing data also increased in recent years. The first human genome sequencing took nearly 10 years with amount in number of billion USD, whereas now it takes only one week with 2000 USD in a single machine due to the different software tools available for big data analytics in an efficient manner that speeds up the processes.

Statistics performed in biological data finds difficult to most of the biological experts including the scientists, teachers etc. since, the problem they faces deals with the probability distribution occurs in the wavelet transform, degrees of freedom, density calculation, path length, formulae selection, etc. In this cases are so far the statistical tools has its major part, which can be making the process in an easier and efficient manner for the performance such as excel, spreadsheets and the programming languages are also to be useful for those strategies such as python etc. these calculations are classified into four major types for their statistical and graphical representations such as network overview, node overview, edge overview and dynamic. Though these types available, the connected components are analyzed and the corresponding nodes and edges are found. Their modularity and page rank with respect to network overview are also calculated. Thus, by this way we can carry out the obtained results and their interpretation can also be performed here in an efficient way.

In a transcriptional regulation, the factors considered for the proteins are the tough section for the given sequences to have the control over it. The major fact it is to find where these DNA bind the protein in to it, in the middle RNA acts in the way by transforming the base from T to U, through which the codon identification done for the amino acid present in the proteins. These aspects can be done efficiently and their scores can also be mentioned graphically. This can also be done for all the available methods for the protein translation. These methods are also to be applied for various biological techniques such as DNA – protein interaction, healthcare etc. Figure 1 shows the methodology for NGS data maintenance by which analysis, interpretation and visualization can be done for the increased biological data. Figure 1 is proposed based on the methods that can be well efficient for maintaining data in the NGS.

Clustering On Structured Proteins With Merge Filter

The protein structure is predicted by using target sequences from BLAST. The predicted protein structure of macropus rufus and structured proteolyzed lysozyme protein are

Figure 1. System Architecture

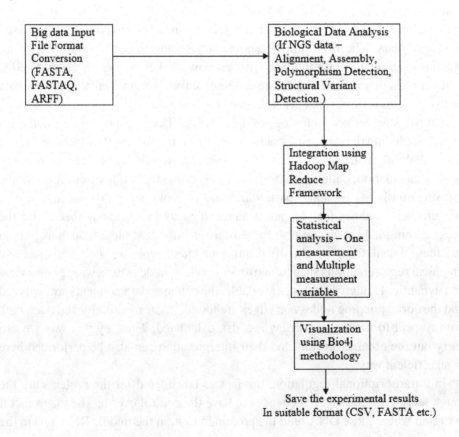

interacted together using merge sets filter for clustering. The selection of a clustering technique for protein clustering is a problem. In order to estimate, performance on three clustering algorithms that are SimpleKMeans, ExpectationMaximization and MakeDensityBasedClusterer are analysed. Comparative analysis with various clustering algorithms illustrates the efficiency of the better clustering algorithm. This method can be applied for the large class of applications such as drug discovery, protein-protein analysis, docking etc. A survey on different types of bioinformatics tools available for next generation sequencing process are done and accumulated extensive experience in sample handling, variant detection and bioinformatics analysis on tools. The research in this area has various advantages to the real time applications, which led to accurate techniques for the process of extracting information related to patterns from a given database.

A survey of NGS data analysis software and methods done on the memory management to provide space for advances in bioinformatics to address big data problems. We have compared various software tools for the de novo NGS data analysis. Big genome paves a way to give more complex repeated structures, which can be overcome by using best alignment and assembler software tools. This survey provides a technical review of NGS data analysis software tools, algorithms and workflow systems to date, which hopefully will be a useful resource for future next generation sequencing research aspects.

CONCLUSION

This chapter explores the big data analysis technique in NGS biological research and EHR technology for health care. This study also deals with the data management aspects in bioinformatics to address the problems in handling big data with the help of efficient Hadoop map reduce framework. NGS analysis methods for processing the big gene expressions are performed in samples. This survey provides a technical review of big data in bioinformatics, which hopefully will be a useful resource for future research applications such as NGS, Health care, Online databases etc. In future, this survey can be extended in deep to the levels involved in NGS such as analysis, interpretation and visualization based on their recent technologies updation.

REFERENCES

Bao, H., Guo, H., Wang, J., Zhou, R., Lu, X., & Shi, S. (2009). MapView: Visualization of short reads alignment on a desktop computer. *Bioinformatics (Oxford, England)*, *25*(12), 1554–1555. doi:10.1093/bioinformatics/btp255 PMID:19369497

Bare, J. C., Koide, T., Reiss, D. J., Tenenbaum, D., & Baliga, N. S. (2010). Integration and visualization of systems biology data in context of the genome. *BMC Bioinformatics*, *11*(1), 382. doi:10.1186/1471-2105-11-382 PMID:20642854

Bonfield, J. K., & Whitwham, A. (2010). Gap5editing the billion fragment sequence assembly. *Bioinformatics (Oxford, England)*, *26*(14), 1699–1703. doi:10.1093/bioinformatics/btq268 PMID:20513662

Carver, T., Harris, S. R., Berriman, M., Parkhill, J., & McQuillan, J. A. (2011). Artemis: An integrated platform for visualization and analysis of high-throughput sequence-based experimental data. *Bioinformatics (Oxford, England)*, *28*(4), 464–469. doi:10.1093/bioinformatics/btr703 PMID:22199388

Carver, T., Harris, S. R., Otto, T. D., Berriman, M., Parkhill, J., & McQuillan, J. A. (2012). BamView: Visualizing and interpretation of next-generation sequencing read alignments. *Briefings in Bioinformatics*, *14*(2), 203–212. doi:10.1093/bib/bbr073 PMID:22253280

Chen, K., Wallis, J. W., McLellan, M. D., Larson, D. E., Kalicki, J. M., Pohl, C. S., & Mardis, E. R. et al. (2009). BreakDancer: An algorithm for high-resolution mapping of genomic structural variation. *Nature Methods*, *6*(9), 677–681. doi:10.1038/nmeth.1363 PMID:19668202

Clark, M. J., Homer, N., OConnor, B. D., Chen, Z., Eskin, A., Lee, H., & Nelson, S. F. et al. (2010). U87MG Decoded: The Genomic sequence of a Cytogenetically aberrant human cancer cell line. *PLOS Genetics*, *6*(1), e1000832. doi:10.1371/journal.pgen.1000832 PMID:20126413

Craven, M., & Page, C. D. (2015). Big Data in Healthcare: Opportunities and Challenges. *Big Data*, *3*(4), 209–210. doi:10.1089/big.2015.29001.mcr PMID:27441403

Engels, R., Yu, T., Burge, C., Mesirov, J. P., DeCaprio, D., & Galagan, J. E. (2006). Combo: A whole genome comparative browser. *Bioinformatics (Oxford, England)*, *22*(14), 1782–1783. doi:10.1093/bioinformatics/btl193 PMID:16709588

Friedel, M., Nikolajewa, S., Suhnel, J., & Wilhelm, T. (2009). DiProGB: The dinucleotide properties genome browser. *Bioinformatics (Oxford, England)*, *25*(19), 2603–2604. doi:10.1093/bioinformatics/btp436 PMID:19605418

Ganesan, H., Rakitianskaia, A. S., Davenport, C. F., Tümmler, B., & Reva, O. N. (2008). The SeqWord genome Browser: An online tool for the identification and visualization of atypical regions of bacterial genomes through oligonucleotide usage. *BMC Bioinformatics*, *9*(1), 333. doi:10.1186/1471-2105-9-333 PMID:18687122

Ge, H., Liu, K., Juan, T., Fang, F., Newman, M., & Hoeck, W. (2011). FusionMap: Detecting fusion genes from next-generation sequencing data at base-pair resolution. *Bioinformatics (Oxford, England), 27*(14), 1922–1928. doi:10.1093/bioinformatics/btr310 PMID:21593131

Ha, G., Roth, A., Lai, D., Bashashati, A., Ding, J., Goya, R., & Shah, S. P. et al. (2012). Integrative analysis of genome-wide loss of heterozygosity and monoallelic expression at nucleotide resolution reveals disrupted pathways in triple-negative breast cancer. *Genome Research, 22*(10), 1995–2007. doi:10.1101/gr.137570.112 PMID:22637570

Haycox, D. A. (1999). Evidence-Based Healthcare Management. *Evidence-based Healthcare, 3*(3), 67–69. doi:10.1054/ebhc.1999.0247

Hou, H., Zhao, F., Zhou, L., Zhu, E., Teng, H., Li, X., Bao, Q., Wu, J. and Sun, Z. (2010). MagicViewer: Integrated solution for next-generation sequencing data visualization and genetic variation detection and annotation. *Nucleic Acids Research, 38*(Web Server), W732–W736.

Huang, W., & Marth, G. (2008). EagleView: A genome assembly viewer for next-generation sequencing technologies. *Genome Research, 18*(9), 1538–1543. doi:10.1101/gr.076067.108 PMID:18550804

Karakoc, E., Alkan, C., ORoak, B. J., Dennis, M. Y., Vives, L., Mark, K., & Eichler, E. E. et al. (2011). Detection of structural variants and indels within exome data. *Nature Methods, 9*(2), 176–178. doi:10.1038/nmeth.1810 PMID:22179552

Kong, L., Wang, J., Zhao, S., Gu, X., Luo, J., & Gao, G. (2012). ABrowse - a customizable next-generation genome browser framework. *BMC Bioinformatics, 13*(1), 2. doi:10.1186/1471-2105-13-2 PMID:22222089

Korbel, J. O., Abyzov, A., Mu, X., Carriero, N., Cayting, P., Zhang, Z., & Gerstein, M. B. et al. (2009). PEMer: A computational framework with simulation-based error models for inferring genomic structural variants from massive paired-end sequencing data. *Genome Biology, 10*(2), R23. doi:10.1186/gb-2009-10-2-r23 PMID:19236709

Manske, H. M., & Kwiatkowski, D. P. (2009). LookSeq: A browser-based viewer for deep sequencing data. *Genome Research, 19*(11), 2125–2132. doi:10.1101/gr.093443.109 PMID:19679872

Masri, , A., & Nasir, M. (2016). Learning machine implementation for big data Analytics, challenges and solutions. *Journal of Data Mining in Genomics & Proteomics, 07*(02).

Miller, J. R., Koren, S., & Sutton, G. (2010). Assembly algorithms for next-generation sequencing data. *Genomics*, *95*(6), 315–327. doi:10.1016/j.ygeno.2010.03.001 PMID:20211242

Nicol, J. W., Helt, G. A., Blanchard, S. G., Raja, A., & Loraine, A. E. (2009). The integrated genome Browser: Free software for distribution and exploration of genome-scale datasets. *Bioinformatics (Oxford, England)*, *25*(20), 2730–2731. doi:10.1093/bioinformatics/btp472 PMID:19654113

Oyelade, J., Soyemi, J., Isewon, I., & Obembe, O. (2015). Bioinformatics, Healthcare Informatics and Analytics: An Imperative for Improved Healthcare System. *International Journal of Applied Information Systems*, *8*(5), 1–6. doi:10.5120/ijais15-451318

Popendorf, K., & Sakakibara, Y. (2012). SAMSCOPE: An OpenGL-based real-time interactive scale-free SAM viewer. *Bioinformatics (Oxford, England)*, *28*(9), 1276–1277. doi:10.1093/bioinformatics/bts122 PMID:22419785

Schatz, M. C., Phillippy, A. M., Sommer, D. D., Delcher, A. L., Puiu, D., Narzisi, G., & Pop, M. et al. (2011). Hawkeye and AMOS: Visualizing and assessing the quality of genome assemblies. *Briefings in Bioinformatics*, *14*(2), 213–224. doi:10.1093/bib/bbr074 PMID:22199379

Sindi, S. S., Önal, S., Peng, L. C., Wu, H.-T., & Raphael, B. J. (2012). An integrative probabilistic model for identification of structural variation in sequencing data. *Genome Biology*, *13*(3), R22. doi:10.1186/gb-2012-13-3-r22 PMID:22452995

Spudich, G. M., & Fernández-Suárez, X. M. (2010). Touring Ensembl: A practical guide to genome browsing. *BMC Genomics*, *11*(1), 295. doi:10.1186/1471-2164-11-295 PMID:20459808

Sun, R., Love, M. I., Zemojtel, T., Emde, A., Chung, H., Vingron, M., & Haas, S. A. (2012). Breakpointer: Using local mapping artifacts to support sequence breakpoint discovery from single-end reads. *Bioinformatics (Oxford, England)*, *28*(7), 1024–1025. doi:10.1093/bioinformatics/bts064 PMID:22302574

Suzuki, S., Yasuda, T., Shiraishi, Y., Miyano, S., & Nagasaki, M. (2011). ClipCrop: A tool for detecting structural variations with single-base resolution using soft-clipping information. *BMC Bioinformatics*, *12*(Suppl 14), S7. doi:10.1186/1471-2105-12-S14-S7 PMID:22373054

Thorvaldsdottir, H., Robinson, J. T., & Mesirov, J. P. (2012). Integrative Genomics viewer (IGV): High-performance genomics data visualization and exploration. *Briefings in Bioinformatics*, *14*(2), 178–192. doi:10.1093/bib/bbs017 PMID:22517427

Wandelt, S., Rheinländer, A., Bux, M., Thalheim, L., Haldemann, B., & Leser, U. (2012). Data management challenges in next generation Sequencing. *Datenbank Spektrum*, *12*(3), 161–171. doi:10.1007/s13222-012-0098-2

Waterhouse, A. M., Procter, J. B., Martin, D. M. A., Clamp, M., & Barton, G. J. (2009). Jalview version 2 a multiple sequence alignment editor and analysis workbench. *Bioinformatics (Oxford, England)*, *25*(9), 1189–1191. doi:10.1093/bioinformatics/btp033 PMID:19151095

Westesson, O., Skinner, M., & Holmes, I. (2012). Visualizing next-generation sequencing data with JBrowse. *Briefings in Bioinformatics*, *14*(2), 172–177. doi:10.1093/bib/bbr078 PMID:22411711

Yoon, S., Xuan, Z., Makarov, V., Ye, K., & Sebat, J. (2009). Sensitive and accurate detection of copy number variants using read depth of coverage. *Genome Research*, *19*(9), 1586–1592. doi:10.1101/gr.092981.109 PMID:19657104

Zeitouni, B., Boeva, V., Janoueix-Lerosey, I., Loeillet, S., Legoix-ne, P., Nicolas, A., & Barillot, E. et al. (2010). SVDetect: A tool to identify genomic structural variations from paired-end and mate-pair sequencing data. *Bioinformatics (Oxford, England)*, *26*(15), 1895–1896. doi:10.1093/bioinformatics/btq293 PMID:20639544

KEY TERMS AND DEFINITIONS

Bio data mining: It is the process of extracting useful information from the biological database for the reference of biological applications.

Clustering: It groups the similar sets of data's under a single window known as cluster and whole process of cluster said to be clustering.

Codon: Combination of three nucleotides in a sequence used for identifying genes in the genome by start and stop codon.

Docking: A secure, protect and efficient interaction of molecules in a protein used for identifying the biopolymer reactions in the chain, etc for biological applications.

Hadoop: This technology supports for the large datasets involved in the process with the distributed systems in an efficient manner.

Interface: Common line for both the side to meet their needs in their understandable manner especially for communication aspect, data formats in the biological sequence.

Mapreduce: A Big data are subdivided in to the chunks and create the virtual distribution to take place the process in a parallel way without making delay under waiting aspect.

NGS: High throughput sequencing effectively concentrates in the visualization prospects to describe the recent technologies for analysis etc.

Pattern: A regular form which can be used for identifying same genes in the genome or to match the data in the database.

Pipelining: Linear Sequence formed by breaking a very large datasets and results in a data format for easy access in the retrieval process.

APPENDIX 1

PROTEIN STRUCTURE REPRESENTATIONS

In the present work, a unstructured protein sequence (Crab - alpha B crystallin, partial [Macropus rufus]) named as query sequence and the target sequences (2KLR - Solid-state NMR structure of the alpha-crystallin domain in alphaB-crystallin oligomers, 3LIG - Human AlphaB crystallin, 2WJ7 - Human AlphaB crystallin, 2Y1Z - Human Alphab crystallin ACD R120G) are given as input to predict the protein structure as shown in Figure 2. was converted to ARFF file format known as input sequence1. Another structured protein (Egg - Crystal Structure of proteolyzed lysozyme) as shown in Figure 3. was converted into ARFF file known as input sequence2. This PPI method done through mergesets filter in Bioweka software and finds the best clustering algorithm for the real world applications.

APPENDIX 2

Python Scripts and Data Mining Technique

The python language helps in coding the scripts for predicting the protein structure in an efficient way with the help of BLAST algorithm. BLAST paves the way to identify the similarities in the pattern structure with the calculation of affinities in the representation of percentage. This results gives the similar proteins with highest matching patterns that paves the way to identify the protein structure. This protein structure was made to combine with another protein structure and applied a data mining technique clustering with their existing algorithms and found the results. The results of the python scripts are the predicted protein structure shown in Figure 2. The execution of these python scripts are shown in the Figure 4. The scripts includes

Figure 2. Predicted protein structure

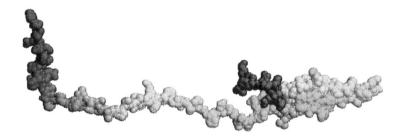

Figure 3. Crystal structure of proteolyzed lysozyme

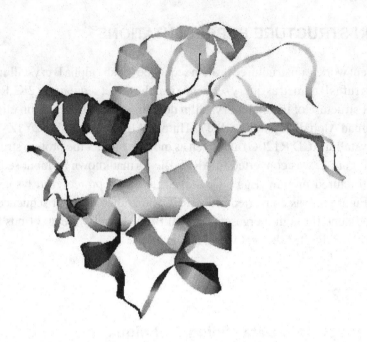

Figure 4. Python scripts execution

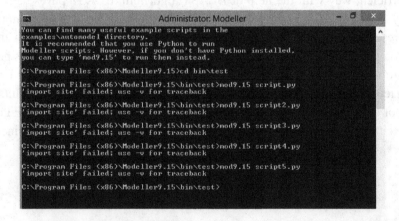

Figure 5. Proteins interaction data clustering

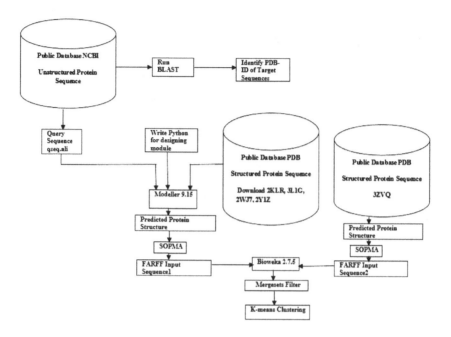

the input structures obtained from the blast results and produce the predicted output of the protein structure.

BIG DATA-BIOINFORMATICS RESEARCH LABS

1. Merck Research Lab, Boston, MA, USA
2. Roche Holding AG, Basel, Switzerland
3. Biodatamics and BioDT, Bethesda, MD, USA
4. Advanced Chemistry Development Lab, Toronto, Canada

Related References

To continue our tradition of advancing information science and technology research, we have compiled a list of recommended IGI Global readings. These references will provide additional information and guidance to further enrich your knowledge and assist you with your own research and future publications.

Abramowicz, W., Stolarski, P., & Tomaszewski, T. (2013). Legal ontologies in ICT and law. In *Digital rights management: Concepts, methodologies, tools, and applications* (pp. 34–49). Hershey, PA: IGI Global. doi:10.4018/978-1-4666-2136-7.ch003

Adamich, T. (2012). Materials-to-standards alignment: How to "chunk" a whole cake and even use the "crumbs": State standards alignment models, learning objects, and formative assessment – methodologies and metadata for education. In L. Tomei (Ed.), *Advancing education with information communication technologies: Facilitating new trends* (pp. 165–178). Hershey, PA: IGI Global. doi:10.4018/978-1-61350-468-0.ch014

Adomi, E. E. (2011). Regulation of internet content. In E. Adomi (Ed.), *Frameworks for ICT policy: Government, social and legal issues* (pp. 233–246). Hershey, PA: IGI Global. doi:10.4018/978-1-61692-012-8.ch015

Aggestam, L. (2011). Guidelines for preparing organizations in developing countries for standards-based B2B. In *Global business: Concepts, methodologies, tools and applications* (pp. 206–228). Hershey, PA: IGI Global. doi:10.4018/978-1-60960-587-2.ch114

Akowuah, F., Yuan, X., Xu, J., & Wang, H. (2012). A survey of U.S. laws for health information security & privacy. *International Journal of Information Security and Privacy*, 6(4), 40–54. doi:10.4018/jisp.2012100102

Akowuah, F., Yuan, X., Xu, J., & Wang, H. (2013). A survey of security standards applicable to health information systems. *International Journal of Information Security and Privacy*, 7(4), 22–36. doi:10.4018/ijisp.2013100103

Al Hadid, I. (2012). Applying the certification's standards to the simulation study steps. In E. Abu-Taieh, A. El Sheikh, & M. Jafari (Eds.), *Technology engineering and management in aviation: Advancements and discoveries* (pp. 294–307). Hershey, PA: IGI Global. doi:10.4018/978-1-60960-887-3.ch017

Al Mohannadi, F., Arif, M., Aziz, Z., & Richardson, P. A. (2013). Adopting BIM standards for managing vision 2030 infrastructure development in Qatar. *International Journal of 3-D Information Modeling (IJ3DIM)*, 2(3), 64-73. doi:10.4018/ij3dim.2013070105

Al-Nuaimi, A. A. (2011). Using watermarking techniques to prove rightful ownership of web images. *International Journal of Information Technology and Web Engineering*, 6(2), 29–39. doi:10.4018/jitwe.2011040103

Alejandre, G. M. (2013). IT security governance legal issues. In D. Mellado, L. Enrique Sánchez, E. Fernández-Medina, & M. Piattini (Eds.), *IT security governance innovations: Theory and research* (pp. 47–73). Hershey, PA: IGI Global. doi:10.4018/978-1-4666-2083-4.ch003

Alexandropoulou-Egyptiadou, E. (2013). The Hellenic framework for computer program copyright protection following the implementation of the relative european union directives. In *Digital rights management: Concepts, methodologies, tools, and applications* (pp. 738–745). Hershey, PA: IGI Global. doi:10.4018/978-1-4666-2136-7.ch033

Ali, S. (2012). Practical web application security audit following industry standards and compliance. In J. Zubairi & A. Mahboob (Eds.), *Cyber security standards, practices and industrial applications: Systems and methodologies* (pp. 259–279). Hershey, PA: IGI Global. doi:10.4018/978-1-60960-851-4.ch013

Alirezaee, M., & Afsharian, M. (2011). Measuring the effect of the rules and regulations on global malmquist index. *International Journal of Operations Research and Information Systems*, 2(3), 64–78. doi:10.4018/joris.2011070105

Alirezaee, M., & Afsharian, M. (2013). Measuring the effect of the rules and regulations on global malmquist index. In J. Wang (Ed.), *Optimizing, innovating, and capitalizing on information systems for operations* (pp. 215–229). Hershey, PA: IGI Global. doi:10.4018/978-1-4666-2925-7.ch011

Alves de Lima, A., Carvalho dos Reis, P., Branco, J. C., Danieli, R., Osawa, C. C., Winter, E., & Santos, D. A. (2013). Scenario-patent protection compared to climate change: The case of green patents. *International Journal of Social Ecology and Sustainable Development*, *4*(3), 61–70. doi:10.4018/jsesd.2013070105

Amirante, A., Castaldi, T., Miniero, L., & Romano, S. P. (2013). Protocol interactions among user agents, application servers, and media servers: Standardization efforts and open issues. In D. Kanellopoulos (Ed.), *Intelligent multimedia technologies for networking applications: Techniques and tools* (pp. 48–63). Hershey, PA: IGI Global. doi:10.4018/978-1-4666-2833-5.ch003

Anker, P. (2013). The impact of regulations on the business case for cognitive radio. In T. Lagkas, P. Sarigiannidis, M. Louta, & P. Chatzimisios (Eds.), *Evolution of cognitive networks and self-adaptive communication systems* (pp. 142–170). Hershey, PA: IGI Global. doi:10.4018/978-1-4666-4189-1.ch006

Antunes, A. M., Mendes, F. M., Schumacher, S. D., Quoniam, L., & Lima de Magalhães, J. (2014). The contribution of information science through intellectual property to innovation in the Brazilian health sector. In G. Jamil, A. Malheiro, & F. Ribeiro (Eds.), *Rethinking the conceptual base for new practical applications in information value and quality* (pp. 83–115). Hershey, PA: IGI Global. doi:10.4018/978-1-4666-4562-2.ch005

Atiskov, A. Y., Novikov, F. A., Fedorchenko, L. N., Vorobiev, V. I., & Moldovyan, N. A. (2013). Ontology-based analysis of cryptography standards and possibilities of their harmonization. In A. Elçi, J. Pieprzyk, A. Chefranov, M. Orgun, H. Wang, & R. Shankaran (Eds.), *Theory and practice of cryptography solutions for secure information systems* (pp. 1–33). Hershey, PA: IGI Global. doi:10.4018/978-1-4666-4030-6.ch001

Ayanso, A., & Herath, T. (2012). Law and technology at crossroads in cyberspace: Where do we go from here? In A. Dudley, J. Braman, & G. Vincenti (Eds.), *Investigating cyber law and cyber ethics: Issues, impacts and practices* (pp. 57–77). Hershey, PA: IGI Global. doi:10.4018/978-1-61350-132-0.ch004

Ayanso, A., & Herath, T. (2014). Law and technology at crossroads in cyberspace: Where do we go from here? In *Cyber behavior: Concepts, methodologies, tools, and applications* (pp. 1990–2010). Hershey, PA: IGI Global. doi:10.4018/978-1-4666-5942-1.ch105

Aydogan-Duda, N. (2012). Branding innovation: The case study of Turkey. In N. Ekekwe & N. Islam (Eds.), *Disruptive technologies, innovation and global redesign: Emerging implications* (pp. 238–248). Hershey, PA: IGI Global. doi:10.4018/978-1-4666-0134-5.ch012

Bagby, J. W. (2011). Environmental standardization for sustainability. In Z. Luo (Ed.), *Green finance and sustainability: Environmentally-aware business models and technologies* (pp. 31–55). Hershey, PA: IGI Global. doi:10.4018/978-1-60960-531-5.ch002

Bagby, J. W. (2013). Insights from U.S. experience to guide international reliance on standardization: Achieving supply chain sustainability. *International Journal of Applied Logistics*, 4(3), 25–46. doi:10.4018/jal.2013070103

Baggio, B., & Beldarrain, Y. (2011). Intellectual property in an age of open source and anonymity. In *Anonymity and learning in digitally mediated communications: Authenticity and trust in cyber education* (pp. 39–57). Hershey, PA: IGI Global. doi:10.4018/978-1-60960-543-8.ch003

Balzli, C. E., & Fragnière, E. (2012). How ERP systems are centralizing and standardizing the accounting function in public organizations for better and worse. In S. Chhabra & M. Kumar (Eds.), *Strategic enterprise resource planning models for e-government: Applications and methodologies* (pp. 55–72). Hershey, PA: IGI Global. doi:10.4018/978-1-60960-863-7.ch004

Banas, J. R. (2011). Standardized, flexible design of electronic learning environments to enhance learning efficiency and effectiveness. In A. Kitchenham (Ed.), *Models for interdisciplinary mobile learning: Delivering information to students* (pp. 66–86). Hershey, PA: IGI Global. doi:10.4018/978-1-60960-511-7.ch004

Bao, C., & Castresana, J. M. (2011). Interoperability approach in e-learning standardization processes. In F. Lazarinis, S. Green, & E. Pearson (Eds.), *Handbook of research on e-learning standards and interoperability: Frameworks and issues* (pp. 399–418). Hershey, PA: IGI Global. doi:10.4018/978-1-61692-789-9.ch020

Bao, C., & Castresana, J. M. (2012). Interoperability approach in e-learning standardization processes. In *Virtual learning environments: Concepts, methodologies, tools and applications* (pp. 542–560). Hershey, PA: IGI Global. doi:10.4018/978-1-4666-0011-9.ch307

Barrett, B. (2011). Evaluating and implementing teaching standards: Providing quality online teaching strategies and techniques standards. In F. Lazarinis, S. Green, & E. Pearson (Eds.), *Developing and utilizing e-learning applications* (pp. 66–83). Hershey, PA: IGI Global. doi:10.4018/978-1-61692-791-2.ch004

Berleur, J. (2011). Ethical and social issues of the internet governance regulations. In D. Haftor & A. Mirijamdotter (Eds.), *Information and communication technologies, society and human beings: Theory and framework (festschrift in honor of Gunilla Bradley)* (pp. 466–476). Hershey, PA: IGI Global. doi:10.4018/978-1-60960-057-0.ch038

Bhattathiripad, V. P. (2014). Software copyright infringement and litigation. In *Judiciary-friendly forensics of software copyright infringement* (pp. 35–55). Hershey, PA: IGI Global. doi:10.4018/978-1-4666-5804-2.ch002

Bin, X., & Chuan, T. K. (2011). The effect of business characteristics on the methods of knowledge protections. *International Journal of Social Ecology and Sustainable Development*, 2(3), 34–60. doi:10.4018/jsesd.2011070103

Bin, X., & Chuan, T. K. (2013). The effect of business characteristics on the methods of knowledge protections. In E. Carayannis (Ed.), *Creating a sustainable ecology using technology-driven solutions* (pp. 172–200). Hershey, PA: IGI Global. doi:10.4018/978-1-4666-3613-2.ch013

Bin, X., & Chuan, T. K. (2013). The effect of business characteristics on the methods of knowledge protections. In *Digital rights management: Concepts, methodologies, tools, and applications* (pp. 1283–1311). Hershey, PA: IGI Global. doi:10.4018/978-1-4666-2136-7.ch063

Bogers, M., Bekkers, R., & Granstrand, O. (2012). Intellectual property and licensing strategies in open collaborative innovation. In C. de Pablos Heredero & D. López (Eds.), *Open innovation in firms and public administrations: Technologies for value creation* (pp. 37–58). Hershey, PA: IGI Global. doi:10.4018/978-1-61350-341-6.ch003

Bogers, M., Bekkers, R., & Granstrand, O. (2013). Intellectual property and licensing strategies in open collaborative innovation. In *Digital rights management: Concepts, methodologies, tools, and applications* (pp. 1204–1224). Hershey, PA: IGI Global. doi:10.4018/978-1-4666-2136-7.ch059

Bourcier, D. (2013). Law and governance: The genesis of the commons. In F. Doridot, P. Duquenoy, P. Goujon, A. Kurt, S. Lavelle, N. Patrignani, & A. Santuccio et al. (Eds.), *Ethical governance of emerging technologies development* (pp. 166–183). Hershey, PA: IGI Global. doi:10.4018/978-1-4666-3670-5.ch011

Bousquet, F., Fomin, V. V., & Drillon, D. (2011). Anticipatory standards development and competitive intelligence. *International Journal of Business Intelligence Research*, 2(1), 16–30. doi:10.4018/jbir.2011010102

Bousquet, F., Fomin, V. V., & Drillon, D. (2013). Anticipatory standards development and competitive intelligence. In R. Herschel (Ed.), *Principles and applications of business intelligence research* (pp. 17–30). Hershey, PA: IGI Global. doi:10.4018/978-1-4666-2650-8.ch002

Brabazon, A. (2013). Optimal patent design: An agent-based modeling approach. In B. Alexandrova-Kabadjova, S. Martinez-Jaramillo, A. Garcia-Almanza, & E. Tsang (Eds.), *Simulation in computational finance and economics: Tools and emerging applications* (pp. 280–302). Hershey, PA: IGI Global. doi:10.4018/978-1-4666-2011-7.ch014

Bracci, F., Corradi, A., & Foschini, L. (2014). Cloud standards: Security and interoperability issues. In H. Mouftah & B. Kantarci (Eds.), *Communication infrastructures for cloud computing* (pp. 465–495). Hershey, PA: IGI Global. doi:10.4018/978-1-4666-4522-6.ch020

Briscoe, D. R. (2012). Globalization and international labor standards, codes of conduct, and ethics: An International HRM perspective. In C. Wankel & S. Malleck (Eds.), *Ethical models and applications of globalization: Cultural, socio-political and economic perspectives* (pp. 1–22). Hershey, PA: IGI Global. doi:10.4018/978-1-61350-332-4.ch001

Briscoe, D. R. (2014). Globalization and international labor standards, codes of conduct, and ethics: An International HRM perspective. In *Cross-cultural interaction: Concepts, methodologies, tools and applications* (pp. 40–62). Hershey, PA: IGI Global. doi:10.4018/978-1-4666-4979-8.ch004

Brooks, R. G., & Geradin, D. (2011). Interpreting and enforcing the voluntary FRAND commitment. *International Journal of IT Standards and Standardization Research*, *9*(1), 1–23. doi:10.4018/jitsr.2011010101

Brown, C. A. (2013). Common core state standards: The promise for college and career ready students in the U.S. In V. Wang (Ed.), *Handbook of research on teaching and learning in K-20 education* (pp. 50–82). Hershey, PA: IGI Global. doi:10.4018/978-1-4666-4249-2.ch004

Buyurgan, N., Rardin, R. L., Jayaraman, R., Varghese, V. M., & Burbano, A. (2011). A novel GS1 data standard adoption roadmap for healthcare providers. *International Journal of Healthcare Information Systems and Informatics*, *6*(4), 42–59. doi:10.4018/jhisi.2011100103

Buyurgan, N., Rardin, R. L., Jayaraman, R., Varghese, V. M., & Burbano, A. (2013). A novel GS1 data standard adoption roadmap for healthcare providers. In J. Tan (Ed.), *Healthcare information technology innovation and sustainability: Frontiers and adoption* (pp. 41–57). Hershey, PA: IGI Global. doi:10.4018/978-1-4666-2797-0.ch003

Campolo, C., Cozzetti, H. A., Molinaro, A., & Scopigno, R. M. (2012). PHY/MAC layer design in vehicular ad hoc networks: Challenges, standard approaches, and alternative solutions. In R. Aquino-Santos, A. Edwards, & V. Rangel-Licea (Eds.), *Wireless technologies in vehicular ad hoc networks: Present and future challenges* (pp. 70–100). Hershey, PA: IGI Global. doi:10.4018/978-1-4666-0209-0.ch004

Cantatore, F. (2014). Copyright support structures. In *Authors, copyright, and publishing in the digital era* (pp. 81–93). Hershey, PA: IGI Global. doi:10.4018/978-1-4666-5214-9.ch005

Cantatore, F. (2014). History and development of copyright. In *Authors, copyright, and publishing in the digital era* (pp. 10–32). Hershey, PA: IGI Global. doi:10.4018/978-1-4666-5214-9.ch002

Cantatore, F. (2014). Research findings: Authors' perceptions and the copyright framework. In Authors, copyright, and publishing in the digital era (pp. 147-189). Hershey, PA: IGI Global. doi:10.4018/978-1-4666-5214-9.ch008

Cassini, J., Medlin, B. D., & Romaniello, A. (2011). Forty years of federal legislation in the area of data protection and information security. In H. Nemati (Ed.), *Pervasive information security and privacy developments: Trends and advancements* (pp. 14–23). Hershey, PA: IGI Global. doi:10.4018/978-1-61692-000-5.ch002

Charlesworth, A. (2012). Addressing legal issues in online research, publication and archiving: A UK perspective. In C. Silva (Ed.), *Online research methods in urban and planning studies: Design and outcomes* (pp. 368–393). Hershey, PA: IGI Global. doi:10.4018/978-1-4666-0074-4.ch022

Chaudhary, C., & Kang, I. S. (2011). Pirates of the copyright and cyberspace: Issues involved. In R. Santanam, M. Sethumadhavan, & M. Virendra (Eds.), *Cyber security, cyber crime and cyber forensics: Applications and perspectives* (pp. 59–68). Hershey, PA: IGI Global. doi:10.4018/978-1-60960-123-2.ch005

Chen, L., Hu, W., Yang, M., & Zhang, L. (2011). Security and privacy issues in secure e-mail standards and services. In H. Nemati (Ed.), *Security and privacy assurance in advancing technologies: New developments* (pp. 174–185). Hershey, PA: IGI Global. doi:10.4018/978-1-60960-200-0.ch013

Ciaghi, A., & Villafiorita, A. (2012). Law modeling and BPR for public administration improvement. In K. Bwalya & S. Zulu (Eds.), *Handbook of research on e-government in emerging economies: Adoption, E-participation, and legal frameworks* (pp. 391–410). Hershey, PA: IGI Global. doi:10.4018/978-1-4666-0324-0.ch019

Ciptasari, R. W., & Sakurai, K. (2013). Multimedia copyright protection scheme based on the direct feature-based method. In K. Kondo (Ed.), *Multimedia information hiding technologies and methodologies for controlling data* (pp. 412–439). Hershey, PA: IGI Global. doi:10.4018/978-1-4666-2217-3.ch019

Clark, L. A., Jones, D. L., & Clark, W. J. (2012). Technology innovation and the policy vacuum: A call for ethics, norms, and laws to fill the void. *International Journal of Technoethics*, *3*(1), 1–13. doi:10.4018/jte.2012010101

Cooklev, T. (2013). The role of standards in engineering education. In K. Jakobs (Ed.), *Innovations in organizational IT specification and standards development* (pp. 129–137). Hershey, PA: IGI Global. doi:10.4018/978-1-4666-2160-2.ch007

Cooper, A. R. (2013). Key challenges in the design of learning technology standards: Observations and proposals. In K. Jakobs (Ed.), *Innovations in organizational IT specification and standards development* (pp. 241–249). Hershey, PA: IGI Global. doi:10.4018/978-1-4666-2160-2.ch014

Cordella, A. (2011). Emerging standardization. *International Journal of Actor-Network Theory and Technological Innovation*, *3*(3), 49–64. doi:10.4018/jantti.2011070104

Cordella, A. (2013). Emerging standardization. In A. Tatnall (Ed.), *Social and professional applications of actor-network theory for technology development* (pp. 221–237). Hershey, PA: IGI Global. doi:10.4018/978-1-4666-2166-4.ch017

Curran, K., & Lautman, R. (2011). The problems of jurisdiction on the internet. *International Journal of Ambient Computing and Intelligence*, *3*(3), 36–42. doi:10.4018/jaci.2011070105

Dani, D. E., Salloum, S., Khishfe, R., & BouJaoude, S. (2013). A tool for analyzing science standards and curricula for 21st century science education. In M. Khine, & I. Saleh (Eds.), *Approaches and strategies in next generation science learning* (pp. 265-289). Hershey, PA: IGI Global. doi:10.4018/978-1-4666-2809-0.ch014

De Silva, S. (2012). Legal issues with FOS-ERP: A UK law perspective. In R. Atem de Carvalho & B. Johansson (Eds.), *Free and open source enterprise resource planning: Systems and strategies* (pp. 102–115). Hershey, PA: IGI Global. doi:10.4018/978-1-61350-486-4.ch007 de Vries, H. J. (2011). Implementing standardization education at the national level. *International Journal of IT Standards and Standardization Research*, *9*(2), 72–83. doi:10.4018/jitsr.2011070104

de Vries, H. J. (2013). Implementing standardization education at the national level. In K. Jakobs (Ed.), *Innovations in organizational IT specification and standards development* (pp. 116–128). Hershey, PA: IGI Global. doi:10.4018/978-1-4666-2160-2.ch006

de Vuyst, B., & Fairchild, A. (2012). Legal and economic justification for software protection. *International Journal of Open Source Software and Processes*, *4*(3), 1–12. doi:10.4018/ijossp.2012070101

Dedeke, A. (2012). Politics hinders open standards in the public sector: The Massachusetts open document format decision. In C. Reddick (Ed.), *Cases on public information management and e-government adoption* (pp. 1–23). Hershey, PA: IGI Global. doi:10.4018/978-1-4666-0981-5.ch001

Delfmann, P., Herwig, S., Lis, L., & Becker, J. (2012). Supporting conceptual model analysis using semantic standardization and structural pattern matching. In S. Smolnik, F. Teuteberg, & O. Thomas (Eds.), *Semantic technologies for business and information systems engineering: Concepts and applications* (pp. 125–149). Hershey, PA: IGI Global. doi:10.4018/978-1-60960-126-3.ch007

den Uijl, S., de Vries, H. J., & Bayramoglu, D. (2013). The rise of MP3 as the market standard: How compressed audio files became the dominant music format. *International Journal of IT Standards and Standardization Research*, *11*(1), 1–26. doi:10.4018/jitsr.2013010101

Dickerson, J., & Coleman, H. V. (2012). Technology, e-leadership and educational administration in schools: Integrating standards with context and guiding questions. In V. Wang (Ed.), *Encyclopedia of e-leadership, counseling and training* (pp. 408–422). Hershey, PA: IGI Global. doi:10.4018/978-1-61350-068-2.ch030

Dindaroglu, B. (2013). R&D productivity and firm size in semiconductors and pharmaceuticals: Evidence from citation yields. In I. Yetkiner, M. Pamukcu, & E. Erdil (Eds.), *Industrial dynamics, innovation policy, and economic growth through technological advancements* (pp. 92–113). Hershey, PA: IGI Global. doi:10.4018/978-1-4666-1978-4.ch006

Ding, W. (2011). Development of intellectual property of communications enterprise and analysis of current situation of patents in emerging technology field. *International Journal of Advanced Pervasive and Ubiquitous Computing*, *3*(2), 21–28. doi:10.4018/japuc.2011040103

Ding, W. (2013). Development of intellectual property of communications enterprise and analysis of current situation of patents in emerging technology field. In T. Gao (Ed.), *Global applications of pervasive and ubiquitous computing* (pp. 89–96). Hershey, PA: IGI Global. doi:10.4018/978-1-4666-2645-4.ch010

Dorloff, F., & Kajan, E. (2012). Balancing of heterogeneity and interoperability in e-business networks: The role of standards and protocols. *International Journal of E-Business Research*, *8*(4), 15–33. doi:10.4018/jebr.2012100102

Dorloff, F., & Kajan, E. (2012). Efficient and interoperable e-business –Based on frameworks, standards and protocols: An introduction. In E. Kajan, F. Dorloff, & I. Bedini (Eds.), *Handbook of research on e-business standards and protocols: Documents, data and advanced web technologies* (pp. 1–20). Hershey, PA: IGI Global. doi:10.4018/978-1-4666-0146-8.ch001

Driouchi, A., & Kadiri, M. (2013). Challenges to intellectual property rights from information and communication technologies, nanotechnologies and microelectronics. In *Digital rights management: Concepts, methodologies, tools, and applications* (pp. 1474–1492). Hershey, PA: IGI Global. doi:10.4018/978-1-4666-2136-7.ch075

Dubey, M., & Hirwade, M. (2013). Copyright relevancy at stake in libraries of the digital era. In T. Ashraf & P. Gulati (Eds.), *Design, development, and management of resources for digital library services* (pp. 379–384). Hershey, PA: IGI Global. doi:10.4018/978-1-4666-2500-6.ch030

Egyedi, T. M. (2011). Between supply and demand: Coping with the impact of standards change. In *Global business: Concepts, methodologies, tools and applications* (pp. 105–120). Hershey, PA: IGI Global. doi:10.4018/978-1-60960-587-2.ch108

Egyedi, T. M., & Koppenhol, A. (2013). The standards war between ODF and OOXML: Does competition between overlapping ISO standards lead to innovation? In K. Jakobs (Ed.), *Innovations in organizational IT specification and standards development* (pp. 79–90). Hershey, PA: IGI Global. doi:10.4018/978-1-4666-2160-2.ch004

Egyedi, T. M., & Muto, S. (2012). Standards for ICT: A green strategy in a grey sector. *International Journal of IT Standards and Standardization Research*, *10*(1), 34–47. doi:10.4018/jitsr.2012010103

El Kharbili, M., & Pulvermueller, E. (2012). Semantic policies for modeling regulatory process compliance. In S. Smolnik, F. Teuteberg, & O. Thomas (Eds.), *Semantic technologies for business and information systems engineering: Concepts and applications* (pp. 311–336). Hershey, PA: IGI Global. doi:10.4018/978-1-60960-126-3.ch016

El Kharbili, M., & Pulvermueller, E. (2013). Semantic policies for modeling regulatory process compliance. In *IT policy and ethics: Concepts, methodologies, tools, and applications* (pp. 218–243). Hershey, PA: IGI Global. doi:10.4018/978-1-4666-2919-6.ch011

Ervin, K. (2014). Legal and ethical considerations in the implementation of electronic health records. In J. Krueger (Ed.), *Cases on electronic records and resource management implementation in diverse environments* (pp. 193–210). Hershey, PA: IGI Global. doi:10.4018/978-1-4666-4466-3.ch012

Escayola, J., Trigo, J., Martínez, I., Martínez-Espronceda, M., Aragüés, A., Sancho, D., & García, J. et al. (2012). Overview of the ISO/ieee11073 family of standards and their applications to health monitoring. In W. Chen, S. Oetomo, & L. Feijs (Eds.), *Neonatal monitoring technologies: Design for integrated solutions* (pp. 148–173). Hershey, PA: IGI Global. doi:10.4018/978-1-4666-0975-4.ch007

Escayola, J., Trigo, J., Martínez, I., Martínez-Espronceda, M., Aragüés, A., Sancho, D., . . . García, J. (2013). Overview of the ISO/IEEE11073 family of standards and their applications to health monitoring. In User-driven healthcare: Concepts, methodologies, tools, and applications (pp. 357–381). Hershey, PA: IGI Global. doi:10.4018/978-1-4666-2770-3.ch018

Espada, J. P., Martínez, O. S., García-Bustelo, B. C., Lovelle, J. M., & Ordóñez de Pablos, P. (2011). Standardization of virtual objects. In M. Lytras, P. Ordóñez de Pablos, & E. Damiani (Eds.), *Semantic web personalization and context awareness: Management of personal identities and social networking* (pp. 7–21). Hershey, PA: IGI Global. doi:10.4018/978-1-61520-921-7.ch002

Falkner, N. J. (2011). Security technologies and policies in organisations. In M. Quigley (Ed.), *ICT ethics and security in the 21st century: New developments and applications* (pp. 196–213). Hershey, PA: IGI Global. doi:10.4018/978-1-60960-573-5.ch010

Ferrer-Roca, O. (2011). Standards in telemedicine. In A. Moumtzoglou & A. Kastania (Eds.), *E-health systems quality and reliability: Models and standards* (pp. 220–243). Hershey, PA: IGI Global. doi:10.4018/978-1-61692-843-8.ch017

Ferullo, D. L., & Soules, A. (2012). Managing copyright in a digital world. *International Journal of Digital Library Systems*, *3*(4), 1–25. doi:10.4018/ijdls.2012100101

Fichtner, J. R., & Simpson, L. A. (2011). Legal issues facing companies with products in a digital format. In T. Strader (Ed.), *Digital product management, technology and practice: Interdisciplinary perspectives* (pp. 32–52). Hershey, PA: IGI Global. doi:10.4018/978-1-61692-877-3.ch003

Fichtner, J. R., & Simpson, L. A. (2013). Legal issues facing companies with products in a digital format. In *Digital rights management: Concepts, methodologies, tools, and applications* (pp. 1334–1354). Hershey, PA: IGI Global. doi:10.4018/978-1-4666-2136-7.ch066

Folmer, E. (2012). BOMOS: Management and development model for open standards. In E. Kajan, F. Dorloff, & I. Bedini (Eds.), *Handbook of research on e-business standards and protocols: Documents, data and advanced web technologies* (pp. 102–128). Hershey, PA: IGI Global. doi:10.4018/978-1-4666-0146-8.ch006

Fomin, V. V. (2012). Standards as hybrids: An essay on tensions and juxtapositions in contemporary standardization. *International Journal of IT Standards and Standardization Research*, *10*(2), 59–68. doi:10.4018/jitsr.2012070105

Fomin, V. V., & Matinmikko, M. (2014). The role of standards in the development of new informational infrastructure. In M. Khosrow-Pour (Ed.), *Systems and software development, modeling, and analysis: New perspectives and methodologies* (pp. 149–160). Hershey, PA: IGI Global. doi:10.4018/978-1-4666-6098-4.ch006

Fomin, V. V., Medeisis, A., & Vitkute-Adžgauskiene, D. (2012). Pre-standardization of cognitive radio systems. *International Journal of IT Standards and Standardization Research*, *10*(1), 1–16. doi:10.4018/jitsr.2012010101

Francia, G., & Hutchinson, F. S. (2012). Regulatory and policy compliance with regard to identity theft prevention, detection, and response. In T. Chou (Ed.), *Information assurance and security technologies for risk assessment and threat management: Advances* (pp. 292–322). Hershey, PA: IGI Global. doi:10.4018/978-1-61350-507-6.ch012

Francia, G. A., & Hutchinson, F. S. (2014). Regulatory and policy compliance with regard to identity theft prevention, detection, and response. In *Crisis management: Concepts, methodologies, tools and applications* (pp. 280–310). Hershey, PA: IGI Global. doi:10.4018/978-1-4666-4707-7.ch012

Fulkerson, D. M. (2012). Copyright. In D. Fulkerson (Ed.), *Remote access technologies for library collections: Tools for library users and managers* (pp. 33–48). Hershey, PA: IGI Global. doi:10.4018/978-1-4666-0234-2.ch003

Galinski, C., & Beckmann, H. (2014). Concepts for enhancing content quality and eaccessibility: In general and in the field of eprocurement. In *Assistive technologies: Concepts, methodologies, tools, and applications* (pp. 180–197). Hershey, PA: IGI Global. doi:10.4018/978-1-4666-4422-9.ch010

Gaur, R. (2013). Facilitating access to Indian cultural heritage: Copyright, permission rights and ownership issues vis-à-vis IGNCA collections. In *Digital rights management: Concepts, methodologies, tools, and applications* (pp. 817–833). Hershey, PA: IGI Global. doi:10.4018/978-1-4666-2136-7.ch038

Geiger, C. (2011). Copyright and digital libraries: Securing access to information in the digital age. In I. Iglezakis, T. Synodinou, & S. Kapidakis (Eds.), *E-publishing and digital libraries: Legal and organizational issues* (pp. 257–272). Hershey, PA: IGI Global. doi:10.4018/978-1-60960-031-0.ch013

Geiger, C. (2013). Copyright and digital libraries: Securing access to information in the digital age. In *Digital rights management: Concepts, methodologies, tools, and applications* (pp. 99–114). Hershey, PA: IGI Global. doi:10.4018/978-1-4666-2136-7.ch007

Gencer, M. (2012). The evolution of IETF standards and their production. *International Journal of IT Standards and Standardization Research*, *10*(1), 17–33. doi:10.4018/jitsr.2012010102

Gillam, L., & Vartapetiance, A. (2014). Gambling with laws and ethics in cyberspace. In R. Luppicini (Ed.), *Evolving issues surrounding technoethics and society in the digital age* (pp. 149–170). Hershey, PA: IGI Global. doi:10.4018/978-1-4666-6122-6.ch010

Grandinetti, L., Pisacane, O., & Sheikhalishahi, M. (2014). Standardization. In *Pervasive cloud computing technologies: Future outlooks and interdisciplinary perspectives* (pp. 75–96). Hershey, PA: IGI Global. doi:10.4018/978-1-4666-4683-4.ch004

Grant, S., & Young, R. (2013). Concepts and standardization in areas relating to competence. In K. Jakobs (Ed.), *Innovations in organizational IT specification and standards development* (pp. 264–280). Hershey, PA: IGI Global. doi:10.4018/978-1-4666-2160-2.ch016

Grassetti, M., & Brookby, S. (2013). Using the iPad to develop preservice teachers' understanding of the common core state standards for mathematical practice. In D. Polly (Ed.), *Common core mathematics standards and implementing digital technologies* (pp. 370–386). Hershey, PA: IGI Global. doi:10.4018/978-1-4666-4086-3.ch025

Gray, P. J. (2012). CDIO Standards and quality assurance: From application to accreditation. *International Journal of Quality Assurance in Engineering and Technology Education*, *2*(2), 1–8. doi:10.4018/ijqaete.2012040101

Graz, J., & Hauert, C. (2011). The INTERNORM project: Bridging two worlds of expert- and lay-knowledge in standardization. *International Journal of IT Standards and Standardization Research*, *9*(1), 52–62. doi:10.4018/jitsr.2011010103

Graz, J., & Hauert, C. (2013). The INTERNORM project: Bridging two worlds of expert- and lay-knowledge in standardization. In K. Jakobs (Ed.), *Innovations in organizational IT specification and standards development* (pp. 154–164). Hershey, PA: IGI Global. doi:10.4018/978-1-4666-2160-2.ch009

Grobler, M. (2012). The need for digital evidence standardisation. *International Journal of Digital Crime and Forensics*, *4*(2), 1–12. doi:10.4018/jdcf.2012040101

Grobler, M. (2013). The need for digital evidence standardisation. In C. Li (Ed.), *Emerging digital forensics applications for crime detection, prevention, and security* (pp. 234–245). Hershey, PA: IGI Global. doi:10.4018/978-1-4666-4006-1.ch016

Guest, C. L., & Guest, J. M. (2011). Legal issues in the use of technology in higher education: Copyright and privacy in the academy. In D. Surry, R. Gray Jr, & J. Stefurak (Eds.), *Technology integration in higher education: Social and organizational aspects* (pp. 72–85). Hershey, PA: IGI Global. doi:10.4018/978-1-60960-147-8.ch006

Gupta, A., Gantz, D. A., Sreecharana, D., & Kreyling, J. (2012). The interplay of offshoring of professional services, law, intellectual property, and international organizations. *International Journal of Strategic Information Technology and Applications*, *3*(2), 47–71. doi:10.4018/jsita.2012040104

Hai-Jew, S. (2011). Staying legal and ethical in global e-learning course and training developments: An exploration. In V. Wang (Ed.), *Encyclopedia of information communication technologies and adult education integration* (pp. 958–970). Hershey, PA: IGI Global. doi:10.4018/978-1-61692-906-0.ch058

Halder, D., & Jaishankar, K. (2012). Cyber space regulations for protecting women in UK. In *Cyber crime and the victimization of women: Laws, rights and regulations* (pp. 95–104). Hershey, PA: IGI Global. doi:10.4018/978-1-60960-830-9.ch007

Han, M., & Cho, C. (2013). XML in library cataloging workflows: Working with diverse sources and metadata standards. In J. Tramullas & P. Garrido (Eds.), *Library automation and OPAC 2.0: Information access and services in the 2.0 landscape* (pp. 59–72). Hershey, PA: IGI Global. doi:10.4018/978-1-4666-1912-8.ch003

Hanseth, O., & Nielsen, P. (2013). Infrastructural innovation: Flexibility, generativity and the mobile internet. *International Journal of IT Standards and Standardization Research*, *11*(1), 27–45. doi:10.4018/jitsr.2013010102

Hartong, M., & Wijesekera, D. (2012). U.S. regulatory requirements for positive train control systems. In F. Flammini (Ed.), *Railway safety, reliability, and security: Technologies and systems engineering* (pp. 1–21). Hershey, PA: IGI Global. doi:10.4018/978-1-4666-1643-1.ch001

Hasan, H. (2011). Formal and emergent standards in KM. In D. Schwartz & D. Te'eni (Eds.), *Encyclopedia of knowledge management* (2nd ed.; pp. 331–342). Hershey, PA: IGI Global. doi:10.4018/978-1-59904-931-1.ch032

Hatzimihail, N. (2011). Copyright infringement of digital libraries and private international law: Jurisdiction issues. In I. Iglezakis, T. Synodinou, & S. Kapidakis (Eds.), *E-publishing and digital libraries: Legal and organizational issues* (pp. 447–460). Hershey, PA: IGI Global. doi:10.4018/978-1-60960-031-0.ch021

Hauert, C. (2013). Where are you? Consumers' associations in standardization: A case study on Switzerland. In K. Jakobs (Ed.), *Innovations in organizational IT specification and standards development* (pp. 139–153). Hershey, PA: IGI Global. doi:10.4018/978-1-4666-2160-2.ch008

Hawks, V. D., & Ekstrom, J. J. (2011). Balancing policies, principles, and philosophy in information assurance. In M. Dark (Ed.), *Information assurance and security ethics in complex systems: Interdisciplinary perspectives* (pp. 32–54). Hershey, PA: IGI Global. doi:10.4018/978-1-61692-245-0.ch003

Henningsson, S. (2012). International e-customs standardization from the perspective of a global company. *International Journal of IT Standards and Standardization Research, 10*(2), 45–58. doi:10.4018/jitsr.2012070104

Hensberry, K. K., Paul, A. J., Moore, E. B., Podolefsky, N. S., & Perkins, K. K. (2013). PhET interactive simulations: New tools to achieve common core mathematics standards. In D. Polly (Ed.), *Common core mathematics standards and implementing digital technologies* (pp. 147–167). Hershey, PA: IGI Global. doi:10.4018/978-1-4666-4086-3.ch010

Heravi, B. R., & Lycett, M. (2012). Semantically enriched e-business standards development: The case of ebXML business process specification schema. In E. Kajan, F. Dorloff, & I. Bedini (Eds.), *Handbook of research on e-business standards and protocols: Documents, data and advanced web technologies* (pp. 655–675). Hershey, PA: IGI Global. doi:10.4018/978-1-4666-0146-8.ch030

Higuera, J., & Polo, J. (2012). Interoperability in wireless sensor networks based on IEEE 1451 standard. In N. Zaman, K. Ragab, & A. Abdullah (Eds.), *Wireless sensor networks and energy efficiency: Protocols, routing and management* (pp. 47–69). Hershey, PA: IGI Global. doi:10.4018/978-1-4666-0101-7.ch004

Hill, D. S. (2012). An examination of standardized product identification and business benefit. In E. Kajan, F. Dorloff, & I. Bedini (Eds.), *Handbook of research on e-business standards and protocols: Documents, data and advanced web technologies* (pp. 387–411). Hershey, PA: IGI Global. doi:10.4018/978-1-4666-0146-8.ch018

Hill, D. S. (2013). An examination of standardized product identification and business benefit. In *Supply chain management: Concepts, methodologies, tools, and applications* (pp. 171–195). Hershey, PA: IGI Global. doi:10.4018/978-1-4666-2625-6.ch011

Holloway, K. (2012). Fair use, copyright, and academic integrity in an online academic environment. In V. Wang (Ed.), *Encyclopedia of e-leadership, counseling and training* (pp. 298–309). Hershey, PA: IGI Global. doi:10.4018/978-1-61350-068-2.ch022

Hoops, D. S. (2011). Legal issues in the virtual world and e-commerce. In B. Ciaramitaro (Ed.), *Virtual worlds and e-commerce: Technologies and applications for building customer relationships* (pp. 186–204). Hershey, PA: IGI Global. doi:10.4018/978-1-61692-808-7.ch010

Hoops, D. S. (2012). Lost in cyberspace: Navigating the legal issues of e-commerce. *Journal of Electronic Commerce in Organizations*, *10*(1), 33–51. doi:10.4018/jeco.2012010103

Hopkinson, A. (2012). Establishing the digital library: Don't ignore the library standards and don't forget the training needed. In A. Tella & A. Issa (Eds.), *Library and information science in developing countries: Contemporary issues* (pp. 195–204). Hershey, PA: IGI Global. doi:10.4018/978-1-61350-335-5.ch014

Hua, G. B. (2013). The construction industry and standardization of information. In *Implementing IT business strategy in the construction industry* (pp. 47–66). Hershey, PA: IGI Global. doi:10.4018/978-1-4666-4185-3.ch003

Huang, C., & Lin, H. (2011). Patent infringement risk analysis using rough set theory. In Q. Zhang, R. Segall, & M. Cao (Eds.), *Visual analytics and interactive technologies: Data, text and web mining applications* (pp. 123–150). Hershey, PA: IGI Global. doi:10.4018/978-1-60960-102-7.ch008

Huang, C., Tseng, T. B., & Lin, H. (2013). Patent infringement risk analysis using rough set theory. In *Digital rights management: Concepts, methodologies, tools, and applications* (pp. 1225–1251). Hershey, PA: IGI Global. doi:10.4018/978-1-4666-2136-7.ch060

Iyamu, T. (2013). The impact of organisational politics on the implementation of IT strategy: South African case in context. In J. Abdelnour-Nocera (Ed.), *Knowledge and technological development effects on organizational and social structures* (pp. 167–193). Hershey, PA: IGI Global. doi:10.4018/978-1-4666-2151-0.ch011

Jacinto, K., Neto, F. M., Leite, C. R., & Jacinto, K. (2014). Accessibility in u-learning: Standards, legislation, and future visions. In F. Neto (Ed.), *Technology platform innovations and forthcoming trends in ubiquitous learning* (pp. 215–236). Hershey, PA: IGI Global. doi:10.4018/978-1-4666-4542-4.ch012

Jakobs, K., Wagner, T., & Reimers, K. (2011). Standardising the internet of things: What the experts think. *International Journal of IT Standards and Standardization Research*, *9*(1), 63–67. doi:10.4018/jitsr.2011010104

Juzoji, H. (2012). Legal bases for medical supervision via mobile telecommunications in Japan. *International Journal of E-Health and Medical Communications*, *3*(1), 33–45. doi:10.4018/jehmc.2012010103

Kallinikou, D., Papadopoulos, M., Kaponi, A., & Strakantouna, V. (2011). Intellectual property issues for digital libraries at the intersection of law, technology, and the public interest. In I. Iglezakis, T. Synodinou, & S. Kapidakis (Eds.), *E-publishing and digital libraries: Legal and organizational issues* (pp. 294–341). Hershey, PA: IGI Global. doi:10.4018/978-1-60960-031-0.ch015

Kallinikou, D., Papadopoulos, M., Kaponi, A., & Strakantouna, V. (2013). Intellectual property issues for digital libraries at the intersection of law, technology, and the public interest. In *Digital rights management: Concepts, methodologies, tools, and applications* (pp. 1043–1090). Hershey, PA: IGI Global. doi:10.4018/978-1-4666-2136-7.ch052

Kaupins, G. (2012). Laws associated with mobile computing in the cloud. *International Journal of Wireless Networks and Broadband Technologies*, *2*(3), 1–9. doi:10.4018/ijwnbt.2012070101

Kaur, P., & Singh, H. (2013). Component certification process and standards. In H. Singh & K. Kaur (Eds.), *Designing, engineering, and analyzing reliable and efficient software* (pp. 22–39). Hershey, PA: IGI Global. doi:10.4018/978-1-4666-2958-5.ch002

Kayem, A. V. (2013). Security in service oriented architectures: Standards and challenges. In *Digital rights management: Concepts, methodologies, tools, and applications* (pp. 50–73). Hershey, PA: IGI Global. doi:10.4018/978-1-4666-2136-7.ch004

Kemp, M. L., Robb, S., & Deans, P. C. (2013). The legal implications of cloud computing. In A. Bento & A. Aggarwal (Eds.), *Cloud computing service and deployment models: Layers and management* (pp. 257–272). Hershey, PA: IGI Global. doi:10.4018/978-1-4666-2187-9.ch014

Khansa, L., & Liginlal, D. (2012). Regulatory influence and the imperative of innovation in identity and access management. *Information Resources Management Journal, 25*(3), 78–97. doi:10.4018/irmj.2012070104

Kim, E. (2012). Government policies to promote production and consumption of renewable electricity in the US. In M. Tortora (Ed.), *Sustainable systems and energy management at the regional level: Comparative approaches* (pp. 1–18). Hershey, PA: IGI Global. doi:10.4018/978-1-61350-344-7.ch001

Kinsell, C. (2014). Technology and disability laws, regulations, and rights. In B. DaCosta & S. Seok (Eds.), *Assistive technology research, practice, and theory* (pp. 75–87). Hershey, PA: IGI Global. doi:10.4018/978-1-4666-5015-2.ch006

Kitsiou, S. (2010). Overview and analysis of electronic health record standards. In J. Rodrigues (Ed.), *Health information systems: Concepts, methodologies, tools, and applications* (pp. 374–392). Hershey, PA: IGI Global. doi:10.4018/978-1-60566-988-5.ch025

Kloss, J. H., & Schickel, P. (2011). X3D: A secure ISO standard for virtual worlds. In A. Rea (Ed.), *Security in virtual worlds, 3D webs, and immersive environments: Models for development, interaction, and management* (pp. 208–220). Hershey, PA: IGI Global. doi:10.4018/978-1-61520-891-3.ch010

Kotsonis, E., & Eliakis, S. (2011). Information security standards for health information systems: The implementer's approach. In A. Chryssanthou, I. Apostolakis, & I. Varlamis (Eds.), *Certification and security in health-related web applications: Concepts and solutions* (pp. 113–145). Hershey, PA: IGI Global. doi:10.4018/978-1-61692-895-7.ch006

Kotsonis, E., & Eliakis, S. (2013). Information security standards for health information systems: The implementer's approach. In *User-driven healthcare: Concepts, methodologies, tools, and applications* (pp. 225–257). Hershey, PA: IGI Global. doi:10.4018/978-1-4666-2770-3.ch013

Koumaras, H., & Kourtis, M. (2013). A survey on video coding principles and standards. In R. Farrugia & C. Debono (Eds.), *Multimedia networking and coding* (pp. 1–27). Hershey, PA: IGI Global. doi:10.4018/978-1-4666-2660-7.ch001

Krupinski, E. A., Antoniotti, N., & Burdick, A. (2011). Standards and guidelines development in the american telemedicine association. In A. Moumtzoglou & A. Kastania (Eds.), *E-health systems quality and reliability: Models and standards* (pp. 244–252). Hershey, PA: IGI Global. doi:10.4018/978-1-61692-843-8.ch018

Kuanpoth, J. (2011). Biotechnological patents and morality: A critical view from a developing country. In S. Hongladarom (Ed.), *Genomics and bioethics: Interdisciplinary perspectives, technologies and advancements* (pp. 141–151). Hershey, PA: IGI Global. doi:10.4018/978-1-61692-883-4.ch010

Kuanpoth, J. (2013). Biotechnological patents and morality: A critical view from a developing country. In *Digital rights management: Concepts, methodologies, tools, and applications* (pp. 1417–1427). Hershey, PA: IGI Global. doi:10.4018/978-1-4666-2136-7.ch071

Kulmala, R., & Kettunen, J. (2012). Intellectual property protection and process modeling in small knowledge intensive enterprises. In *Organizational learning and knowledge: Concepts, methodologies, tools and applications* (pp. 2963–2980). Hershey, PA: IGI Global. doi:10.4018/978-1-60960-783-8.ch809

Kulmala, R., & Kettunen, J. (2013). Intellectual property protection in small knowledge intensive enterprises. *International Journal of Cyber Warfare & Terrorism*, *3*(1), 29–45. doi:10.4018/ijcwt.2013010103

Küster, M. W. (2012). Standards for achieving interoperability of egovernment in Europe. In E. Kajan, F. Dorloff, & I. Bedini (Eds.), *Handbook of research on e-business standards and protocols: Documents, data and advanced web technologies* (pp. 249–268). Hershey, PA: IGI Global. doi:10.4018/978-1-4666-0146-8.ch012

Kyobe, M. (2011). Factors influencing SME compliance with government regulation on use of IT: The case of South Africa. In F. Tan (Ed.), *International enterprises and global information technologies: Advancing management practices* (pp. 85–116). Hershey, PA: IGI Global. doi:10.4018/978-1-60960-605-3.ch005

Lam, J. C., & Hills, P. (2011). Promoting technological environmental innovations: What is the role of environmental regulation? In Z. Luo (Ed.), *Green finance and sustainability: Environmentally-aware business models and technologies* (pp. 56–73). Hershey, PA: IGI Global. doi:10.4018/978-1-60960-531-5.ch003

Lam, J. C., & Hills, P. (2013). Promoting technological environmental innovations: The role of environmental regulation. In Z. Luo (Ed.), *Technological solutions for modern logistics and supply chain management* (pp. 230–247). Hershey, PA: IGI Global. doi:10.4018/978-1-4666-2773-4.ch015

Laporte, C., & Vargas, E. P. (2012). The development of international standards to facilitate process improvements for very small entities. In S. Fauzi, M. Nasir, N. Ramli, & S. Sahibuddin (Eds.), *Software process improvement and management: Approaches and tools for practical development* (pp. 34–61). Hershey, PA: IGI Global. doi:10.4018/978-1-61350-141-2.ch003

Laporte, C., & Vargas, E. P. (2014). The development of international standards to facilitate process improvements for very small entities. In *Software design and development: Concepts, methodologies, tools, and applications* (pp. 1335–1361). Hershey, PA: IGI Global. doi:10.4018/978-1-4666-4301-7.ch065

Lautman, R., & Curran, K. (2013). The problems of jurisdiction on the internet. In K. Curran (Ed.), *Pervasive and ubiquitous technology innovations for ambient intelligence environments* (pp. 164–170). Hershey, PA: IGI Global. doi:10.4018/978-1-4666-2041-4.ch016

Layne-Farrar, A. (2011). Innovative or indefensible? An empirical assessment of patenting within standard setting. *International Journal of IT Standards and Standardization Research*, *9*(2), 1–18. doi:10.4018/jitsr.2011070101

Layne-Farrar, A. (2013). Innovative or indefensible? An empirical assessment of patenting within standard setting. In K. Jakobs (Ed.), *Innovations in organizational IT specification and standards development* (pp. 1–18). Hershey, PA: IGI Global. doi:10.4018/978-1-4666-2160-2.ch001

Layne-Farrar, A., & Padilla, A. J. (2011). Assessing the link between standards and patents. *International Journal of IT Standards and Standardization Research*, *9*(2), 19–49. doi:10.4018/jitsr.2011070102

Layne-Farrar, A., & Padilla, A. J. (2013). Assessing the link between standards and patents. In K. Jakobs (Ed.), *Innovations in organizational IT specification and standards development* (pp. 19–51). Hershey, PA: IGI Global. doi:10.4018/978-1-4666-2160-2.ch002

Lee, H., & Huh, J. C. (2012). Koreas strategies for ICT standards internationalisation: A comparison with Chinas. *International Journal of IT Standards and Standardization Research*, *10*(2), 1–13. doi:10.4018/jitsr.2012070101

Li, Y., & Wei, C. (2011). Digital image authentication: A review. *International Journal of Digital Library Systems*, *2*(2), 55–78. doi:10.4018/jdls.2011040104

Li, Y., Xiao, X., Feng, X., & Yan, H. (2012). Adaptation and localization: Metadata research and development for Chinese digital resources. *International Journal of Digital Library Systems*, *3*(1), 1–21. doi:10.4018/jdls.2012010101

Lim, W., & Kim, D. (2013). Do technologies support the implementation of the common core state standards in mathematics of high school probability and statistics? In D. Polly (Ed.), *Common core mathematics standards and implementing digital technologies* (pp. 168–183). Hershey, PA: IGI Global. doi:10.4018/978-1-4666-4086-3.ch011

Linton, J., & Stegall, D. (2013). Common core standards for mathematical practice and TPACK: An integrated approach to instruction. In D. Polly (Ed.), *Common core mathematics standards and implementing digital technologies* (pp. 234–249). Hershey, PA: IGI Global. doi:10.4018/978-1-4666-4086-3.ch016

Liotta, A., & Liotta, A. (2011). Privacy in pervasive systems: Legal framework and regulatory challenges. In A. Malatras (Ed.), *Pervasive computing and communications design and deployment: Technologies, trends and applications* (pp. 263–277). Hershey, PA: IGI Global. doi:10.4018/978-1-60960-611-4.ch012

Lissoni, F. (2013). Academic patenting in Europe: Recent research and new perspectives. In I. Yetkiner, M. Pamukcu, & E. Erdil (Eds.), *Industrial dynamics, innovation policy, and economic growth through technological advancements* (pp. 75–91). Hershey, PA: IGI Global. doi:10.4018/978-1-4666-1978-4.ch005

Litaay, T., Prananingrum, D. H., & Krisanto, Y. A. (2011). Indonesian legal perspectives on biotechnology and intellectual property rights. In S. Hongladarom (Ed.), *Genomics and bioethics: Interdisciplinary perspectives, technologies and advancements* (pp. 171–183). Hershey, PA: IGI Global. doi:10.4018/978-1-61692-883-4.ch012

Litaay, T., Prananingrum, D. H., & Krisanto, Y. A. (2013). Indonesian legal perspectives on biotechnology and intellectual property rights. In *Digital rights management: Concepts, methodologies, tools, and applications* (pp. 834–845). Hershey, PA: IGI Global. doi:10.4018/978-1-4666-2136-7.ch039

Losavio, M., Pastukhov, P., & Polyakova, S. (2014). Regulatory aspects of cloud computing in business environments. In S. Srinivasan (Ed.), *Security, trust, and regulatory aspects of cloud computing in business environments* (pp. 156–169). Hershey, PA: IGI Global. doi:10.4018/978-1-4666-5788-5.ch009

Lu, B., Tsou, B. K., Jiang, T., Zhu, J., & Kwong, O. Y. (2011). Mining parallel knowledge from comparable patents. In W. Wong, W. Liu, & M. Bennamoun (Eds.), *Ontology learning and knowledge discovery using the web: Challenges and recent advances* (pp. 247–271). Hershey, PA: IGI Global. doi:10.4018/978-1-60960-625-1.ch013

Lucas-Schloetter, A. (2011). Digital libraries and copyright issues: Digitization of contents and the economic rights of the authors. In I. Iglezakis, T. Synodinou, & S. Kapidakis (Eds.), *E-publishing and digital libraries: Legal and organizational issues* (pp. 159–179). Hershey, PA: IGI Global. doi:10.4018/978-1-60960-031-0.ch009

Lyytinen, K., Keil, T., & Fomin, V. (2010). A framework to build process theories of anticipatory information and communication technology (ICT) standardizing. In K. Jakobs (Ed.), *New applications in IT standards: Developments and progress* (pp. 147–186). Hershey, PA: IGI Global. doi:10.4018/978-1-60566-946-5.ch008

Macedo, M., & Isaías, P. (2013). Standards related to interoperability in EHR & HS. In M. Sicilia & P. Balazote (Eds.), *Interoperability in healthcare information systems: Standards, management, and technology* (pp. 19–44). Hershey, PA: IGI Global. doi:10.4018/978-1-4666-3000-0.ch002

Madden, P. (2011). Greater accountability, less red tape: The Australian standard business reporting experience. *International Journal of E-Business Research, 7*(2), 1–10. doi:10.4018/jebr.2011040101

Maravilhas, S. (2014). Quality improves the value of patent information to promote innovation. In G. Jamil, A. Malheiro, & F. Ribeiro (Eds.), *Rethinking the conceptual base for new practical applications in information value and quality* (pp. 61–82). Hershey, PA: IGI Global. doi:10.4018/978-1-4666-4562-2.ch004

Marshall, S. (2011). E-learning standards: Beyond technical standards to guides for professional practice. In F. Lazarinis, S. Green, & E. Pearson (Eds.), *Handbook of research on e-learning standards and interoperability: Frameworks and issues* (pp. 170–192). Hershey, PA: IGI Global. doi:10.4018/978-1-61692-789-9.ch008

Martino, L., & Bertino, E. (2012). Security for web services: Standards and research issues. In L. Jie-Zhang (Ed.), *Innovations, standards and practices of web services: Emerging research topics* (pp. 336–362). Hershey, PA: IGI Global. doi:10.4018/978-1-61350-104-7.ch015

McCarthy, V., & Hulsart, R. (2012). Management education for integrity: Raising ethical standards in online management classes. In C. Wankel & A. Stachowicz-Stanusch (Eds.), *Handbook of research on teaching ethics in business and management education* (pp. 413–425). Hershey, PA: IGI Global. doi:10.4018/978-1-61350-510-6.ch024

McGrath, T. (2012). The reality of using standards for electronic business document formats. In E. Kajan, F. Dorloff, & I. Bedini (Eds.), *Handbook of research on e-business standards and protocols: Documents, data and advanced web technologies* (pp. 21–32). Hershey, PA: IGI Global. doi:10.4018/978-1-4666-0146-8.ch002

Medlin, B. D., & Chen, C. C. (2012). A global perspective of laws and regulations dealing with information security and privacy. In *Cyber crime: Concepts, methodologies, tools and applications* (pp. 1349–1363). Hershey, PA: IGI Global. doi:10.4018/978-1-61350-323-2.ch609

Mehrfard, H., & Hamou-Lhadj, A. (2011). The impact of regulatory compliance on agile software processes with a focus on the FDA guidelines for medical device software. *International Journal of Information System Modeling and Design*, 2(2), 67–81. doi:10.4018/jismd.2011040104

Mehrfard, H., & Hamou-Lhadj, A. (2013). The impact of regulatory compliance on agile software processes with a focus on the FDA guidelines for medical device software. In J. Krogstie (Ed.), *Frameworks for developing efficient information systems: Models, theory, and practice* (pp. 298–314). Hershey, PA: IGI Global. doi:10.4018/978-1-4666-4161-7.ch013

Mendoza, R. A., & Ravichandran, T. (2011). An exploratory analysis of the relationship between organizational and institutional factors shaping the assimilation of vertical standards. *International Journal of IT Standards and Standardization Research*, 9(1), 24–51. doi:10.4018/jitsr.2011010102

Mendoza, R. A., & Ravichandran, T. (2012). An empirical evaluation of the assimilation of industry-specific data standards using firm-level and community-level constructs. In M. Tavana (Ed.), *Enterprise information systems and advancing business solutions: Emerging models* (pp. 287–312). Hershey, PA: IGI Global. doi:10.4018/978-1-4666-1761-2.ch017

Mendoza, R. A., & Ravichandran, T. (2012). Drivers of organizational participation in XML-based industry standardization efforts. In M. Tavana (Ed.), *Enterprise information systems and advancing business solutions: Emerging models* (pp. 268–286). Hershey, PA: IGI Global. doi:10.4018/978-1-4666-1761-2.ch016

Mendoza, R. A., & Ravichandran, T. (2013). An exploratory analysis of the relationship between organizational and institutional factors shaping the assimilation of vertical standards. In K. Jakobs (Ed.), *Innovations in organizational IT specification and standards development* (pp. 193–221). Hershey, PA: IGI Global. doi:10.4018/978-1-4666-2160-2.ch012

Mense, E. G., Fulwiler, J. H., Richardson, M. D., & Lane, K. E. (2011). Standardization, hybridization, or individualization: Marketing IT to a diverse clientele. In U. Demiray & S. Sever (Eds.), *Marketing online education programs: Frameworks for promotion and communication* (pp. 291–299). Hershey, PA: IGI Global. doi:10.4018/978-1-60960-074-7.ch019

Related References

Metaxa, E., Sarigiannidis, M., & Folinas, D. (2012). Legal issues of the French law on creation and internet (Hadopi 1 and 2). *International Journal of Technoethics*, *3*(3), 21–36. doi:10.4018/jte.2012070102

Meyer, N. (2012). Standardization as governance without government: A critical reassessment of the digital video broadcasting projects success story. *International Journal of IT Standards and Standardization Research*, *10*(2), 14–28. doi:10.4018/jitsr.2012070102

Miguel da Silva, F., Neto, F. M., Burlamaqui, A. M., Pinto, J. P., Fernandes, C. E., & Castro de Souza, R. (2014). T-SCORM: An extension of the SCORM standard to support the project of educational contents for t-learning. In F. Neto (Ed.), *Technology platform innovations and forthcoming trends in ubiquitous learning* (pp. 94–119). Hershey, PA: IGI Global. doi:10.4018/978-1-4666-4542-4.ch006

Moon, A. (2014). Copyright and licensing essentials for librarians and copyright owners in the digital age. In N. Patra, B. Kumar, & A. Pani (Eds.), *Progressive trends in electronic resource management in libraries* (pp. 106–117). Hershey, PA: IGI Global. doi:10.4018/978-1-4666-4761-9.ch006

Moralis, A., Pouli, V., Grammatikou, M., Kalogeras, D., & Maglaris, V. (2012). Security standards and issues for grid computing. In *Grid and cloud computing: Concepts, methodologies, tools and applications* (pp. 1656–1671). Hershey, PA: IGI Global. doi:10.4018/978-1-4666-0879-5.ch708

Moreno, L., Iglesias, A., Calvo, R., Delgado, S., & Zaragoza, L. (2012). Disability standards and guidelines for learning management systems: Evaluating accessibility. In R. Babo & A. Azevedo (Eds.), *Higher education institutions and learning management systems: Adoption and standardization* (pp. 199–218). Hershey, PA: IGI Global. doi:10.4018/978-1-60960-884-2.ch010

Moro, N. (2013). Digital rights management and corporate hegemony: Avenues for reform. In H. Rahman & I. Ramos (Eds.), *Ethical data mining applications for socio-economic development* (pp. 281–299). Hershey, PA: IGI Global. doi:10.4018/978-1-4666-4078-8.ch013

Mula, D., & Lobina, M. L. (2012). Legal protection of the web page. In H. Sasaki (Ed.), *Information technology for intellectual property protection: Interdisciplinary advancements* (pp. 213–236). Hershey, PA: IGI Global. doi:10.4018/978-1-61350-135-1.ch008

Mula, D., & Lobina, M. L. (2013). Legal protection of the web page. In *Digital rights management: Concepts, methodologies, tools, and applications* (pp. 1–18). Hershey, PA: IGI Global. doi:10.4018/978-1-4666-2136-7.ch001

Mulcahy, D. (2011). Performativity in practice: An actor-network account of professional teaching standards. *International Journal of Actor-Network Theory and Technological Innovation*, *3*(2), 1–16. doi:10.4018/jantti.2011040101

Mulcahy, D. (2013). Performativity in practice: An actor-network account of professional teaching standards. In A. Tatnall (Ed.), *Social and professional applications of actor-network theory for technology development* (pp. 1–16). Hershey, PA: IGI Global. doi:10.4018/978-1-4666-2166-4.ch001

Mustaffa, M. T. (2012). Multi-standard multi-band reconfigurable LNA. In A. Marzuki, A. Rahim, & M. Loulou (Eds.), *Advances in monolithic microwave integrated circuits for wireless systems: Modeling and design technologies* (pp. 1–23). Hershey, PA: IGI Global. doi:10.4018/978-1-60566-886-4.ch001

Nabi, S. I., Al-Ghmlas, G. S., & Alghathbar, K. (2012). Enterprise information security policies, standards, and procedures: A survey of available standards and guidelines. In M. Gupta, J. Walp, & R. Sharman (Eds.), *Strategic and practical approaches for information security governance: Technologies and applied solutions* (pp. 67–89). Hershey, PA: IGI Global. doi:10.4018/978-1-4666-0197-0.ch005

Nabi, S. I., Al-Ghmlas, G. S., & Alghathbar, K. (2014). Enterprise information security policies, standards, and procedures: A survey of available standards and guidelines. In *Crisis management: Concepts, methodologies, tools and applications* (pp. 750–773). Hershey, PA: IGI Global. doi:10.4018/978-1-4666-4707-7.ch036

Naixiao, Z., & Chunhua, H. (2012). Research on open innovation in China: Focus on intellectual property rights and their operation in Chinese enterprises. *International Journal of Asian Business and Information Management*, *3*(1), 65–71. doi:10.4018/jabim.2012010106

Naixiao, Z., & Chunhua, H. (2013). Research on open innovation in China: Focus on intellectual property rights and their operation in Chinese enterprises. In *Digital rights management: Concepts, methodologies, tools, and applications* (pp. 714–720). Hershey, PA: IGI Global. doi:10.4018/978-1-4666-2136-7.ch031

Ndjetcheu, L. (2013). Social responsibility and legal financial communication in African companies in the south of the Sahara: Glance from the OHADA accounting law viewpoint. *International Journal of Innovation in the Digital Economy*, *4*(4), 1–17. doi:10.4018/ijide.2013100101

Ng, W. L. (2013). Improving long-term financial risk forecasts using high-frequency data and scaling laws. In B. Alexandrova-Kabadjova, S. Martinez-Jaramillo, A. Garcia-Almanza, & E. Tsang (Eds.), *Simulation in computational finance and economics: Tools and emerging applications* (pp. 255–278). Hershey, PA: IGI Global. doi:10.4018/978-1-4666-2011-7.ch013

Noury, N., Bourquard, K., Bergognon, D., & Schroeder, J. (2013). Regulations initiatives in France for the interoperability of communicating medical devices. *International Journal of E-Health and Medical Communications*, 4(2), 50–64. doi:10.4018/jehmc.2013040104

Null, E. (2013). Legal and political barriers to municipal networks in the United States. In A. Abdelaal (Ed.), *Social and economic effects of community wireless networks and infrastructures* (pp. 27–56). Hershey, PA: IGI Global. doi:10.4018/978-1-4666-2997-4.ch003

OConnor, R. V., & Laporte, C. Y. (2014). An innovative approach to the development of an international software process lifecycle standard for very small entities. *International Journal of Information Technologies and Systems Approach*, 7(1), 1–22. doi:10.4018/ijitsa.2014010101

Onat, I., & Miri, A. (2013). RFID standards. In A. Miri (Ed.), *Advanced security and privacy for RFID technologies* (pp. 14–22). Hershey, PA: IGI Global. doi:10.4018/978-1-4666-3685-9.ch002

Orton, I., Alva, A., & Endicott-Popovsky, B. (2013). Legal process and requirements for cloud forensic investigations. In K. Ruan (Ed.), *Cybercrime and cloud forensics: Applications for investigation processes* (pp. 186–229). Hershey, PA: IGI Global. doi:10.4018/978-1-4666-2662-1.ch008

Ortt, J. R., & Egyedi, T. M. (2014). The effect of pre-existing standards and regulations on the development and diffusion of radically new innovations. *International Journal of IT Standards and Standardization Research*, 12(1), 17–37. doi:10.4018/ijitsr.2014010102

Ozturk, Y., & Sharma, J. (2011). mVITAL: A standards compliant vital sign monitor. In C. Röcker, & M. Ziefle (Eds.), Smart healthcare applications and services: Developments and practices (pp. 174-196). Hershey, PA: IGI Global. doi:10.4018/978-1-60960-180-5.ch008

Ozturk, Y., & Sharma, J. (2013). mVITAL: A standards compliant vital sign monitor. In IT policy and ethics: Concepts, methodologies, tools, and applications (pp. 515-538). Hershey, PA: IGI Global. doi:10.4018/978-1-4666-2919-6.ch024

Parsons, T. D. (2011). Affect-sensitive virtual standardized patient interface system. In D. Surry, R. Gray Jr, & J. Stefurak (Eds.), *Technology integration in higher education: Social and organizational aspects* (pp. 201–221). Hershey, PA: IGI Global. doi:10.4018/978-1-60960-147-8.ch015

Parveen, S., & Pater, C. (2012). Utilizing innovative video chat technology to meet national standards: A Case study on a STARTALK Hindi language program. *International Journal of Virtual and Personal Learning Environments*, *3*(3), 1–20. doi:10.4018/jvple.2012070101

Pawlowski, J. M., & Kozlov, D. (2013). Analysis and validation of learning technology models, standards and specifications: The reference model analysis grid (RMAG). In K. Jakobs (Ed.), *Innovations in organizational IT specification and standards development* (pp. 223–240). Hershey, PA: IGI Global. doi:10.4018/978-1-4666-2160-2.ch013

Pina, P. (2011). The private copy issue: Piracy, copyright and consumers' rights. In T. Strader (Ed.), *Digital product management, technology and practice: Interdisciplinary perspectives* (pp. 193–205). Hershey, PA: IGI Global. doi:10.4018/978-1-61692-877-3.ch011

Pina, P. (2013). Between Scylla and Charybdis: The balance between copyright, digital rights management and freedom of expression. In Digital rights management: Concepts, methodologies, tools, and applications (pp. 1355-1367). Hershey, PA: IGI Global. doi:10.4018/978-1-4666-2136-7.ch067

Pina, P. (2013). Computer games and intellectual property law: Derivative works, copyright and copyleft. In *Digital rights management: Concepts, methodologies, tools, and applications* (pp. 777–788). Hershey, PA: IGI Global. doi:10.4018/978-1-4666-2136-7.ch035

Pina, P. (2013). The private copy issue: Piracy, copyright and consumers' rights. In *Digital rights management: Concepts, methodologies, tools, and applications* (pp. 1546–1558). Hershey, PA: IGI Global. doi:10.4018/978-1-4666-2136-7.ch078

Piotrowski, M. (2011). QTI: A failed e-learning standard? In F. Lazarinis, S. Green, & E. Pearson (Eds.), *Handbook of research on e-learning standards and interoperability: Frameworks and issues* (pp. 59–82). Hershey, PA: IGI Global. doi:10.4018/978-1-61692-789-9.ch004

Ponte, D., & Camussone, P. F. (2013). Neither heroes nor chaos: The victory of VHS against Betamax. *International Journal of Actor-Network Theory and Technological Innovation*, *5*(1), 40–54. doi:10.4018/jantti.2013010103

Pradhan, A. (2011). Pivotal role of the ISO 14001 standard in the carbon economy. *International Journal of Green Computing, 2*(1), 38–46. doi:10.4018/jgc.2011010104

Pradhan, A. (2011). Standards and legislation for the carbon economy. In B. Unhelkar (Ed.), *Handbook of research on green ICT: Technology, business and social perspectives* (pp. 592–606). Hershey, PA: IGI Global. doi:10.4018/978-1-61692-834-6.ch043

Pradhan, A. (2013). Pivotal role of the ISO 14001 standard in the carbon economy. In K. Ganesh & S. Anbuudayasankar (Eds.), *International and interdisciplinary studies in green computing* (pp. 38–46). Hershey, PA: IGI Global. doi:10.4018/978-1-4666-2646-1.ch004

Prentzas, J., & Hatzilygeroudis, I. (2011). Techniques, technologies and patents related to intelligent educational systems. In G. Magoulas (Ed.), *E-infrastructures and technologies for lifelong learning: Next generation environments* (pp. 1–28). Hershey, PA: IGI Global. doi:10.4018/978-1-61520-983-5.ch001

Ramos, I., & Fernandes, J. (2011). Web-based intellectual property marketplace: A survey of current practices. *International Journal of Information Communication Technologies and Human Development, 3*(3), 58–68. doi:10.4018/jicthd.2011070105

Ramos, I., & Fernandes, J. (2013). Web-based intellectual property marketplace: A survey of current practices. In S. Chhabra (Ed.), *ICT influences on human development, interaction, and collaboration* (pp. 203–213). Hershey, PA: IGI Global. doi:10.4018/978-1-4666-1957-9.ch012

Rashmi, R. (2011). Biopharma drugs innovation in India and foreign investment and technology transfer in the changed patent regime. In P. Ordóñez de Pablos, W. Lee, & J. Zhao (Eds.), *Regional innovation systems and sustainable development: Emerging technologies* (pp. 210–225). Hershey, PA: IGI Global. doi:10.4018/978-1-61692-846-9.ch016

Rashmi, R. (2011). Optimal policy for biopharmaceutical drugs innovation and access in India. In P. Ordóñez de Pablos, W. Lee, & J. Zhao (Eds.), *Regional innovation systems and sustainable development: Emerging technologies* (pp. 74–114). Hershey, PA: IGI Global. doi:10.4018/978-1-61692-846-9.ch007

Rashmi, R. (2013). Biopharma drugs innovation in India and foreign investment and technology transfer in the changed patent regime. In *Digital rights management: Concepts, methodologies, tools, and applications* (pp. 846–859). Hershey, PA: IGI Global. doi:10.4018/978-1-4666-2136-7.ch040

Reed, C. N. (2011). The open geospatial consortium and web services standards. In P. Zhao & L. Di (Eds.), *Geospatial web services: Advances in information interoperability* (pp. 1–16). Hershey, PA: IGI Global. doi:10.4018/978-1-60960-192-8.ch001

Rejas-Muslera, R., Davara, E., Abran, A., & Buglione, L. (2013). Intellectual property systems in software. *International Journal of Cyber Warfare & Terrorism*, *3*(1), 1–14. doi:10.4018/ijcwt.2013010101

Rejas-Muslera, R. J., García-Tejedor, A. J., & Rodriguez, O. P. (2011). Open educational resources in e-learning: standards and environment. In F. Lazarinis, S. Green, & E. Pearson (Eds.), *Handbook of research on e-learning standards and interoperability: Frameworks and issues* (pp. 346–359). Hershey, PA: IGI Global. doi:10.4018/978-1-61692-789-9.ch017

Ries, N. M. (2011). Legal issues in health information and electronic health records. In *Clinical technologies: Concepts, methodologies, tools and applications* (pp. 1948–1961). Hershey, PA: IGI Global. doi:10.4018/978-1-60960-561-2.ch708

Riillo, C. A. (2013). Profiles and motivations of standardization players. *International Journal of IT Standards and Standardization Research*, *11*(2), 17–33. doi:10.4018/jitsr.2013070102

Rodriguez, E., & Lolas, F. (2011). Social issues related to gene patenting in Latin America: A bioethical reflection. In S. Hongladarom (Ed.), *Genomics and bioethics: Interdisciplinary perspectives, technologies and advancements* (pp. 152–170). Hershey, PA: IGI Global. doi:10.4018/978-1-61692-883-4.ch011

Rutherford, M. (2013). Implementing common core state standards using digital curriculum. In D. Polly (Ed.), *Common core mathematics standards and implementing digital technologies* (pp. 38–44). Hershey, PA: IGI Global. doi:10.4018/978-1-4666-4086-3.ch003

Rutherford, M. (2014). Implementing common core state standards using digital curriculum. In *K-12 education: Concepts, methodologies, tools, and applications* (pp. 383–389). Hershey, PA: IGI Global. doi:10.4018/978-1-4666-4502-8.ch022

Ryan, G., & Shinnick, E. (2011). Knowledge and intellectual property rights: An economics perspective. In D. Schwartz & D. Te'eni (Eds.), *Encyclopedia of knowledge management* (2nd ed.; pp. 489–496). Hershey, PA: IGI Global. doi:10.4018/978-1-59904-931-1.ch047

Ryoo, J., & Choi, Y. (2011). A taxonomy of green information and communication protocols and standards. In B. Unhelkar (Ed.), *Handbook of research on green ICT: Technology, business and social perspectives* (pp. 364–376). Hershey, PA: IGI Global. doi:10.4018/978-1-61692-834-6.ch026

Saeed, K., Ziegler, G., & Yaqoob, M. K. (2013). Management practices in exploration and production industry. In S. Saeed, M. Khan, & R. Ahmad (Eds.), *Business strategies and approaches for effective engineering management* (pp. 151–187). Hershey, PA: IGI Global. doi:10.4018/978-1-4666-3658-3.ch010

Saiki, T. (2014). Intellectual property in mergers & acquisitions. In J. Wang (Ed.), *Encyclopedia of business analytics and optimization* (pp. 1275–1283). Hershey, PA: IGI Global. doi:10.4018/978-1-4666-5202-6.ch117

Santos, O., & Boticario, J. (2011). A general framework for inclusive lifelong learning in higher education institutions with adaptive web-based services that support standards. In G. Magoulas (Ed.), *E-infrastructures and technologies for lifelong learning: Next generation environments* (pp. 29–58). Hershey, PA: IGI Global. doi:10.4018/978-1-61520-983-5.ch002

Santos, O., Boticario, J., Raffenne, E., Granado, J., Rodriguez-Ascaso, A., & Gutierrez y Restrepo, E. (2011). A standard-based framework to support personalisation, adaptation, and interoperability in inclusive learning scenarios. In F. Lazarinis, S. Green, & E. Pearson (Eds.), *Handbook of research on e-learning standards and interoperability: Frameworks and issues* (pp. 126–169). Hershey, PA: IGI Global. doi:10.4018/978-1-61692-789-9.ch007

Sarabdeen, J. (2012). Legal issues in e-healthcare systems. In M. Watfa (Ed.), *E-healthcare systems and wireless communications: Current and future challenges* (pp. 23–48). Hershey, PA: IGI Global. doi:10.4018/978-1-61350-123-8.ch002

Scheg, A. G. (2014). Common standards for online education found in accrediting organizations. In *Reforming teacher education for online pedagogy development* (pp. 50–76). Hershey, PA: IGI Global. doi:10.4018/978-1-4666-5055-8.ch003

Sclater, N. (2012). Legal and contractual issues of cloud computing for educational institutions. In L. Chao (Ed.), *Cloud computing for teaching and learning: Strategies for design and implementation* (pp. 186–199). Hershey, PA: IGI Global. doi:10.4018/978-1-4666-0957-0.ch013

Selwyn, L., & Eldridge, V. (2013). Governance and organizational structures. In *Public law librarianship: Objectives, challenges, and solutions* (pp. 41–71). Hershey, PA: IGI Global. doi:10.4018/978-1-4666-2184-8.ch003

Seo, D. (2012). The significance of government's role in technology standardization: Two cases in the wireless communications industry. In C. Reddick (Ed.), *Cases on public information management and e-government adoption* (pp. 219–231). Hershey, PA: IGI Global. doi:10.4018/978-1-4666-0981-5.ch009

Seo, D. (2013). Analysis of various structures of standards setting organizations (SSOs) that impact tension among members. *International Journal of IT Standards and Standardization Research*, *11*(2), 46–60. doi:10.4018/jitsr.2013070104

Seo, D. (2013). Background of standards strategy. In *Evolution and standardization of mobile communications technology* (pp. 1–17). Hershey, PA: IGI Global. doi:10.4018/978-1-4666-4074-0.ch001

Seo, D. (2013). Developing a theoretical model. In *Evolution and standardization of mobile communications technology* (pp. 18–42). Hershey, PA: IGI Global. doi:10.4018/978-1-4666-4074-0.ch002

Seo, D. (2013). The 1G (first generation) mobile communications technology standards. In *Evolution and standardization of mobile communications technology* (pp. 54–75). Hershey, PA: IGI Global. doi:10.4018/978-1-4666-4074-0.ch005

Seo, D. (2013). The 2G (second generation) mobile communications technology standards. In *Evolution and standardization of mobile communications technology* (pp. 76–114). Hershey, PA: IGI Global. doi:10.4018/978-1-4666-4074-0.ch006

Seo, D. (2013). The 3G (third generation) of mobile communications technology standards. In *Evolution and standardization of mobile communications technology* (pp. 115–161). Hershey, PA: IGI Global. doi:10.4018/978-1-4666-4074-0.ch007

Seo, D. (2013). The significance of government's role in technology standardization: Two cases in the wireless communications industry. In K. Jakobs (Ed.), *Innovations in organizational IT specification and standards development* (pp. 183–192). Hershey, PA: IGI Global. doi:10.4018/978-1-4666-2160-2.ch011

Seo, D., & Koek, J. W. (2012). Are Asian countries ready to lead a global ICT standardization? *International Journal of IT Standards and Standardization Research*, *10*(2), 29–44. doi:10.4018/jitsr.2012070103

Sharp, R. J., Ewald, J. A., & Kenward, R. (2013). Central information flows and decision-making requirements. In J. Papathanasiou, B. Manos, S. Arampatzis, & R. Kenward (Eds.), *Transactional environmental support system design: Global solutions* (pp. 7–32). Hershey, PA: IGI Global. doi:10.4018/978-1-4666-2824-3.ch002

Shen, X., Graham, I., Stewart, J., & Williams, R. (2013). Standards development as hybridization. *International Journal of IT Standards and Standardization Research*, *11*(2), 34–45. doi:10.4018/jitsr.2013070103

Sherman, M. (2013). Using technology to engage students with the standards for mathematical practice: The case of DGS. In D. Polly (Ed.), *Common core mathematics standards and implementing digital technologies* (pp. 78–101). Hershey, PA: IGI Global. doi:10.4018/978-1-4666-4086-3.ch006

Singh, J., & Kumar, V. (2013). Compliance and regulatory standards for cloud computing. In R. Khurana & R. Aggarwal (Eds.), *Interdisciplinary perspectives on business convergence, computing, and legality* (pp. 54–64). Hershey, PA: IGI Global. doi:10.4018/978-1-4666-4209-6.ch006

Singh, S., & Paliwal, M. (2014). Exploring a sense of intellectual property valuation for Indian SMEs. *International Journal of Asian Business and Information Management*, *5*(1), 15–36. doi:10.4018/ijabim.2014010102

Singh, S., & Siddiqui, T. J. (2013). Robust image data hiding technique for copyright protection. *International Journal of Information Security and Privacy*, *7*(2), 44–56. doi:10.4018/jisp.2013040103

Spies, M., & Tabet, S. (2012). Emerging standards and protocols for governance, risk, and compliance management. In E. Kajan, F. Dorloff, & I. Bedini (Eds.), *Handbook of research on e-business standards and protocols: Documents, data and advanced web technologies* (pp. 768–790). Hershey, PA: IGI Global. doi:10.4018/978-1-4666-0146-8.ch035

Spinello, R. A., & Tavani, H. T. (2008). Intellectual property rights: From theory to practical implementation. In H. Sasaki (Ed.), *Intellectual property protection for multimedia information technology* (pp. 25–69). Hershey, PA: IGI Global. doi:10.4018/978-1-59904-762-1.ch002

Spyrou, S., Bamidis, P., & Maglaveras, N. (2010). Health information standards: Towards integrated health information networks. In J. Rodrigues (Ed.), *Health information systems: Concepts, methodologies, tools, and applications* (pp. 2145–2159). Hershey, PA: IGI Global. doi:10.4018/978-1-60566-988-5.ch136

Stanfill, D. (2012). Standards-based educational technology professional development. In V. Wang (Ed.), *Encyclopedia of e-leadership, counseling and training* (pp. 819–834). Hershey, PA: IGI Global. doi:10.4018/978-1-61350-068-2.ch060

Steen, H. U. (2011). The battle within: An analysis of internal fragmentation in networked technologies based on a comparison of the DVB-H and T-DMB mobile digital multimedia broadcasting standards. *International Journal of IT Standards and Standardization Research*, 9(2), 50–71. doi:10.4018/jitsr.2011070103

Steen, H. U. (2013). The battle within: An analysis of internal fragmentation in networked technologies based on a comparison of the DVB-H and T-DMB mobile digital multimedia broadcasting standards. In K. Jakobs (Ed.), *Innovations in organizational IT specification and standards development* (pp. 91–114). Hershey, PA: IGI Global. doi:10.4018/978-1-4666-2160-2.ch005

Stoll, M., & Breu, R. (2012). Information security governance and standard based management systems. In M. Gupta, J. Walp, & R. Sharman (Eds.), *Strategic and practical approaches for information security governance: Technologies and applied solutions* (pp. 261–282). Hershey, PA: IGI Global. doi:10.4018/978-1-4666-0197-0.ch015

Suzuki, O. (2013). Search efforts, selective appropriation, and the usefulness of new knowledge: Evidence from a comparison across U.S. and non-U.S. patent applicants. *International Journal of Knowledge Management (IJKM)*, 9(1), 42-59. doi:10.4018/jkm.2013010103

Tajima, M. (2012). The role of technology standardization in RFID adoption: The pharmaceutical context. *International Journal of IT Standards and Standardization Research*, 10(1), 48–67. doi:10.4018/jitsr.2012010104

Talevi, A., Castro, E. A., & Bruno-Blanch, L. E. (2012). Virtual screening: An emergent, key methodology for drug development in an emergent continent: A bridge towards patentability. In E. Castro & A. Haghi (Eds.), *Advanced methods and applications in chemoinformatics: Research progress and new applications* (pp. 229–245). Hershey, PA: IGI Global. doi:10.4018/978-1-60960-860-6.ch011

Tauber, A. (2012). Requirements and properties of qualified electronic delivery systems in egovernment: An Austrian experience. In S. Sharma (Ed.), *E-adoption and technologies for empowering developing countries: Global advances* (pp. 115–128). Hershey, PA: IGI Global. doi:10.4018/978-1-4666-0041-6.ch009

Telesko, R., & Nikles, S. (2012). Semantic-enabled compliance management. In S. Smolnik, F. Teuteberg, & O. Thomas (Eds.), *Semantic technologies for business and information systems engineering: Concepts and applications* (pp. 292–310). Hershey, PA: IGI Global. doi:10.4018/978-1-60960-126-3.ch015

Tella, A., & Afolabi, A. K. (2013). Internet policy issues and digital libraries' management of intellectual property. In S. Thanuskodi (Ed.), *Challenges of academic library management in developing countries* (pp. 272–284). Hershey, PA: IGI Global. doi:10.4018/978-1-4666-4070-2.ch019

Tiwari, S. C., Gupta, M., Khan, M. A., & Ansari, A. Q. (2013). Intellectual property rights in semi-conductor industries: An Indian perspective. In S. Saeed, M. Khan, & R. Ahmad (Eds.), *Business strategies and approaches for effective engineering management* (pp. 97–110). Hershey, PA: IGI Global. doi:10.4018/978-1-4666-3658-3.ch006

Truyen, F., & Buekens, F. (2013). Professional ICT knowledge, epistemic standards, and social epistemology. In T. Takševa (Ed.), *Social software and the evolution of user expertise: Future trends in knowledge creation and dissemination* (pp. 274–294). Hershey, PA: IGI Global. doi:10.4018/978-1-4666-2178-7.ch016

Tummons, J. (2011). Deconstructing professionalism: An actor-network critique of professional standards for teachers in the UK lifelong learning sector. *International Journal of Actor-Network Theory and Technological Innovation, 3*(4), 22–31. doi:10.4018/jantti.2011100103

Tummons, J. (2013). Deconstructing professionalism: An actor-network critique of professional standards for teachers in the UK lifelong learning sector. In A. Tatnall (Ed.), *Social and professional applications of actor-network theory for technology development* (pp. 78–87). Hershey, PA: IGI Global. doi:10.4018/978-1-4666-2166-4.ch007

Tuohey, W. G. (2014). Lessons from practices and standards in safety-critical and regulated sectors. In I. Ghani, W. Kadir, & M. Ahmad (Eds.), *Handbook of research on emerging advancements and technologies in software engineering* (pp. 369–391). Hershey, PA: IGI Global. doi:10.4018/978-1-4666-6026-7.ch016

Tzoulia, E. (2013). Legal issues to be considered before setting in force consumer-centric marketing strategies within the European Union. In H. Kaufmann & M. Panni (Eds.), *Customer-centric marketing strategies: Tools for building organizational performance* (pp. 36–56). Hershey, PA: IGI Global. doi:10.4018/978-1-4666-2524-2.ch003

Unland, R. (2012). Interoperability support for e-business applications through standards, services, and multi-agent systems. In E. Kajan, F. Dorloff, & I. Bedini (Eds.), *Handbook of research on e-business standards and protocols: Documents, data and advanced web technologies* (pp. 129–153). Hershey, PA: IGI Global. doi:10.4018/978-1-4666-0146-8.ch007

Uslar, M., Grüning, F., & Rohjans, S. (2013). A use case for ontology evolution and interoperability: The IEC utility standards reference framework 62357. In M. Khosrow-Pour (Ed.), *Cases on performance measurement and productivity improvement: Technology integration and maturity* (pp. 387–415). Hershey, PA: IGI Global. doi:10.4018/978-1-4666-2618-8.ch018

van de Kaa, G. (2013). Responsible innovation and standardization: A new research approach? *International Journal of IT Standards and Standardization Research, 11*(2), 61–65. doi:10.4018/jitsr.2013070105

van de Kaa, G., Blind, K., & de Vries, H. J. (2013). The challenge of establishing a recognized interdisciplinary journal: A citation analysis of the international journal of IT standards and standardization research. *International Journal of IT Standards and Standardization Research, 11*(2), 1–16. doi:10.4018/jitsr.2013070101

Venkataraman, H., Ciubotaru, B., & Muntean, G. (2012). System design perspective: WiMAX standards and IEEE 802.16j based multihop WiMAX. In G. Cornetta, D. Santos, & J. Vazquez (Eds.), *Wireless radio-frequency standards and system design: Advanced techniques* (pp. 287–309). Hershey, PA: IGI Global. doi:10.4018/978-1-4666-0083-6.ch012

Vishwakarma, P., & Mukherjee, B. (2014). Knowing protection of intellectual contents in digital era. In N. Patra, B. Kumar, & A. Pani (Eds.), *Progressive trends in electronic resource management in libraries* (pp. 147–165). Hershey, PA: IGI Global. doi:10.4018/978-1-4666-4761-9.ch008

Wasilko, P. J. (2011). Law, architecture, gameplay, and marketing. In M. Cruz-Cunha, V. Varvalho, & P. Tavares (Eds.), *Business, technological, and social dimensions of computer games: Multidisciplinary developments* (pp. 476–493). Hershey, PA: IGI Global. doi:10.4018/978-1-60960-567-4.ch029

Wasilko, P. J. (2012). Law, architecture, gameplay, and marketing. In *Computer engineering: concepts, methodologies, tools and applications* (pp. 1660–1677). Hershey, PA: IGI Global. doi:10.4018/978-1-61350-456-7.ch703

Wasilko, P. J. (2014). Beyond compliance: Understanding the legal aspects of information system administration. In I. Portela & F. Almeida (Eds.), *Organizational, legal, and technological dimensions of information system administration* (pp. 57–75). Hershey, PA: IGI Global. doi:10.4018/978-1-4666-4526-4.ch004

White, G. L., Mediavilla, F. A., & Shah, J. R. (2011). Information privacy: Implementation and perception of laws and corporate policies by CEOs and managers. *International Journal of Information Security and Privacy, 5*(1), 50–66. doi:10.4018/jisp.2011010104

White, G. L., Mediavilla, F. A., & Shah, J. R. (2013). Information privacy: Implementation and perception of laws and corporate policies by CEOs and managers. In H. Nemati (Ed.), *Privacy solutions and security frameworks in information protection* (pp. 52–69). Hershey, PA: IGI Global. doi:10.4018/978-1-4666-2050-6. ch004

Whyte, K. P., List, M., Stone, J. V., Grooms, D., Gasteyer, S., Thompson, P. B., & Bouri, H. et al. (2014). Uberveillance, standards, and anticipation: A case study on nanobiosensors in U.S. cattle. In M. Michael & K. Michael (Eds.), *Uberveillance and the social implications of microchip implants: Emerging technologies* (pp. 260–279). Hershey, PA: IGI Global. doi:10.4018/978-1-4666-4582-0.ch012

Wilkes, W., Reusch, P. J., & Moreno, L. E. (2012). Flexible classification standards for product data exchange. In E. Kajan, F. Dorloff, & I. Bedini (Eds.), *Handbook of research on e-business standards and protocols: Documents, data and advanced web technologies* (pp. 448–466). Hershey, PA: IGI Global. doi:10.4018/978-1-4666-0146-8.ch021

Wittkower, D. E. (2011). Against strong copyright in e-business. In *Global business: Concepts, methodologies, tools and applications* (pp. 2157–2176). Hershey, PA: IGI Global. doi:10.4018/978-1-60960-587-2.ch720

Wright, D. (2012). Evolution of standards for smart grid communications. *International Journal of Interdisciplinary Telecommunications and Networking*, *4*(1), 47–55. doi:10.4018/jitn.2012010103

Wurster, S. (2013). Development of a specification for data interchange between information systems in public hazard prevention: Dimensions of success and related activities identified by case study research. *International Journal of IT Standards and Standardization Research*, *11*(1), 46–66. doi:10.4018/jitsr.2013010103

Wyburn, M. (2011). Copyright and ethical issues in emerging models for the digital media reporting of sports news in Australia. In M. Quigley (Ed.), *ICT ethics and security in the 21st century: New developments and applications* (pp. 66–85). Hershey, PA: IGI Global. doi:10.4018/978-1-60960-573-5.ch004

Wyburn, M. (2013). Copyright and ethical issues in emerging models for the digital media reporting of sports news in Australia. In *Digital rights management: Concepts, methodologies, tools, and applications* (pp. 290–309). Hershey, PA: IGI Global. doi:10.4018/978-1-4666-2136-7.ch014

Xiaohui, T., Yaohui, Z., & Yi, Z. (2012). The management system of enterprises intellectual property rights: A case study from China. *International Journal of Asian Business and Information Management*, *3*(1), 50–64. doi:10.4018/jabim.2012010105

Xiaohui, T., Yaohui, Z., & Yi, Z. (2013). The management system of enterprises' intellectual property rights: A case study from China. In *Digital rights management: Concepts, methodologies, tools, and applications* (pp. 1092–1106). Hershey, PA: IGI Global. doi:10.4018/978-1-4666-2136-7.ch053

Xuan, X., & Xiaowei, Z. (2012). The dilemma and resolution: The patentability of traditional Chinese medicine. *International Journal of Asian Business and Information Management*, *3*(3), 1–8. doi:10.4018/jabim.2012070101

Yang, C., & Lu, Z. (2011). A blind image watermarking scheme utilizing BTC bitplanes. *International Journal of Digital Crime and Forensics*, *3*(4), 42–53. doi:10.4018/jdcf.2011100104

Yastrebenetsky, M., & Gromov, G. (2014). International standard bases and safety classification. In M. Yastrebenetsky & V. Kharchenko (Eds.), *Nuclear power plant instrumentation and control systems for safety and security* (pp. 31–60). Hershey, PA: IGI Global. doi:10.4018/978-1-4666-5133-3.ch002

Zouag, N., & Kadiri, M. (2014). Intellectual property rights, innovation, and knowledge economy in Arab countries. In A. Driouchi (Ed.), *Knowledge-based economic policy development in the Arab world* (pp. 245–272). Hershey, PA: IGI Global. doi:10.4018/978-1-4666-5210-1.ch010

Compilation of References

Abbasi, A., France, S., Zhang, Z., & Chen, H. (2011). Selecting Attributes for Sentiment Classification Using Feature Relation Networks. *IEEE Transactions on Knowledge and Data Engineering, 23*(3), 447–462. doi:10.1109/TKDE.2010.110

Abramowicz, W., Stolarski, P., & Tomaszewski, T. (2013). Legal ontologies in ICT and law. In *Digital rights management: Concepts, methodologies, tools, and applications* (pp. 34–49). Hershey, PA: IGI Global. doi:10.4018/978-1-4666-2136-7.ch003

Adamich, T. (2012). Materials-to-standards alignment: How to "chunk" a whole cake and even use the "crumbs": State standards alignment models, learning objects, and formative assessment – methodologies and metadata for education. In L. Tomei (Ed.), *Advancing education with information communication technologies: Facilitating new trends* (pp. 165–178). Hershey, PA: IGI Global. doi:10.4018/978-1-61350-468-0.ch014

Adomi, E. E. (2011). Regulation of internet content. In E. Adomi (Ed.), *Frameworks for ICT policy: Government, social and legal issues* (pp. 233–246). Hershey, PA: IGI Global. doi:10.4018/978-1-61692-012-8.ch015

Aggarwal, C. C. (2014). *Data Mining: The Textbook*. Springer International Publishing.

Aggarwal, C., Han, J., Wang, J., & Yu, P. (2003). A framework for clustering evolving data streams. *Proc. Int. Conf. Very Large Databases*, 81–92. doi:10.1016/B978-012722442-8/50016-1

Aggestam, L. (2011). Guidelines for preparing organizations in developing countries for standards-based B2B. In *Global business: Concepts, methodologies, tools and applications* (pp. 206–228). Hershey, PA: IGI Global. doi:10.4018/978-1-60960-587-2.ch114

Agrawal, R., Gollapudi, S., Kannan, A., & Kenthapadi, K. (2012). Data mining for improving textbooks. *SIGKDD Explor. Newsl, 13*(2).

Agrawal, R., Gollapudi, S., Kenthapadi, K., Srivastava, N., & Velu, R. (2010). Enriching textbooks through data mining. *Proceedings of the First ACM Symposium on Computing for Development*. doi:10.1145/1926180.1926204

Aji, A., Wang, F., Vo, H., Lee, R., Liu, Q., Zhang, X., & Saltz, J. (2013). Hadoop GIS: A high performance spatial data warehousing system over mapreduce. *Proceedings of the VLDB Endowment*, 6(11), 1009–1020. doi:10.14778/2536222.2536227 PMID:24187650

Akowuah, F., Yuan, X., Xu, J., & Wang, H. (2012). A survey of U.S. laws for health information security & privacy. *International Journal of Information Security and Privacy*, 6(4), 40–54. doi:10.4018/jisp.2012100102

Akowuah, F., Yuan, X., Xu, J., & Wang, H. (2013). A survey of security standards applicable to health information systems. *International Journal of Information Security and Privacy*, 7(4), 22–36. doi:10.4018/ijisp.2013100103

Al Hadid, I. (2012). Applying the certification's standards to the simulation study steps. In E. Abu-Taieh, A. El Sheikh, & M. Jafari (Eds.), *Technology engineering and management in aviation: Advancements and discoveries* (pp. 294–307). Hershey, PA: IGI Global. doi:10.4018/978-1-60960-887-3.ch017

Al Mohannadi, F., Arif, M., Aziz, Z., & Richardson, P. A. (2013). Adopting BIM standards for managing vision 2030 infrastructure development in Qatar. *International Journal of 3-D Information Modeling (IJ3DIM)*, 2(3), 64-73. doi:10.4018/ij3dim.2013070105

Alejandre, G. M. (2013). IT security governance legal issues. In D. Mellado, L. Enrique Sánchez, E. Fernández-Medina, & M. Piattini (Eds.), *IT security governance innovations: Theory and research* (pp. 47–73). Hershey, PA: IGI Global. doi:10.4018/978-1-4666-2083-4.ch003

Alexandropoulou-Egyptiadou, E. (2013). The Hellenic framework for computer program copyright protection following the implementation of the relative european union directives. In *Digital rights management: Concepts, methodologies, tools, and applications* (pp. 738–745). Hershey, PA: IGI Global. doi:10.4018/978-1-4666-2136-7.ch033

Alirezaee, M., & Afsharian, M. (2011). Measuring the effect of the rules and regulations on global malmquist index. *International Journal of Operations Research and Information Systems*, 2(3), 64–78. doi:10.4018/joris.2011070105

Alirezaee, M., & Afsharian, M. (2013). Measuring the effect of the rules and regulations on global malmquist index. In J. Wang (Ed.), *Optimizing, innovating, and capitalizing on information systems for operations* (pp. 215–229). Hershey, PA: IGI Global. doi:10.4018/978-1-4666-2925-7.ch011

Ali, S. (2012). Practical web application security audit following industry standards and compliance. In J. Zubairi & A. Mahboob (Eds.), *Cyber security standards, practices and industrial applications: Systems and methodologies* (pp. 259–279). Hershey, PA: IGI Global. doi:10.4018/978-1-60960-851-4.ch013

Al-Nuaimi, A. A. (2011). Using watermarking techniques to prove rightful ownership of web images. *International Journal of Information Technology and Web Engineering*, 6(2), 29–39. doi:10.4018/jitwe.2011040103

Alsaffar, A., & Omar, N. (2014). Study on Feature Selection and Machine Learning Algorithms For Malay Sentiment Classification. *IEEE International Conference on Information Technology and Multimedia (ICIMU)*, 270-275. doi:10.1109/ICIMU.2014.7066643

Alves de Lima, A., Carvalho dos Reis, P., Branco, J. C., Danieli, R., Osawa, C. C., Winter, E., & Santos, D. A. (2013). Scenario-patent protection compared to climate change: The case of green patents. *International Journal of Social Ecology and Sustainable Development, 4*(3), 61–70. doi:10.4018/jsesd.2013070105

Amirante, A., Castaldi, T., Miniero, L., & Romano, S. P. (2013). Protocol interactions among user agents, application servers, and media servers: Standardization efforts and open issues. In D. Kanellopoulos (Ed.), *Intelligent multimedia technologies for networking applications: Techniques and tools* (pp. 48–63). Hershey, PA: IGI Global. doi:10.4018/978-1-4666-2833-5.ch003

Anderberg, M. R. (1973). *Cluster analysis for applications*. Academic Press.

Anker, P. (2013). The impact of regulations on the business case for cognitive radio. In T. Lagkas, P. Sarigiannidis, M. Louta, & P. Chatzimisios (Eds.), *Evolution of cognitive networks and self-adaptive communication systems* (pp. 142–170). Hershey, PA: IGI Global. doi:10.4018/978-1-4666-4189-1.ch006

Antunes, A. M., Mendes, F. M., Schumacher, S. D., Quoniam, L., & Lima de Magalhães, J. (2014). The contribution of information science through intellectual property to innovation in the Brazilian health sector. In G. Jamil, A. Malheiro, & F. Ribeiro (Eds.), *Rethinking the conceptual base for new practical applications in information value and quality* (pp. 83–115). Hershey, PA: IGI Global. doi:10.4018/978-1-4666-4562-2.ch005

Appel, Chiclana, Carter, & Fujita. (2016). A hybrid approach to the sentiment analysis problem at the sentence level. *Knowledge-Based Systems*, 1-15.

Atiskov, A. Y., Novikov, F. A., Fedorchenko, L. N., Vorobiev, V. I., & Moldovyan, N. A. (2013). Ontology-based analysis of cryptography standards and possibilities of their harmonization. In A. Elçi, J. Pieprzyk, A. Chefranov, M. Orgun, H. Wang, & R. Shankaran (Eds.), *Theory and practice of cryptography solutions for secure information systems* (pp. 1–33). Hershey, PA: IGI Global. doi:10.4018/978-1-4666-4030-6.ch001

Ayanso, A., & Herath, T. (2012). Law and technology at crossroads in cyberspace: Where do we go from here? In A. Dudley, J. Braman, & G. Vincenti (Eds.), *Investigating cyber law and cyber ethics: Issues, impacts and practices* (pp. 57–77). Hershey, PA: IGI Global. doi:10.4018/978-1-61350-132-0.ch004

Ayanso, A., & Herath, T. (2014). Law and technology at crossroads in cyberspace: Where do we go from here? In *Cyber behavior: Concepts, methodologies, tools, and applications* (pp. 1990–2010). Hershey, PA: IGI Global. doi:10.4018/978-1-4666-5942-1.ch105

Aydogan-Duda, N. (2012). Branding innovation: The case study of Turkey. In N. Ekekwe & N. Islam (Eds.), *Disruptive technologies, innovation and global redesign: Emerging implications* (pp. 238–248). Hershey, PA: IGI Global. doi:10.4018/978-1-4666-0134-5.ch012

Babu, V. S., & Viswanath, P. (2007, December). Weighted k-nearest leader classifier for large data sets. In *International Conference on Pattern Recognition and Machine Intelligence* (pp. 17-24). Springer Berlin Heidelberg. doi:10.1007/978-3-540-77046-6_3

Babu, T. R., Chatterjee, A., Khandeparker, S., Subhash, A. V., & Gupta, A. (2015). Geographical address classification without using geolocation coordinates. *Proceedings of the 9th Workshop on Geographic Information Retrieval*, 8. doi:10.1145/2837689.2837696

Babu, T. R., Murty, M. N., & Subrahmanya, S. V. (2013). *Compression Schemes for Mining Large Datasets*. London: Springer-Verlag. doi:10.1007/978-1-4471-5607-9

Bação, F. L. (2006). *Geospatial Data Mining. ISEGI*. New University of Lisbon.

Baeza-Yates, R., & Ribeiro-Neto, B. (1999). *Modern Information retrieval*. Reading, MA: Addison Wesley Longman.

Bagby, J. W. (2011). Environmental standardization for sustainability. In Z. Luo (Ed.), *Green finance and sustainability: Environmentally-aware business models and technologies* (pp. 31–55). Hershey, PA: IGI Global. doi:10.4018/978-1-60960-531-5.ch002

Bagby, J. W. (2013). Insights from U.S. experience to guide international reliance on standardization: Achieving supply chain sustainability. *International Journal of Applied Logistics*, *4*(3), 25–46. doi:10.4018/jal.2013070103

Baggio, B., & Beldarrain, Y. (2011). Intellectual property in an age of open source and anonymity. In *Anonymity and learning in digitally mediated communications: Authenticity and trust in cyber education* (pp. 39–57). Hershey, PA: IGI Global. doi:10.4018/978-1-60960-543-8.ch003

Balzli, C. E., & Fragnière, E. (2012). How ERP systems are centralizing and standardizing the accounting function in public organizations for better and worse. In S. Chhabra & M. Kumar (Eds.), *Strategic enterprise resource planning models for e-government: Applications and methodologies* (pp. 55–72). Hershey, PA: IGI Global. doi:10.4018/978-1-60960-863-7.ch004

Banas, J. R. (2011). Standardized, flexible design of electronic learning environments to enhance learning efficiency and effectiveness. In A. Kitchenham (Ed.), *Models for interdisciplinary mobile learning: Delivering information to students* (pp. 66–86). Hershey, PA: IGI Global. doi:10.4018/978-1-60960-511-7.ch004

Bao, C., & Castresana, J. M. (2011). Interoperability approach in e-learning standardization processes. In F. Lazarinis, S. Green, & E. Pearson (Eds.), *Handbook of research on e-learning standards and interoperability: Frameworks and issues* (pp. 399–418). Hershey, PA: IGI Global. doi:10.4018/978-1-61692-789-9.ch020

Bao, C., & Castresana, J. M. (2012). Interoperability approach in e-learning standardization processes. In *Virtual learning environments: Concepts, methodologies, tools and applications* (pp. 542–560). Hershey, PA: IGI Global. doi:10.4018/978-1-4666-0011-9.ch307

Bao, H., Guo, H., Wang, J., Zhou, R., Lu, X., & Shi, S. (2009). MapView: Visualization of short reads alignment on a desktop computer. *Bioinformatics (Oxford, England)*, *25*(12), 1554–1555. doi:10.1093/bioinformatics/btp255 PMID:19369497

Barbu, A., She, Y., Ding, L., & Gramajo, G. (2017). Feature Selection with Annealing for Computer Vision and Big Data Learning. *IEEE Transactions on Pattern Analysis and Machine Intelligence*, *39*(2), 272–286. doi:10.1109/TPAMI.2016.2544315 PMID:27019473

Bare, J. C., Koide, T., Reiss, D. J., Tenenbaum, D., & Baliga, N. S. (2010). Integration and visualization of systems biology data in context of the genome. *BMC Bioinformatics*, *11*(1), 382. doi:10.1186/1471-2105-11-382 PMID:20642854

Barrett, B. (2011). Evaluating and implementing teaching standards: Providing quality online teaching strategies and techniques standards. In F. Lazarinis, S. Green, & E. Pearson (Eds.), *Developing and utilizing e-learning applications* (pp. 66–83). Hershey, PA: IGI Global. doi:10.4018/978-1-61692-791-2.ch004

Bello-Orgaz, G., Jung, J. J., & Camacho, D. (2016). Social big data: Recent achievements and new challenges. *Information Fusion*, *28*, 45–59. doi:10.1016/j.inffus.2015.08.005

Berkhin, P. (2006). A survey of clustering data mining techniques. In *Grouping multidimensional data* (pp. 25–71). Springer Berlin Heidelberg. doi:10.1007/3-540-28349-8_2

Berleur, J. (2011). Ethical and social issues of the internet governance regulations. In D. Haftor & A. Mirijamdotter (Eds.), *Information and communication technologies, society and human beings: Theory and framework (festschrift in honor of Gunilla Bradley)* (pp. 466–476). Hershey, PA: IGI Global. doi:10.4018/978-1-60960-057-0.ch038

Bezdek, J. C. (1981). Pattern recognition with Fuzzy Objective Function Algorithms. Kluwer Academic Publishers.

Bhattathiripad, V. P. (2014). Software copyright infringement and litigation. In *Judiciary-friendly forensics of software copyright infringement* (pp. 35–55). Hershey, PA: IGI Global. doi:10.4018/978-1-4666-5804-2.ch002

Bhosale, H. S., & Gadekar, D. P. (2014). A review paper on big data and hadoop. International Journal of Scientific and Research Publications, 756.

Bhushan, S. B., Danti, A., & Fernandes, S. L. (2017). A Novel Integer Representation-Based Approach for Classification of Text Documents. *Proceedings of the International Conference on Data Engineering and Communication Technology*, 557-564.

Bin, X., & Chuan, T. K. (2011). The effect of business characteristics on the methods of knowledge protections. *International Journal of Social Ecology and Sustainable Development*, *2*(3), 34–60. doi:10.4018/jsesd.2011070103

Bin, X., & Chuan, T. K. (2013). The effect of business characteristics on the methods of knowledge protections. In E. Carayannis (Ed.), *Creating a sustainable ecology using technology-driven solutions* (pp. 172–200). Hershey, PA: IGI Global. doi:10.4018/978-1-4666-3613-2.ch013

Bin, X., & Chuan, T. K. (2013). The effect of business characteristics on the methods of knowledge protections. In *Digital rights management: Concepts, methodologies, tools, and applications* (pp. 1283–1311). Hershey, PA: IGI Global. doi:10.4018/978-1-4666-2136-7.ch063

Blake, C., & Merz, C. J. (1998). *{UCI} Repository of machine learning databases*. Academic Press.

Blum, A. L., & Langley, P. (1997). Selection of relevant features and examples in machine learning. *Artificial Intelligence*, *97*(1), 245–271. doi:10.1016/S0004-3702(97)00063-5

Bogers, M., Bekkers, R., & Granstrand, O. (2012). Intellectual property and licensing strategies in open collaborative innovation. In C. de Pablos Heredero & D. López (Eds.), *Open innovation in firms and public administrations: Technologies for value creation* (pp. 37–58). Hershey, PA: IGI Global. doi:10.4018/978-1-61350-341-6.ch003

Bogers, M., Bekkers, R., & Granstrand, O. (2013). Intellectual property and licensing strategies in open collaborative innovation. In *Digital rights management: Concepts, methodologies, tools, and applications* (pp. 1204–1224). Hershey, PA: IGI Global. doi:10.4018/978-1-4666-2136-7.ch059

Bondi, A. B. (2000). Characteristics of scalability and their impact on performance. *Proceedings of the 2nd international workshop on Software and performance,* 195-203. doi:10.1145/350391.350432

Bonfield, J. K., & Whitwham, A. (2010). Gap5editing the billion fragment sequence assembly. *Bioinformatics (Oxford, England)*, *26*(14), 1699–1703. doi:10.1093/bioinformatics/btq268 PMID:20513662

Bottou, L. (2012). Stochastic Gradient Descent Tricks. *Neural Networks, Tricks of the Trade, Reloaded, Springer*, *7700*, 430–445.

Bourcier, D. (2013). Law and governance: The genesis of the commons. In F. Doridot, P. Duquenoy, P. Goujon, A. Kurt, S. Lavelle, N. Patrignani, & A. Santuccio et al. (Eds.), *Ethical governance of emerging technologies development* (pp. 166–183). Hershey, PA: IGI Global. doi:10.4018/978-1-4666-3670-5.ch011

Bousquet, F., Fomin, V. V., & Drillon, D. (2011). Anticipatory standards development and competitive intelligence. *International Journal of Business Intelligence Research*, *2*(1), 16–30. doi:10.4018/jbir.2011010102

Bousquet, F., Fomin, V. V., & Drillon, D. (2013). Anticipatory standards development and competitive intelligence. In R. Herschel (Ed.), *Principles and applications of business intelligence research* (pp. 17–30). Hershey, PA: IGI Global. doi:10.4018/978-1-4666-2650-8.ch002

Brabazon, A. (2013). Optimal patent design: An agent-based modeling approach. In B. Alexandrova-Kabadjova, S. Martinez-Jaramillo, A. Garcia-Almanza, & E. Tsang (Eds.), *Simulation in computational finance and economics: Tools and emerging applications* (pp. 280–302). Hershey, PA: IGI Global. doi:10.4018/978-1-4666-2011-7.ch014

Bracci, F., Corradi, A., & Foschini, L. (2014). Cloud standards: Security and interoperability issues. In H. Mouftah & B. Kantarci (Eds.), *Communication infrastructures for cloud computing* (pp. 465–495). Hershey, PA: IGI Global. doi:10.4018/978-1-4666-4522-6.ch020

Brants, Thorsten, & Franz. (2006). *Web 1t 5-gram version 1*. Academic Press.

Bratko, A., Cormack, G. V., Filipič, B., Lynam, T. R., & Zupan, B. (2006). Spam filtering using statistical data compression models. *Journal of Machine Learning Research, 7*(Dec), 2673–2698.

Bravo-Marquez, F., Mendoza, M., & Poblete, B. (2014). Meta-level sentiment models for big social data analysis. *Knowledge-Based Systems, 69*, 86–99. doi:10.1016/j.knosys.2014.05.016

Breiger. (2004). *The Analysis of Social Networks*. Sage Publications Ltd.

Briscoe, D. R. (2012). Globalization and international labor standards, codes of conduct, and ethics: An International HRM perspective. In C. Wankel & S. Malleck (Eds.), *Ethical models and applications of globalization: Cultural, socio-political and economic perspectives* (pp. 1–22). Hershey, PA: IGI Global. doi:10.4018/978-1-61350-332-4.ch001

Briscoe, D. R. (2014). Globalization and international labor standards, codes of conduct, and ethics: An International HRM perspective. In *Cross-cultural interaction: Concepts, methodologies, tools and applications* (pp. 40–62). Hershey, PA: IGI Global. doi:10.4018/978-1-4666-4979-8.ch004

Brooks, R. G., & Geradin, D. (2011). Interpreting and enforcing the voluntary FRAND commitment. *International Journal of IT Standards and Standardization Research, 9*(1), 1–23. doi:10.4018/jitsr.2011010101

Brown, C. A. (2013). Common core state standards: The promise for college and career ready students in the U.S. In V. Wang (Ed.), *Handbook of research on teaching and learning in K-20 education* (pp. 50–82). Hershey, PA: IGI Global. doi:10.4018/978-1-4666-4249-2.ch004

Bu, H., Howe, B., Balazinska, M., & Ernst, M. D. (2010). HaLoop: Efficient Iterative Data Processing on Large Clusters. *Proceedings of the VLDB Endowment, 3*(1), 285-296.

Buyurgan, N., Rardin, R. L., Jayaraman, R., Varghese, V. M., & Burbano, A. (2011). A novel GS1 data standard adoption roadmap for healthcare providers. *International Journal of Healthcare Information Systems and Informatics, 6*(4), 42–59. doi:10.4018/jhisi.2011100103

Buyurgan, N., Rardin, R. L., Jayaraman, R., Varghese, V. M., & Burbano, A. (2013). A novel GS1 data standard adoption roadmap for healthcare providers. In J. Tan (Ed.), *Healthcare information technology innovation and sustainability: Frontiers and adoption* (pp. 41–57). Hershey, PA: IGI Global. doi:10.4018/978-1-4666-2797-0.ch003

Campolo, C., Cozzetti, H. A., Molinaro, A., & Scopigno, R. M. (2012). PHY/MAC layer design in vehicular ad hoc networks: Challenges, standard approaches, and alternative solutions. In R. Aquino-Santos, A. Edwards, & V. Rangel-Licea (Eds.), *Wireless technologies in vehicular ad hoc networks: Present and future challenges* (pp. 70–100). Hershey, PA: IGI Global. doi:10.4018/978-1-4666-0209-0.ch004

Can, F. (1993). Incremental clustering for dynamic information processing. *ACM Transactions on Information Systems, 11*(2), 143–164. doi:10.1145/130226.134466

Can, F., Fox, E., Snavely, C., & France, R. (1995). Incremental clustering for very large document databases: Initial MARIAN experience. *Information Sciences*, *84*(1–2), 101–114. doi:10.1016/0020-0255(94)00111-N

Cantatore, F. (2014). Research findings: Authors' perceptions and the copyright framework. In Authors, copyright, and publishing in the digital era (pp. 147-189). Hershey, PA: IGI Global. doi:10.4018/978-1-4666-5214-9.ch008

Cantatore, F. (2014). Copyright support structures. In *Authors, copyright, and publishing in the digital era* (pp. 81–93). Hershey, PA: IGI Global. doi:10.4018/978-1-4666-5214-9.ch005

Cantatore, F. (2014). History and development of copyright. In *Authors, copyright, and publishing in the digital era* (pp. 10–32). Hershey, PA: IGI Global. doi:10.4018/978-1-4666-5214-9.ch002

Cao, L. (Ed.). (2009). *Data mining and multi-agent integration*. Springer Science & Business Media. doi:10.1007/978-1-4419-0522-2

Carpenter, G. A., & Grossberg, S. (1987). A massively parallel architecture for a self-organizing neural pattern recognition machine. *Computer Vision Graphics and Image Processing*, *37*(1), 54–115. doi:10.1016/S0734-189X(87)80014-2

Carpenter, G. A., & Grossberg, S. (1990). ART 3: Hierarchical search using chemical transmitters in self–organizing pattern recognition architectures. *Neural Networks*, *3*(2), 129–152. doi:10.1016/0893-6080(90)90085-Y

Carver, T., Harris, S. R., Berriman, M., Parkhill, J., & McQuillan, J. A. (2011). Artemis: An integrated platform for visualization and analysis of high-throughput sequence-based experimental data. *Bioinformatics (Oxford, England)*, *28*(4), 464–469. doi:10.1093/bioinformatics/btr703 PMID:22199388

Carver, T., Harris, S. R., Otto, T. D., Berriman, M., Parkhill, J., & McQuillan, J. A. (2012). BamView: Visualizing and interpretation of next-generation sequencing read alignments. *Briefings in Bioinformatics*, *14*(2), 203–212. doi:10.1093/bib/bbr073 PMID:22253280

Cary, A., Sun, Z., Hristidis, V., & Rishe, N. (2009, June). Experiences on processing spatial data with mapreduce. In *International Conference on Scientific and Statistical Database Management* (pp. 302-319). Springer Berlin Heidelberg. doi:10.1007/978-3-642-02279-1_24

Cassini, J., Medlin, B. D., & Romaniello, A. (2011). Forty years of federal legislation in the area of data protection and information security. In H. Nemati (Ed.), *Pervasive information security and privacy developments: Trends and advancements* (pp. 14–23). Hershey, PA: IGI Global. doi:10.4018/978-1-61692-000-5.ch002

Catal, C., & Mehmet, N. (2017). A sentiment classification model based on multiple classifiers. *Applied Soft Computing*, *50*, 135–141. doi:10.1016/j.asoc.2016.11.022

Chaira, T. (2015). *Medical Image Processing: Advanced Fuzzy Set Theoretic Techniques*. CRC Press.

Chakraborty, T. (2015). Leveraging disjoint communities for detecting overlapping community structure. *Journal of Statistical Mechanics, 2015*(5), P05017. doi:10.1088/1742-5468/2015/05/P05017

Chandrashekar, G., & Ferat, S. (2014). A survey on feature selection methods. *Computers & Electrical Engineering, 40*(1), 16–28. doi:10.1016/j.compeleceng.2013.11.024

Charlesworth, A. (2012). Addressing legal issues in online research, publication and archiving: A UK perspective. In C. Silva (Ed.), *Online research methods in urban and planning studies: Design and outcomes* (pp. 368–393). Hershey, PA: IGI Global. doi:10.4018/978-1-4666-0074-4.ch022

Chaudhary, C., & Kang, I. S. (2011). Pirates of the copyright and cyberspace: Issues involved. In R. Santanam, M. Sethumadhavan, & M. Virendra (Eds.), *Cyber security, cyber crime and cyber forensics: Applications and perspectives* (pp. 59–68). Hershey, PA: IGI Global. doi:10.4018/978-1-60960-123-2.ch005

Chen, C. P., & Zhang, C. Y. (2014). Data-intensive applications, challenges, techniques and technologies: A survey on Big Data. *Information Sciences, 275*, 314–347. doi:10.1016/j.ins.2014.01.015

Cheng, T. W., Goldgof, D. B., & Hall, L. O. (1995). Fast clustering with application to fuzzy rule generation. *Proceedings of the IEEE international Conference on Fuzzy Systems*, 2289-2295.

Chen, H., Jiang, W., Li, C., & Li, R. (2013). A heuristic feature selection approach for text categorization by using chaos optimization and genetic algorithm. *Mathematical Problems in Engineering, 2013*, 1–6. doi:10.1155/2013/524017

Chen, K. (2014). Optimizing star-coordinate visualization models for effective interactive cluster exploration on big data. *Intelligent Data Analysis, 18*(2), 117–136.

Chen, K., Wallis, J. W., McLellan, M. D., Larson, D. E., Kalicki, J. M., Pohl, C. S., & Mardis, E. R. et al. (2009). BreakDancer: An algorithm for high-resolution mapping of genomic structural variation. *Nature Methods, 6*(9), 677–681. doi:10.1038/nmeth.1363 PMID:19668202

Chen, L., Hu, W., Yang, M., & Zhang, L. (2011). Security and privacy issues in secure e-mail standards and services. In H. Nemati (Ed.), *Security and privacy assurance in advancing technologies: New developments* (pp. 174–185). Hershey, PA: IGI Global. doi:10.4018/978-1-60960-200-0.ch013

Chen, M. S., Jiawei, H., & Yu, P. S. (1996). Data Mining: An Overview from Database Perspective. *IEEE Transactions on Knowledge and Data Engineering, 8*(6), 866–883. doi:10.1109/69.553155

Chen, Y., Zhang, X., Li, Z., & Ng, J. P. (2015). Search engine reinforced semi-supervised classification and graph-based summarization of microblogs. *Neurocomputing, 152*, 274–286. doi:10.1016/j.neucom.2014.10.068

Chen, Z., Wen, Y., Cao, J., Zheng, W., Chang, J., Wu, Y., & Peng, G. et al. (2015). A survey of bitmap index compression algorithms for big data. *Tsinghua Science and Technology, 20*(1), 100–115. doi:10.1109/TST.2015.7040519

Chitta, R., Jin, R., Havens, T., & Jain, A. (2011). Approximate kernel k-means: Solutions to large scale kernel clustering. Proc. ACM SIGKDD Conf. Knowl Discovery and Data Mining, 895-903.

Ciaghi, A., & Villafiorita, A. (2012). Law modeling and BPR for public administration improvement. In K. Bwalya & S. Zulu (Eds.), *Handbook of research on e-government in emerging economies: Adoption, E-participation, and legal frameworks* (pp. 391–410). Hershey, PA: IGI Global. doi:10.4018/978-1-4666-0324-0.ch019

Ciptasari, R. W., & Sakurai, K. (2013). Multimedia copyright protection scheme based on the direct feature-based method. In K. Kondo (Ed.), *Multimedia information hiding technologies and methodologies for controlling data* (pp. 412–439). Hershey, PA: IGI Global. doi:10.4018/978-1-4666-2217-3.ch019

Clark, L. A., Jones, D. L., & Clark, W. J. (2012). Technology innovation and the policy vacuum: A call for ethics, norms, and laws to fill the void. *International Journal of Technoethics*, *3*(1), 1–13. doi:10.4018/jte.2012010101

Clark, M. J., Homer, N., OConnor, B. D., Chen, Z., Eskin, A., Lee, H., & Nelson, S. F. et al. (2010). U87MG Decoded: The Genomic sequence of a Cytogenetically aberrant human cancer cell line. *PLOS Genetics*, *6*(1), e1000832. doi:10.1371/journal.pgen.1000832 PMID:20126413

Claster, W. B., Dinh, Q. H., & Shanmuganathan, S. (2010). Unsupervised Artificial Neural Nets for Modeling Movie Sentiment. *Second International Conference on Computational Intelligence, Communication Systems and Networks*, 349-353. doi:10.1109/CICSyN.2010.23

Cooklev, T. (2013). The role of standards in engineering education. In K. Jakobs (Ed.), *Innovations in organizational IT specification and standards development* (pp. 129–137). Hershey, PA: IGI Global. doi:10.4018/978-1-4666-2160-2.ch007

Cooper, A. R. (2013). Key challenges in the design of learning technology standards: Observations and proposals. In K. Jakobs (Ed.), *Innovations in organizational IT specification and standards development* (pp. 241–249). Hershey, PA: IGI Global. doi:10.4018/978-1-4666-2160-2.ch014

Cordeiro, F., Traina, C. Jr, Traina, A. J. M., Lopez, J., Kang, U., & Taloutsos, C. (2011). Clustering very large multi-dimensional datasets with MapReduce. *Proceedings of KDD'11*, 690-698.

Cordella, A. (2011). Emerging standardization. *International Journal of Actor-Network Theory and Technological Innovation*, *3*(3), 49–64. doi:10.4018/jantti.2011070104

Cordella, A. (2013). Emerging standardization. In A. Tatnall (Ed.), *Social and professional applications of actor-network theory for technology development* (pp. 221–237). Hershey, PA: IGI Global. doi:10.4018/978-1-4666-2166-4.ch017

Cover, T. M., & Thomas, J. A. (2006). *Elements of Information Theory*. John Wiley & Sons.

Cover, T., & Hart, P. (1967). Nearest neighbor pattern classification. *IEEE Transactions on Information Theory*, *13*(1), 21–27. doi:10.1109/TIT.1967.1053964

Craven, M., & Page, C. D. (2015). Big Data in Healthcare: Opportunities and Challenges. *Big Data*, *3*(4), 209–210. doi:10.1089/big.2015.29001.mcr PMID:27441403

Curran, K., & Lautman, R. (2011). The problems of jurisdiction on the internet. *International Journal of Ambient Computing and Intelligence*, *3*(3), 36–42. doi:10.4018/jaci.2011070105

Cutting, D. R., Karger, D. R., Pederson, J. O., & Tukey, J. W. (1992). Scatter/gather: a cluster-based approach to browsing large document collections. Proceedings of the ACM SIGIR'92, 318-329.

da Silva, N. F. F., Hruschka, E. R., & Hruschka, E. R. Jr. (2014). Tweet sentiment analysis with classifier ensembles. *Decision Support Systems*, *66*, 170–179. doi:10.1016/j.dss.2014.07.003

D'Andrea, A. (2009). An Overview of Methods for Virtual Social Network Analysis. In *Computational Social Network Analysis: Trends, Tools and Research Advances* (p. 8). Springer.

Dang, Y., Zhang, Y., & Chen, H. (2010). A Lexicon-Enhanced Method for Sentiment Classification: An Experiment on Online Product Reviews. *IEEE Intelligent Systems*, *25*(4), 46–53. doi:10.1109/MIS.2009.105

Dani, D. E., Salloum, S., Khishfe, R., & BouJaoude, S. (2013). A tool for analyzing science standards and curricula for 21st century science education. In M. Khine, & I. Saleh (Eds.), *Approaches and strategies in next generation science learning* (pp. 265-289). Hershey, PA: IGI Global. doi:10.4018/978-1-4666-2809-0.ch014

Davis, D. L., & Bouldin, D. W. (1979). A cluster separation measure. *IEEE Transactions on Pattern Analysis and Machine Intelligence*, *PAMI-1*(2), 224–227. doi:10.1109/TPAMI.1979.4766909 PMID:21868852

De Silva, S. (2012). Legal issues with FOS-ERP: A UK law perspective. In R. Atem de Carvalho & B. Johansson (Eds.), *Free and open source enterprise resource planning: Systems and strategies* (pp. 102–115). Hershey, PA: IGI Global. doi:10.4018/978-1-61350-486-4.ch007

de Vries, H. J. (2011). Implementing standardization education at the national level. *International Journal of IT Standards and Standardization Research*, *9*(2), 72–83. doi:10.4018/jitsr.2011070104

de Vries, H. J. (2013). Implementing standardization education at the national level. In K. Jakobs (Ed.), *Innovations in organizational IT specification and standards development* (pp. 116–128). Hershey, PA: IGI Global. doi:10.4018/978-1-4666-2160-2.ch006

de Vuyst, B., & Fairchild, A. (2012). Legal and economic justification for software protection. *International Journal of Open Source Software and Processes*, *4*(3), 1–12. doi:10.4018/ijossp.2012070101

Dean, J., & Ghemawat, S. (2004). MapReduce: simplified data processing on large clusters. *Proceedings of the 6th conference on Symposium on Operating Systems Design and Implementation*, 6, 10.

Dedeke, A. (2012). Politics hinders open standards in the public sector: The Massachusetts open document format decision. In C. Reddick (Ed.), *Cases on public information management and e-government adoption* (pp. 1–23). Hershey, PA: IGI Global. doi:10.4018/978-1-4666-0981-5.ch001

Delfmann, P., Herwig, S., Lis, L., & Becker, J. (2012). Supporting conceptual model analysis using semantic standardization and structural pattern matching. In S. Smolnik, F. Teuteberg, & O. Thomas (Eds.), *Semantic technologies for business and information systems engineering: Concepts and applications* (pp. 125–149). Hershey, PA: IGI Global. doi:10.4018/978-1-60960-126-3.ch007

den Uijl, S., de Vries, H. J., & Bayramoglu, D. (2013). The rise of MP3 as the market standard: How compressed audio files became the dominant music format. *International Journal of IT Standards and Standardization Research*, *11*(1), 1–26. doi:10.4018/jitsr.2013010101

Deng, Z.-H., Luo, K.-H., & Yu, H.-L. (2014). A study of supervised term weighting scheme for sentiment analysis. *Expert Systems with Applications*, *41*(7), 3506–3513. doi:10.1016/j.eswa.2013.10.056

Department of the Army. (n.d.). Social Network Analysis. *Field Manual 3-24: Counterinsurgency (PDF). Headquarters*, (pp. B–11 – B–12). Author.

Developers, T. (n.d.a). *REST APIs | Twitter Developers*. Retrieved on June 30, 2016 from https://dev.twitter.com/rest/public

Developers, T. (n.d.b). *The Streaming APIs |Twitter Developers*. Retrieved on June 30, 2016, from https://dev.twitter.com/streaming/overview

Devi, V. S., & Murty, M. N. (2002). An incremental prototype set building technique. *Pattern Recognition*, *35*(2), 505–513. doi:10.1016/S0031-3203(00)00184-9

Dickerson, J., & Coleman, H. V. (2012). Technology, e-leadership and educational administration in schools: Integrating standards with context and guiding questions. In V. Wang (Ed.), *Encyclopedia of e-leadership, counseling and training* (pp. 408–422). Hershey, PA: IGI Global. doi:10.4018/978-1-61350-068-2.ch030

Dindaroglu, B. (2013). R&D productivity and firm size in semiconductors and pharmaceuticals: Evidence from citation yields. In I. Yetkiner, M. Pamukcu, & E. Erdil (Eds.), *Industrial dynamics, innovation policy, and economic growth through technological advancements* (pp. 92–113). Hershey, PA: IGI Global. doi:10.4018/978-1-4666-1978-4.ch006

Ding, W. (2011). Development of intellectual property of communications enterprise and analysis of current situation of patents in emerging technology field. *International Journal of Advanced Pervasive and Ubiquitous Computing*, *3*(2), 21–28. doi:10.4018/japuc.2011040103

Ding, W. (2013). Development of intellectual property of communications enterprise and analysis of current situation of patents in emerging technology field. In T. Gao (Ed.), *Global applications of pervasive and ubiquitous computing* (pp. 89–96). Hershey, PA: IGI Global. doi:10.4018/978-1-4666-2645-4.ch010

Dionisios, N., Sotiropoulos, C. D., Kounavis, P. K., & Giaglis, G. M. (2014). What drives social sentiment? An entropic measure-based clustering approach towards identifying factors that influence social sentiment polarity. *The 5th International Conference on Information, Intelligence, Systems and Applications*, 361 – 373.

Donalek, C., Djorgovski, S. G., Cioc, A., Wang, A., Zhang, J., Lawler, E., . . . Davidoff, S. (2014, October). Immersive and collaborative data visualization using virtual reality platforms. In *Big Data (Big Data), 2014 IEEE International Conference on* (pp. 609-614). IEEE. doi:10.1109/BigData.2014.7004282

Dorloff, F., & Kajan, E. (2012). Balancing of heterogeneity and interoperability in e-business networks: The role of standards and protocols. *International Journal of E-Business Research*, *8*(4), 15–33. doi:10.4018/jebr.2012100102

Dorloff, F., & Kajan, E. (2012). Efficient and interoperable e-business –Based on frameworks, standards and protocols: An introduction. In E. Kajan, F. Dorloff, & I. Bedini (Eds.), *Handbook of research on e-business standards and protocols: Documents, data and advanced web technologies* (pp. 1–20). Hershey, PA: IGI Global. doi:10.4018/978-1-4666-0146-8.ch001

Douglas, L. (2011). *3D Data Management: Controlling Data Volume, Velocity and Variety*. Meta Group.

Driouchi, A., & Kadiri, M. (2013). Challenges to intellectual property rights from information and communication technologies, nanotechnologies and microelectronics. In *Digital rights management: Concepts, methodologies, tools, and applications* (pp. 1474–1492). Hershey, PA: IGI Global. doi:10.4018/978-1-4666-2136-7.ch075

Dubey, M., & Hirwade, M. (2013). Copyright relevancy at stake in libraries of the digital era. In T. Ashraf & P. Gulati (Eds.), *Design, development, and management of resources for digital library services* (pp. 379–384). Hershey, PA: IGI Global. doi:10.4018/978-1-4666-2500-6.ch030

Dubois, D., & Prade, H. (1990). Rough Fuzzy Sets and Fuzzy Rough Sets. *International Journal of General Systems*, *17*(2-3), 191–209. doi:10.1080/03081079008935107

Duda, R. O., Hart, P. E., & Stork, D. G. (2012). *Pattern classification*. John Wiley & Sons.

Dunn, J. C. (1973). *A fuzzy relative of the ISODATA process and its use in detecting compact well-separated clusters*. Academic Press.

Ebrahimpour, M. K., & Eftekhari, M. (2017). Ensemble of feature selection methods: A hesitant fuzzy sets approach. *Applied Soft Computing*, *50*, 300–312. doi:10.1016/j.asoc.2016.11.021

Egyedi, T. M. (2011). Between supply and demand: Coping with the impact of standards change. In *Global business: Concepts, methodologies, tools and applications* (pp. 105–120). Hershey, PA: IGI Global. doi:10.4018/978-1-60960-587-2.ch108

Egyedi, T. M., & Koppenhol, A. (2013). The standards war between ODF and OOXML: Does competition between overlapping ISO standards lead to innovation? In K. Jakobs (Ed.), *Innovations in organizational IT specification and standards development* (pp. 79–90). Hershey, PA: IGI Global. doi:10.4018/978-1-4666-2160-2.ch004

Egyedi, T. M., & Muto, S. (2012). Standards for ICT: A green strategy in a grey sector. *International Journal of IT Standards and Standardization Research*, *10*(1), 34–47. doi:10.4018/jitsr.2012010103

El Kharbili, M., & Pulvermueller, E. (2012). Semantic policies for modeling regulatory process compliance. In S. Smolnik, F. Teuteberg, & O. Thomas (Eds.), *Semantic technologies for business and information systems engineering: Concepts and applications* (pp. 311–336). Hershey, PA: IGI Global. doi:10.4018/978-1-60960-126-3.ch016

El Kharbili, M., & Pulvermueller, E. (2013). Semantic policies for modeling regulatory process compliance. In *IT policy and ethics: Concepts, methodologies, tools, and applications* (pp. 218–243). Hershey, PA: IGI Global. doi:10.4018/978-1-4666-2919-6.ch011

Eldawy, A., & Mokbel, M. F. (2014, March). Pigeon: A spatial mapreduce language. In *2014 IEEE 30th International Conference on Data Engineering* (pp. 1242-1245). IEEE. doi:10.1109/ICDE.2014.6816751

Eldawy, A. (2014, June). SpatialHadoop: towards flexible and scalable spatial processing using mapreduce. In *Proceedings of the 2014 SIGMOD PhD symposium* (pp. 46-50). ACM. doi:10.1145/2602622.2602625

Eldawy, A., & Mokbel, M. F. (2013). A demonstration of SpatialHadoop: An efficient mapreduce framework for spatial data. *Proceedings of the VLDB Endowment*, *6*(12), 1230–1233. doi:10.14778/2536274.2536283

Ene, A., Im, S., & Moseley, B. (2011). Fast clustering using MapReduce. *Proceedings of KDD'11*, 681-689.

Engels, R., Yu, T., Burge, C., Mesirov, J. P., DeCaprio, D., & Galagan, J. E. (2006). Combo: A whole genome comparative browser. *Bioinformatics (Oxford, England)*, *22*(14), 1782–1783. doi:10.1093/bioinformatics/btl193 PMID:16709588

Ervin, K. (2014). Legal and ethical considerations in the implementation of electronic health records. In J. Krueger (Ed.), *Cases on electronic records and resource management implementation in diverse environments* (pp. 193–210). Hershey, PA: IGI Global. doi:10.4018/978-1-4666-4466-3.ch012

Escayola, J., Trigo, J., Martínez, I., Martínez-Espronceda, M., Aragüés, A., Sancho, D., . . . García, J. (2013). Overview of the ISO/IEEE11073 family of standards and their applications to health monitoring. In User-driven healthcare: Concepts, methodologies, tools, and applications (pp. 357-381). Hershey, PA: IGI Global. doi:10.4018/978-1-4666-2770-3.ch018

Escayola, J., Trigo, J., Martínez, I., Martínez-Espronceda, M., Aragüés, A., Sancho, D., & García, J. et al. (2012). Overview of the ISO/ieee11073 family of standards and their applications to health monitoring. In W. Chen, S. Oetomo, & L. Feijs (Eds.), *Neonatal monitoring technologies: Design for integrated solutions* (pp. 148–173). Hershey, PA: IGI Global. doi:10.4018/978-1-4666-0975-4.ch007

Espada, J. P., Martínez, O. S., García-Bustelo, B. C., Lovelle, J. M., & Ordóñez de Pablos, P. (2011). Standardization of virtual objects. In M. Lytras, P. Ordóñez de Pablos, & E. Damiani (Eds.), *Semantic web personalization and context awareness: Management of personal identities and social networking* (pp. 7–21). Hershey, PA: IGI Global. doi:10.4018/978-1-61520-921-7.ch002

Esterich, S., & Ke, J. (2003). Fast accurate fuzzy clustering through data reduction. *IEEE Transactions on Fuzzy Systems, 11*(2), 262–269. doi:10.1109/TFUZZ.2003.809902

Ester, M., Kriegel, H. P., Sander, J., & Xu, X. (1996). A Density-Based Algorithm for Discovering Clusters in Large Spatial Databases with Noise. *Proceedings of KDD-96*, 226–231.

Everitt, B. J. & Marina E. W. (2002). Psychomotor Stimulant Addiction: A Neural Systems Perspective. *The Journal of Neuroscience, 22*(9), 3312–3320.

Everitt, B. S., Landau, S., Leese, M., & Daniel, S. (2011). *Cluster Analysis* (5th ed.). John Wiley & Sons, Ltd. doi:10.1002/9780470977811

Fahad, A., Alshatri, N., Tari, Z., Alamri, A., Khalil, I., Zomaya, A. Y., & Boura, A. et al. (2014). A Survey of Clustering Algorithms for Big Data: Taxonomy and Empirical Analysis. *IEEE Transactions on Emerging Topics in Computing, 2*(3), 267–279. doi:10.1109/TETC.2014.2330519

Falkner, N. J. (2011). Security technologies and policies in organisations. In M. Quigley (Ed.), *ICT ethics and security in the 21st century: New developments and applications* (pp. 196–213). Hershey, PA: IGI Global. doi:10.4018/978-1-60960-573-5.ch010

Fan, W., & Bifet, A. (2013). Mining big data: current status, and forecast to the future. *ACM SIGKDD Explorations Newsletter, 14*(2), 1-5.

Feldman, R. (2013). Techniques and applications for sentiment analysis. *Communications of the ACM, 56*(4), 82–89. doi:10.1145/2436256.2436274

Felipe da Silva, N. F., Coletta, L. F. S., Hruschka, E. R., & Hruschka, E. R. Jr. (2016). Using unsupervised information to improve semi-supervised tweet sentiment classification. *Information Sciences, 355*, 348–365. doi:10.1016/j.ins.2016.02.002

Feng, S., Pang, J., Wang, D., Yu, G., Yang, F., & Xu, D. (2011). A novel approach for clustering sentiments in Chinese blogs based on graph similarity. *Computers & Mathematics with Applications (Oxford, England), 62*(7), 2770–2778. doi:10.1016/j.camwa.2011.07.043

Fernández-Gavilanes, M., Álvarez-López, T., Juncal-Martínez, J., Costa-Montenegro, E., & González-Castaño, F. J. (2016). Unsupervised method for sentiment analysis in online texts. *Expert Systems with Applications, 58*, 57–75. doi:10.1016/j.eswa.2016.03.031

Ferrer-Roca, O. (2011). Standards in telemedicine. In A. Moumtzoglou & A. Kastania (Eds.), *E-health systems quality and reliability: Models and standards* (pp. 220–243). Hershey, PA: IGI Global. doi:10.4018/978-1-61692-843-8.ch017

Ferri, F., Pudil, P., Hatef, M., & Kittler, J. (1994). Comparative study of techniques for large-scale feature selection. *Pattern Recognition in Practice, 4*, 403–413.

Ferullo, D. L., & Soules, A. (2012). Managing copyright in a digital world. *International Journal of Digital Library Systems, 3*(4), 1–25. doi:10.4018/ijdls.2012100101

Fichtner, J. R., & Simpson, L. A. (2011). Legal issues facing companies with products in a digital format. In T. Strader (Ed.), *Digital product management, technology and practice: Interdisciplinary perspectives* (pp. 32–52). Hershey, PA: IGI Global. doi:10.4018/978-1-61692-877-3.ch003

Fichtner, J. R., & Simpson, L. A. (2013). Legal issues facing companies with products in a digital format. In *Digital rights management: Concepts, methodologies, tools, and applications* (pp. 1334–1354). Hershey, PA: IGI Global. doi:10.4018/978-1-4666-2136-7.ch066

Fielding, A. T. (2000). *Architectural Styles and the Design of Network-based Software Architectures.* Irvine, CA: University of California.

Flynn, , Reagans, R. E., & Guillory, L. (2010). Do you two know each other? Transitivity, homophily, and the need for (network) closure. *Journal of Personality and Social Psychology, 99*(5), 855–869. doi:10.1037/a0020961 PMID:20954787

Folmer, E. (2012). BOMOS: Management and development model for open standards. In E. Kajan, F. Dorloff, & I. Bedini (Eds.), *Handbook of research on e-business standards and protocols: Documents, data and advanced web technologies* (pp. 102–128). Hershey, PA: IGI Global. doi:10.4018/978-1-4666-0146-8.ch006

Fomin, V. V. (2012). Standards as hybrids: An essay on tensions and juxtapositions in contemporary standardization. *International Journal of IT Standards and Standardization Research, 10*(2), 59–68. doi:10.4018/jitsr.2012070105

Fomin, V. V., & Matinmikko, M. (2014). The role of standards in the development of new informational infrastructure. In M. Khosrow-Pour (Ed.), *Systems and software development, modeling, and analysis: New perspectives and methodologies* (pp. 149–160). Hershey, PA: IGI Global. doi:10.4018/978-1-4666-6098-4.ch006

Fomin, V. V., Medeisis, A., & Vitkute-Adžgauskiene, D. (2012). Pre-standardization of cognitive radio systems. *International Journal of IT Standards and Standardization Research, 10*(1), 1–16. doi:10.4018/jitsr.2012010101

Forman, G. (2003). An extensive empirical study of feature selection metrics for text classification. *Journal of Machine Learning Research, 3*, 1289–1305.

Fox, P., & Hendler, J. (2011). Changing the equation on scientific data visualization. *Science, 331*(6018), 705–708. doi:10.1126/science.1197654 PMID:21311008

Francia, G. A., & Hutchinson, F. S. (2014). Regulatory and policy compliance with regard to identity theft prevention, detection, and response. In *Crisis management: Concepts, methodologies, tools and applications* (pp. 280–310). Hershey, PA: IGI Global. doi:10.4018/978-1-4666-4707-7.ch012

Francia, G., & Hutchinson, F. S. (2012). Regulatory and policy compliance with regard to identity theft prevention, detection, and response. In T. Chou (Ed.), *Information assurance and security technologies for risk assessment and threat management: Advances* (pp. 292–322). Hershey, PA: IGI Global. doi:10.4018/978-1-61350-507-6.ch012

Franco-Salvador, M., Cruz, F. L., Troyano, J. A., & Rosso, P. (2015). Cross-domain polarity classification using a knowledge-enhanced meta-classifier. *Knowledge-Based Systems, 86*, 46–56. doi:10.1016/j.knosys.2015.05.020

Freeman & Linton. (2006). *The Development of Social Network Analysis Vancouver*. Empirical Press.

Friedel, M., Nikolajewa, S., Suhnel, J., & Wilhelm, T. (2009). DiProGB: The dinucleotide properties genome browser. *Bioinformatics (Oxford, England), 25*(19), 2603–2604. doi:10.1093/bioinformatics/btp436 PMID:19605418

Friedman, J., Trevor, H., & Tibshirani, R. (2001). The elements of statistical learning (vol. 1). Springer.

Fulkerson, D. M. (2012). Copyright. In D. Fulkerson (Ed.), *Remote access technologies for library collections: Tools for library users and managers* (pp. 33–48). Hershey, PA: IGI Global. doi:10.4018/978-1-4666-0234-2.ch003

Galinski, C., & Beckmann, H. (2014). Concepts for enhancing content quality and eaccessibility: In general and in the field of eprocurement. In *Assistive technologies: Concepts, methodologies, tools, and applications* (pp. 180–197). Hershey, PA: IGI Global. doi:10.4018/978-1-4666-4422-9.ch010

Ganesan, H., Rakitianskaia, A. S., Davenport, C. F., Tümmler, B., & Reva, O. N. (2008). The SeqWord genome Browser: An online tool for the identification and visualization of atypical regions of bacterial genomes through oligonucleotide usage. *BMC Bioinformatics, 9*(1), 333. doi:10.1186/1471-2105-9-333 PMID:18687122

Ganti, V., Gehrke, J., & Ramakrishnan, R. (1999a). Mining very large databases. *Computer, 32*(August), 38–45. doi:10.1109/2.781633

Ganti, V., Ramakrishnan, R., Gehrke, J., Powel, A. L., & French, J. C. (1999b) Clustering large datasets in arbitrary metric spaces. *Proceedings of the 14th international conference on Data Engineering*, 502-511. doi:10.1109/ICDE.1999.754966

Gao, D., Li, W., Cai, X., Zhang, R., & Ouyang, Y. (2014). Sequential summarization: A full view of twitter trending topics. *IEEE/ACM Transactions on Audio, Speech, and Language Processing, 22*(2), 293-302.

Gao, D., Wei, F., Li, W., Liu, X., & Zhou, M. (2014). Cross-lingual Sentiment Lexicon Learning with Bilingual Word Graph Label Propagation. Association for Computational Linguistics.

Gaur, R. (2013). Facilitating access to Indian cultural heritage: Copyright, permission rights and ownership issues vis-à-vis IGNCA collections. In *Digital rights management: Concepts, methodologies, tools, and applications* (pp. 817–833). Hershey, PA: IGI Global. doi:10.4018/978-1-4666-2136-7.ch038

Ge, H., Liu, K., Juan, T., Fang, F., Newman, M., & Hoeck, W. (2011). FusionMap: Detecting fusion genes from next-generation sequencing data at base-pair resolution. *Bioinformatics (Oxford, England)*, 27(14), 1922–1928. doi:10.1093/bioinformatics/btr310 PMID:21593131

Geiger, C. (2011). Copyright and digital libraries: Securing access to information in the digital age. In I. Iglezakis, T. Synodinou, & S. Kapidakis (Eds.), *E-publishing and digital libraries: Legal and organizational issues* (pp. 257–272). Hershey, PA: IGI Global. doi:10.4018/978-1-60960-031-0.ch013

Geiger, C. (2013). Copyright and digital libraries: Securing access to information in the digital age. In *Digital rights management: Concepts, methodologies, tools, and applications* (pp. 99–114). Hershey, PA: IGI Global. doi:10.4018/978-1-4666-2136-7.ch007

Gencer, M. (2012). The evolution of IETF standards and their production. *International Journal of IT Standards and Standardization Research*, 10(1), 17–33. doi:10.4018/jitsr.2012010102

Ghareb, A. S., Bakar, A. A., & Hamdan, A. R. (2016). Hybrid feature selection based on enhanced genetic algorithm for text categorization. *Expert Systems with Applications*, 49, 31–47. doi:10.1016/j.eswa.2015.12.004

Gillam, L., & Vartapetiance, A. (2014). Gambling with laws and ethics in cyberspace. In R. Luppicini (Ed.), *Evolving issues surrounding technoethics and society in the digital age* (pp. 149–170). Hershey, PA: IGI Global. doi:10.4018/978-1-4666-6122-6.ch010

Goldberg, D. (1989). *Genetic Algorithms in search, optimization and machine learning*. Addison-Wesley.

Gorodov, E. Y. E., & Gubarev, V. V. E. (2013). Analytical review of data visualization methods in application to big data. *Journal of Electrical and Computer Engineering*, 2013, 22. doi:10.1155/2013/969458

Grandinetti, L., Pisacane, O., & Sheikhalishahi, M. (2014). Standardization. In *Pervasive cloud computing technologies: Future outlooks and interdisciplinary perspectives* (pp. 75–96). Hershey, PA: IGI Global. doi:10.4018/978-1-4666-4683-4.ch004

Granovetter. (1973). The strength of weak ties. *American Journal of Sociology, 78*, 1360–1380.

Granovetter, M. (2007). Introduction for the French Reader. *Sociologica, 2*, 1–8.

Grant, S., & Young, R. (2013). Concepts and standardization in areas relating to competence. In K. Jakobs (Ed.), *Innovations in organizational IT specification and standards development* (pp. 264–280). Hershey, PA: IGI Global. doi:10.4018/978-1-4666-2160-2.ch016

Grassetti, M., & Brookby, S. (2013). Using the iPad to develop preservice teachers' understanding of the common core state standards for mathematical practice. In D. Polly (Ed.), *Common core mathematics standards and implementing digital technologies* (pp. 370–386). Hershey, PA: IGI Global. doi:10.4018/978-1-4666-4086-3.ch025

Gray, P. J. (2012). CDIO Standards and quality assurance: From application to accreditation. *International Journal of Quality Assurance in Engineering and Technology Education*, *2*(2), 1–8. doi:10.4018/ijqaete.2012040101

Graz, J., & Hauert, C. (2011). The INTERNORM project: Bridging two worlds of expert- and lay-knowledge in standardization. *International Journal of IT Standards and Standardization Research*, *9*(1), 52–62. doi:10.4018/jitsr.2011010103

Graz, J., & Hauert, C. (2013). The INTERNORM project: Bridging two worlds of expert- and lay-knowledge in standardization. In K. Jakobs (Ed.), *Innovations in organizational IT specification and standards development* (pp. 154–164). Hershey, PA: IGI Global. doi:10.4018/978-1-4666-2160-2.ch009

Gregory, S. (2007). An algorithm to find overlapping community structure in networks. In J. N. Kok, J. Koronacki, R. Lopez de Mantras, S. Matwin, D. Mladenic, & A. Skowron (Eds.), *PKDD 2007, LNAI* (Vol. 4702, pp. 91–102). Heidelberg, Germany: Springer. doi:10.1007/978-3-540-74976-9_12

Gregory, S. (2008). A fast algorithm to find overlapping communities in networks. In W. Daelemans (Ed.), *ECML PKDD 2008, LNAI* (Vol. 5212, pp. 408–423). Berlin: Springer. doi:10.1007/978-3-540-87479-9_45

Gregory, S. (2010). Finding overlapping communities in networks by label propagation. *New Journal of Physics*, *12*(10), 10301. doi:10.1088/1367-2630/12/10/103018

Grobler, M. (2012). The need for digital evidence standardisation. *International Journal of Digital Crime and Forensics*, *4*(2), 1–12. doi:10.4018/jdcf.2012040101

Grobler, M. (2013). The need for digital evidence standardisation. In C. Li (Ed.), *Emerging digital forensics applications for crime detection, prevention, and security* (pp. 234–245). Hershey, PA: IGI Global. doi:10.4018/978-1-4666-4006-1.ch016

Guest, C. L., & Guest, J. M. (2011). Legal issues in the use of technology in higher education: Copyright and privacy in the academy. In D. Surry, R. Gray Jr, & J. Stefurak (Eds.), *Technology integration in higher education: Social and organizational aspects* (pp. 72–85). Hershey, PA: IGI Global. doi:10.4018/978-1-60960-147-8.ch006

Guha, S., Meyerson, A., Mishra, N., Motwani, R., & OCallaghan, L. (2003). Clustering data streams: Theory and practice. *IEEE Transactions on Knowledge and Data Engineering*, *15*(3), 515–528. doi:10.1109/TKDE.2003.1198387

Guha, S., Rastogi, R., & Shim, K. (1998). CURE: An efficient clustering algorithm for large databases. *Proceedings of ACM SIGMOD*, 73–84 doi:10.1145/276304.276312

Guha, S., Rastogi, R., & Shim, K. (2000). ROCK: A Robust Clustering Algorithm for Categorical Attributes. *15th International Conference on Data Engineering*, 512-521. doi:10.1016/S0306-4379(00)00022-3

Guille, A. (n.d.). *SONDY.* Retrieved June 30, 2016, from https://github.com/AdrienGuille/SONDY

Guille, A., & Hacid, H. (2012) A predictive model for the temporal dynamics of information diffusion in online social networks. *Proceedings of the 21st international conference on World Wide Web.* doi:10.1145/2187980.2188254

Günal, S. (2012). Hybrid feature selection for text classification. *Turkish Journal of Electrical Engineering & Computer Sciences, 20*(Sup. 2), 1296-1311.

Gupta, A., Gantz, D. A., Sreecharana, D., & Kreyling, J. (2012). The interplay of offshoring of professional services, law, intellectual property, and international organizations. *International Journal of Strategic Information Technology and Applications, 3*(2), 47–71. doi:10.4018/jsita.2012040104

Guyon, I., & Elisseeff, A. (2003). An introduction to variable and feature selection. *Journal of Machine Learning Research, 3*(Mar), 1157–1182.

Guyon, I., Weston, J., Barnhill, S., & Vapnik, V. (2003). Gene Selection for Cancer Classification using Support Vector Machines. *Journal of Machine Learning Research, 3*(March), 1439–1461.

Ha, G., Roth, A., Lai, D., Bashashati, A., Ding, J., Goya, R., & Shah, S. P. et al. (2012). Integrative analysis of genome-wide loss of heterozygosity and monoallelic expression at nucleotide resolution reveals disrupted pathways in triple-negative breast cancer. *Genome Research, 22*(10), 1995–2007. doi:10.1101/gr.137570.112 PMID:22637570

Hai-Jew, S. (2011). Staying legal and ethical in global e-learning course and training developments: An exploration. In V. Wang (Ed.), *Encyclopedia of information communication technologies and adult education integration* (pp. 958–970). Hershey, PA: IGI Global. doi:10.4018/978-1-61692-906-0.ch058

Hajmohammadi, M. S., Ibrahim, R., & Selamat, A. (2014). Bi-view semi-supervised active learning for cross-lingual sentiment classification. *Information Processing & Management, 50*(5), 718–732. doi:10.1016/j.ipm.2014.03.005

Halder, D., & Jaishankar, K. (2012). Cyber space regulations for protecting women in UK. In *Cyber crime and the victimization of women: Laws, rights and regulations* (pp. 95–104). Hershey, PA: IGI Global. doi:10.4018/978-1-60960-830-9.ch007

Han, M., & Cho, C. (2013). XML in library cataloging workflows: Working with diverse sources and metadata standards. In J. Tramullas & P. Garrido (Eds.), *Library automation and OPAC 2.0: Information access and services in the 2.0 landscape* (pp. 59–72). Hershey, PA: IGI Global. doi:10.4018/978-1-4666-1912-8.ch003

Hanneman, A., & Riddle, M. (2005). *Introduction to social network methods.* Online at http://www.faculty.ucr.edu/ hanneman/nettext/

Hanneman, . (2011). *Concepts and Measures for Basic Network Analysis. In The Sage Handbook of Social Network Analysis* (pp. 364–367). SAGE.

Hansen, D. (2010). *Analyzing Social Media Networks with NodeXL*. Morgan Kaufmann.

Hanseth, O., & Nielsen, P. (2013). Infrastructure innovation: Flexibility, generativity and the mobile internet. *International Journal of IT Standards and Standardization Research*, *11*(1), 27–45. doi:10.4018/jitsr.2013010102

Harenberg, S., Bello, G., Gjeltema, L., Ranshous, S., Jitendra, H., Ramona, S., Padmanabhan, K., & Samatova, N. (2014). Community detection in large-scale networks: a survey and empirical evaluation. *WIREs Comput Stat, 6*, 426-439.

HarPeled, S., & Mazumdar, S. (2004). On core sets for K-means and k-median clustering. *Proc. ACM Symposium on Theory Compute*, 291–300.

Hartigan, J. A. (1975). Clustering Algorithms. John Wiley & Sons, Inc.

Hartong, M., & Wijesekera, D. (2012). U.S. regulatory requirements for positive train control systems. In F. Flammini (Ed.), *Railway safety, reliability, and security: Technologies and systems engineering* (pp. 1–21). Hershey, PA: IGI Global. doi:10.4018/978-1-4666-1643-1.ch001

Hasan, H. (2011). Formal and emergent standards in KM. In D. Schwartz & D. Te'eni (Eds.), *Encyclopedia of knowledge management* (2nd ed.; pp. 331–342). Hershey, PA: IGI Global. doi:10.4018/978-1-59904-931-1.ch032

Hathaway, R., & Bezdek, Z. (2006). Extending fuzzy and probabilistic clustering to very large data sets. *Computational Statistics & Data Analysis*, *51*(1), 215–234. doi:10.1016/j.csda.2006.02.008

Hatzimihail, N. (2011). Copyright infringement of digital libraries and private international law: Jurisdiction issues. In I. Iglezakis, T. Synodinou, & S. Kapidakis (Eds.), *E-publishing and digital libraries: Legal and organizational issues* (pp. 447–460). Hershey, PA: IGI Global. doi:10.4018/978-1-60960-031-0.ch021

Hauert, C. (2013). Where are you? Consumers' associations in standardization: A case study on Switzerland. In K. Jakobs (Ed.), *Innovations in organizational IT specification and standards development* (pp. 139–153). Hershey, PA: IGI Global. doi:10.4018/978-1-4666-2160-2.ch008

Havens, T. C., Bezdek, J. C., Leckie, C., Hall, L. O., & Palaniswami, M. (2012). Fuzzy c-Means Algorithms for Very Large Data. *IEEE Transactions on Fuzzy Systems*, *20*(6), 1130–1146. doi:10.1109/TFUZZ.2012.2201485

Havens, T. C., Chitta, R., Jain, A. K., & Rong, J. (2011). Speedup of fuzzy and possibilistic kernel C-Means for Large scale clustering. *2011 IEEE International Conference on Fuzzy Systems (FUZZ)*, 463-470. doi:10.1109/FUZZY.2011.6007618

Hawks, V. D., & Ekstrom, J. J. (2011). Balancing policies, principles, and philosophy in information assurance. In M. Dark (Ed.), *Information assurance and security ethics in complex systems: Interdisciplinary perspectives* (pp. 32–54). Hershey, PA: IGI Global. doi:10.4018/978-1-61692-245-0.ch003

Haycox, D. A. (1999). Evidence-Based Healthcare Management. *Evidence-based Healthcare, 3*(3), 67–69. doi:10.1054/ebhc.1999.0247

He, Y., Tan, H., Luo, W., Feng, S., & Fan, J. (2014). Mr-dB scan: a scalable MapReduce based dB scan algorithm for heavily skewed data. *Frontiers of Computer Science, 8*(1), 83-99.

Henningsson, S. (2012). International e-customs standardization from the perspective of a global company. *International Journal of IT Standards and Standardization Research, 10*(2), 45–58. doi:10.4018/jitsr.2012070104

Hensberry, K. K., Paul, A. J., Moore, E. B., Podolefsky, N. S., & Perkins, K. K. (2013). PhET interactive simulations: New tools to achieve common core mathematics standards. In D. Polly (Ed.), *Common core mathematics standards and implementing digital technologies* (pp. 147–167). Hershey, PA: IGI Global. doi:10.4018/978-1-4666-4086-3.ch010

Heravi, B. R., & Lycett, M. (2012). Semantically enriched e-business standards development: The case of ebXML business process specification schema. In E. Kajan, F. Dorloff, & I. Bedini (Eds.), *Handbook of research on e-business standards and protocols: Documents, data and advanced web technologies* (pp. 655–675). Hershey, PA: IGI Global. doi:10.4018/978-1-4666-0146-8.ch030

Higuera, J., & Polo, J. (2012). Interoperability in wireless sensor networks based on IEEE 1451 standard. In N. Zaman, K. Ragab, & A. Abdullah (Eds.), *Wireless sensor networks and energy efficiency: Protocols, routing and management* (pp. 47–69). Hershey, PA: IGI Global. doi:10.4018/978-1-4666-0101-7.ch004

Hill, D. S. (2012). An examination of standardized product identification and business benefit. In E. Kajan, F. Dorloff, & I. Bedini (Eds.), *Handbook of research on e-business standards and protocols: Documents, data and advanced web technologies* (pp. 387–411). Hershey, PA: IGI Global. doi:10.4018/978-1-4666-0146-8.ch018

Hill, D. S. (2013). An examination of standardized product identification and business benefit. In *Supply chain management: Concepts, methodologies, tools, and applications* (pp. 171–195). Hershey, PA: IGI Global. doi:10.4018/978-1-4666-2625-6.ch011

Hoffman, M., Blei, D., & Bach, F. (2010). On-line learning for latent Dirichlet allocation. *Neural Information Processing Systems*.

Hollander, J. B., Graves, E., Renski, H., Foster-Karim, C., Wiley, A., & Das, D. (2016). *A (Short) History of Social Media Sentiment Analysis*. Urban Social Listening. doi:10.1057/978-1-137-59491-4_2

Holloway, K. (2012). Fair use, copyright, and academic integrity in an online academic environment. In V. Wang (Ed.), *Encyclopedia of e-leadership, counseling and training* (pp. 298–309). Hershey, PA: IGI Global. doi:10.4018/978-1-61350-068-2.ch022

Hoops, D. S. (2011). Legal issues in the virtual world and e-commerce. In B. Ciaramitaro (Ed.), *Virtual worlds and e-commerce: Technologies and applications for building customer relationships* (pp. 186–204). Hershey, PA: IGI Global. doi:10.4018/978-1-61692-808-7.ch010

Hoops, D. S. (2012). Lost in cyberspace: Navigating the legal issues of e-commerce. *Journal of Electronic Commerce in Organizations, 10*(1), 33–51. doi:10.4018/jeco.2012010103

Hopkinson, A. (2012). Establishing the digital library: Don't ignore the library standards and don't forget the training needed. In A. Tella & A. Issa (Eds.), *Library and information science in developing countries: Contemporary issues* (pp. 195–204). Hershey, PA: IGI Global. doi:10.4018/978-1-61350-335-5.ch014

Hore, P., Hall, L., & Goldgof, D. (2007). Single pass fuzzy c-means. *Proc. IEEE Int. Conf. Fuzzy Syst.*, 1-7.

Hore, P., Hall, L., Goldgof, D., Gu, Y., & Maudsley, A. (2009). A scalable framework for segmenting magnetic resonance images, J. Signal process. *Syst., 54*(1-3), 183–203.

Hou, H., Zhao, F., Zhou, L., Zhu, E., Teng, H., Li, X., Bao, Q., Wu, J. and Sun, Z. (2010). MagicViewer: Integrated solution for next-generation sequencing data visualization and genetic variation detection and annotation. *Nucleic Acids Research, 38*(Web Server), W732–W736.

Hua, G. B. (2013). The construction industry and standardization of information. In *Implementing IT business strategy in the construction industry* (pp. 47–66). Hershey, PA: IGI Global. doi:10.4018/978-1-4666-4185-3.ch003

Huang, C., & Lin, H. (2011). Patent infringement risk analysis using rough set theory. In Q. Zhang, R. Segall, & M. Cao (Eds.), *Visual analytics and interactive technologies: Data, text and web mining applications* (pp. 123–150). Hershey, PA: IGI Global. doi:10.4018/978-1-60960-102-7.ch008

Huang, C., Tseng, T. B., & Lin, H. (2013). Patent infringement risk analysis using rough set theory. In *Digital rights management: Concepts, methodologies, tools, and applications* (pp. 1225–1251). Hershey, PA: IGI Global. doi:10.4018/978-1-4666-2136-7.ch060

Huang, S., Niu, Z., & Shi, C. (2014). Automatic construction of domain-specific sentiment lexicon based on constrained label propagation. *Knowledge-Based Systems, 56*, 191–200. doi:10.1016/j.knosys.2013.11.009

Huang, W., & Marth, G. (2008). EagleView: A genome assembly viewer for next-generation sequencing technologies. *Genome Research, 18*(9), 1538–1543. doi:10.1101/gr.076067.108 PMID:18550804

Huang, W., Zhao, Y., Yang, S., & Lu, Y. (2008). Analysis of the user behavior and opinion classification based on the BBS. *Applied Mathematics and Computation, 205*(2), 668–676. doi:10.1016/j.amc.2008.01.038

Huang, Z. (1997). Clustering Large Data Sets With Mixed Numeric And Categorical Values. *Proceedings of the first Pacific-Asia Conference on Knowledge Discovery and Data Mining.*

Hu, M., & Liu, B. (2004, August). Mining and summarizing customer reviews. *Proceedings of the tenth ACM SIGKDD international conference on Knowledge discovery and data mining,* 168-177.

Hung, C., & Lin, H.-K. (2013). Using Objective Words in SentiWordNet to Improve Word-ofMouth Sentiment Classification. *IEEE Intelligent Systems, Volume, 28*(2), 47–54. doi:10.1109/MIS.2013.1

Hwang. (n.d.). *An ltv model and customer segmentation based on customer value: a case.* Academic Press.

IBM. (2005). *Improving india's education system through information technology.* IBM.

Iyamu, T. (2013). The impact of organisational politics on the implementation of IT strategy: South African case in context. In J. Abdelnour-Nocera (Ed.), *Knowledge and technological development effects on organizational and social structures* (pp. 167–193). Hershey, PA: IGI Global. doi:10.4018/978-1-4666-2151-0.ch011

Izenman, A. J. (2008). Modern multivariate statistical techniques. *Regression, Classification and Manifold Learning.*

Jacinto, K., Neto, F. M., Leite, C. R., & Jacinto, K. (2014). Accessibility in u-learning: Standards, legislation, and future visions. In F. Neto (Ed.), *Technology platform innovations and forthcoming trends in ubiquitous learning* (pp. 215–236). Hershey, PA: IGI Global. doi:10.4018/978-1-4666-4542-4.ch012

Jain, A. K., Murty, M.N., & Flynn, P.J. (1999). Data clustering: A Review. *ACM Computing Surveys (CSUR), 31*(3), 264-323.

Jain, A. K., & Dubes, R. C. (1988). *Algorithms for clustering Data.* Upper Saddle River, NJ: Prentice-Hall, Inc.

Jain, A., & Zongker, D. (1997). Feature selection: Evaluation, application, and small sample performance. *IEEE Transactions on Pattern Analysis and Machine Intelligence, 19*(2), 153–158. doi:10.1109/34.574797

Jakobs, K., Wagner, T., & Reimers, K. (2011). Standardising the internet of things: What the experts think. *International Journal of IT Standards and Standardization Research, 9*(1), 63–67. doi:10.4018/jitsr.2011010104

Jiang, C., Chen, Y., & Liu, K. R. (2014). Evolutionary dynamics of information diffusion over social networks. *IEEE Transactions on Signal Processing, 62*(17), 4573–4586. doi:10.1109/TSP.2014.2339799

Jurek, Mulvenna, & Bi. (2015). Improved lexicon-based sentiment analysis for social media analytics. *Security Informatics*, 4-9.

Juzoji, H. (2012). Legal bases for medical supervision via mobile telecommunications in Japan. *International Journal of E-Health and Medical Communications*, *3*(1), 33–45. doi:10.4018/jehmc.2012010103

Kadushin. (2012). *Understanding social networks: Theories, concepts, and findings.* Oxford, UK: Oxford University Press.

Kallinikou, D., Papadopoulos, M., Kaponi, A., & Strakantouna, V. (2011). Intellectual property issues for digital libraries at the intersection of law, technology, and the public interest. In I. Iglezakis, T. Synodinou, & S. Kapidakis (Eds.), *E-publishing and digital libraries: Legal and organizational issues* (pp. 294–341). Hershey, PA: IGI Global. doi:10.4018/978-1-60960-031-0.ch015

Kallinikou, D., Papadopoulos, M., Kaponi, A., & Strakantouna, V. (2013). Intellectual property issues for digital libraries at the intersection of law, technology, and the public interest. In *Digital rights management: Concepts, methodologies, tools, and applications* (pp. 1043–1090). Hershey, PA: IGI Global. doi:10.4018/978-1-4666-2136-7.ch052

Karakoc, E., Alkan, C., ORoak, B. J., Dennis, M. Y., Vives, L., Mark, K., & Eichler, E. E. et al. (2011). Detection of structural variants and indels within exome data. *Nature Methods*, *9*(2), 176–178. doi:10.1038/nmeth.1810 PMID:22179552

Karamibekr, M., & Ghorbani, A. A. (2012). Verb Oriented Sentiment Classification. *IEEE/WIC/ACM International Conferences on Web Intelligence and Intelligent Agent Technology*, 327-331.

Kaupins, G. (2012). Laws associated with mobile computing in the cloud. *International Journal of Wireless Networks and Broadband Technologies*, *2*(3), 1–9. doi:10.4018/ijwnbt.2012070101

Kaur, P., & Singh, H. (2013). Component certification process and standards. In H. Singh & K. Kaur (Eds.), *Designing, engineering, and analyzing reliable and efficient software* (pp. 22–39). Hershey, PA: IGI Global. doi:10.4018/978-1-4666-2958-5.ch002

Kayem, A. V. (2013). Security in service oriented architectures: Standards and challenges. In *Digital rights management: Concepts, methodologies, tools, and applications* (pp. 50–73). Hershey, PA: IGI Global. doi:10.4018/978-1-4666-2136-7.ch004

Kemp, M. L., Robb, S., & Deans, P. C. (2013). The legal implications of cloud computing. In A. Bento & A. Aggarwal (Eds.), *Cloud computing service and deployment models: Layers and management* (pp. 257–272). Hershey, PA: IGI Global. doi:10.4018/978-1-4666-2187-9.ch014

Khan, F. H., Bashir, S., & Qamar, U. (2014). TOM: Twitter opinion mining framework using hybrid classification scheme. *Decision Support Systems*, *57*, 245–257. doi:10.1016/j.dss.2013.09.004

Khan, F. H., Qamar, U., & Bashir, S. (2016). SWIMS: Semi-supervised subjective feature weighting and intelligent model selection for sentiment analysis. *Knowledge-Based Systems*, *100*, 97–111. doi:10.1016/j.knosys.2016.02.011

Khan, M., & Khan, S. S. (2011). Data and information visualization methods, and interactive mechanisms: A survey. *International Journal of Computers and Applications*, *34*(1), 1–14.

Khansa, L., & Liginlal, D. (2012). Regulatory influence and the imperative of innovation in identity and access management. *Information Resources Management Journal*, *25*(3), 78–97. doi:10.4018/irmj.2012070104

Kilduff & Tsai. (2003). *Social networks and organisations*. Sage Publications.

Kim, E. (2012). Government policies to promote production and consumption of renewable electricity in the US. In M. Tortora (Ed.), *Sustainable systems and energy management at the regional level: Comparative approaches* (pp. 1–18). Hershey, PA: IGI Global. doi:10.4018/978-1-61350-344-7.ch001

Kim, K., & Lee, J. (2014). Sentiment visualization and classification via semi-supervised nonlinear dimensionality reduction. *Pattern Recognition*, *47*(2), 758–768. doi:10.1016/j.patcog.2013.07.022

Kim, Y. I., Ji, Y. K., & Park, S. (2014). Social network visualization method using inherence relationship of user based on cloud. *International Journal of Multimedia and Ubiquitous Engineering*, *9*(4), 13–20. doi:10.14257/ijmue.2014.9.4.02

Kinsell, C. (2014). Technology and disability laws, regulations, and rights. In B. DaCosta & S. Seok (Eds.), *Assistive technology research, practice, and theory* (pp. 75–87). Hershey, PA: IGI Global. doi:10.4018/978-1-4666-5015-2.ch006

Kitsiou, S. (2010). Overview and analysis of electronic health record standards. In J. Rodrigues (Ed.), *Health information systems: Concepts, methodologies, tools, and applications* (pp. 374–392). Hershey, PA: IGI Global. doi:10.4018/978-1-60566-988-5.ch025

Kloss, J. H., & Schickel, P. (2011). X3D: A secure ISO standard for virtual worlds. In A. Rea (Ed.), *Security in virtual worlds, 3D webs, and immersive environments: Models for development, interaction, and management* (pp. 208–220). Hershey, PA: IGI Global. doi:10.4018/978-1-61520-891-3.ch010

Kohavi, R., & John, G. H. (1997). Wrappers for feature subset selection. *Artificial Intelligence*, *97*(1), 273–324. doi:10.1016/S0004-3702(97)00043-X

Kong, L., Wang, J., Zhao, S., Gu, X., Luo, J., & Gao, G. (2012). ABrowse - a customizable next-generation genome browser framework. *BMC Bioinformatics*, *13*(1), 2. doi:10.1186/1471-2105-13-2 PMID:22222089

Korbel, J. O., Abyzov, A., Mu, X., Carriero, N., Cayting, P., Zhang, Z., & Gerstein, M. B. et al. (2009). PEMer: A computational framework with simulation-based error models for inferring genomic structural variants from massive paired-end sequencing data. *Genome Biology*, *10*(2), R23. doi:10.1186/gb-2009-10-2-r23 PMID:19236709

Kothari, D., Narayanan, S. T., & Devi, K. K. (2014). Extended Fuzzy C-Means with Random Sampling Techniques for Clustering Large Data. *Int. Jour. of Innovative Research in Advanced Engineering*, *3*(1), 1–4.

Kotsonis, E., & Eliakis, S. (2011). Information security standards for health information systems: The implementer's approach. In A. Chryssanthou, I. Apostolakis, & I. Varlamis (Eds.), *Certification and security in health-related web applications: Concepts and solutions* (pp. 113–145). Hershey, PA: IGI Global. doi:10.4018/978-1-61692-895-7.ch006

Kotsonis, E., & Eliakis, S. (2013). Information security standards for health information systems: The implementer's approach. In *User-driven healthcare: Concepts, methodologies, tools, and applications* (pp. 225–257). Hershey, PA: IGI Global. doi:10.4018/978-1-4666-2770-3.ch013

Koumaras, H., & Kourtis, M. (2013). A survey on video coding principles and standards. In R. Farrugia & C. Debono (Eds.), *Multimedia networking and coding* (pp. 1–27). Hershey, PA: IGI Global. doi:10.4018/978-1-4666-2660-7.ch001

Krishnapuram, R., & Keller, J. M. (1993). A Possibilistic Approach to Clustering. *IEEE Transactions on Fuzzy Systems*, *1*(2), 98–110. doi:10.1109/91.227387

Krishnapuram, R., & Keller, J. M. (1996). The possibilistic c-means algorithm: Insights and recommendations. Fuzzy Systems. *IEEE Transactions on*, *4*(3), 385–393.

Krupinski, E. A., Antoniotti, N., & Burdick, A. (2011). Standards and guidelines development in the american telemedicine association. In A. Moumtzoglou & A. Kastania (Eds.), *E-health systems quality and reliability: Models and standards* (pp. 244–252). Hershey, PA: IGI Global. doi:10.4018/978-1-61692-843-8.ch018

Kuanpoth, J. (2011). Biotechnological patents and morality: A critical view from a developing country. In S. Hongladarom (Ed.), *Genomics and bioethics: Interdisciplinary perspectives, technologies and advancements* (pp. 141–151). Hershey, PA: IGI Global. doi:10.4018/978-1-61692-883-4.ch010

Kuanpoth, J. (2013). Biotechnological patents and morality: A critical view from a developing country. In *Digital rights management: Concepts, methodologies, tools, and applications* (pp. 1417–1427). Hershey, PA: IGI Global. doi:10.4018/978-1-4666-2136-7.ch071

Kulmala, R., & Kettunen, J. (2012). Intellectual property protection and process modeling in small knowledge intensive enterprises. In *Organizational learning and knowledge: Concepts, methodologies, tools and applications* (pp. 2963–2980). Hershey, PA: IGI Global. doi:10.4018/978-1-60960-783-8.ch809

Kulmala, R., & Kettunen, J. (2013). Intellectual property protection in small knowledge intensive enterprises. *International Journal of Cyber Warfare & Terrorism*, *3*(1), 29–45. doi:10.4018/ijcwt.2013010103

Kumar, R. R., Viswanath, P., & Bindu, C. S. (2016, February). Nearest Neighbor Classifiers: Reducing the Computational Demands. In *Advanced Computing (IACC), 2016 IEEE 6th International Conference on* (pp. 45-50). IEEE.

Kumar, R. R., Viswanath, P., & Bindu, C. S. (2017). A Cascaded Method to Reduce the Computational Burden of Nearest Neighbor Classifier. In *Proceedings of the First International Conference on Computational Intelligence and Informatics* (pp. 275-288). Springer Singapore. doi:10.1007/978-981-10-2471-9_27

Kumar, R. R., Viswanath, P., & Bindu, C. S. (2016). An Approach to Reduce the Computational Burden of Nearest Neighbor Classifier. *Procedia Computer Science, 85*, 588–597. doi:10.1016/j.procs.2016.05.225

Kuncheva, L. I. (2001). *Reducing the computational demand of the nearest neighbor classifier.* Academic Press.

Kuncheva, L. I., & Jain, L. C. (1999). Nearest neighbor classifier: Simultaneous editing and feature selection. *Pattern Recognition Letters, 20*(11), 1149–1156. doi:10.1016/S0167-8655(99)00082-3

Küster, M. W. (2012). Standards for achieving interoperability of egovernment in Europe. In E. Kajan, F. Dorloff, & I. Bedini (Eds.), *Handbook of research on e-business standards and protocols: Documents, data and advanced web technologies* (pp. 249–268). Hershey, PA: IGI Global. doi:10.4018/978-1-4666-0146-8.ch012

Kyobe, M. (2011). Factors influencing SME compliance with government regulation on use of IT: The case of South Africa. In F. Tan (Ed.), *International enterprises and global information technologies: Advancing management practices* (pp. 85–116). Hershey, PA: IGI Global. doi:10.4018/978-1-60960-605-3.ch005

Lal, T. N., Chapelle, O., Weston, J., & Elisseeff, A. (2006). Embedded methods. In *Feature extraction* (pp. 137–165). Springer Berlin Heidelberg. doi:10.1007/978-3-540-35488-8_6

Lam, J. C., & Hills, P. (2011). Promoting technological environmental innovations: What is the role of environmental regulation? In Z. Luo (Ed.), *Green finance and sustainability: Environmentally-aware business models and technologies* (pp. 56–73). Hershey, PA: IGI Global. doi:10.4018/978-1-60960-531-5.ch003

Lam, J. C., & Hills, P. (2013). Promoting technological environmental innovations: The role of environmental regulation. In Z. Luo (Ed.), *Technological solutions for modern logistics and supply chain management* (pp. 230–247). Hershey, PA: IGI Global. doi:10.4018/978-1-4666-2773-4.ch015

Lancichinetti, A., Fortunato, S., & Kertesz, J. (2009). Detecting the overlapping and hierarchical community structure of complex networks. *New Journal of Physics, 11*(3), 033015. doi:10.1088/1367-2630/11/3/033015

Lancichinetti, A., Radicchi, F., Ramasco, J. J., & Fortunato, S. (2011). Finding statistically significant communities in networks. *PLoS ONE, 6*(4), e18961. doi:10.1371/journal.pone.0018961 PMID:21559480

Laporte, C., & Vargas, E. P. (2012). The development of international standards to facilitate process improvements for very small entities. In S. Fauzi, M. Nasir, N. Ramli, & S. Sahibuddin (Eds.), *Software process improvement and management: Approaches and tools for practical development* (pp. 34–61). Hershey, PA: IGI Global. doi:10.4018/978-1-61350-141-2.ch003

Laporte, C., & Vargas, E. P. (2014). The development of international standards to facilitate process improvements for very small entities. In *Software design and development: Concepts, methodologies, tools, and applications* (pp. 1335–1361). Hershey, PA: IGI Global. doi:10.4018/978-1-4666-4301-7.ch065

Lautman, R., & Curran, K. (2013). The problems of jurisdiction on the internet. In K. Curran (Ed.), *Pervasive and ubiquitous technology innovations for ambient intelligence environments* (pp. 164–170). Hershey, PA: IGI Global. doi:10.4018/978-1-4666-2041-4.ch016

Layne-Farrar, A. (2011). Innovative or indefensible? An empirical assessment of patenting within standard setting. *International Journal of IT Standards and Standardization Research, 9*(2), 1–18. doi:10.4018/jitsr.2011070101

Layne-Farrar, A. (2013). Innovative or indefensible? An empirical assessment of patenting within standard setting. In K. Jakobs (Ed.), *Innovations in organizational IT specification and standards development* (pp. 1–18). Hershey, PA: IGI Global. doi:10.4018/978-1-4666-2160-2.ch001

Layne-Farrar, A., & Padilla, A. J. (2011). Assessing the link between standards and patents. *International Journal of IT Standards and Standardization Research, 9*(2), 19–49. doi:10.4018/jitsr.2011070102

Layne-Farrar, A., & Padilla, A. J. (2013). Assessing the link between standards and patents. In K. Jakobs (Ed.), *Innovations in organizational IT specification and standards development* (pp. 19–51). Hershey, PA: IGI Global. doi:10.4018/978-1-4666-2160-2.ch002

Lee, H., & Huh, J. C. (2012). Koreas strategies for ICT standards internationalisation: A comparison with Chinas. *International Journal of IT Standards and Standardization Research, 10*(2), 1–13. doi:10.4018/jitsr.2012070101

Leskovec, J., & Krevl, A. (2015). *SNAP Datasets: Stanford Large Network Dataset Collection.* Retrieved from http://snap.stanford.edu/data

Leskovec, J., Rajaraman, A., & Ullman, J. D. (2014). *Mining of massive datasets.* Cambridge University Press. doi:10.1017/CBO9781139924801

Li, H. G., Wu, G. Q., Hu, X. G., Zhang, J., Li, L., & Wu, X. (2011). K-means clustering with bagging and MapReduce. *Proceedings of the 2011 44th Hawaii International conference on System Sciences,* 1-8.

Li, Xiao, & Xue. (2012). An unsupervised Approach for sentiment classification. *IEEE symposium on Robotics and Applications (ISRA),* 638-640.

Liao, L., & Lin, T. (2007). A fast constrained fuzzy kernel clustering algorithm for MRI brain image segmentation. *Proc. Int. Conf. Wavelet Analysis and Pattern Recognition,* 82–87.

Liben-Nowell & Kleinberg. (2003). The Link Prediction problem for social networks. Proceedings of the Twelfth International Conference on Information and Knowledge Management, 556-559.

Lichman, M. (2013). *UCI Machine Learning Repository*. Irvine, CA: University of California, School of Information and Computer Science.

Li, G., & Liu, F. (2010). A Clustering-based Approach on Sentiment Analysis. *International Conference on Intelligent Systems and Knowledge Engineering (ISKE)*, 331-337.

Lim, K. W., Chen, C., & Buntine, W. (2016). *Twitter-Network Topic Model: A Full Bayesian Treatment for Social Network and Text Modeling. NIPS 2013 Topic Models: Computation* (pp. 1–5). Application, and Evaluation.

Lim, W., & Kim, D. (2013). Do technologies support the implementation of the common core state standards in mathematics of high school probability and statistics? In D. Polly (Ed.), *Common core mathematics standards and implementing digital technologies* (pp. 168–183). Hershey, PA: IGI Global. doi:10.4018/978-1-4666-4086-3.ch011

Lin, Z., Jin, X., Xu, X., Wang, Y., Cheng, X., Wang, W., & Meng, D. (2016). An Unsupervised Cross-Lingual Topic Model Framework for Sentiment Classification. IEEE/ACM Transactions On Audio, Speech, And Language Processing, 24(3).

Lingras, P., & West, C. (2004). Interval Set Clustering of Web Users with Rough K-Means. *Journal of Intelligent Information Systems, 23*(1), 5–16. doi:10.1023/B:JIIS.0000029668.88665.1a

Linton, J., & Stegall, D. (2013). Common core standards for mathematical practice and TPACK: An integrated approach to instruction. In D. Polly (Ed.), *Common core mathematics standards and implementing digital technologies* (pp. 234–249). Hershey, PA: IGI Global. doi:10.4018/978-1-4666-4086-3.ch016

Liotta, A., & Liotta, A. (2011). Privacy in pervasive systems: Legal framework and regulatory challenges. In A. Malatras (Ed.), *Pervasive computing and communications design and deployment: Technologies, trends and applications* (pp. 263–277). Hershey, PA: IGI Global. doi:10.4018/978-1-60960-611-4.ch012

Li, P., Zhu, Q., & Zhang, W. (2011). A Dependency Tree Based Approach for Sentence-level Classification. *12th ACIS International Conference on Software Engineering, Artificial Intelligence, Networking and Parallel/Distributed Computing*, 166-171. doi:10.1109/SNPD.2011.20

Li, S.-T., & Tsai, F.-C. (2013). A fuzzy conceptualization model for text mining with application in opinion polarity classification. *Knowledge-Based Systems, 39*, 23–33. doi:10.1016/j.knosys.2012.10.005

Lissoni, F. (2013). Academic patenting in Europe: Recent research and new perspectives. In I. Yetkiner, M. Pamukcu, & E. Erdil (Eds.), *Industrial dynamics, innovation policy, and economic growth through technological advancements* (pp. 75–91). Hershey, PA: IGI Global. doi:10.4018/978-1-4666-1978-4.ch005

Litaay, T., Prananingrum, D. H., & Krisanto, Y. A. (2011). Indonesian legal perspectives on biotechnology and intellectual property rights. In S. Hongladarom (Ed.), *Genomics and bioethics: Interdisciplinary perspectives, technologies and advancements* (pp. 171–183). Hershey, PA: IGI Global. doi:10.4018/978-1-61692-883-4.ch012

Litaay, T., Prananingrum, D. H., & Krisanto, Y. A. (2013). Indonesian legal perspectives on biotechnology and intellectual property rights. In *Digital rights management: Concepts, methodologies, tools, and applications* (pp. 834–845). Hershey, PA: IGI Global. doi:10.4018/978-1-4666-2136-7.ch039

Liu, B. (2011). *Web Data Mining: Exploring Hyperlinks, Contents, and Usage Data.* Springer. doi:10.1007/978-3-642-19460-3

Liu, B., Blasch, E., Chen, Y., Shen, D., & Chen, G. (2013). Scalable Sentiment Classification for Big Data Analysis Using Na¨ıve Bayes Classifier. *IEEE International Conference on Big Data*, 99-104.

Liu, B., Cong, G., Zeng, Y., Xu, D., & Chee, Y. M. (2014). Influence spreading path and its application to the time constrained social influence maximization problem and beyond. *IEEE Transactions on Knowledge and Data Engineering*, 26(8), 1904–1917. doi:10.1109/TKDE.2013.106

Liu, F., Liu, Y., & Weng, F. (2011, June). Why is sxsw trending?: exploring multiple text sources for twitter topic summarization. In *Proceedings of the Workshop on Languages in Social Media* (pp. 66-75). Association for Computational Linguistics.

Liu, S. M., & Chen, J.-H. (2015). A multi-label classification based approach for sentiment classification. *Expert Systems with Applications*, 42(3), 1083–1093. doi:10.1016/j.eswa.2014.08.036

Liu, S., Cheng, X., Li, F., & Li, F. (2015). TASC:Topic-Adaptive Sentiment Classification on Dynamic Tweets. *IEEE Transactions on Knowledge and Data Engineering*, 27(6), 1696–1709. doi:10.1109/TKDE.2014.2382600

Liu, X., Li, M., Li, S., Peng, S., Liao, X., & Lu, X. (2014). IMGPU: GPU-accelerated influence maximization in large-scale social networks. *IEEE Transactions on Parallel and Distributed Systems*, 25(1), 136–145. doi:10.1109/TPDS.2013.41

Li, Y., Algarni, A., Albathan, M., Shen, Y., & Bijaksana, M. A. (2015). Relevance feature discovery for text mining. *IEEE Transactions on Knowledge and Data Engineering*, 27(6), 1656–1669. doi:10.1109/TKDE.2014.2373357

Li, Y., Chen, C. Y., & Wasserman, W. W. (2015) Deep feature selection: Theory and application to identify enhancers and promoters. *International Conference on Research in Computational Molecular Biology.* Springer International Publishing. doi:10.1007/978-3-319-16706-0_20

Li, Y., & Wei, C. (2011). Digital image authentication: A review. *International Journal of Digital Library Systems*, 2(2), 55–78. doi:10.4018/jdls.2011040104

Li, Y., Xiao, X., Feng, X., & Yan, H. (2012). Adaptation and localization: Metadata research and development for Chinese digital resources. *International Journal of Digital Library Systems*, *3*(1), 1–21. doi:10.4018/jdls.2012010101

Losavio, M., Pastukhov, P., & Polyakova, S. (2014). Regulatory aspects of cloud computing in business environments. In S. Srinivasan (Ed.), *Security, trust, and regulatory aspects of cloud computing in business environments* (pp. 156–169). Hershey, PA: IGI Global. doi:10.4018/978-1-4666-5788-5.ch009

Lowagie, B. (2010). iText in Action (2nd ed.). Manning Publications.

Lu, B., Tsou, B. K., Jiang, T., Zhu, J., & Kwong, O. Y. (2011). Mining parallel knowledge from comparable patents. In W. Wong, W. Liu, & M. Bennamoun (Eds.), *Ontology learning and knowledge discovery using the web: Challenges and recent advances* (pp. 247–271). Hershey, PA: IGI Global. doi:10.4018/978-1-60960-625-1.ch013

Lucas-Schloetter, A. (2011). Digital libraries and copyright issues: Digitization of contents and the economic rights of the authors. In I. Iglezakis, T. Synodinou, & S. Kapidakis (Eds.), *E-publishing and digital libraries: Legal and organizational issues* (pp. 159–179). Hershey, PA: IGI Global. doi:10.4018/978-1-60960-031-0.ch009

Ludwig, S. A. (2015). MapReduce-based Fuzzy C-Means Clustering Algorithm: Implementation and Scalability. *Int. Jour. of Machine Learning and Cybernetics*, *6*(6), 923–934. doi:10.1007/s13042-015-0367-0

Luo, M., Nie, F., Chang, X., Yang, Y., Hauptmann, A. G., & Zheng, Q. (2017). *Adaptive Unsupervised Feature Selection With Structure Regularization. IEEE Transactions on Neural Networks and Learning Systems*.

Lyytinen, K., Keil, T., & Fomin, V. (2010). A framework to build process theories of anticipatory information and communication technology (ICT) standardizing. In K. Jakobs (Ed.), *New applications in IT standards: Developments and progress* (pp. 147–186). Hershey, PA: IGI Global. doi:10.4018/978-1-60566-946-5.ch008

Macedo, M., & Isaías, P. (2013). Standards related to interoperability in EHR & HS. In M. Sicilia & P. Balazote (Eds.), *Interoperability in healthcare information systems: Standards, management, and technology* (pp. 19–44). Hershey, PA: IGI Global. doi:10.4018/978-1-4666-3000-0.ch002

Madden, P. (2011). Greater accountability, less red tape: The Australian standard business reporting experience. *International Journal of E-Business Research*, *7*(2), 1–10. doi:10.4018/jebr.2011040101

Maji, P., & Pal, S. K. (2007). RFCM: A Hybrid Clustering Algorithm using rough and fuzzy set. *Fundamenta Informaticae*, *8*(4), 475–496.

Maks, I., & Vossen, P. (2012). A lexicon model for deep sentiment analysis and opinion mining applications. *Decision Support Systems*, *53*(4), 680–688. doi:10.1016/j.dss.2012.05.025

Mane, M. G., & Kulkarni, M. A. (2015). Twitter Event Summarization Using Phrase Reinforcement Algorithm and NLP Features. In Proceedings of International Journal of Advanced Research in Computer and Communication Engineering (vol. 4.5 pp. 427-430). doi:10.17148/IJARCCE.2015.45157

Manning, C. D., Raghavan, P., & Schutze, H. (2009). *An Introduction to Information Retrieval.* Cambridge University Press.

Manske, H. M., & Kwiatkowski, D. P. (2009). LookSeq: A browser-based viewer for deep sequencing data. *Genome Research, 19*(11), 2125–2132. doi:10.1101/gr.093443.109 PMID:19679872

Maravilhas, S. (2014). Quality improves the value of patent information to promote innovation. In G. Jamil, A. Malheiro, & F. Ribeiro (Eds.), *Rethinking the conceptual base for new practical applications in information value and quality* (pp. 61–82). Hershey, PA: IGI Global. doi:10.4018/978-1-4666-4562-2.ch004

Marshall, S. (2011). E-learning standards: Beyond technical standards to guides for professional practice. In F. Lazarinis, S. Green, & E. Pearson (Eds.), *Handbook of research on e-learning standards and interoperability: Frameworks and issues* (pp. 170–192). Hershey, PA: IGI Global. doi:10.4018/978-1-61692-789-9.ch008

Martino, L., & Bertino, E. (2012). Security for web services: Standards and research issues. In L. Jie-Zhang (Ed.), *Innovations, standards and practices of web services: Emerging research topics* (pp. 336–362). Hershey, PA: IGI Global. doi:10.4018/978-1-61350-104-7.ch015

Masri, , A., & Nasir, M. (2016). Learning machine implementation for big data Analytics, challenges and solutions. *Journal of Data Mining in Genomics & Proteomics, 07*(02).

Mathew, J., & Vijayakumar, R. (2014). Scalable parallel clustering approach for large data using parallel K-means and firefly algorithms. *Proceedings of International Conference on High Computing and Applications*, 1–8.

McCarthy, V., & Hulsart, R. (2012). Management education for integrity: Raising ethical standards in online management classes. In C. Wankel & A. Stachowicz-Stanusch (Eds.), *Handbook of research on teaching ethics in business and management education* (pp. 413–425). Hershey, PA: IGI Global. doi:10.4018/978-1-61350-510-6.ch024

McDaid, A. F., Greene, D., & Hurley, N. (2013). *Normalized Mutual Information to evaluate overlapping community finding algorithms.* CORR,abs/1110.2515

McGrath, T. (2012). The reality of using standards for electronic business document formats. In E. Kajan, F. Dorloff, & I. Bedini (Eds.), *Handbook of research on e-business standards and protocols: Documents, data and advanced web technologies* (pp. 21–32). Hershey, PA: IGI Global. doi:10.4018/978-1-4666-0146-8.ch002

McQueen, J. (1967). Some Methods for Classification and Analysis of Multivariate Observations. *Proc. Fifth Berkeley Symposium on Mathematics Statistics and Probability*, 281–297.

Medlin, B. D., & Chen, C. C. (2012). A global perspective of laws and regulations dealing with information security and privacy. In *Cyber crime: Concepts, methodologies, tools and applications* (pp. 1349–1363). Hershey, PA: IGI Global. doi:10.4018/978-1-61350-323-2.ch609

Meek, C., Thiesson, B., & Heckerman, D. (2002). The learning curve sampling method applied to model based clustering. *Journal of Machine Learning Research*, 2, 397–418.

Mehrfard, H., & Hamou-Lhadj, A. (2011). The impact of regulatory compliance on agile software processes with a focus on the FDA guidelines for medical device software. *International Journal of Information System Modeling and Design*, 2(2), 67–81. doi:10.4018/jismd.2011040104

Mehrfard, H., & Hamou-Lhadj, A. (2013). The impact of regulatory compliance on agile software processes with a focus on the FDA guidelines for medical device software. In J. Krogstie (Ed.), *Frameworks for developing efficient information systems: Models, theory, and practice* (pp. 298–314). Hershey, PA: IGI Global. doi:10.4018/978-1-4666-4161-7.ch013

Mendoza, R. A., & Ravichandran, T. (2011). An exploratory analysis of the relationship between organizational and institutional factors shaping the assimilation of vertical standards. *International Journal of IT Standards and Standardization Research*, 9(1), 24–51. doi:10.4018/jitsr.2011010102

Mendoza, R. A., & Ravichandran, T. (2012). An empirical evaluation of the assimilation of industry-specific data standards using firm-level and community-level constructs. In M. Tavana (Ed.), *Enterprise information systems and advancing business solutions: Emerging models* (pp. 287–312). Hershey, PA: IGI Global. doi:10.4018/978-1-4666-1761-2.ch017

Mendoza, R. A., & Ravichandran, T. (2012). Drivers of organizational participation in XML-based industry standardization efforts. In M. Tavana (Ed.), *Enterprise information systems and advancing business solutions: Emerging models* (pp. 268–286). Hershey, PA: IGI Global. doi:10.4018/978-1-4666-1761-2.ch016

Mendoza, R. A., & Ravichandran, T. (2013). An exploratory analysis of the relationship between organizational and institutional factors shaping the assimilation of vertical standards. In K. Jakobs (Ed.), *Innovations in organizational IT specification and standards development* (pp. 193–221). Hershey, PA: IGI Global. doi:10.4018/978-1-4666-2160-2.ch012

Mense, E. G., Fulwiler, J. H., Richardson, M. D., & Lane, K. E. (2011). Standardization, hybridization, or individualization: Marketing IT to a diverse clientele. In U. Demiray & S. Sever (Eds.), *Marketing online education programs: Frameworks for promotion and communication* (pp. 291–299). Hershey, PA: IGI Global. doi:10.4018/978-1-60960-074-7.ch019

Metaxa, E., Sarigiannidis, M., & Folinas, D. (2012). Legal issues of the French law on creation and internet (Hadopi 1 and 2). *International Journal of Technoethics*, 3(3), 21–36. doi:10.4018/jte.2012070102

Meyer, N. (2012). Standardization as governance without government: A critical reassessment of the digital video broadcasting projects success story. *International Journal of IT Standards and Standardization Research*, 10(2), 14–28. doi:10.4018/jitsr.2012070102

Microsoft. (2011). Retrieved October 11, 2013, from http://web-ngram.research.microsoft.com/info/

Miguel da Silva, F., Neto, F. M., Burlamaqui, A. M., Pinto, J. P., Fernandes, C. E., & Castro de Souza, R. (2014). T-SCORM: An extension of the SCORM standard to support the project of educational contents for t-learning. In F. Neto (Ed.), *Technology platform innovations and forthcoming trends in ubiquitous learning* (pp. 94–119). Hershey, PA: IGI Global. doi:10.4018/978-1-4666-4542-4.ch006

Miller, J. R., Koren, S., & Sutton, G. (2010). Assembly algorithms for next-generation sequencing data. *Genomics*, *95*(6), 315–327. doi:10.1016/j.ygeno.2010.03.001 PMID:20211242

Mitra, S., Banka, H., & Pedrycz, W. (2006). Rough-Fuzzy Collaborative Clustering. *IEEE Transactions on Systems, Man, and Cybernetics. Part B, Cybernetics*, *36*(4), 795–805. doi:10.1109/TSMCB.2005.863371 PMID:16903365

Mller, C., Zesch, T., & Gurevych, I. (2008). Extracting lexical semantic knowledge from wikipedia and wiktionary. In *Proceedings of the Sixth International Conference on Language Resources and Evaluation (LREC'08)*. European Language Resources Association (ELRA).

Modenesi, M. V., Costa, M. C. A., Evsukoff, A. G., & Ebecken, N. F. (2007). Parallel Fuzz C-means Cluster Analysis. In *Lecture Notes in Computer Science on High Performance Computing for Computational Science- VECPAR*. Springer.

Montejo-Ráez, A., Martínez-Cámara, E., Martín-Valdivia, M. T., & Urena-López, L. A. (2014). Ranked WordNet graph for Sentiment Polarity Classification in Twitter. *Computer Speech & Language*, *28*(1), 93–107. doi:10.1016/j.csl.2013.04.001

Moody-White. (2003). In *Wikipedia*. Retrieved from https://en.wikipedia.org/wiki/Structural_cohesion

Moody, , & White, D. R. (2003). Structural Cohesion and Embeddedness: A Hierarchical Concept of Social Groups. *American Sociological Review*, *68*(1), 103–127. doi:10.2307/3088904

Moon, A. (2014). Copyright and licensing essentials for librarians and copyright owners in the digital age. In N. Patra, B. Kumar, & A. Pani (Eds.), *Progressive trends in electronic resource management in libraries* (pp. 106–117). Hershey, PA: IGI Global. doi:10.4018/978-1-4666-4761-9.ch006

Moralis, A., Pouli, V., Grammatikou, M., Kalogeras, D., & Maglaris, V. (2012). Security standards and issues for grid computing. In *Grid and cloud computing: Concepts, methodologies, tools and applications* (pp. 1656–1671). Hershey, PA: IGI Global. doi:10.4018/978-1-4666-0879-5.ch708

Moreno, L., Iglesias, A., Calvo, R., Delgado, S., & Zaragoza, L. (2012). Disability standards and guidelines for learning management systems: Evaluating accessibility. In R. Babo & A. Azevedo (Eds.), *Higher education institutions and learning management systems: Adoption and standardization* (pp. 199–218). Hershey, PA: IGI Global. doi:10.4018/978-1-60960-884-2.ch010

Moreo, A., Romero, M., Castro, J. L., & Zurita, J. M. (2012). Lexicon-based Comments-oriented News Sentiment Analyzer system. *Expert Systems with Applications*, *39*(10), 9166–9180. doi:10.1016/j.eswa.2012.02.057

Moro, N. (2013). Digital rights management and corporate hegemony: Avenues for reform. In H. Rahman & I. Ramos (Eds.), *Ethical data mining applications for socio-economic development* (pp. 281–299). Hershey, PA: IGI Global. doi:10.4018/978-1-4666-4078-8.ch013

Mula, D., & Lobina, M. L. (2012). Legal protection of the web page. In H. Sasaki (Ed.), *Information technology for intellectual property protection: Interdisciplinary advancements* (pp. 213–236). Hershey, PA: IGI Global. doi:10.4018/978-1-61350-135-1.ch008

Mula, D., & Lobina, M. L. (2013). Legal protection of the web page. In *Digital rights management: Concepts, methodologies, tools, and applications* (pp. 1–18). Hershey, PA: IGI Global. doi:10.4018/978-1-4666-2136-7.ch001

Mulcahy, D. (2011). Performativity in practice: An actor-network account of professional teaching standards. *International Journal of Actor-Network Theory and Technological Innovation*, *3*(2), 1–16. doi:10.4018/jantti.2011040101

Mulcahy, D. (2013). Performativity in practice: An actor-network account of professional teaching standards. In A. Tatnall (Ed.), *Social and professional applications of actor-network theory for technology development* (pp. 1–16). Hershey, PA: IGI Global. doi:10.4018/978-1-4666-2166-4.ch001

Mulvancy, N. (2005). *Indexing books*. Chicago: University of Chicago Press. doi:10.7208/chicago/9780226550176.001.0001

Mustaffa, M. T. (2012). Multi-standard multi-band reconfigurable LNA. In A. Marzuki, A. Rahim, & M. Loulou (Eds.), *Advances in monolithic microwave integrated circuits for wireless systems: Modeling and design technologies* (pp. 1–23). Hershey, PA: IGI Global. doi:10.4018/978-1-60566-886-4.ch001

Nabi, S. I., Al-Ghmlas, G. S., & Alghathbar, K. (2012). Enterprise information security policies, standards, and procedures: A survey of available standards and guidelines. In M. Gupta, J. Walp, & R. Sharman (Eds.), *Strategic and practical approaches for information security governance: Technologies and applied solutions* (pp. 67–89). Hershey, PA: IGI Global. doi:10.4018/978-1-4666-0197-0.ch005

Nabi, S. I., Al-Ghmlas, G. S., & Alghathbar, K. (2014). Enterprise information security policies, standards, and procedures: A survey of available standards and guidelines. In *Crisis management: Concepts, methodologies, tools and applications* (pp. 750–773). Hershey, PA: IGI Global. doi:10.4018/978-1-4666-4707-7.ch036

Nair, S., & Mehta, J. (2011). Clustering with apache Hadoo. *Proceedings of the International Conference, Workshop on Emerging Trends in technology, ICWET'11*, 505-509.

Naixiao, Z., & Chunhua, H. (2012). Research on open innovation in China: Focus on intellectual property rights and their operation in Chinese enterprises. *International Journal of Asian Business and Information Management, 3*(1), 65–71. doi:10.4018/jabim.2012010106

Naixiao, Z., & Chunhua, H. (2013). Research on open innovation in China: Focus on intellectual property rights and their operation in Chinese enterprises. In *Digital rights management: Concepts, methodologies, tools, and applications* (pp. 714–720). Hershey, PA: IGI Global. doi:10.4018/978-1-4666-2136-7.ch031

Najafabadi, M. M., Villanustre, F., Khoshgoftaar, T. M., Seliya, N., Wald, R., & Muharemagic, E. (2015). Deep learning applications and challenges in big data analytics. *Journal of Big Data, 2*(1), 1. doi:10.1186/s40537-014-0007-7

Namdev, A., & Tripathy, B. K. (2016). Scalable Rough C-Means clustering using Firefly algorithm. *International Journal of Computer Science and Business Informatics, 16*(2), 1–14.

Namgay, P., & Singha, A. (2016). Evaluation and Analysis of Grammatical Linguistic Pattern over Social Science and Technology Textbooks. In *Proceedings of the Sixth International Conference on Advances in Computing & Communications (ICACC'16)* (*vol. 93*, pp. 521-532). Procedia Computer Science. doi:10.1016/j.procs.2016.07.247

Narendra, P., & Fukunaga, K. (1977). A branch and bound algorithm for feature subset section. *IEEE Transactions on Computers, 26*(9), 917–922. doi:10.1109/TC.1977.1674939

Ndjetcheu, L. (2013). Social responsibility and legal financial communication in African companies in the south of the Sahara: Glance from the OHADA accounting law viewpoint. *International Journal of Innovation in the Digital Economy, 4*(4), 1–17. doi:10.4018/ijide.2013100101

Newman, M. E. J. (2015). *Real world network datasets*. Retrieved from http://www-personal. umich.edu/~mejn/netdata/

Ng, R. T., & Han, J. (1994). Efficient and Effective clustering methods for spatial data mining. *Proceedings of the 20th international conference on very large databases*, 144-155.

Ng, W. L. (2013). Improving long-term financial risk forecasts using high-frequency data and scaling laws. In B. Alexandrova-Kabadjova, S. Martinez-Jaramillo, A. Garcia-Almanza, & E. Tsang (Eds.), *Simulation in computational finance and economics: Tools and emerging applications* (pp. 255–278). Hershey, PA: IGI Global. doi:10.4018/978-1-4666-2011-7.ch013

Nicol, J. W., Helt, G. A., Blanchard, S. G., Raja, A., & Loraine, A. E. (2009). The integrated genome Browser: Free software for distribution and exploration of genome-scale datasets. *Bioinformatics (Oxford, England), 25*(20), 2730–2731. doi:10.1093/bioinformatics/btp472 PMID:19654113

Nicosia, V., Mangioni, G., Carchiolo, V., & Malgeri, M. (2009). Extending the definition of modularity to directed graphs with overlapping communities. *Journal of Statistical Mechanics, 2009*(03), 03024. doi:10.1088/1742-5468/2009/03/P03024

Noury, N., Bourquard, K., Bergognon, D., & Schroeder, J. (2013). Regulations initiatives in France for the interoperability of communicating medical devices. *International Journal of E-Health and Medical Communications*, 4(2), 50–64. doi:10.4018/jehmc.2013040104

Null, E. (2013). Legal and political barriers to municipal networks in the United States. In A. Abdelaal (Ed.), *Social and economic effects of community wireless networks and infrastructures* (pp. 27–56). Hershey, PA: IGI Global. doi:10.4018/978-1-4666-2997-4.ch003

Nunzio, G. M. D., & Orio, N. (2016). A game theory approach to feature selection for text classification. *Proc. of 7th Italian Information Retrieval Workshop, 1653*.

O'Connor, B., Krieger, M., & Ahn, D. (2010, May). TweetMotif: Exploratory Search and Topic Summarization for Twitter. *Proceedings of the Fourth International AAAI Conference on Weblogs and Social Media*, 384-385.

OConnor, R. V., & Laporte, C. Y. (2014). An innovative approach to the development of an international software process lifecycle standard for very small entities. *International Journal of Information Technologies and Systems Approach*, 7(1), 1–22. doi:10.4018/ijitsa.2014010101

Oh, I. S., Lee, J. S., & Moon, B. R. (2004). Hybrid genetic algorithms for feature selection. *IEEE Transactions on Pattern Analysis and Machine Intelligence*, 26(11), 1424–1437. doi:10.1109/TPAMI.2004.105 PMID:15521491

Onan, A., Korukoglu, S., & Bulut, H. (2016). A multiobjective weighted voting ensemble classifier based on differential evolution algorithm for text sentiment classification. *Expert Systems with Applications*, 62, 1–16. doi:10.1016/j.eswa.2016.06.005

Onat, I., & Miri, A. (2013). RFID standards. In A. Miri (Ed.), *Advanced security and privacy for RFID technologies* (pp. 14–22). Hershey, PA: IGI Global. doi:10.4018/978-1-4666-3685-9.ch002

Opsahl, , Agneessens, F., & Skvoretz, J. (2010). Node centrality in weighted networks: Generalizing degree and shortest paths. *Social Networks*, 32(3), 245–251. doi:10.1016/j.socnet.2010.03.006

Orlandia, R., Lai, Y., & Lee, W. (2005). Clustering high dimensional data using an efficient and effective data space reduction. *Proc. ACM Conference on Information and Knowledge Management*, 201–208.

Ortigosa-Hernandez, J., Rodrıguez, J. D., Alzate, L., Lucania, M., Inza, I., & Lozano, J. A. (2012). Approaching Sentiment Analysis by using semi-supervised learning of multi-dimensional classifiers. *Neurocomputing*, 92, 98–115. doi:10.1016/j.neucom.2012.01.030

Orton, I., Alva, A., & Endicott-Popovsky, B. (2013). Legal process and requirements for cloud forensic investigations. In K. Ruan (Ed.), *Cybercrime and cloud forensics: Applications for investigation processes* (pp. 186–229). Hershey, PA: IGI Global. doi:10.4018/978-1-4666-2662-1.ch008

Ortt, J. R., & Egyedi, T. M. (2014). The effect of pre-existing standards and regulations on the development and diffusion of radically new innovations. *International Journal of IT Standards and Standardization Research*, 12(1), 17–37. doi:10.4018/ijitsr.2014010102

Otte, E., & Rousseau, R. (2002). Social network analysis: A powerful strategy, also for the information sciences. *Journal of Information Science*, *28*(6), 441–453. doi:10.1177/016555150202800601

Oyelade, J., Soyemi, J., Isewon, I., & Obembe, O. (2015). Bioinformatics, Healthcare Informatics and Analytics: An Imperative for Improved Healthcare System. *International Journal of Applied Information Systems*, *8*(5), 1–6. doi:10.5120/ijais15-451318

Ozturk, Y., & Sharma, J. (2011). mVITAL: A standards compliant vital sign monitor. In C. Röcker, & M. Ziefle (Eds.), Smart healthcare applications and services: Developments and practices (pp. 174-196). Hershey, PA: IGI Global. doi:10.4018/978-1-60960-180-5.ch008

Ozturk, Y., & Sharma, J. (2013). mVITAL: A standards compliant vital sign monitor. In IT policy and ethics: Concepts, methodologies, tools, and applications (pp. 515-538). Hershey, PA: IGI Global. doi:10.4018/978-1-4666-2919-6.ch024

Palla, G., Derenyi, I., Farkas, I., & Vicsek, T. (2005). Uncovering the overlapping community structure of complex networks in nature and society. *Nature*, *435*(7043), 814–818. doi:10.1038/nature03607 PMID:15944704

Pal, N. R., Pal, K., Keller, J. M., & Bezdek, J. C. (2005). A Possibilistic Fuzzy C-Means Clustering Algorithm. *IEEE Transactions on Fuzzy Systems*, *13*(4), 517–530. doi:10.1109/TFUZZ.2004.840099

Pan, S. J., Ni, X., Sun, J. T., Yang, Q., & Chen, Z. (2010, April). Cross-domain sentiment classification via spectral feature alignment. In *Proceedings of the 19th international conference on World wide web* (pp. 751-760). ACM. doi:10.1145/1772690.1772767

Pan, S. J., Ni, X., Sun, J.-T., Yang, Q., & Chen, Z. (2010). Cross-Domain Sentiment Classification via Spectral Feature Alignment. *WWW*, *2010*(April), 26–30.

Papadimitriou, S., & Sun, J. (2008). Disco: distributed co-clustering with MapReduce: A case study towards petabyte-scale end-to-end mining. *Proc. of the IEEE ICDM'08*, 512–521. doi:10.1109/ICDM.2008.142

Park, S., Lee, W., & Moon, I.-C. (2015). Efficient extraction of domain specific sentiment lexicon with active learning. *Pattern Recognition Letters*, *56*, 38–44. doi:10.1016/j.patrec.2015.01.004

Parsons, L., Ehtesham, H., & Liu, H. (2004). Subspace clustering for high dimensional data: A review. *ACM SIGKDD Explorations Newsletter*, *6*(1), 90–105. doi:10.1145/1007730.1007731

Parsons, T. D. (2011). Affect-sensitive virtual standardized patient interface system. In D. Surry, R. Gray Jr, & J. Stefurak (Eds.), *Technology integration in higher education: Social and organizational aspects* (pp. 201–221). Hershey, PA: IGI Global. doi:10.4018/978-1-60960-147-8.ch015

Parveen, S., & Pater, C. (2012). Utilizing innovative video chat technology to meet national standards: A Case study on a STARTALK Hindi language program. *International Journal of Virtual and Personal Learning Environments*, *3*(3), 1–20. doi:10.4018/jvple.2012070101

Pattillo, J. (2011). Clique relaxation models in social network analysis. In Handbook of Optimization in Complex Networks: Communication and Social Networks. Springer.

Pawlak, Z. (1991). *Rough Sets, Theoretical Aspects of Reasoning about Data*. Dordrecht, The Netherlands: Kluwer.

Pawlowski, J. M., & Kozlov, D. (2013). Analysis and validation of learning technology models, standards and specifications: The reference model analysis grid (RMAG). In K. Jakobs (Ed.), *Innovations in organizational IT specification and standards development* (pp. 223–240). Hershey, PA: IGI Global. doi:10.4018/978-1-4666-2160-2.ch013

Pedro, M. D. C., & Roy, A. (2016). Sentiment Lexicon Creation using Continuous Latent Space and Neural Networks. *Proceedings of NAACL-HLT*, *2016*, 37–42.

Peng, T.-C., & Shih, C.-C. (2010). An Unsupervised Snippet-based Sentiment Classification Method for Chinese Unknown Phrases without using Reference Word Pairs. *IEEE/WIC/ACM International Conference on Web Intelligence and Intelligent Agent Technology*. 243-248. doi:10.1109/WI-IAT.2010.229

Pherson, . (2001). Birds of a feather: Homophily in social networks. *Annual Review of Sociology*, *27*(1), 415–444. doi:10.1146/annurev.soc.27.1.415

Pina, P. (2013). Between Scylla and Charybdis: The balance between copyright, digital rights management and freedom of expression. In Digital rights management: Concepts, methodologies, tools, and applications (pp. 1355-1367). Hershey, PA: IGI Global. doi:10.4018/978-1-4666-2136-7.ch067

Pina, P. (2011). The private copy issue: Piracy, copyright and consumers' rights. In T. Strader (Ed.), *Digital product management, technology and practice: Interdisciplinary perspectives* (pp. 193–205). Hershey, PA: IGI Global. doi:10.4018/978-1-61692-877-3.ch011

Pina, P. (2013). Computer games and intellectual property law: Derivative works, copyright and copyleft. In *Digital rights management: Concepts, methodologies, tools, and applications* (pp. 777–788). Hershey, PA: IGI Global. doi:10.4018/978-1-4666-2136-7.ch035

Pina, P. (2013). The private copy issue: Piracy, copyright and consumers' rights. In *Digital rights management: Concepts, methodologies, tools, and applications* (pp. 1546–1558). Hershey, PA: IGI Global. doi:10.4018/978-1-4666-2136-7.ch078

Pinheiro, C. A. R. (2011). *Social Network Analysis in Telecommunications*. John Wiley & Sons.

Piotrowski, M. (2011). QTI: A failed e-learning standard? In F. Lazarinis, S. Green, & E. Pearson (Eds.), *Handbook of research on e-learning standards and interoperability: Frameworks and issues* (pp. 59–82). Hershey, PA: IGI Global. doi:10.4018/978-1-61692-789-9.ch004

Podolny, J. M., & Baron, J. N. (1997). Resources and relationships: Social networks and mobility in the workplace. *American Sociological Review*, *62*(5), 673–693. doi:10.2307/2657354

Ponte, D., & Camussone, P. F. (2013). Neither heroes nor chaos: The victory of VHS against Betamax. *International Journal of Actor-Network Theory and Technological Innovation, 5*(1), 40–54. doi:10.4018/jantti.2013010103

Popendorf, K., & Sakakibara, Y. (2012). SAMSCOPE: An OpenGL-based real-time interactive scale-free SAM viewer. *Bioinformatics (Oxford, England), 28*(9), 1276–1277. doi:10.1093/bioinformatics/bts122 PMID:22419785

Pradhan, A. (2011). Pivotal role of the ISO 14001 standard in the carbon economy. *International Journal of Green Computing, 2*(1), 38–46. doi:10.4018/jgc.2011010104

Pradhan, A. (2011). Standards and legislation for the carbon economy. In B. Unhelkar (Ed.), *Handbook of research on green ICT: Technology, business and social perspectives* (pp. 592–606). Hershey, PA: IGI Global. doi:10.4018/978-1-61692-834-6.ch043

Pradhan, A. (2013). Pivotal role of the ISO 14001 standard in the carbon economy. In K. Ganesh & S. Anbuudayasankar (Eds.), *International and interdisciplinary studies in green computing* (pp. 38–46). Hershey, PA: IGI Global. doi:10.4018/978-1-4666-2646-1.ch004

Prekopcsák, Z., Makrai, G., Henk, T., & Gaspar-Papanek, C. (2011, June). Radoop: Analyzing big data with rapidminer and hadoop. *Proceedings of the 2nd RapidMiner community meeting and conference (RCOMM 2011)*, 865-874.

Prentzas, J., & Hatzilygeroudis, I. (2011). Techniques, technologies and patents related to intelligent educational systems. In G. Magoulas (Ed.), *E-infrastructures and technologies for lifelong learning: Next generation environments* (pp. 1–28). Hershey, PA: IGI Global. doi:10.4018/978-1-61520-983-5.ch001

Ptaszynski, M., Masui, F., Rzepka, R., & Araki, K. (2017). *Subjective? Emotional? Emotive?: Language Combinatorics based Automatic Detection of Emotionally Loaded Sentences*. Academic Press.

Pudil, P., Novovicova, J., & Kittler, J. (1994). Floating search methods in feature selection. *Pattern Recognition Letters, 15*(11), 1119–1125. doi:10.1016/0167-8655(94)90127-9

Pu, I. M. (2005). *Fundamental data compression*. Butterworth-Heinemann.

Ramos, I., & Fernandes, J. (2011). Web-based intellectual property marketplace: A survey of current practices. *International Journal of Information Communication Technologies and Human Development, 3*(3), 58–68. doi:10.4018/jicthd.2011070105

Ramos, I., & Fernandes, J. (2013). Web-based intellectual property marketplace: A survey of current practices. In S. Chhabra (Ed.), *ICT influences on human development, interaction, and collaboration* (pp. 203–213). Hershey, PA: IGI Global. doi:10.4018/978-1-4666-1957-9.ch012

Rao, Y., Li, Q., Mao, X., & Wenyin, L. (2014). Sentiment topic models for social emotion mining. *Information Sciences, 266*, 90–100. doi:10.1016/j.ins.2013.12.059

Raschka, S. (2014). *About feature scaling and normalization*. Academic Press.

Rashmi, R. (2011). Biopharma drugs innovation in India and foreign investment and technology transfer in the changed patent regime. In P. Ordóñez de Pablos, W. Lee, & J. Zhao (Eds.), *Regional innovation systems and sustainable development: Emerging technologies* (pp. 210–225). Hershey, PA: IGI Global. doi:10.4018/978-1-61692-846-9.ch016

Rashmi, R. (2011). Optimal policy for biopharmaceutical drugs innovation and access in India. In P. Ordóñez de Pablos, W. Lee, & J. Zhao (Eds.), *Regional innovation systems and sustainable development: Emerging technologies* (pp. 74–114). Hershey, PA: IGI Global. doi:10.4018/978-1-61692-846-9.ch007

Rashmi, R. (2013). Biopharma drugs innovation in India and foreign investment and technology transfer in the changed patent regime. In *Digital rights management: Concepts, methodologies, tools, and applications* (pp. 846–859). Hershey, PA: IGI Global. doi:10.4018/978-1-4666-2136-7.ch040

Reed, C. N. (2011). The open geospatial consortium and web services standards. In P. Zhao & L. Di (Eds.), *Geospatial web services: Advances in information interoperability* (pp. 1–16). Hershey, PA: IGI Global. doi:10.4018/978-1-60960-192-8.ch001

Rejas-Muslera, R. J., García-Tejedor, A. J., & Rodriguez, O. P. (2011). Open educational resources in e-learning: standards and environment. In F. Lazarinis, S. Green, & E. Pearson (Eds.), *Handbook of research on e-learning standards and interoperability: Frameworks and issues* (pp. 346–359). Hershey, PA: IGI Global. doi:10.4018/978-1-61692-789-9.ch017

Rejas-Muslera, R., Davara, E., Abran, A., & Buglione, L. (2013). Intellectual property systems in software. *International Journal of Cyber Warfare & Terrorism*, *3*(1), 1–14. doi:10.4018/ijcwt.2013010101

Reza, Z., Abbasi, M. A., & Liu, H. (2014). *Social Media Mining: An Introduction*. Cambridge University Press.

Ries, N. M. (2011). Legal issues in health information and electronic health records. In *Clinical technologies: Concepts, methodologies, tools and applications* (pp. 1948–1961). Hershey, PA: IGI Global. doi:10.4018/978-1-60960-561-2.ch708

Riillo, C. A. (2013). Profiles and motivations of standardization players. *International Journal of IT Standards and Standardization Research*, *11*(2), 17–33. doi:10.4018/jitsr.2013070102

Rodriguez, E., & Lolas, F. (2011). Social issues related to gene patenting in Latin America: A bioethical reflection. In S. Hongladarom (Ed.), *Genomics and bioethics: Interdisciplinary perspectives, technologies and advancements* (pp. 152–170). Hershey, PA: IGI Global. doi:10.4018/978-1-61692-883-4.ch011

Rui, H., Liu, Y., & Whinston, A. (2013). Whose and what chatter matters? The effect of tweets on movie sales. *Decision Support Systems*, *55*(4), 863–870. doi:10.1016/j.dss.2012.12.022

Ruspini, E. H. (1970). Numerical methods for fuzzy clustering. *Information Sciences*, *2*(3), 319–350. doi:10.1016/S0020-0255(70)80056-1

Rutherford, M. (2013). Implementing common core state standards using digital curriculum. In D. Polly (Ed.), *Common core mathematics standards and implementing digital technologies* (pp. 38–44). Hershey, PA: IGI Global. doi:10.4018/978-1-4666-4086-3.ch003

Rutherford, M. (2014). Implementing common core state standards using digital curriculum. In *K-12 education: Concepts, methodologies, tools, and applications* (pp. 383–389). Hershey, PA: IGI Global. doi:10.4018/978-1-4666-4502-8.ch022

Ryan, G., & Shinnick, E. (2011). Knowledge and intellectual property rights: An economics perspective. In D. Schwartz & D. Te'eni (Eds.), *Encyclopedia of knowledge management* (2nd ed.; pp. 489–496). Hershey, PA: IGI Global. doi:10.4018/978-1-59904-931-1.ch047

Ryoo, J., & Choi, Y. (2011). A taxonomy of green information and communication protocols and standards. In B. Unhelkar (Ed.), *Handbook of research on green ICT: Technology, business and social perspectives* (pp. 364–376). Hershey, PA: IGI Global. doi:10.4018/978-1-61692-834-6.ch026

Saeed, K., Ziegler, G., & Yaqoob, M. K. (2013). Management practices in exploration and production industry. In S. Saeed, M. Khan, & R. Ahmad (Eds.), *Business strategies and approaches for effective engineering management* (pp. 151–187). Hershey, PA: IGI Global. doi:10.4018/978-1-4666-3658-3.ch010

Sahami, M., Dumais, S., Heckerman, D., & Horvitz, E. (1998, July). A Bayesian approach to filtering junk e-mail. *Learning for Text Categorization: Papers from the 1998 Workshop, 62*, 98-105.

Saiki, T. (2014). Intellectual property in mergers & acquisitions. In J. Wang (Ed.), *Encyclopedia of business analytics and optimization* (pp. 1275–1283). Hershey, PA: IGI Global. doi:10.4018/978-1-4666-5202-6.ch117

Saleha, R., Haider, J. N., & Danish, N. (2002). Rough Intuitionistic Fuzzy Sets. *Proceedings of the 8th Int. conf. on Fuzzy Theory and Technology (FT & T)*.

Salomon, D. (2004). *Data compression: the complete reference*. Springer Science & Business Media.

Salomon, D., & Motta, G. (2010). *Handbook of data compression*. Springer Science & Business Media. doi:10.1007/978-1-84882-903-9

Sangiorgi, P., Augello, A., & Pilato, G. (2013). An unsupervised data-driven cross-lingual method for building high precision sentiment lexicons. *IEEE Seventh International Conference on Semantic Computing*. 184-190. doi:10.1109/ICSC.2013.40

Santos, O., & Boticario, J. (2011). A general framework for inclusive lifelong learning in higher education institutions with adaptive web-based services that support standards. In G. Magoulas (Ed.), *E-infrastructures and technologies for lifelong learning: Next generation environments* (pp. 29–58). Hershey, PA: IGI Global. doi:10.4018/978-1-61520-983-5.ch002

Santos, O., Boticario, J., Raffenne, E., Granado, J., Rodriguez-Ascaso, A., & Gutierrez y Restrepo, E. (2011). A standard-based framework to support personalisation, adaptation, and interoperability in inclusive learning scenarios. In F. Lazarinis, S. Green, & E. Pearson (Eds.), *Handbook of research on e-learning standards and interoperability: Frameworks and issues* (pp. 126–169). Hershey, PA: IGI Global. doi:10.4018/978-1-61692-789-9.ch007

Sarabdeen, J. (2012). Legal issues in e-healthcare systems. In M. Watfa (Ed.), *E-healthcare systems and wireless communications: Current and future challenges* (pp. 23–48). Hershey, PA: IGI Global. doi:10.4018/978-1-61350-123-8.ch002

Sayood, K. (2012). *Introduction to data compression*. Newnes.

Schatz, M. C., Phillippy, A. M., Sommer, D. D., Delcher, A. L., Puiu, D., Narzisi, G., & Pop, M. et al. (2011). Hawkeye and AMOS: Visualizing and assessing the quality of genome assemblies. *Briefings in Bioinformatics*, *14*(2), 213–224. doi:10.1093/bib/bbr074 PMID:22199379

Scheg, A. G. (2014). Common standards for online education found in accrediting organizations. In *Reforming teacher education for online pedagogy development* (pp. 50–76). Hershey, PA: IGI Global. doi:10.4018/978-1-4666-5055-8.ch003

Sclater, N. (2012). Legal and contractual issues of cloud computing for educational institutions. In L. Chao (Ed.), *Cloud computing for teaching and learning: Strategies for design and implementation* (pp. 186–199). Hershey, PA: IGI Global. doi:10.4018/978-1-4666-0957-0.ch013

Sebastiani, F. (2002). Machine learning in automated text categorization. *ACM Computing Surveys*, *34*(1), 1–47. doi:10.1145/505282.505283

Selwyn, L., & Eldridge, V. (2013). Governance and organizational structures. In *Public law librarianship: Objectives, challenges, and solutions* (pp. 41–71). Hershey, PA: IGI Global. doi:10.4018/978-1-4666-2184-8.ch003

Seo, D. (2012). The significance of government's role in technology standardization: Two cases in the wireless communications industry. In C. Reddick (Ed.), *Cases on public information management and e-government adoption* (pp. 219–231). Hershey, PA: IGI Global. doi:10.4018/978-1-4666-0981-5.ch009

Seo, D. (2013). Analysis of various structures of standards setting organizations (SSOs) that impact tension among members. *International Journal of IT Standards and Standardization Research*, *11*(2), 46–60. doi:10.4018/jitsr.2013070104

Seo, D. (2013). Background of standards strategy. In *Evolution and standardization of mobile communications technology* (pp. 1–17). Hershey, PA: IGI Global. doi:10.4018/978-1-4666-4074-0.ch001

Seo, D. (2013). Developing a theoretical model. In *Evolution and standardization of mobile communications technology* (pp. 18–42). Hershey, PA: IGI Global. doi:10.4018/978-1-4666-4074-0.ch002

Seo, D. (2013). The 1G (first generation) mobile communications technology standards. In *Evolution and standardization of mobile communications technology* (pp. 54–75). Hershey, PA: IGI Global. doi:10.4018/978-1-4666-4074-0.ch005

Seo, D. (2013). The 2G (second generation) mobile communications technology standards. In *Evolution and standardization of mobile communications technology* (pp. 76–114). Hershey, PA: IGI Global. doi:10.4018/978-1-4666-4074-0.ch006

Seo, D. (2013). The 3G (third generation) of mobile communications technology standards. In *Evolution and standardization of mobile communications technology* (pp. 115–161). Hershey, PA: IGI Global. doi:10.4018/978-1-4666-4074-0.ch007

Seo, D. (2013). The significance of government's role in technology standardization: Two cases in the wireless communications industry. In K. Jakobs (Ed.), *Innovations in organizational IT specification and standards development* (pp. 183–192). Hershey, PA: IGI Global. doi:10.4018/978-1-4666-2160-2.ch011

Seo, D., & Koek, J. W. (2012). Are Asian countries ready to lead a global ICT standardization? *International Journal of IT Standards and Standardization Research, 10*(2), 29–44. doi:10.4018/jitsr.2012070103

Shankar, B. U., & Pal, N. (1994). FFCM: An effective approach for large data sets. *Proc. Int. Conf. Fuzzy Logic, Neural Nets, Soft Computing, 332.*

Shapiro, G. P., & Frawley, W. J. (1991). *Knowledge Discovery in Databases.* AAAI/MIT Press.

Sharp, R. J., Ewald, J. A., & Kenward, R. (2013). Central information flows and decision-making requirements. In J. Papathanasiou, B. Manos, S. Arampatzis, & R. Kenward (Eds.), *Transactional environmental support system design: Global solutions* (pp. 7–32). Hershey, PA: IGI Global. doi:10.4018/978-1-4666-2824-3.ch002

Shen, D., Ruvini, J. D., & Sarwar, B. (2012). Large-scale item categorization for e-commerce. *Proceedings of the 21st ACM international conference on Information and knowledge management,* 595-604.

Shen, X., Graham, I., Stewart, J., & Williams, R. (2013). Standards development as hybridization. *International Journal of IT Standards and Standardization Research, 11*(2), 34–45. doi:10.4018/jitsr.2013070103

Sherman, M. (2013). Using technology to engage students with the standards for mathematical practice: The case of DGS. In D. Polly (Ed.), *Common core mathematics standards and implementing digital technologies* (pp. 78–101). Hershey, PA: IGI Global. doi:10.4018/978-1-4666-4086-3.ch006

Sindi, S. S., Önal, S., Peng, L. C., Wu, H.-T., & Raphael, B. J. (2012). An integrative probabilistic model for identification of structural variation in sequencing data. *Genome Biology, 13*(3), R22. doi:10.1186/gb-2012-13-3-r22 PMID:22452995

Singh, J., & Kumar, V. (2013). Compliance and regulatory standards for cloud computing. In R. Khurana & R. Aggarwal (Eds.), *Interdisciplinary perspectives on business convergence, computing, and legality* (pp. 54–64). Hershey, PA: IGI Global. doi:10.4018/978-1-4666-4209-6.ch006

Singh, S., & Paliwal, M. (2014). Exploring a sense of intellectual property valuation for Indian SMEs. *International Journal of Asian Business and Information Management*, 5(1), 15–36. doi:10.4018/ijabim.2014010102

Singh, S., & Siddiqui, T. J. (2013). Robust image data hiding technique for copyright protection. *International Journal of Information Security and Privacy*, 7(2), 44–56. doi:10.4018/jisp.2013040103

Sivaram, D. (2005). *Soap-simple object access protocol*. Academic Press.

Song, G., Zhou, X., Wang, Y., & Xie, K. (2015). Influence maximization on large-scale mobile social network: A divide-and-conquer method. *IEEE Transactions on Parallel and Distributed Systems*, 26(5), 1379–1392. doi:10.1109/TPDS.2014.2320515

Song, Q. (2013). A fast clustering-based feature subset selection algorithm for high-dimensional data. *IEEE Transactions on Knowledge and Data Engineering*, 25(1), 1–14. doi:10.1109/TKDE.2011.181

Song, Y., Zhou, G., & Zhu, Y. (2013). Present status and challenges of big data processing in smart grid. *Power System Technology*, 37(4), 927–935.

Spies, M., & Tabet, S. (2012). Emerging standards and protocols for governance, risk, and compliance management. In E. Kajan, F. Dorloff, & I. Bedini (Eds.), *Handbook of research on e-business standards and protocols: Documents, data and advanced web technologies* (pp. 768–790). Hershey, PA: IGI Global. doi:10.4018/978-1-4666-0146-8.ch035

Spinello, R. A., & Tavani, H. T. (2008). Intellectual property rights: From theory to practical implementation. In H. Sasaki (Ed.), *Intellectual property protection for multimedia information technology* (pp. 25–69). Hershey, PA: IGI Global. doi:10.4018/978-1-59904-762-1.ch002

Spudich, G. M., & Fernández-Suárez, X. M. (2010). Touring Ensembl: A practical guide to genome browsing. *BMC Genomics*, 11(1), 295. doi:10.1186/1471-2164-11-295 PMID:20459808

Spyrou, S., Bamidis, P., & Maglaveras, N. (2010). Health information standards: Towards integrated health information networks. In J. Rodrigues (Ed.), *Health information systems: Concepts, methodologies, tools, and applications* (pp. 2145–2159). Hershey, PA: IGI Global. doi:10.4018/978-1-60566-988-5.ch136

Sriram, B., Fuhry, D., Demir, E., Ferhatosmanoglu, H., & Demirbas, M. (2010, July). Short text classification in twitter to improve information filtering. *Proceedings of the 33rd international ACM SIGIR conference on Research and development in information retrieval*, 841-842. doi:10.1145/1835449.1835643

Srujan, C., Jain, A., & Tripathy, B. K. (2017). Image segmentation using Hybridized Firefly Algorithm and Intuitionistic Fuzzy C-Means. *First International Conference on Smart Systems, Innovation and Computing*. Manipal University.

Srujan, C., Jain, A., & Tripathy, B. K. (2017). Stabilizing Rough Set Based Clustering Algorithms using Firefly Algorithm over Image Datasets. *Second International Conference on Information and Communication technology for Intelligent Systems*.

Stamatatos, E. (2009). A survey of modern authorship attribution methods. *Journal of the American Society for Information Science and Technology*, *60*(3), 538–556. doi:10.1002/asi.21001

Stanfill, D. (2012). Standards-based educational technology professional development. In V. Wang (Ed.), *Encyclopedia of e-leadership, counseling and training* (pp. 819–834). Hershey, PA: IGI Global. doi:10.4018/978-1-61350-068-2.ch060

Steen, H. U. (2011). The battle within: An analysis of internal fragmentation in networked technologies based on a comparison of the DVB-H and T-DMB mobile digital multimedia broadcasting standards. *International Journal of IT Standards and Standardization Research*, *9*(2), 50–71. doi:10.4018/jitsr.2011070103

Steen, H. U. (2013). The battle within: An analysis of internal fragmentation in networked technologies based on a comparison of the DVB-H and T-DMB mobile digital multimedia broadcasting standards. In K. Jakobs (Ed.), *Innovations in organizational IT specification and standards development* (pp. 91–114). Hershey, PA: IGI Global. doi:10.4018/978-1-4666-2160-2.ch005

Stoll, M., & Breu, R. (2012). Information security governance and standard based management systems. In M. Gupta, J. Walp, & R. Sharman (Eds.), *Strategic and practical approaches for information security governance: Technologies and applied solutions* (pp. 261–282). Hershey, PA: IGI Global. doi:10.4018/978-1-4666-0197-0.ch015

Stoppiglia, H., Dreyfus, G., Dubois, R., & Oussar, Y. (2003). Ranking a Random Feature for Variable and Feature Selection. *Journal of Machine Learning Research*, *3*, 1399–1414.

Suarjaya, I. M. A. D. (2012). *A new algorithm for data compression optimization*. arXiv preprint arXiv:1209.1045

Sucharitha, V., Subash, S. R., & Prakash, P. (2014). Visualization of big data: Its tools and challenges. *International Journal of Applied Engineering Research*, *9*(18), 5277–5290.

Sun, R., Love, M. I., Zemojtel, T., Emde, A., Chung, H., Vingron, M., & Haas, S. A. (2012). Breakpointer: Using local mapping artifacts to support sequence breakpoint discovery from single-end reads. *Bioinformatics (Oxford, England)*, *28*(7), 1024–1025. doi:10.1093/bioinformatics/bts064 PMID:22302574

Sun, X., Li, C., Xu, W., & Ren, F. (2014), Chinese Microblog Sentiment Classification Based on Deep Belief Nets with Extended Multi-modality Features. *IEEE International Conference on Data Mining Workshop*, 928-935. doi:10.1109/ICDMW.2014.101

Suzuki, O. (2013). Search efforts, selective appropriation, and the usefulness of new knowledge: Evidence from a comparison across U.S. and non-U.S. patent applicants. *International Journal of Knowledge Management (IJKM), 9*(1), 42-59. doi:10.4018/jkm.2013010103

Suzuki, S., Yasuda, T., Shiraishi, Y., Miyano, S., & Nagasaki, M. (2011). ClipCrop: A tool for detecting structural variations with single-base resolution using soft-clipping information. *BMC Bioinformatics, 12*(Suppl 14), S7. doi:10.1186/1471-2105-12-S14-S7 PMID:22373054

Swonger, C. W. (1972). *Sample set condensation for a condensed nearest neighbor decision rule for pattern recognition*. Academic Press.

Tajima, M. (2012). The role of technology standardization in RFID adoption: The pharmaceutical context. *International Journal of IT Standards and Standardization Research, 10*(1), 48–67. doi:10.4018/jitsr.2012010104

Talevi, A., Castro, E. A., & Bruno-Blanch, L. E. (2012). Virtual screening: An emergent, key methodology for drug development in an emergent continent: A bridge towards patentability. In E. Castro & A. Haghi (Eds.), *Advanced methods and applications in chemoinformatics: Research progress and new applications* (pp. 229–245). Hershey, PA: IGI Global. doi:10.4018/978-1-60960-860-6.ch011

Tan, S., Li, Y., Sun, H., Guan, Z., Yan, X., Bu, J., & He, X. (2014). Interpreting the public sentiment variations on twitter. *IEEE Transactions on Knowledge and Data Engineering, 26*(5), 1158–1170. doi:10.1109/TKDE.2013.116

Tan, S., & Wu, Q. (2011). A random walk algorithm for automatic construction of domain-oriented sentiment lexicon. *Expert Systems with Applications, 38*(10), 12094–12100. doi:10.1016/j.eswa.2011.02.105

Tauber, A. (2012). Requirements and properties of qualified electronic delivery systems in egovernment: An Austrian experience. In S. Sharma (Ed.), *E-adoption and technologies for empowering developing countries: Global advances* (pp. 115–128). Hershey, PA: IGI Global. doi:10.4018/978-1-4666-0041-6.ch009

Taxidou, I., & Fischer, P. (2013). Realtime analysis of information diffusion in social media. *Proceedings of the VLDB Endowment, 6*(12), 1416–1421. doi:10.14778/2536274.2536328

Taylor, A., Marcus, M., & Santorini, B. (2003). *The Penn Treebank: An overview*. Academic Press.

Telesko, R., & Nikles, S. (2012). Semantic-enabled compliance management. In S. Smolnik, F. Teuteberg, & O. Thomas (Eds.), *Semantic technologies for business and information systems engineering: Concepts and applications* (pp. 292–310). Hershey, PA: IGI Global. doi:10.4018/978-1-60960-126-3.ch015

Tella, A., & Afolabi, A. K. (2013). Internet policy issues and digital libraries' management of intellectual property. In S. Thanuskodi (Ed.), *Challenges of academic library management in developing countries* (pp. 272–284). Hershey, PA: IGI Global. doi:10.4018/978-1-4666-4070-2.ch019

Thorvaldsdottir, H., Robinson, J. T., & Mesirov, J. P. (2012). Integrative Genomics viewer (IGV): High-performance genomics data visualization and exploration. *Briefings in Bioinformatics, 14*(2), 178–192. doi:10.1093/bib/bbs017 PMID:22517427

Tiwari, S. C., Gupta, M., Khan, M. A., & Ansari, A. Q. (2013). Intellectual property rights in semi-conductor industries: An Indian perspective. In S. Saeed, M. Khan, & R. Ahmad (Eds.), *Business strategies and approaches for effective engineering management* (pp. 97–110). Hershey, PA: IGI Global. doi:10.4018/978-1-4666-3658-3.ch006

Tomek, I. (1976). Two modifications of CNN. *IEEE Transactions on Systems, Man, and Cybernetics, 6*(11), 769–772. doi:10.1109/TSMC.1976.4309452

Toutanova, K., Klein, D., Manning, C. D., & Singer, Y. (2003). Feature-rich part-of-speech tagging with a cyclic dependency network. In *Proceedings of the 2003 Conference of the North American Chapter of the Association for Computational Linguistics on Human Language Technology* (Vol. 1) Association for Computational Linguistics. doi:10.3115/1073445.1073478

Trindade, Wang, Blackburn, & Philip. (2014). Taylor. Enhanced Factored Sequence Kernel for Sentiment Classification. *IEEE/WIC/ACM International Joint Conferences on Web Intelligence (WI) and Intelligent Agent Technologies (IAT)*, 519-525.

Tripathy, B. K., & Ghosh, A. (2011a). SDR: An algorithm for clustering categorical data using rough set theory. Recent Advances in Intelligent Computational Systems (RAICS), 2011 IEEE, Trivandrum, 867-872.

Tripathy, B. K., & Ghosh, A. (2012). Data Clustering Algorithms Using Rough Sets. Handbook of Research on Computational Intelligence for Engineering, Science, and Business, 297.

Tripathy, B. K., Mittal, D., & Hudedagaddi, D. P. (2016). Hadoop with Intuitionistic Fuzzy C-Means for Clustering in Big Data. *Proceedings of the International Congress on Information and Communication Technology*, 599-610. doi:10.1007/978-981-10-0767-5_62

Tripathy, B. K., Tripathy, A. & Govindarajulu, K. (2014b). Possibilistic rough fuzzy C-means algorithm in data clustering and image segmentation. *Proceedings of the IEEE ICCIC 2014*, 981-986.

Tripathy, B. K., Tripathy, A. & Govindarajulu, K. (2015). On PRIFCM Algorithm for Data Clustering, Image Segmentation and Comparative Analysis. *Proceedings of the IEEE IACC 2015*, 333 – 336.

Tripathy, B. K., Tripathy, A., Govindarajulu, K., & Bhargav, R. (2014a). On Kernel Based Rough Intuitionistic Fuzzy C-means Algorithm and a Comparative Analysis. Advanced Computing, Networking and Informatics, 1, 349-359.

Tripathy, A., Agrawal, A., & Rath, S. K. (2016). Classification of sentiment reviews using n-gram machine learning approach. *Expert Systems with Applications, 57*, 117–126. doi:10.1016/j.eswa.2016.03.028

Tripathy, B. K., Bhargava, R., Tripathy, A., Dhull, R., Verma, E., & Swarnalatha, P. (2013). *Rough Intuitionistic Fuzzy C-Means Algorithm and a Comparative Analysis in proceedings of ACM Compute 2013*. VIT University.

Tripathy, B. K., & Ghosh, A. (2011b). SSDR: An Algorithm for Clustering Categorical Data Using Rough Set Theory. *Advances in Applied Science Research*, *2*(3), 314–326.

Tripathy, B. K., Ghosh, S. K., & Jena, S. P. (2002). Intuitionistic Fuzzy Rough Sets. *Notes on Intuitionistic Fuzzy Sets (Bulgaria)*, *8*(1), 1–18.

Tripathy, B. K., Goyal, A., Chowdhury, R., & Patra, A. S. (2017). *MMeMeR: An Algorithm for Clustering Heterogeneous Data using Rough Set Theory*. Communicated to International Journal of Intelligent Systems and Applications.

Tripathy, B. K., Goyal, A., & Patra, A. S. (2016). A Comparative Analysis of Rough Intuitionistic Fuzzy K-mode for Clustering Categorical Data. *Research Journal of Pharmaceutical, Biological and Chemical Sciences*, *7*(5), 2787–2802.

Tripathy, B. K., Goyal, A., & Patra, A. S. (2016). Clustering Categorical Data Using Intuitionistic Fuzzy K-mode. *International Journal of Pharmacy and Technology*, *8*(3), 16688–16701.

Tripathy, B. K., & Kumar, M. S. P. (2009). MMeR: An algorithm for clustering Heterogeneous data using rough Set Theory. *International Journal of Rapid Manufacturing*, *1*(2), 189–207. doi:10.1504/IJRAPIDM.2009.029382

Tripathy, B. K., & Mittal, D. (2016). Hadoop based Uncertain Possibilistic Kernelized C-Means Algorithms for Image Segmentation and a Comparative analysis. *Applied Soft Computing*, *46*, 886–923. doi:10.1016/j.asoc.2016.01.045

Truyen, F., & Buekens, F. (2013). Professional ICT knowledge, epistemic standards, and social epistemology. In T. Takševa (Ed.), *Social software and the evolution of user expertise: Future trends in knowledge creation and dissemination* (pp. 274–294). Hershey, PA: IGI Global. doi:10.4018/978-1-4666-2178-7.ch016

Tsvetovat, . (2011). *Social Network Analysis for Startups: Finding Connections on the Social Web*. O'Reilly.

Tummons, J. (2011). Deconstructing professionalism: An actor-network critique of professional standards for teachers in the UK lifelong learning sector. *International Journal of Actor-Network Theory and Technological Innovation*, *3*(4), 22–31. doi:10.4018/jantti.2011100103

Tummons, J. (2013). Deconstructing professionalism: An actor-network critique of professional standards for teachers in the UK lifelong learning sector. In A. Tatnall (Ed.), *Social and professional applications of actor-network theory for technology development* (pp. 78–87). Hershey, PA: IGI Global. doi:10.4018/978-1-4666-2166-4.ch007

Tuohey, W. G. (2014). Lessons from practices and standards in safety-critical and regulated sectors. In I. Ghani, W. Kadir, & M. Ahmad (Eds.), *Handbook of research on emerging advancements and technologies in software engineering* (pp. 369–391). Hershey, PA: IGI Global. doi:10.4018/978-1-4666-6026-7.ch016

Tzoulia, E. (2013). Legal issues to be considered before setting in force consumer-centric marketing strategies within the European Union. In H. Kaufmann & M. Panni (Eds.), *Customer-centric marketing strategies: Tools for building organizational performance* (pp. 36–56). Hershey, PA: IGI Global. doi:10.4018/978-1-4666-2524-2.ch003

Unland, R. (2012). Interoperability support for e-business applications through standards, services, and multi-agent systems. In E. Kajan, F. Dorloff, & I. Bedini (Eds.), *Handbook of research on e-business standards and protocols: Documents, data and advanced web technologies* (pp. 129–153). Hershey, PA: IGI Global. doi:10.4018/978-1-4666-0146-8.ch007

Uslar, M., Grüning, F., & Rohjans, S. (2013). A use case for ontology evolution and interoperability: The IEC utility standards reference framework 62357. In M. Khosrow-Pour (Ed.), *Cases on performance measurement and productivity improvement: Technology integration and maturity* (pp. 387–415). Hershey, PA: IGI Global. doi:10.4018/978-1-4666-2618-8.ch018

Uysal, A. K. (2016). An improved global feature selection scheme for text classification. *Expert Systems with Applications*, *43*, 82–92. doi:10.1016/j.eswa.2015.08.050

van de Kaa, G. (2013). Responsible innovation and standardization: A new research approach? *International Journal of IT Standards and Standardization Research*, *11*(2), 61–65. doi:10.4018/jitsr.2013070105

van de Kaa, G., Blind, K., & de Vries, H. J. (2013). The challenge of establishing a recognized interdisciplinary journal: A citation analysis of the international journal of IT standards and standardization research. *International Journal of IT Standards and Standardization Research*, *11*(2), 1–16. doi:10.4018/jitsr.2013070101

Venkataraman, H., Ciubotaru, B., & Muntean, G. (2012). System design perspective: WiMAX standards and IEEE 802.16j based multihop WiMAX. In G. Cornetta, D. Santos, & J. Vazquez (Eds.), *Wireless radio-frequency standards and system design: Advanced techniques* (pp. 287–309). Hershey, PA: IGI Global. doi:10.4018/978-1-4666-0083-6.ch012

Verikas, A., & Bacauskiene, M. (2002). Feature selection with neural networks. *Pattern Recognition Letters*, *23*(11), 1323–1335. doi:10.1016/S0167-8655(02)00081-8

Verleysen, M., & François, D. (2005, June). The curse of dimensionality in data mining and time series prediction. In *International Work-Conference on Artificial Neural Networks* (pp. 758–770). Springer Berlin Heidelberg. doi:10.1007/11494669_93

Vishwakarma, P., & Mukherjee, B. (2014). Knowing protection of intellectual contents in digital era. In N. Patra, B. Kumar, & A. Pani (Eds.), *Progressive trends in electronic resource management in libraries* (pp. 147–165). Hershey, PA: IGI Global. doi:10.4018/978-1-4666-4761-9.ch008

Viswanath, P., & Sarma, T. H. (2011, September). An improvement to k-nearest neighbor classifier. In Recent Advances in Intelligent Computational Systems (RAICS), 2011 IEEE (pp. 227-231). IEEE. doi:10.1109/RAICS.2011.6069307

Viswanath, P., Murty, N., & Bhatnagar, S. (2005). Overlap pattern synthesis with an efficient nearest neighbor classifier. *Pattern Recognition*, *38*(8), 1187–1195. doi:10.1016/j.patcog.2004.10.007

Voss, J. (2006). *Collaborative thesaurus tagging the Wikipedia way*. Academic Press.

Wan & Gao. (2015). An Ensemble Sentiment Classification System of Twitter Data for Airline Services Analysis. *IEEE 15th International Conference on Data Mining Workshops*, 1318-1325.

Wandelt, S., Rheinländer, A., Bux, M., Thalheim, L., Haldemann, B., & Leser, U. (2012). Data management challenges in next generation Sequencing. *Datenbank Spektrum*, *12*(3), 161–171. doi:10.1007/s13222-012-0098-2

Wang, F., Wang, H., & Xu, K. (2012). Diffusive logistic model towards predicting information diffusion in online social networks. *2012 32nd International Conference on Distributed Computing Systems Workshops*. IEEE. doi:10.1109/ICDCSW.2012.16

Wang, K., Thrasher, C., Viegas, E., Li, X., & Hsu, B. (2010). An overview of microsoft web n-gram corpus and applications. In *Proceedings of the NAACL HLT 2010 Demonstration Session*, (pp. 45-48). Association for Computational Linguistics.

Wang, G., Zhang, Z., Sun, J., Yang, S., & Larson, C. A. (2015). POS-RS: A Random Subspace method for sentiment classification based on part-of-speech analysis. *Information Processing & Management*, *51*(4), 458–479. doi:10.1016/j.ipm.2014.09.004

Wang, L., Wang, G., & Alexander, C. A. (2015). Big data and visualization: Methods, challenges and technology progress. *Digital Technologies*, *1*(1), 33–38.

Wang, S., Yin, X., Zhang, J., Li, R., & Lv, Y. (2012). Sentiment Clustering of Product Object Based on Feature Reduction. *9th International Conference on Fuzzy Systems and Knowledge Discovery (FSKD 2012)*, 742-746. doi:10.1109/FSKD.2012.6234203

Wang, X., & Fu, G. (2010). Chinese Sentence-Level Sentiment Classification Based on Sentiment Morphemes. *International Conference on Asian Language Processing*, 203-206. doi:10.1109/IALP.2010.21

Wasilko, P. J. (2011). Law, architecture, gameplay, and marketing. In M. Cruz-Cunha, V. Varvalho, & P. Tavares (Eds.), *Business, technological, and social dimensions of computer games: Multidisciplinary developments* (pp. 476–493). Hershey, PA: IGI Global. doi:10.4018/978-1-60960-567-4.ch029

Wasilko, P. J. (2012). Law, architecture, gameplay, and marketing. In *Computer engineering: concepts, methodologies, tools and applications* (pp. 1660–1677). Hershey, PA: IGI Global. doi:10.4018/978-1-61350-456-7.ch703

Wasilko, P. J. (2014). Beyond compliance: Understanding the legal aspects of information system administration. In I. Portela & F. Almeida (Eds.), *Organizational, legal, and technological dimensions of information system administration* (pp. 57–75). Hershey, PA: IGI Global. doi:10.4018/978-1-4666-4526-4.ch004

Wasserman, . (1994). *Social Networks Analysis: Methods and Applications.* Cambridge, UK: Cambridge University Press. doi:10.1017/CBO9780511815478

Waterhouse, A. M., Procter, J. B., Martin, D. M. A., Clamp, M., & Barton, G. J. (2009). Jalview version 2a multiple sequence alignment editor and analysis workbench. *Bioinformatics (Oxford, England)*, *25*(9), 1189–1191. doi:10.1093/bioinformatics/btp033 PMID:19151095

Wei, W., & Zou, L. (2016). LDA-TM: A two-step approach to twitter topic data clustering. *Proceedings of the 2016 IEEE International Conference on Cloud Computing and Big Data Analysis*, 342-347. doi:10.1109/ICCCBDA.2016.7529581

Wellman, B. (n.d.). *The Networked Individual.* Retrieved from http://www.semioticon.com/semiotix/semiotix14/sem-14-05.html

Wen, D., & Marshall, G. (2014, December). Automatic twitter topic summarization. In *Computational Science and Engineering (CSE), 2014 IEEE 17th International Conference on* (pp. 207-212). doi:10.1109/CSE.2014.69

Westesson, O., Skinner, M., & Holmes, I. (2012). Visualizing next-generation sequencing data with JBrowse. *Briefings in Bioinformatics*, *14*(2), 172–177. doi:10.1093/bib/bbr078 PMID:22411711

Weston, J., Mukherjee, S., Chapelle, O., Pontil, M., Poggio, T., & Vapnik, V. (2000). In S. A. Solla, T. K. Leen, & K.-R. Muller (Eds.), *Feature Selection for SVMs* (Vol. 12, pp. 526–532). Cambridge, MA: MIT Press.

White, G. L., Mediavilla, F. A., & Shah, J. R. (2011). Information privacy: Implementation and perception of laws and corporate policies by CEOs and managers. *International Journal of Information Security and Privacy*, *5*(1), 50–66. doi:10.4018/jisp.2011010104

White, G. L., Mediavilla, F. A., & Shah, J. R. (2013). Information privacy: Implementation and perception of laws and corporate policies by CEOs and managers. In H. Nemati (Ed.), *Privacy solutions and security frameworks in information protection* (pp. 52–69). Hershey, PA: IGI Global. doi:10.4018/978-1-4666-2050-6.ch004

Whyte, K. P., List, M., Stone, J. V., Grooms, D., Gasteyer, S., Thompson, P. B., & Bouri, H. et al. (2014). Uberveillance, standards, and anticipation: A case study on nanobiosensors in U.S. cattle. In M. Michael & K. Michael (Eds.), *Uberveillance and the social implications of microchip implants: Emerging technologies* (pp. 260–279). Hershey, PA: IGI Global. doi:10.4018/978-1-4666-4582-0.ch012

Wilbur, J. W., & Sirotkin, K. (1992). The automatic identification of stop words. *Journal of Information Science*, *18*(1), 45–55. doi:10.1177/016555159201800106

Wilkes, W., Reusch, P. J., & Moreno, L. E. (2012). Flexible classification standards for product data exchange. In E. Kajan, F. Dorloff, & I. Bedini (Eds.), *Handbook of research on e-business standards and protocols: Documents, data and advanced web technologies* (pp. 448–466). Hershey, PA: IGI Global. doi:10.4018/978-1-4666-0146-8.ch021

Wittkower, D. E. (2011). Against strong copyright in e-business. In *Global business: Concepts, methodologies, tools and applications* (pp. 2157–2176). Hershey, PA: IGI Global. doi:10.4018/978-1-60960-587-2.ch720

Wright, D. (2012). Evolution of standards for smart grid communications. *International Journal of Interdisciplinary Telecommunications and Networking, 4*(1), 47–55. doi:10.4018/jitn.2012010103

Wu, F., Huang, Y., & Song, Y. (2016). Structured microblog sentiment classification via social context regularization. *Neurocomputing, 175*, 599–609. doi:10.1016/j.neucom.2015.10.101

Wurster, S. (2013). Development of a specification for data interchange between information systems in public hazard prevention: Dimensions of success and related activities identified by case study research. *International Journal of IT Standards and Standardization Research, 11*(1), 46–66. doi:10.4018/jitsr.2013010103

Wyburn, M. (2011). Copyright and ethical issues in emerging models for the digital media reporting of sports news in Australia. In M. Quigley (Ed.), *ICT ethics and security in the 21st century: New developments and applications* (pp. 66–85). Hershey, PA: IGI Global. doi:10.4018/978-1-60960-573-5.ch004

Wyburn, M. (2013). Copyright and ethical issues in emerging models for the digital media reporting of sports news in Australia. In *Digital rights management: Concepts, methodologies, tools, and applications* (pp. 290–309). Hershey, PA: IGI Global. doi:10.4018/978-1-4666-2136-7.ch014

Xiaohui, T., Yaohui, Z., & Yi, Z. (2012). The management system of enterprises intellectual property rights: A case study from China. *International Journal of Asian Business and Information Management, 3*(1), 50–64. doi:10.4018/jabim.2012010105

Xiaohui, T., Yaohui, Z., & Yi, Z. (2013). The management system of enterprises' intellectual property rights: A case study from China. In *Digital rights management: Concepts, methodologies, tools, and applications* (pp. 1092–1106). Hershey, PA: IGI Global. doi:10.4018/978-1-4666-2136-7.ch053

Xia, R., Zong, C., Hu, X., & Cambria, E. (2013). Feature Ensemble Plus Sample Selection: Domain Adaptation for Sentiment Classification. *IEEE Intelligent Systems, 28*(3), 10–18. doi:10.1109/MIS.2013.27

Xia, R., Zong, C., & Li, S. (2011). Ensemble of feature sets and classification algorithms for sentiment classification. *Information Sciences, 181*(6), 1138–1152. doi:10.1016/j.ins.2010.11.023

Xie, J. R., Kelley, S., & Szymanski, B. K. (2013). Overlapping community detection in networks: The state of the art and comparative study. *ACM Computing Surveys, 45*(4), 1–43. doi:10.1145/2501654.2501657

Xie, J., & Szymanski, B. K. (2012). Towards linear time overlapping community detection in social networks. *Proceedings of PAKDD Conf.* (pp. 25-36). doi:10.1007/978-3-642-30220-6_3

Xie, J., Szymanski, B. K., & Liu, X. (2011). SLPA: Uncovering Overlapping communities in Social Networks via A Speaker-listener Interaction Dynamic Process. *Proceedings of 11th IEEE International Conference on Data Mining Workshops (ICDM)* (pp. 344-349). IEEE. doi:10.1109/ICDMW.2011.154

Xuan, X., & Xiaowei, Z. (2012). The dilemma and resolution: The patentability of traditional Chinese medicine. *International Journal of Asian Business and Information Management, 3*(3), 1–8. doi:10.4018/jabim.2012070101

Xu, G. (2010). *Web Mining and Social Networking: Techniques and Applications*. Springer.

Xu, X., Ester, M., Kriegel, H. P., & Sander, J. (1998). A Distribution-Based Clustering Algorithm for Mining in Large Spatial Databases. *Proceedings of 14th International Conference on Data Engineering (ICDE'98)*.

Yang, Y., & Pedersen, J.O. (1997). A comparative study on feature selection in text categorization. *ICML, 97*, 412-420.

Yang, C., & Lu, Z. (2011). A blind image watermarking scheme utilizing BTC bitplanes. *International Journal of Digital Crime and Forensics, 3*(4), 42–53. doi:10.4018/jdcf.2011100104

Yang, J., & Honavar, V. (1998). Feature subset selection using a genetic algorithm. *Feature extraction, construction and selection. Springer US, 1998*, 117–136.

Yang, J., & Leskovec, J. (2013). Overlapping Community Detection at Scale: A Nonnegative Matrix Factorization Approach. *Proceedings of WSDM* (pp. 587-596). Rome, Italy: ACM. doi:10.1145/2433396.2433471

Yang, J., & Li, X. (2013). MapReduce based method for big data semantic clustering. *Proceedings of the 2013 IEEE International Conference on Systems, Man and Cybernetics, SMC'13*, 2814-2819. doi:10.1109/SMC.2013.480

Yastrebenetsky, M., & Gromov, G. (2014). International standard bases and safety classification. In M. Yastrebenetsky & V. Kharchenko (Eds.), *Nuclear power plant instrumentation and control systems for safety and security* (pp. 31–60). Hershey, PA: IGI Global. doi:10.4018/978-1-4666-5133-3.ch002

Ye, Zhang, & Law. (2014). Sentiment classification of online reviews to travel destinations by supervised machine learning approaches. *Expert Systems with Applications, 36*, 6527–6535.

Yoon, S., Xuan, Z., Makarov, V., Ye, K., & Sebat, J. (2009). Sensitive and accurate detection of copy number variants using read depth of coverage. *Genome Research, 19*(9), 1586–1592. doi:10.1101/gr.092981.109 PMID:19657104

Zadeh, L. A. (1965). Fuzzy Sets. *Information and Control, 8*(11), 338–353. doi:10.1016/S0019-9958(65)90241-X

Zeitouni, B., Boeva, V., Janoueix-Lerosey, I., Loeillet, S., Legoix-ne, P., Nicolas, A., & Barillot, E. et al. (2010). SVDetect: A tool to identify genomic structural variations from paired-end and mate-pair sequencing data. *Bioinformatics (Oxford, England)*, *26*(15), 1895–1896. doi:10.1093/bioinformatics/btq293 PMID:20639544

Zhang, D., Ma, J., Yi, J., Niu, X., & Xu, X. (2015). An Ensemble Method for Unbalanced Sentiment Classification. *IEEE 11th International Conference on Natural Computation (ICNC)*, 440-445.

Zhang, Wang, Xu, & Yin. (2009). Chinese Text Sentiment Classification based on Granule Network. GRC '09. *IEEE International Conference on Granular Computing*. 775 – 778.

Zhang, C., Zuo, W., Peng, T., & He, F. (2008). Sentiment Classification for Chinese Reviews Using Machine Learning Methods Based on String Kernel. *Third International Conference on Convergence and Hybrid Information Technology*. doi:10.1109/ICCIT.2008.51

Zhang, D., & Chen, S. (2002). Fuzzy Clustering Using Kernel Method. *Proceedings of the international conference on control and automation*, 123–127.

Zhang, , Li, , & Zhu, . (2010). Sentiment Classification Based on Syntax Tree Pruning and Tree Kernel. *Seventh Web Information Systems and Applications Conference*, 101-105.

Zhang, T., Ramakrishnan, R., & Livny, M. (1996). BIRCH: An efficient data clustering method for very large databases. *Proc. ACM SIGMOD Int. Conf. Management Data*, 103–114. doi:10.1145/233269.233324

Zhao, W., Ma, H., & He, Q. (2009). *Parallel k-means clustering based on MapReduce. In proceedings of the CloudCom'09* (pp. 674–679). Berlin, Heidelberg: Springer Verlag.

Zhou, P., Lei, J., & Ye, W. (2011). Large-scale data sets clustering based on MapReduce and Hadoop, Computational. *Information Systems*, *7*(16), 5956–5963.

Zhou, S., Chen, Q., & Wang, X. (2013). Active deep learning method for semi-supervised sentiment classification. *Neurocomputing*, *120*, 536–546. doi:10.1016/j.neucom.2013.04.017

Zhou, S., Chen, Q., & Wang, X. (2014). Fuzzy deep belief networks for semi-supervised sentiment classification. *Neurocomputing*, *131*, 312–322. doi:10.1016/j.neucom.2013.10.011

Zhou, T., Zhang, Y., Lu, H., Deng, F., & Wang, F. (2008). Rough Cluster Algorithm Based on Kernel Function. In G. Wang, T. Li, J. W. Grzymala-Busse, D. Miao, A. Skowron, & Y. Yao (Eds.), *RSKT 2008, LNAI* (Vol. 5009, pp. 172–179). doi:10.1007/978-3-540-79721-0_27

Zongker, D., & Jain, A. (1996, August). Algorithms for feature selection: An evaluation. In *Pattern Recognition, 1996. Proceedings of the 13th International Conference on* (Vol. 2, pp. 18-22). IEEE.

Zouag, N., & Kadiri, M. (2014). Intellectual property rights, innovation, and knowledge economy in Arab countries. In A. Driouchi (Ed.), *Knowledge-based economic policy development in the Arab world* (pp. 245–272). Hershey, PA: IGI Global. doi:10.4018/978-1-4666-5210-1.ch010

About the Contributors

B. K. Tripathy is a Senior Professor in SCOPE, VIT University, Vellore, India. He has received fellowships from UGC, DST, SERC and DOE of Govt. of India. He has published more than 320 technical papers and has produced 21 PhDs, 13 MPhils and 2 M.S (By research) under his supervision. Dr. Tripathy has published two text books on Soft Computing and Computer Graphics and has edited two research volumes for IGI publications. He is a life-time/ senior member of IEEE, ACM, IRSS, CSI and IMS. He is an editorial board member/reviewer of more than 60 journals. His research interest includes fuzzy sets and systems, rough sets and knowledge engineering, data clustering, social network analysis, soft computing, granular computing, content based learning, neighbourhood systems, soft set theory and applications, multiset theory, list theory and multi-criteria decision making.

* * *

C. Shoba Bindu is currently working as an Associate Professor in the Department of Computer Science and Engineering at Jawaharlal Nehru Technological University Anantapur college of Engineering, Ananthapuramu. She obtained her Bachelor degree in Electronics and Communication Engineering, Master's in Computer Science and Ph.D. in Computer Science & Engineering from Jawaharlal Nehru Technological University Anantapur. She has published several Research papers in National /International Conferences and Journals. Her research interests are network security.

S Rao Chintalapudi received both Bachelor of Technology and Master of Technology from Bonam Venkata Chalamayya Engineering College, Odalarevu, affiliated to JNTU Kakinada. Currently, he is working as a full time research scholar in the department of computer science and engineering, University College of Engineering Kakinada (Autonomous), Jawaharlal Nehru Technological University Kakinada, Andhra Pradesh, India. He worked as assistant professor in Bharat Institute of Engineering and Technology and CMR Technical Campus in Hyderabad. He is a member of CSI, IEEE and ACM. He has six research papers published in international conferences and peer reviewed journals. He is a member of the board of reviewers in International journal of Rough Sets and Data Analysis (IJRSDA). His research interests are Social Network Analysis, Graph Mining, High Performance Computing, Big Data Analytics and Data Mining. Visit my website for more details: https://sites.google.com/site/sraochintalapudi/.

Ashok Kumar J received the Bachelor of Science (BSc) degree in mathematics from University of Madras, the Master of Computer Applications (MCA) degree in computer applications from Anna University. He is currently a research scholar in the department of Information Science and Technology, Anna University, Chennai. His research interests include opinion mining, analytics, data mining and machine learning.

Manas Kirti is working as Software Development Engineer at Flipkart Internet Private Limited, Bangalore. Previously, he worked as Software Engineer at Samsung Research Institute, Bangalore. He graduated in Computer Science & Engineering from Birla Institute of Technology, Mesra in 2014. His areas of interests include developing Machine Learning models.

R. Raja Kumar received his M.Tech in Computer Science from Jawahar Lal Technological University, Kakinada. Currently He is working as Assistant professor in Computer Science and Engineering Department, at RGMCET, Nandyal. Currently he is working for his Ph.d at Jawahar Lal TechnologicalUnviersity, Anantapur. His areas of interest are Pattern Recognition, Data Mining, Machine Learning.

H. M. Krishna Prasad M is currently Full Professor, Department of Computer Science and Engineering, University College of Engineering Kakinada (Autonomous), JNTUK, Andhra Pradesh. He did his B.E. from Osmania University, Hyderabad, M.Tech and Ph.D. in data mining from JNTU, Hyderabad. Dr. Munaga successfully completed a two year MIUR fellowship (Jan 2007 – Dec 08) at University of Udine, Udine, Italy. He has about 50+ research papers in various International Journals and Conferences, and attended many national and international conferences in India and abroad. He is a member of Association for Computing Machinery (ACM), ISTE and IAENG (Germany). He is an active member of the board of reviewers in various International Journals and Conferences. His research interests include Data mining, BigData Analytics and High Performance Computing.

Brojo Kishore Mishra obtained his Doctor of Philosophy (Ph.D.) in Computer Science from Berhampur University, India. He is presently working as Associate Professor in the Department of Information Technology, C. V. Raman College of Engineering, Bhubaneswar, India. His experience and areas of interest focus on Data / Web / Opinion Mining, Soft Computing, Cloud Computing, E-Learning and Social Network. He has published more than 20 research papers in reputed International journal & conference including IEEE. He is the CSI Regional Student Coordinator, Odisha. (2016-17) and IEEE Day-2015 Ambassador in Kolkata section, India. He is the life member of CSI, ISTE and member of IEEE, IAENG, UACEE professional societies.

Monalisa Mishra completed M.Tech (CS & IS) from KIIT University in the year 2011. Currently she is pursuing Ph.D. (Computer Application) in NIT Durgapur. Also, she is continuing as Asst. Professor in CSE Dept of C. V. Raman College of Engineering, Bhubaneswar.

Sushruta Mishra completed his M.Tech from IIIT, BBSR and now perusing his Ph.D. from KIIT University, Bhubaneswar, INDIA. He is very much active in research and development works and has several publications to his credit in reputed Journals and conferences.

Phub Namgay obtained his Master degree in Computer Applications (MCA) from South Asian University, New Delhi, India in the year 2013. He is currently working at Sherubtse College, Royal University of Bhutan, Bhutan. He is the first Bhutanese to receive SAARC-India Silver Jubilee Scholarship, a grant that allows students from South Asian region to study at South Asian University, New Delhi, India. Before joining Royal Thimphu College, he interned for Six months at Rigsum Institute of Information Technology, Thimphu, Bhutan.

Viswanath Pulabaigari received his PhD degree from Indian Institute of Science Bangalore, India. He published several papers in reputed International Journals and International Conferences. At present, he is working as a Visiting Professor in the Computer Science and Engineering department at IIIT Chittoor, India. His area of interest includes Pattern Recognition, Data Mining and Algorithms.

Parvathi R is an Associate Professor of School of Computing Science and Engineering at VIT University, Chenna since 2011. She received the Doctoral degree in the field of spatial data mining in the same year. Her teaching experience in the area of computer science includes more than two decades and her research interests include data mining, big data and computational biology.

Abirami S is an Assistant Professor in the department of information science and technology at Anna University, Chennai. She received her ME degree in computer science and engineering, and obtained PhD in the area of document imaging from Anna University. Her research interests include video analytics, text mining, artificial intelligence, programming languages, and Bigdata analytics.

Chitrakala S is an Associate Professor, Department of Computer Science and Engineering at Anna University, Chennai, Tamil Nadu. Her research interests include Data mining, Computer Vision, Artificial Intelligence, Web Information Retrieval, Natural Language Processing, Text mining, and Big Data Analytics. Her research contributions have culminated in 130 publications which include 45 International journals and 85 International conferences. She has organized various Conferences, Workshops and seminars. She is the reviewer for various Journals and International conferences. She is a life member of CSI and life member of Indian Society of Technical Education ISTE, New Delhi.

Bangaru Kamatchi Seethapathy completed bachelor degree in Information Technology and Masters in Computer Science, currently pursuing PhD in the area of Big Data in VIT University Chennai.

Anu Singha obtained his first Masters' degree in Computer Applications (MCA) from South Asian University, New Delhi, India, in the year 2013, and second Masters' degree in Computer Science and Engineering (M.Tech) from Tripura University, Agartala, India, in 2015. Currently, he is a PhD scholar at Tripura University, India.

Ravindra Babu Tallamraju is currently working as Principal Data Scientist in Flipkart Internet Private Limited, Bangalore. Previously he worked as Principal Researcher at Infosys Limited and as Scientist at Indian Space Research Organization. His areas of interest include Large data clustering and classification, evolutionary algorithms, image processing and data mining.

Hrudaya Kumar Tripathy is presently working as Associate Professor at School of Computer Engineering, KIIT University, Bhubaneswar, Odisha, India. Having 16 years of teaching experience with 6 years of post-doctorate research experience in the field of Soft Computing, Machine Learning, Speech Processing, Mobile Robotics and Big Data Analysis. Invited as visiting faculty to Asia Pacific University (APU), Kuala Lumpur, Malyasia and University Utara Malaysia (UUM), Sintok, Kedah, Malaysia. Worked as Center Head in APTECH Ltd., Bhubaneswar for 3 years. Appointed as Centre Coordinator by IGNOU, New Delhi for study centre at IACR, Rayagada. Published around 60 No.(s) of research papers in reputed international referred journals & IEEE conferences. Technical reviewer and member of technical committee of many International conferences. Awarded as Young IT professional award 2013 on regional level from Computer Society of India (CSI). Received many certificates of merits and highly applauded in presentation of research papers at International conferences of different Asian countries (Thailand, Singapore, Hong Kong, Malaysia). Member of International Association of Computer Science and Information Technology (IACSIT), Singapore, Member of International Association of Engineers (IAENG), Hong Kong, Senior Member of IEEE, India Chapter, Member if IET, India, Associate Member of Indian Institute of Ceramics, Kolkatta, and Life Member of Computer Society of India, New Delhi.

Tina Esther Trueman is a Teaching Fellow and Research Scholar in the department of information science and technology at Anna University, Chennai. She received her BE degree in computer science and engineering from University of Madras, and ME degree in computer science and engineering from Anna University. Her research interests include Data analytics, soft computing, artificial intelligence, and Cloud computing.

Vignesh Umapathy received his Bachelor of Technology degree from the department of Information Technology at Anna University, Chennai in 2010. He received his Master of Technology degree from the Department of Information Technology from same university in 2012. After receiving his education, he worked as Assistant Professor at Mookambigai College of Engineering for 3 years. He is currently a PhD student in the field of biological data analysis in School of Computing Science and Engineering at VIT University, Chennai. He has co-authored over 15 refereed articles in journals and conference proceedings. His research interests are in the area of big data, data mining and bioinformatics.

Index

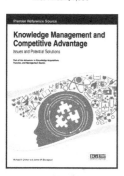

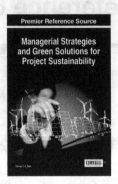

Printed in the United States
By Bookmasters